The Modern Girl Around the World

NEXT WAVE

New Directions in Women's Studies

A series edited by

INDERPAL GREWAL, CAREN KAPLAN,

and ROBYN WIEGMAN

The Modern Girl Around the World

Consumption, Modernity, and Globalization

The Modern Girl

Around the World Research Group

(ALYS EVE WEINBAUM, LYNN M. THOMAS, PRITI RAMAMURTHY,

UTA G. POIGER, MADELEINE YUE DONG,

and TANI E. BARLOW, editors)

DUKE UNIVERSITY PRESS

DURHAM AND LONDON

2008

© 2008

DUKE UNIVERSITY PRESS

ALL RIGHTS RESERVED

PRINTED IN THE UNITED STATES

OF AMERICA ON ACID-FREE PAPER ∞

DESIGNED BY KATY CLOVE

TYPESET IN SABON BY KEYSTONE TYPESETTING, INC.

LIBRARY OF CONGRESS CATALOGING-IN-PUBLICATION

DATA AND REPUBLICATION ACKNOWLEDGMENTS APPEAR

ON THE LAST PRINTED PAGES OF THIS BOOK.

Duke University Press gratefully acknowledges the support of the University of Washington and the Simpson Center for the Humanities, both of which provided support for the production of this book.

In memory of MIRIAM SILVERBERG

Contents

Acknowledgments

In our collaborative research project spanning six years we have accumulated numerous debts. At the University of Washington, we hosted a number of speakers' series and workshops on the Modern Girl. In addition to Davarian Baldwin, Timothy Burke, Liz Conor, Anne Gorsuch, Mary Louise Roberts, and Miriam Silverberg, whose work appears in this volume, Antoinette Burton, Judith Henchy, Ali Igmen, Miyako Inoue, William Mazzarella, Linda Mizejewski, Vicki Ruiz, Yiman Wang, Claire Wilkinson Weber, Richard Wilk, and Paola Zamperini participated in those forums and contributed to the development of our project. We also thank colleagues at the University of California, Los Angeles, Duke University, and the Radcliffe Institute for Advanced Study, Harvard University, who invited us to present our collaborative work in progress. Those who attended our presentations at the University of Washington and the meetings of the Berkshire Conference on the History of Women (2002), the Modern Studies Association (2003), the Modern Language Association (2004), and the American Historical Association (2005) similarly offered insightful commentary.

We have learned a great deal from engagement with members of our Tokyo-based sister research group, The Modern Girl and Colonial Modernity in East Asia, which includes Angelina Chin, Kim Eunshil, Sakamoto Hiroko, Ko Ikujo, Dai Jinhua, Tachi Kaoru, Muta Kazue, Vera Mackie, Adachi Mariko, Kohiyama Rui, Ito Ruri, Barbara Sato, and Tani E. Barlow. In September 2004, our two groups cosponsored a workshop at Ochanomizu Women's University in Tokyo. We appreciated the members of the audience who so actively participated in that four-day event.

We gratefully acknowledge support from the following units at the University of Washington: the Walter Chapin Simpson Center for the Humanities and especially its director, Kathleen Woodward; the Institute for Transnational Studies; the Office of the Divisional Dean of Social Sciences; the Graduate School; the Henry M. Jackson School of International Studies; the International Studies Center; and the Center for Comparative Study of Law and Society. We extend our gratitude to librarians Susan Kane, Alan Grosenheider, Richard Karkeek, Theresa Mudrock, Siew-Choo Poh, and Dianna Xu. In addition, we thank the Kenneth S. Allen Foundation for its generous support of acquisitions by the University of Washington libraries.

This project would not be possible without the contributions of our undergraduate and graduate research assistants Michelle Acupanda, Phoebe Ayers, Amanda Berman, Amy Bhatt, Catherine Brueckner, Kate Brumage, Glorya Cho, Cara Codekas, Kendra Dupuy, Betsy Fomon, Ian Foster, Breona Gutschmidt, Mara Hobler, Chenee' Holcomb, Rachelle Longe, Serena Maurer, Sarah McKay, Kristen McTighe, Shalini Miskelly, Jamaica Morris, Dipika Nath, Amy Piedalue, Gazelle Samizay, Pamela Samson, Kacie Sisel, Eric Stowe, Pamela Tang, Riki Thompson, Alexis Wheeler, Jessica Woznak, Anne Wessel, Stella Yee, Sumei Yi, Mengliang Zhang, and Kasa Zipfel. Special thanks go to our graduate project assistants John Foster, Katrina Hagen, Kristy Leissle, Teresa Mares, Rebecca McColl, and Helen Schneider. Over the last two and a half years of the project, Teresa Mares has worked on matters ranging from conference organization to manuscript preparation with remarkable efficiency and tact.

1

The Modern Girl
as Heuristic Device

Collaboration, Connective Comparison,

Multidirectional Citation

MODERN GIRL AROUND THE WORLD
RESEARCH GROUP (ALYS EVE WEINBAUM,
LYNN M. THOMAS, PRITI RAMAMURTHY,
UTA G. POIGER, MADELEINE Y. DONG,
and TANI E. BARLOW)

The Modern Girl emerged quite literally around the world in the first half of the twentieth century. In cities from Beijing to Bombay, Tokyo to Berlin, Johannesburg to New York, the Modern Girl made her sometimes flashy, always fashionable appearance. What identified Modern Girls was their use of specific commodities and their explicit eroticism. Modern Girls were known by a variety of names including flappers, *garçonnes*, *moga*, *modeng xiaojie*, schoolgirls, *kallege ladki*, vamps, and *neue Frauen*. Adorned in provocative fashions, in pursuit of romantic love, Modern Girls appeared to disregard roles of dutiful daughter, wife, and mother. Contemporary journalists, politicians, social scientists, and the general public debated whether Modern Girls were looking for sexual, economic, or political emancipation. They also raised the possibility that the Modern Girl was little more than an image, a hollow product of clever advertising campaigns in the new commodity culture.

The signal contribution of our collaboration has been the discovery of the Modern Girl as a global phenomenon in the 1920s and 1930s. Our group, which has engaged in collaborative research and writing for seven years, is composed of faculty members at the University of Washington trained in literary criticism, history, cultural and feminist studies, and political economy and possesses regional expertise in Africa, Asia, Europe, and North America. This volume contains our efforts — in this introduction, in a case study that appears as chapter 2, and in individual chapters — to trace the Modern Girl's various colonial and national incarnations and to reveal linkages among the many geographic locations in which she appeared. This volume also includes chapters by scholars whose work on gender, modernity, and consumption has influenced our own, and with whom we have been in dialogue. We invited these scholars to consider, or to reconsider, their research in light of our group's two central questions: How was the Modern Girl global? And what made her so?

The first section of this introduction elaborates two techniques our group developed for answering these questions and entering debates about gender and globalization.[1] These are the *Modern Girl as heuristic device* and the *method of connective comparison*.[2] Subsequent sections discuss chapters in this volume in relation to six thematics that repeatedly emerge in our work and in that of other volume contributors: the modern, the girl, visual economies, nationalisms, commodities, and consumption.

The Modern Girl as Heuristic Device and the Method of Connective Comparison

We intentionally elected, at the outset, to employ the Modern Girl as a heuristic device. The adjective "heuristic" means "serving to find out or discover." A heuristic device cannot be taken as given a priori; rather, it emerges in and through the research process and possesses a future orientation. Visual representations of the Modern Girl allowed us to track her across the globe. Numerous iconic visual elements including bobbed hair, painted lips, provocative clothing, elongated body, and open, easy smile enabled us to locate the Modern Girl around the world in approximately the same years between World War I and World War II. These visual elements also allowed us to discern the linkages shaping specific phenomena across geographic and political boundaries. Our ability to call upon each other's regional expertise promoted recognition of underlying structures of commonality and difference specific to various nation-

1.1 Ad in the South African newspaper *Bantu World* (1933)
that depicts a Modern Girl with an elongated body and
promotes products manufactured by an African
American–owned cosmetics company.

states, to different colonial and semicolonial regimes, and to diverse national and international corporate strategies.

Equally important, using the Modern Girl as a heuristic device allowed us to capitalize on unexpected research findings. In tracking corporate deployments of the Modern Girl in Indian and South African advertising campaigns, for example, Priti Ramamurthy and Lynn M. Thomas discovered the existence of Indian, black, and mixed-race Modern Girls in the late 1920s and early 1930s, more than a decade earlier than previous scholarship had suggested. This discovery of the near simultaneous appearance of Modern Girls around the world complicates widely accepted histories of commercial capitalism, consumption, and visual culture that presume the dissemination of "modernity" from Europe and North America to the rest of the world in the post–World War II period.

In using the Modern Girl as a heuristic device we were able to learn from each other about economic and political processes in geographic locales other than those in which we individually conducted research, and, consequently, we were able to develop the method we label connective comparison.[3] Connective comparison avoids recourse to abstract types and instead focuses on how specific local processes condition each other. It scrutinizes the idea of discrete

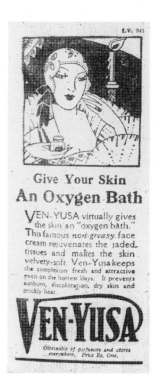

Give Your Skin An Oxygen Bath

VEN-YUSA virtually gives the skin an "oxygen bath." This famous *non-greasy* face cream rejuvenates the jaded tissues and makes the skin velvety-soft. Ven-Yusa keeps the complexion fresh and attractive even on the hottest days. It prevents sunburn, discoloration, dry skin and prickly heat.

VEN-YUSA

Obtainable of perfumers and stores everywhere. Price Re. One.

1.2 Ad in the Indian newspaper *The Statesman* (1930) for the perfume company Ven-Yusa that depicts a Modern Girl with stylized features.

temporal and geographic locations by positioning specific local developments *in conversation with* those occurring elsewhere in the world. In so doing, it highlights the inchoate manner in which things previously understood to be local come into being through complex global dynamics. Connective comparison is, thus, a method that neither reads peculiar phenomena as deviations from an abstracted "norm" nor one that measures such developments against those postulated by theories of inevitable modernization. Rather, it puts into practice Johannes Fabian's insight that the time of modernity is lateral and simultaneous, not evolutionary or stagist.[4] Connective comparison avoids establishing temporal priority in a manner that privileges linear causality.[5]

Notably, working in collaboration facilitated the method of connective comparison. Only in very rare instances can one person handle the multiple languages and historical contexts that such research demands. To pay more than lip service to the diversity and commonality that characterize globalization, regional and disciplinary specialists must agree, as we have, to bring individual expertise to bear on a shared set of questions. Members of our group, who work in Chinese, English, French, German, Hindi, and Swahili, have thus together employed the method of connective comparison. In turn, this enabled us to track the Modern Girl's specific manifestations and also to demonstrate the simultaneity of modernist aesthetics and aspirations without turning the simultaneity discovered into either sameness or equivalence.

Among our most important findings is that in any given geopolitical location, above all else, the Modern Girl was distinguished from other female figures and representations by her continual incorporation of local elements with those drawn from elsewhere. We have termed such incorporation *multidirectional citation*. We define it as the mutual, though asymmetrical, influences and circuits of exchange that produce common figurations and practices in multiple locations. In our usage, multidirectional citation pertains to both *actual* Modern Girls, historical agents who produced and performed new appearances and subjectivities by incorporating elements from disparate locations, and to *representations* of these new appearances and subjectivities. Figures 1.1 through 1.5 in this introduction are examples of such representations. In chapter 2, our collaborative case study on cosmetics advertising, we illustrate our method of connective comparison and the existence of multidirectional citation by locating the circulation, interaction, and entanglement of images and ideas of the Modern Girl within and across specific colonial, national, and international hierarchies.

Taken together, the Modern Girl as a heuristic device, the method of connective comparison, and the associated concept of multidirectional citation have enabled us to engage current debates about globalization. In most recent scholarship globalization describes processes of economic and cultural integration specific to the second half of the twentieth century. By contrast, this volume provides a study of globalization before the invention of the term. Though some scholars have argued that economic globalization is as old as capitalism,[6] we are less interested in identifying its origins than in providing a nuanced analysis of how global commodity and cultural flows shaped modern femininity across geopolitical locations. To this end, and in contrast to previous studies of *moga, garçonnes, modeng xiaojie, neue Frauen,* and flappers that focus on one nation or, at best, bilateral relations between a nation and its formal colonies,[7] we examine the Modern Girl's global emergence through economic structures and cultural flows stretching beyond such discrete and circumscribed boundaries. In our case study of cosmetics advertising and in individual chapters, U.S. corporations emerge as a major source and as the most important international distributor of imagery associated with the Modern Girl, especially because of U.S. preeminence in the international distribution of advertising and film. However, we suggest that processes of Americanization were not uniform and should instead be understood in relation to British, European, and Japanese colonialism and the international circuits through which corporations, cultural workers, and image makers operated.[8] On this point our analysis resonates with Richard Wilk's argument that globalization comprises a series of social and economic processes through which commonalities are expressed differentially — as what he calls "structures of common difference."[9] For us, the multidirectional citations that shaped the Modern Girl reveal such "structures of common difference."

Our group arrived at a shared set of questions about the Modern Girl through our prior individual research on gender, political economy, and cultures of consumption in twentieth-century Africa, Asia, Europe, and North America. Over the course of our collaboration we have disagreed on numerous

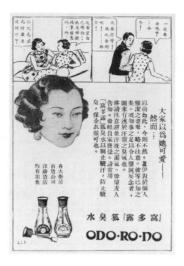

1.3 Ad in an elite Chinese magazine, *Young Companion* (1937) for
"Odorono," a deodorant licensed around the world by a U.S. company.

1.4 Ad in the German magazine *Leipziger Illustrirte Zeitung* (1928)
for the U.S.–licensed deodorant "Odorono," highlighting abstracted
facial features and exposed body parts.

issues about how to ask and answer questions. At times, our divergent disciplinary frameworks have proven difficult to reconcile. These differences are
evident in our individual chapters. And, yet, it is our sense — more vivid now in
retrospect — that these differences have also constituted an invaluable asset.
Sharing area and disciplinary expertise as well as our individual research findings with one another, each of us was continually reminded that no one place or
single process can stand as the "model" or the determinative force in making
the Modern Girl global. Such sharing prompted us to develop a methodology
that refuses temporal progression as the basis of comparison.

Once formed in 2000, our Seattle-based research group organized a multi-
year speakers' series, inviting scholars from other institutions to the University
of Washington to engage with our questions and findings. Miriam Silverberg
was the first scholar whom we invited, as her pioneering essay on the Modern
Girl in interwar Japan had inspired our initial work.[10] Her comments, along
with those by Timothy Burke and Kathy Peiss, conclude this volume. Chapters
by other scholars who shared their work with us follow this introduction. In
2001, Tani Barlow spent six months at the Institute for Gender Studies at
Ochanomizu Women's University in Tokyo, where she worked with Ruri Ito to
form a Tokyo-based sister research group, "The Modern Girl and Colonial

Modernity in East Asia." In September 2004, our two groups cosponsored a workshop at Ochanomizu at which several of the chapters collected in this volume were first presented.[11] What you are reading may aptly be described as a retrospective account of our journey: an introduction by way of conclusion.

The Modern

The Modern Girl as heuristic device opens up an obvious, if difficult, question: What made her "modern"? In answering this question, volume contributors examine how the Modern Girl was singled out as a marker of "modernity"—a concept that scholars in the humanities and social sciences have long sought to limn and define. Earlier conflation of "modern"

1.5 Ad in U.S. *Vogue* (1928) for Marie Earle cosmetics, featuring a Modern Girl with a svelte, elongated body who wears a "skyscraper frock" and holds the world in her hands.

and "Western" has been challenged by those who have sought to emphasize how academic and popular discussions of modernity inevitably create hierarchies that posit some societies as "ahead" and others as "catching up."[12] Others have treated the problem of fascist modernity and its relationship to capitalism and liberal democracy.[13] Still others have challenged the notion of a singular modernity, arguing that modernity ought to be understood as "multiple" — as composed of "alternative" or "parallel" forms forged through the complex interplay of imperial and indigenous social formations and politics.[14] Some scholars working in regional Asia have put forward "colonial modernity," a concept that stresses the colonial roots of revolutionary modernization and the markets and civic institutions that linked "semicolonial" areas, including parts of China, to the larger capitalist world system.[15] Others remind us that those living in areas of Africa that have experienced profound economic decline in recent decades often feel "cheated" out of modernity's promises.[16]

This volume intervenes in discussions that decenter the idea of Western modernity through treatment of the multifaceted linkages — ideological, aesthetic, and material — among the locales in which the Modern Girl emerged. It pays attention to how people in different contexts understood the Modern Girl as *modern*. And it explores how dominant modernist ideologies — such as those of individual autonomy, scientific racism, and social reform — conditioned the Modern Girl's global emergence. This volume also pays particularly close attention to how modernist aesthetics emanating from multiple contexts shaped and were shaped by what we refer to as "the Modern Girl look": the Modern Girl's surface or image and its representation. Indeed, most contributors to this volume examine how a Modern Girl — either an actual historical actor or a representational strategy — became recognizable, consumable, and locally intelligible. For, ultimately, this volume argues that debates over the Modern Girl always relied upon and reworked notions of modernity and femininity (and, consequently, also ideas of masculinity) in specific locales. For contemporaries the Modern Girl was a harbinger of both the possibilities and dangers of modern life.[17]

The volume's focus, the turbulent period between World War I and World War II, is marked by two contradictory forces: increasing global economic interdependence, and ascendance of forms of political nationalism that often challenged such interdependence. From 1919 to 1939 manufacture of consumer products was further industrialized and new markets for domestic and foreign working classes were created. Interdependency also led in the United States to the stock market crash of 1929, the Great Depression, and a cascade of uneven effects on global employment and economic restructuring. Germany and the United Kingdom, for instance, responded with high tariffs as a measure of protection from outside influences. Japan, and later Germany, undertook aggressive territorial expansion to increase access to raw materials and markets and to effect a racist reordering of populations. In the British colony of India and in the British dominion of South Africa, the shift to grow domestic markets benefited local entrepreneurs. The political nationalism that emerged in this period took various forms: Fascism in Italy, Germany, and Japan; Stalinism in the Soviet Union; and racial nationalism in the United States, Australia, and South Africa. Movements for self-determination, often led by bourgeoisies in Asia and Africa, also ascribed to various political nationalisms, but these were aligned against colonial and semicolonial forces, not with them. As this volume demonstrates, the Modern Girl's emergence reflected major economic trends and the rise of modern nationalisms; however, her emergence was not always synchronic with the development of nationalism, nor did it necessarily coincide with the development of bourgeoisies.

The Girl

The first product of our collaboration was a presentation titled "The Modern Girl Around the World." Instructively, each time we gave it, our use of the term "girl" was challenged from the floor. On one occasion we also noticed that "girl" had been struck from several posters advertising the presentation and replaced with "woman." And yet, it is precisely the troublesomeness of "girl" that has attracted us. "Girl" signifies the contested status of young women, no longer children, and their unstable and sometimes subversive relationship to social norms relating to heterosexuality, marriage, and motherhood. An easily identifiable figure of feminine adolescence emerged during the Victorian period, encompassing the mid- to late nineteenth century. By the 1880s the term "girl" came into popular usage in England, where it referred to working-class and middle-class unmarried women who occupied an ephemeral free space between childhood and adulthood.[18] Our research has shown that during the 1920s and 1930s "girl" and its equivalent translations appeared around the globe. In these decades, "girl" denoted young women with the wherewithal and desire to define themselves in excess of conventional female roles and as transgressive of national, imperial, and racial boundaries. Indeed, our research strongly suggests the historical emergence of "girl" as a modern social and representational category and as a style of self-expression largely delinked from biological age.

Sometimes contemporaries picked up "girl" wholesale. In Germany, critics frequently used the English word "girl" interchangeably with "*neue Frau*" (literally New Woman) when referring to fashionable women who involved themselves in the emergent media culture as shop girls, film fans, and cabaret entertainers. In the United States, the phrase "It Girl," closely identified with the silent screen star Clara Bow, became a common euphemism for flapper. In the Anglophone black African press, "modern girl" referred to schoolgirls or graduates with panache for fashion and for choosing their own lovers. In Japan, the term "modern girl" was reworked into *modan garu* through a process of phonetic translation and then shortened to *moga*. In China, where *modeng xiaojie* (modern young lady) and India where *kallege ladki* (college girl) were used, preexisting terms for unmarried young women were modified through affiliation with modernity or with the institution of schooling. In all cases, these monikers denoted an up-to-date and youthful femininity, provocative and unseemly in its intimacy with foreign aesthetic and commodity influences.

Queries about our use of "girl" have often turned into questions about the distinction between the Modern Girl and the so-called New Woman. In answering these, we note that the New Woman is frequently figured as the mother of the Modern Girl: contemporaries identified the New Woman with reform and with social and political advocacy and associated her daughter with the "frivolous" pursuits of consumption, romance, and fashion. While our research suggests a close association between the Modern Girl and commodity capitalism in all contexts, it also questions hard and fast distinctions that align New Women with political activism and Modern Girls with consumption. New Women were often avid consumers and passionate advocates of "free love," and Modern Girls embraced a variety of political projects including socialism and nationalism. Women as politically diverse as the Nazi filmmaker Leni Riefenstahl and the West African author of antiracist plays Mabel Dove used Modern Girl commodities and styles in their artistic production and their self-presentation.[19]

Both New Women and Modern Girls found political inspiration in popular female performance and spectacle. As Mary Louise Roberts's chapter explains, the French New Woman (as personified by the *éclaireuse* Marguerite Durand) and *garçonne*, though distinct, shared enthusiasm for mass, consumer culture and a "distinctly feminine glamour." In particular, Durand challenged French stereotypes of New Women as Anglo-Saxon, unattractive, and threatening by mobilizing an "aesthetic politics" aimed at middle-class audiences of mass print media and theater. These developments had parallels elsewhere. New Women and suffragists in the United States — the very same women whom French contemporaries dismissed as embittered "prudes" and "plain-Janes" — embraced advertising and consumer culture in their efforts to popularize their political causes.[20]

Several chapters in this volume further illuminate how often it was women themselves who intertwined the New Woman and the Modern Girl. Young women labeled and dismissed as Modern Girls responded by claiming to be New Women. In semicolonial and colonial contexts in which these two figures surfaced simultaneously in the interwar period, entanglement of the Modern Girl and New Woman was exacerbated.[21] As Ruri Ito's chapter demonstrates, in the Japanese colony of Okinawa young women students, teachers, and journalists who were referred to as New Women sympathized with Japanese feminist literary magazines. Together with Okinawan migration to and from the Japanese metropole, an intensified interest in female literacy and education created a productive matrix for Okinawan women, compelling them to exhibit a keen interest in modern fashion and self-portrayal. The multiplicity of mobilizations and engagements of the Modern Girl reveals how important it is to avoid measuring each against predetermined ideals or types, such as the feminist or emancipated woman antagonistic to consumer culture, or the respectable national citizen aspiring to motherhood or education. Indeed, the method of connective comparison reveals that by the interwar period the Modern Girl was an effect of globe-straddling multidirectional citation practices, which included the travel of iconography, commodities, and ideas. In turn, these practices were reworked as they were locally deployed.

In many instances "girl" functioned as a racialized category. In those contexts structured by eugenics, racial segregation, and colonial rule, the Modern Girl could not be envisioned apart from hierarchical racial formations. Chapters by Liz Conor and Alys Eve Weinbaum demonstrate how dominant white culture in both Australia and the United States presumed the Modern Girl to be white. In Australia, Conor argues, the Modern Girl's whiteness was established through distancing her from Aboriginal women. Racist cartoons portrayed white Australian flappers as superior to Aboriginal women whose "uncivilized" blackness rendered them allegedly incapable of "proper" display of modern fashion and style. In the United States, the white Modern Girl secured her designation as "modern" through a process that Weinbaum terms "racial masquerade," a performance of the self that involved both putting on and taking off the superficial markers of racial "otherness" made available through the new consumer culture. In particular, the white American Modern Girl's play with "Oriental" or "primitive" clothing and makeup allowed her to underscore her robust possession of whiteness, national belonging, and the status of "modern." By contrast, Weinbaum argues, African American women and women recently immigrated from Asia — those whose full participation in commodity culture was circumscribed by poverty and racism — most often could not make recourse to "racial masquerade" as a means of securing racial prestige or "modernity."

"Girl" was racialized in other ways as well. As a diminutive of woman, "girl," like "boy," was evoked as a racial insult in Jim Crow United States and in colonial and white minority–ruled Africa. In his chapter on black U.S. beauty culture, Davarian Baldwin argues that African American women sought to resist "racist taxonomies of girlhood," while creating a gendered politics of "Black re-creation" through their participation in commercial leisure culture. Out of respect for the spirit of this politics of re-creation, Baldwin refrains from using the term "girl" in his discussion of the African American entrepreneur Madam C. J. Walker's "makeover" of "Black womanhood." By contrast, other chapters employ "girl" in recognition of its historic and ongoing usage by people of color, and in appreciation of its analytical potential in racist contexts. Chapters by Ramamurthy, Weinbaum, and Thomas reveal Anglo-Indian film stars, African and Asian Americans, and black school graduates in South Africa engaging "girlness" to challenge racist ideas of "primitive," "backward," and "uncivilized" femininity, and to claim a fashionable, "respectable" modernity. Although "woman" is the ideologically "correct" choice within much contemporary feminist scholarship, we elect "girl" because of the fresh political possibilities it offers for rethinking race and femininity in the twentieth century.

The Modern Girl needs to be examined in her manifestation as a style, an icon, and a performance. It is in these guises that "modern girlness" was appropriated by married as well as unmarried women, and as easily invoked in advertisements for anti–bed bug remedies as in those for cosmetics. Tani Barlow's chapter on advertising in Shanghai focuses on what she terms "the other scene of use value." Out of fantasies that illuminated the new logic of capitalist commodification in visual form, the Shanghai advertising industry developed an immediately identifiable "sexy Modern Girl icon" and placed it in scenes that modeled the emotional life imputed to moderns who used commodities. Banalization of this icon in the Shanghai-based commercial press spread the iconic image far and wide. The trite visual language of "the sexy Modern Girl icon" was consequently applied to an array of commodities ranging from fertilizer to real estate and food products. Madeleine Dong's chapter, also on China, argues that the Modern Girl emerged as an archetypal figure marking the unprecedented public visibility of young women in the early twentieth century. As Dong explains, a "Modern Girl look" was singled out by commentators as a key mechanism that allowed women to disrupt class boundaries and to challenge established gender relations. In elite and popular publications, class and gender anxieties were interwoven: the Modern Girl threatened male authority, the elite's privileged claim to "being modern," and she polluted the elite marriage market. Overall, the Modern Girl's "girlness" could work to trouble or shore up social conventions and raced and gendered hierarchies.

Visual Economies

For both sociological and technological reasons, the preponderance of evidence for our claim that the Modern Girl was a global phenomenon is visual in nature. Sociologically, Modern Girls were women who became visible as urban migrants, factory and domestic workers, waitresses, cinema stars, citizens, freedom fighters, revolutionaries, consumers, and leisure seekers in new public realms — city streets, train stations, factories, offices, department stores, ballrooms, film studios, theaters, clubs, cafes, beaches, and tennis courts. Being seen was a quintessential feature of the Modern Girl. By the 1920s, lithography, photography, and cinema together enabled the easy reproduction of visual representations. These durable and cheap technologies were the sine qua non of the Modern Girls' near-simultaneity since everywhere she became visible in and through these common media. Multinational corporations, film industries, international reporting and artistic circuits, and the distribution of illustrated magazines from metropoles to colonies, and from urban centers to remote locations, facilitated the circulation of a Modern Girl iconography. In particular, the graphic designs circulated on posters and in illustrated magazines and design journals were adopted across contexts, as such visual (as opposed to literary) representations were accessible to those lacking literacy or foreign linguistic expertise. For similar reasons, films, especially silent films, circulated widely. Many more representations of the Modern Girl were locally produced and consumed, including the photographs of South African, Indian, and Okinawan women that chapters by Thomas, Ramamurthy, and Ito discuss (see especially figures 5.3 and 7.4). By the 1930s visual representations of women with bobbed hair, cloche hats, elongated bodies, and open, easy smiles could be found on all five continents in a range of visual media.

Visuality was important to the self-representation of all women (and men) who considered themselves "modern." Since the nineteenth century, women had used

Lassen Sie den Reiz Ihres Lächelns nicht durch Film zerstören!

Entfernen Sie den Film um auffallend schöne Zähne zu erhalten!

Pepsodent tut zweierlei: es entfernt den Film und poliert den Zahnschmelz.
Film ist ein schlüpfriger, die Zahnverfall verursachenden Bakterien beherbergender Belag. Seine Entfernung ist wichtig für Ihre Gesundheit. Die Zahnpasta, die Sie verwenden, bestimmt das Aussehen Ihrer Zähne. Das schonend wirkende Pepsodent verleiht ihnen unvergleichlichen Glanz durch die Entfernung des Films.
Verlangen Sie noch heute gratis eine 10-Tage-Tube von dem Apotheken-Bedarfs-Contor, Berlin SW. 68, Friedrichstraße 19.

Pepsodent die spezielle filmentfernende Zahnpasta

1.6 Ad run in the German magazines *Die Dame* and *Leipziger Illustrirte Zeitung* (1931) for the U.S. toothpaste Pepsodent featuring a Modern Girl with an open, easy smile.

photography along with older media such as painting, drawing, and literary representations of female spectacle and performance to stage the self. As numerous chapters document, visual means of portrayal were a component of the New Woman and the Modern Girl when she emerged in the United States, Europe, Japan, and various colonies. As has already been noted, Roberts found the French *éclaireuse*, Durand, using her newspaper as a vehicle to portray the New Woman as independent and beautiful; and Dong shows the Modern Girl emerging through cartoons as both an object of the gaze and as herself in possession of the gaze and thus as capable of objectifying those who would objectify her.

As exciting as is the recognition of the visual ubiquity of the Modern Girl, it raises thorny conceptual questions. Over the last three decades, scholars of visual culture have carefully attended to "scopic regimes," "visual regimes," and "visual economies" and have questioned the universal intelligibility of visual representations.[22] Aided by the method of connective comparison, we have engaged this scholarship and have added to it by situating visual representations of the Modern Girl in specific circuits of production, distribution, and reception. We have found that uneven power relations shaped representations of the Modern Girl differently across contexts, influencing her image in a variety of genres including newspapers, illustrated magazines, studio photographs, films, cartoons, novels, and sociological commentary. Barbara Sato, in her chapter on the Japanese Modern Girl, argues that it was her visual representation in popular women's magazines that made it possible for less privileged and rural women to partake in her appeal.

Even as these representations literally made the Modern Girl visible to contemporaries everywhere, the conditions of her visuality varied dramatically. Gorsuch's chapter on the Soviet Union suggests that political paintings critical of the bourgeois lifestyle and ads for commodities such as shoes surreptitiously featured the Modern Girl, while "Bolshevik moralists" attacked her as incompatible with Communism. Through recovery of the culture of the Indian starlet (*sitara*) in the interwar years, Ramamurthy's chapter illustrates the past existence of a local style of Modern Girl, especially in the few extant film stills. These images feature languidly posed women with bobbed hair, "kiss curls," plucked eyebrows, and painted lips. As Ramamurthy explains, the fact that these often racially ambiguous and erotic images were dropped from nationalist historiography indicates nationalist hostility to this imagery and demonstrates the importance of redeeming the Modern Girl for an alternative feminist historiography — one that includes the now vanished film culture of female self-invention. Similarly, Thomas finds evidence of the Modern Girl in 1930s photographs that South African women sent to the black newspaper *Bantu World*, which asked readers to participate in a beauty competition for "African ladies." The top-place finisher distinguished herself from other competitors by wearing a cloche hat and drop neckline and sporting a teeth-revealing smile, thus creating an image resonant with movie star stills and toothpaste ads then in international circulation.

While the method of connective comparison reveals continuities in the visual representation of the Modern Girl across contexts, our research suggests that similar visuals did not always carry similar meanings. In our discussion of cosmetics advertising in chapter 2, for example, we examine adjustments in advertising copy made by multinational companies in order to present nearly identical visuals to audiences in disparate regions. Efforts to identify the specific grammar of local representation clearly requires attention to multiple genres of visual representation and to the interplay between written word and visual text, as well as careful (re)construction of the context of reception.

The visual coding of race in representations of the Modern Girl in the 1920s and 1930s highlights these general points. As we suggest in the next chapter, graphic artists created representations of women with highly abstract facial and bodily features in a broad range of contexts. Some of these images, for example in the U.S. and German presses and in the Indian and South African presses that catered to white colonial populations, presented Modern Girls with stylized, possibly "East Asian" eyes. Our group has hotly debated these "Asianized" images. They are clearly part of a larger art deco trend that abstracts the human form.[23] And yet, this does not entirely explain the manner in which such otherwise abstract representations traded in racially coded visual signifiers that were both local and global (see figure 1.2). In order to explore these images and the production of this specific bodily, sartorial, and design aesthetic in cosmetics ads from many parts of the world, chapter 2 introduces the term "Asianization." Despite the complexities involved in using the term to demarcate aesthetic features (for further discussion see chapter 2), some of us have found the term useful in describing the efforts of companies and designers to produce and sell an exoticized Asian aesthetic as "modern." As has already been noted, Weinbaum's chapter on the U.S. Modern Girl explores "Asianization" as a form of "racial masquerade." Uta Poiger's chapter on the international frameworks that produced cosmetics advertising in Weimar and Nazi Germany also elaborates on these issues. Poiger describes what she calls the "cosmopolitan aesthetic" that characterizes imagery combining a range of racial markers, including blond hair, brown skin, and stylized eyes. This aesthetic became attractive to export-oriented cosmetics advertisers in the United States, Germany, and elsewhere in the 1920s as part of an international business logic that imagined a convergence of lifestyles and looks from around the world. In Germany, Poiger explains, the cosmopolitan aesthetic marked a departure from earlier racist conventions; it was also an aesthetic that largely disappeared with the onset of the Great Depression and the rise of National Socialism.

Nationalisms

The Modern Girl was an object of nationalist scrutiny and thus provoked a full range of nationalist desires. In all national contexts in which she appeared she was a contested figure and image, either an object of celebration or of attempted control. Her sexual adventurousness was viewed as inextricable from her implication in commodity culture and often both were seen as threatening to national sovereignty. To contemporaries, Modern Girls appeared to challenge "proper" female commitments to the nation — be it as active participants in nationalist struggles for liberation; as mothers, the biological reproducers of national subjects and populations; as transmitters of national culture; as upholders of the boundaries of nations through restrictions on sexual behavior and the circumscription of "marriage" within clearly defined ethnic and racial groups; or as symbols and signifiers of nations.[24] In particular, the Modern Girl's supposed sexual transgressions — her expression of sexuality as such, her interest in same-sex or interracial sexuality and in sexuality outside marriage — made the Modern Girl into a body in need of policing by nation-states, social reformers, and missionaries as well as national bourgeoisies.[25] The chapters of this volume principally treat the heterosexual modern girl whose sexual transgressions involved the sheer act of being sexual in public and actively choosing her male partners. While scholars who focus on literary and psychoanalytic texts, including "underground" publications, have begun to investigate same-sex desire in the interwar years, most chapters in this volume cover dominant media cultures, which rarely depicted same-sex or interracial intimacy. Historiography on the New Woman has treated her lesbianism and her often androgynous self-expression. Further scholarship on the lesbian Modern Girl, distinct from the figure whom Carroll Smith-Rosenberg famously labeled the "androgyn," remains to be done, as does work on the Modern Girl and interracial sex.[26]

In general, policing of the Modern Girl was carried out as a representational project, and sometimes also as a governmental or juridical one. In the various representations of the Modern Girl treated in this volume, whether textual or visual, we see pitched contestation over the Modern Girl's sexuality and public display, its representation in a variety of media and genres, and its imbrication within commodity culture. Indeed, both policing of actual Modern Girls and of representations of Modern Girls characterized modern nationalism worldwide in the 1920s and 1930s. In order to ensure their continuous production and consolidation, hegemonic nationalisms seem to have required control over Modern Girls as historical agents and as images — thus the vigilant containment of the Modern Girl's sexuality, consumption, and not least her representation in the variety of cultural texts, including literature, film, advertising, and social theory, analyzed in this volume.

While everywhere there was a response to the presence and representation of the Modern Girl, the political dimensions of this response varied widely. In some instances, Modern Girl iconography was used to cement nationalist ideals. Conversely, in others, nationalism was expressed through denigration of the Modern Girl as agent and image of antinationalist subjectivity. As individual volume chapters attest, this variation depended on a range of factors, including the presence or absence of social revolution, colonialism, indigenous nationalist and anticolonial struggles, and alternative models and icons of femininity. Where the Modern Girl was condemned or censored she was most often regarded and represented as a threat to national cohesion and social control. In the Soviet Union, China, and South Africa, for instance, the Modern Girl was frequently represented as in need of discipline. As Gorsuch argues in her chapter on Soviet flappers who emerged in the wake of the Bolshevik revolution, their "playful attitude" toward style and fashion was associated with American decadence; consequently, they represented a threat to "a healthy communist body politic." Bolshevik moralists sought to transform the youth culture to which flappers belonged, but even they found it necessary, at least during the New Economic Policy of the 1920s, to support the relative freedoms, such as access to commodities and expressive dance styles, that ran counter to the more sober collectivist ideals. Similarly, Dong's chapter shows that in China in the same period, the ample space granted to cartoons condemning Modern Girls indicated an abiding mainstream interest in the Modern Girl alongside, and perhaps despite, vocal condemnation of her.

Frequently, public condemnation of the Modern Girl was aimed not only at controlling her social interactions and public display but also at shaping the production of historical and thus nationalist memory. As Ramamurthy demonstrates, erasure of Indian Modern Girl culture from subsequent nationalist historiography powerfully reveals the manner in which hegemonic nationalism distanced itself from women's participation in a Westernized culture of consumption. As Thomas argues, in South Africa the discourse of "racial respectability" that was used to police the African Modern Girl produced ambiguous political results. Black male journalists and intellectuals viewed black women's use of white powder and red lipstick as a misguided imitation of white women, and thus as catering to segregationist rather than nationalist ideas. However, some black women appear to have regarded their own cosmetic use as necessary to crafting an urbane and "respectable" appearance, one partly inspired by African American role models.

Whereas anticolonial struggles tended to view the Modern Girl with suspicion, nationalist projects often mobilized the white Modern Girl as a signifier of "healthy" and "civilized" national femininity in the United States and Australia and, with much ambivalence, in Nazi Germany. In white-dominated contexts, various forms of racial nationalism were shored up through circulation of idealized representations of the white Modern Girl that contrasted her with her dark and thus "premodern" sister. While the Modern Girl's instrumentalization by racial nationalists was most evident in white settler contexts (the United States and Australia) where being white was often viewed as tantamount to being a "proper" national subject, she was also instrumentalized by nationalists in Europe, especially fascist Germany. As Poiger argues, the Great Depression and the rise of National Socialism in Germany coincided with a shift in cosmetics advertising from preference for a "cosmopolitan aesthetic" in depiction of the Modern Girl to embrace of a more decisively white-looking Modern Girl. While some of the latter images were of "Aryan" or "Nordic" types whose blond athleticism complied with the emergent fascist ideals of racial and national superiority, others were "vamp" or "girl" types against whom commentators from across the political spectrum had railed since the days of the Weimar Republic.

Although in the United States the Modern Girl icon was most often used to shore up racial nationalism, intellectuals and antiracist pundits who wished to critique ideas of nationalism predicated on white racial superiority created competing representations of the Modern Girl that critiqued her exclusive whiteness. As Weinbaum demonstrates through her reading of the work of the African American novelist Nella Larsen, black intellectuals in the 1920s used representations of black sartorial and beauty culture to contest white aesthetic and social supremacy. Larsen's writings are also important in that they expose the class bias and hypocrisy of elite blacks whose "racial uplift" philosophy denigrated poor and working-class black cultural expression. Similarly, as Baldwin's chapter on U.S. black beauty culture reveals, black beauty culturalists' promotion of black beauty ideals functioned as an implicit critique of Jim Crow racial hierarchies, and thus of the forms of racism and nationalism pervasive in the United States in the same period.

Commodities

Early on, the Modern Girl research group recognized that a particular bundle of commodities including lipstick, nail polish, face creams and powders, skin lighteners, tanning lotions, shampoos, hair styling products, fancy soaps, perfumes, deodorants, toothpastes, cigarettes, high-heel shoes, cloche hats, and fashionable, sexy clothes was advertised globally. We also realized that such commodities were linked in each local context to the expression of modern femininity. We thus designated them "Modern Girl commodities."

As is evident from the list of Modern Girl commodities, they are robustly corporeal. They literally changed how bodies appeared, how they were "worked on and through," how they were fashioned, fragmented, abstracted, and calibrated to the seasons, or even, as some hoped, permanently transformed.[27] These commodities created new relationships to the body and enabled women to craft themselves as modern. In her influential book on U.S. beauty culture, Kathy Peiss argues that new commodities associated modernity, novelty, and self-care with consciousness of bodily autonomy, freedom, and sexual desire.[28] This volume builds on these insights through discussion of the corporality and performativity of Modern Girl commodities in two ways. First, several chapters explore how such commodities fostered young women's yearnings for public life by outfitting them with faces and bodies that emboldened them to cross the domestic threshold into the public sphere. And second, several chapters examine how such commodities publicized women's everyday lives by putting private cares about the body and bodily functions on display.

What we have called multidirectional citation characterized the representation of Modern Girl commodities in advertisements found around the world. And yet, what gave these commodities, and through them the Modern Girl, an "internationalist" valence in the United States or South Africa, for example, was quite different from what gave them a "cosmopolitan" valence in Germany. In the former locations, as Baldwin and Thomas demonstrate, cosmetics could be used by African American and African consumers to express race pride and a sense of participation in a larger internationalist, African diaspora. By contrast, in pre-Depression Germany, the United States, and Japan cosmetics companies deployed the "cosmopolitan aesthetic" that Poiger discusses —an aesthetic composed of racial markers connoting exoticism and, in some instances, worldliness.

Not only did Modern Girl commodities traffic in ideas about gender, race, and modernity; trade flows enabled them to materially connect different parts of the world. As marketed and exchanged goods with monetary values, their spread and sale was driven by the capitalist logic of supply, demand, and profitability. From the beginning, in collaborative and individual work, we have sought to situate Modern Girl commodities in the context of the broad transformations in political economy in the 1920s and 1930s, including increasing interdependency of markets and the global impact of the Great Depression. This volume demonstrates that Modern Girl commodities appeared not only in the capitalist core but also in communist and fascist states, and in imperial domains. In the Soviet Union, as Gorsuch shows, and in fascist Germany, as Poiger reveals, state domination of commercial processes was attempted in the interest of generating a politically palatable gendered modernity. In general, we find that during periods of economic and political upheaval, in these nations and others, demands for national sovereignty were carefully balanced with those of mass consumption.

Around the world the production of a new form of femininity centered on purchased products for the body created enormous social anxiety, much of which was targeted at consumption. In Conor's chapter, racist cartoons depict the consumption of Modern Girl commodities by Australian Aboriginal

Modern Girls as unbecoming, comical, and anxiety making for white settler women. As Dong's treatment of satirical Modern Girl cartoons and magazine stories shows, the Chinese public was fixated on the spousal tensions caused by the wife's consumption of commodities, including cosmetics. For Dong, this fixation was symptomatic of a crisis in the Chinese family as it shifted from being principally defined as a unit of production to one of consumption.

Several chapters address the use of the Modern Girl icon and advertising's solicitation of the Modern Girl consumer in the development of national markets and industries in metropole and colony. Our method of connective comparison establishes that advertising agencies played a central role as mediator of Modern Girl culture and global flows of Modern Girl commodities. In chapter 2 we discuss J. Walter Thompson as an example of one such agency with international reach. Because, in most instances, the emergence of commodity capitalism and nationalism were tightly bound, there was a necessary but at once ambivalent embrace of the Modern Girl as an advertising icon. Especially in those contexts in which Modern Girls were viewed as less than respectable, this complicity of capitalism and economic development produced tension. In her chapter on India, Ramamurthy demonstrates that by the 1930s it was only "cultured" Modern Girl cinema stars possessing respectable patrilines whose images were used to sell products to an emerging Indian national market.

Consumption and the Question of Agency

Notwithstanding the overarching calculations of corporations and the regulatory functions of states, many volume chapters attest to the fact that Modern Girls exercised agency as consumers and social actors. In recent years, social scientists have debated and explored consumption as an important site of individual agency, some arguing that consumption allows people to be creative actors, meaningfully presenting and defining themselves through purchase and use. Others, usually Marxist, argue that commodities attach people to economic structures that create deprivation and dependency.[29] Although not all contributors to this volume are sanguine about the liberatory potential of consumer culture, most concur that Modern Girl commodities were involved in fashioning both individual and social bodies (see figure 1.8).

Often the question of Modern Girl consumer agency was related to her participation, implicit or explicit, in racial politics. As chapters by Thomas, Weinbaum, and Baldwin show, albeit in divergent ways, the Modern Girl used consumption as a means to participate in hegemonic racial identity and, in some instances, to contest it. Faced with the question of whether consumption

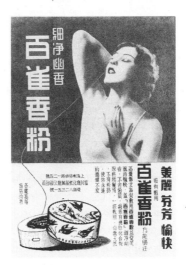

1.7 Ad for facial cream in *Times of India* (1940) that was marketed by British multinational Burroughs Welcome and features an Indian Modern Girl with short hair and exposed arms.

1.8 An act of self-creation? A Chinese consumer applies "Sparrow Face Powder" in an ad from *Young Companion* (1940).

of Modern Girl commodities by black women in South Africa was racial mimicry or an alternative cultural politics, Thomas refuses an either/or conclusion through exploration of the contested story of "racial respectability." Baldwin tracks how use of Modern Girl commodities enabled working-class black women in the United States to explore the possibilities of "re-creation." Black women's consumption of cosmetics was, Baldwin argues, both part of the capitalist economy and simultaneously liberatory in that it allowed consumers to separate leisure from work and to develop systemic health. In contrast to Baldwin, Weinbaum explores the existence of an emergent critique of U.S. consumer capitalism across a variety of sociological and literary texts from the 1920s. As she demonstrates, early race theorists and U.S. women of color, including African American and Asian American women, were acutely aware of the limitations of recourse to consumption as a liberatory practice. After all, commodities were not equally accessible to all women and the transformation of bodily surfaces that they enabled was only possible in certain contexts and within certain racial formations.

In other chapters the Modern Girl's consumer agency is treated in relation to class politics. In her chapter on Soviet flappers, Gorsuch underscores that these

Modern Girls were working girls, "factory youth" for whom the silk stockings and red lipstick signified that the consumer of these goods was "modern," though not necessarily Western or bourgeois. Sato's chapter on the Japanese Modern Girl similarly positions her as a consumer whose participation in commodity culture opened the possibility of social and cultural redefinition. In making this argument Sato challenges assertions by other scholars who have argued that Japanese Modern Girls were urban and upper-class women who indulged in glamorous consumption. As she demonstrates, less privileged and rural women also partook in consumerism — albeit a less conspicuous form of consumerism grounded in everyday life — by buying, looking at, and reading women's magazines.

Through the course of our project, we have found that an alternative approach to the Modern Girl's agency involves forgoing the desire to decide unequivocally whether Modern Girls were dupes or resistors of consumer capitalism and instead asking how Modern Girl commodities functioned pedagogically and as technologies of the self. Such an approach involves an exploration of commodity advertising as a key technique for schooling consumers in the "cultural practices of modernity."[30] It resists assessment of consumption as positive or negative, oppressive or liberatory, and instead emphasizes how commodity advertising and consumption were productive of the Modern Girl as both representational strategy and social agent formed in and through early processes of gendered globalization. The implications of these processes with regard to social stratification, political emancipation, and consolidation or contestation of national political regimes defy easy generalization as they necessarily vary from context to context and over time. This volume explores these issues of consumption, representation, and social and political agency through a variety of approaches. Our hope is that the chapters collected here will inspire others to engage the Modern Girl as a heuristic device, to employ the method of connective comparison, and to recognize multidirectional citation as a useful tool in the study of gendered modernity in a global frame.

Notes

All authors contributed equally to this chapter, chapter 2, and the editing of the volume.

1. The group's first publication of these ideas is in Modern Girl Around the World Research Group (Tani E. Barlow, Madeleine Yue Dong, Uta G. Poiger, Priti Ramamurthy, Lynn M. Thomas, and Alys Eve Weinbaum), "The Modern Girl around the World."

2. Tani E. Barlow prefers her own conceptual framework in dealing with this question. See Barlow, *The Question of Women in Chinese Feminism*, Barlow, "History and the Border," and Barlow, " 'What Is a Poem?' "

3. Our method resonates with Gillian Hart's method of "relational comparisons" and Anna Lowenhaupt Tsing's formulation of "friction." See Hart, "Denaturalizing Dispossession," and Lowenhaupt Tsing, *Friction*.

4. Fabian, *Time and the Other*.

5. Afsaneh Najmabadi, "Comments on the Modern Girl as Heuristic: Collaboration, Connective Comparison, Multidirectional Citation," remarks presented at "The Modern Girl Around the World" symposium, Radcliffe Institute for Advanced Study, Harvard University, 16 March 2007.

6. Bairoch, "Globalization Myths and Realities," Cooper, "What Is the Concept of Globalization Good For?"

7. For Japan, see Silverberg, "The Modern Girl as Militant" and "The Café Waitress Serving Modern Japan"; Harootunian, *Overcome by Modernity*; and Sato, *The New Japanese Woman*. For the United States, see Peiss, *Cheap Amusements* and *Hope in a Jar*; Mizejewski, *Ziegfeld Girl*; Latham, *Posing a Threat*; and Glenn, *Female Spectacle*. For China, see Shih, "Gender, Race and Semicolonialism." For Africa, see Glazier Schuster, *New Women of Lusaka*. For India, see Mohan, *Of Wayward Girls and Wicked Women*. For Europe, see Roberts, *Civilization without Sexes*; Chadwick and Latimer, eds., *The Modern Woman Revisited*; Grossmann, "Girlkultur, or Thoroughly Rationalized Female?"; von Ankum, ed., *Women in the Metropolis*; Søland, *Becoming Modern*.

8. On "Americanization" and "globalization," see Fehrenbach and Poiger, eds., *Transactions, Transgressions, Transformations*; and Weinbaum and Edwards, "On Critical Globality."

9. Wilk, "The Local and the Global in the Political Economy of Beauty."

10. See Silverberg, "The Café Waitress Serving Modern Japan."

11. The Tokyo-based group's edited volume is forthcoming in Japanese: Ruri Ito, Hiroko Sakamoto, and Tani Barlow, eds., *The Modern Girl and Colonial Modernity in East Asia* (Tokyo: Iwanami Shoten).

12. See, for example, Fabian, *Time and the Other*, and Donham, *Marxist Modern*.

13. See, for example, Harootunian, *Overcome by Modernity*; Peukert, *The Weimar Republic*; and Ben-Ghiat, *Fascist Modernities*.

14. See, for example, Chakrabarty, *Provincializing Europe*; Comaroff and Comaroff, eds., *Modernity and Its Malcontents*; Gaonkar, "On Alternative Modernities"; Larkin, "Indian Films and Nigerian Lovers"; Rofel, *Other Modernities*; Sivaramakrishnan and Agrawal, "Regional Modernities in Stories and Practices of Development"; and essays collected in Knauft, ed., *Critically Modern*.

15. See Barlow, ed., *Formations of Colonial Modernity in East Asia* and Barlow, "Eugenic Woman, Semi-Colonialism and Colonial Modernity as Problems for Postcolonial Theory"; and Jones, *Yellow Music*.

16. See Ferguson, *Expectations of Modernity*.

17. Felski, *The Gender of Modernity*; Rofel, *Other Modernities*; Wardlow, " 'Hands-Up'-ing Buses and Harvesting Cheese-Pops."

18. Mitchell, *The New Girl*, 3. On girlhood, also see Driscoll, *Girls*; and Maynes, Søland, and Benninghaus, eds., *Secret Gardens, Satanic Mills*.

19. Trimborn, *Leni Riefenstahl*; Newell, "An Incident of Colonial Intertextuality"; Newell, "White Cargoes/Black Cargoes on the West Coast of Africa."

20. Also see Finnegan, *Selling Suffrage*; Glenn, *Female Spectacle*.

21. On the distinction between New Woman and Modern Girl in China, see Stevens, "Figuring Modernity."

22. See Brennan and Jay, eds., *Vision in Context*; Poole, *Vision, Race, and Modernity*; Landau and Kaspin, *Images and Empires*; Wexler, *Tender Violence*; Pratt, *Imperial Eyes*; and Mitchell, *Picture Theory*.

23. See Fischer, *Designing Women*; and Ward, *Weimar Surfaces*.

24. See Yuval Davis and Anthias, Introduction.

25. On the nationalist policing of interracial sexuality, see Weinbaum, *Wayward Reproductions*; and Stevens, *Reproducing the State*.

26. See Doan, *Fashioning Sapphism*; Dean, *The Frail Social Body*; Chadwick and Latimer, eds., *The Modern Woman Revisited*; Smith-Rosenberg, *Disorderly Conduct*; and Halberstam, *Female Masculinity*.

27. Burke, *Lifebuoy Men, Lux Women*, 4.

28. Peiss, *Hope in a Jar*.

29. See Wilk, "Consumer Goods as Dialogue about Development," 83; Peiss, *Hope in a Jar*, 4; and the commentary by Timothy Burke in this volume.

30. Harvey, *The Condition of Postmodernity*.

2

The Modern Girl
Around the World

Cosmetics Advertising

and the Politics of Race and Style

MODERN GIRL AROUND THE WORLD
RESEARCH GROUP (ALYS EVE WEINBAUM,
LYNN M. THOMAS, PRITI RAMAMURTHY,
UTA G. POIGER, MADELEINE Y. DONG,
and TANI E. BARLOW)

Advertising was one of the primary means through which a distinct Modern Girl style simultaneously appeared around the globe in the 1920s and 1930s. With large advertising budgets, multinational and local cosmetics companies created and transmitted this Modern Girl style in the print media, portraying Modern Girls with carefully made-up faces, bobbed hair, exposed arms and backs, and bodies clad in the latest fashions. Cosmetics ads placed Modern Girls in new social situations — romancing in public, playing sports, posing as film stars, or caring for the self in the bathroom — and, frequently, represented them using a unique aesthetic that emphasized an elongated body and abstracted facial features. Such ads also frequently depicted Modern Girls as involved in efforts to alter their skin color through use of makeup, whitening, coloring, and tanning products. It is in this way that cosmetics presented the Modern Girl's various acts of self-fashioning and public display as tightly knit into national as well as transnational processes of racial formation.

The richness of Modern Girl cosmetics ads, their depiction of Modern Girl style and aesthetics, and, not least, their participation in racial formation encouraged our research group to track the Modern Girl as a global phenomenon in and through them. Over the last several years we have created a diverse collection of advertisements spanning four continents, multiple languages, and a range of print media. In this chapter we explore the global prevalence of the Modern Girl in cosmetics ads and suggest ways that capitalist enterprises created and transmitted representations of femininity and race. The visual nature of these ads was especially useful in that it enabled us to work together using a method we call connective comparison — a method of reading texts that allows us to identify connections among disparate locales and to explore the overlap and distinction among Modern Girl representations, as discussed in chapter 1. Overall, we have relied on two research strategies: first, we have simultaneously examined multinational and local companies that marketed Modern Girl cosmetics; and second, we have tracked imagery associated with select categories of cosmetics, those designed to alter skin color. As we will see, in depicting processes of cleansing, coloring, and transforming facial and bodily surfaces, cosmetics ads indexed new, modern technologies of the self and revealed a set of newly emergent social practices.[1]

Our method of connective comparison has also allowed us to pay close attention to the peculiarities of local manifestations of the Modern Girl style and aesthetic and to discern the repeated citation of specific styles and aesthetics across contexts. As this chapter argues, local understandings of skin color and their relationship to national racial formations shaped Modern Girl style and aesthetics and at once contributed to the global Modern Girl phenomenon. Put differently, the chapter illustrates the phenomenon that we term *multidirectional citation:* the mutual, though nonequivalent influences and circuits of exchange that actively connected disparate parts of the globe, shaping and transforming the representation and enactment of the Modern Girl around the world.

Modern Girl Cosmetics and Toiletry Advertising

Although multinational and local companies in all locales drew on Modern Girl imagery to market cosmetics and toiletry products, she was not equally visible everywhere. In the United States, Germany, and China, advertisements featuring the Modern Girl were more frequent than in Africa and South Asia. During the 1920s, U.S. companies were at the forefront of these developments as they consciously employed advertising to create new markets abroad.[2] Ads appearing in newspapers and magazines around the world featured U.S. more often than German, British, or other European products. In the periodicals that we examined, we found no evidence that cosmetics companies based outside the United States, Europe, and Japan were able to market their products abroad before World War II. The United States, by the 1920s, moreover, was the biggest producer of magazines and print advertising.

We have principally drawn ads from three American publications catering to middle-class and upper-class readers, *Vogue, Ladies Home Journal,* and *Cosmopolitan,* and from two publications specifically targeted at black readers, *The Crisis,* the journal of the National Association for the Advancement of Colored People (NAACP) that was edited during the 1920s by W. E. B. Du Bois, and the more populist weekly newspaper, the *Baltimore Afro-American.*[3] For Germany, we have collected ads from four illustrated magazines directed at middle-class and upper-class audiences, the *Leipziger Illustrirte Zeitung, Berliner Illustrirte Zeitung, Die Woche,* and the women's magazine *Die Dame.* For China, the cosmetics and toiletry ads we have collected are from treaty-port newspapers including *North China Daily News* and *South China Morning Post,* both of which were published in English as well as Chinese, and from the illustrated Chinese-language magazines *Ladies' Journal (Funü zazhi)* and *Young Companion (Liang You),* which addressed an upper-class and middle-class audience. Lower-class and communist tabloids, such as the German *Arbeiter-Illustrierte-Zeitung (Illustrated Worker Press),* or the Chinese *Luobinhan (Robin Hood)* and *Fuermosi (Sherlock Holmes)* rarely contained cosmetics ads, either because of leftist hostilities toward such luxury products or because workers were not seen as cosmetics consumers.

By comparison with the U.S., German, and Chinese contexts, we have found that in Africa and India, cosmetics and toiletry ads featuring the Modern Girl were not as commonplace in the 1920s. For Africa in the 1920s and 1930s, we collected ads from the *Cape Times* (Cape Town), a newspaper catering to the white and, to a lesser extent, "coloured" populations in the British dominion of South Africa.[4] The *Cape Times* often carried ads featuring white Modern Girls similar to those that appeared in the U.S., German, and Chinese press. For the early 1930s onward, we focused on the black newspapers *Bantu World* (Johannesburg), *Bantu Mirror* (Salisbury), and the *Times of West Africa* (Accra), which carried some ads for facial creams that featured the black Modern Girl. Finally, we gathered ads from *Drum* (Johannesburg and, later, Lagos, Accra, and Nairobi), a monthly magazine established in 1951, in which the black Modern Girl became widely visible. For India, we collected ads from the *Statesman* (Calcutta) and the *Times of India* (Bombay), major English-language pan-subcontinental dailies catering to British colonials and Indian elites. In these papers, advertisements mainly featured the white Modern Girl until 1930, after which time some ads for toiletry and cosmetics products began to feature the Indian Modern Girl. We also drew ads from the *Illustrated Weekly of India* (Bombay), one of the first English-language magazines to publish ads explicitly targeted at elite Indian women. Here, the Indian Modern Girl appeared more frequently in the late 1930s, becoming commonplace by the 1940s.[5]

Modern Girl advertising varied in kind. Some multinational companies simply recycled the same ad in a number of national and colonial contexts. One vivid example is the ubiquitous advertising for Pepsodent toothpaste, a product made by a U.S.-based company of the same name. In three ads that appeared in the Shanghai-based Chinese language magazine *Funü zazhi* (*Ladies' Journal*), the *Times of India* newspaper, and U.S. *Vogue* between 1926 and 1931, the image of the Modern Girl varies little (see figures 2.1, 2.2, and 2.3). In fact, apart from translation into Chinese, these three Pepsodent ads are nearly identical. All feature a young white woman with bobbed hair (while two of these ads also feature an older man resembling future U.S. president Franklin Roosevelt). All proclaim that Pepsodent removes the "dingy film" from teeth and encourage readers to send away for a free sample with the clip-out coupon provided. Advertisers used such coupons to track the effectiveness of their campaigns. Similar ads, featuring a lone white Modern Girl appeared in the *Times of West Africa* in 1934 and in the German press around the same time. In each, a young woman with bobbed hair flashes her bright teeth thanks to Pepsodent (see figure 1.6). The Modern Girl in all of these Pepsodent ads exhibits an aesthetic that evokes "Americanness": a wide smile, big white teeth, and a body that is noticeably athletic, sensual, relaxed, at leisure.

By contrast, other ads that we have found indicate that international companies adjusted advertisements — images and copy — in order to appeal to specific colonial and national markets. For example, from the 1920s to the 1950s the U.S.-based Pond's Extract Company (after 1955, Chesebrough-Pond's) adapted advertisements for its so-called vanishing cream to a wide array of local contexts. The Pond's campaigns were designed by the New York–based advertising agency J. Walter Thompson (JWT), which, by 1950, had offices in at least twenty-five foreign locations, including Bombay and Johannesburg. Pond's was, in fact, JWT's oldest client, dating back to 1886. Once JWT went global they used the Pond's account to showcase the value of working with an agency whose international offices could tailor a company's message for local markets. Instructively, an ad from a 1925 issue of the Chinese *Ladies' Journal* renames the product as Pond's White Jade Cream and explains how the cream can be applied underneath powder to "keep your makeup in place for the day." While one side of the cream bottle featured in the ad carries an English trademark, the

Ads for the U.S. toothpaste Pepsodent that circulated, (2.1) in China (1926), (2.2) in India (1926), (2.3) in the United States (1931), and elsewhere, with the claim to remove "dingy film" from teeth.

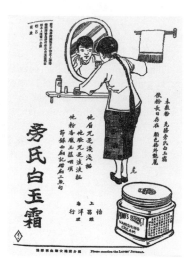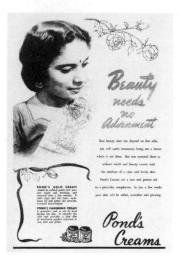

2.4 Ad for the U.S. product Pond's Cream in the Chinese magazine *Fünu Zazhi* (Ladies' Journal, 1925) featuring contemporary fashions and a long braid.

2.5 Ad in *Illustrated Weekly of India* (1942) for Pond's, featuring an Indian Modern Girl with *bindi*, stylish hair, and sari.

other side offers explanations in Chinese of the virtues of the product. The same ad also evokes verses from a famous fourteenth-century drama to allude to the beauty achievable through use of Pond's (see figure 2.4). In Germany JWT and Pond's told magazine readers in ads in 1930 that "trendsetting women" in fifty countries depended on Pond's cold cream and vanishing cream to make their skin "smooth."[6] Another Pond's ad from a 1942 issue of the *Illustrated Weekly of India* proclaims that "Beauty needs no adornment—real beauty does not depend on fine silks." According to this ad, Pond's enables women to achieve "real beauty" regardless of their class and caste (see figure 2.5). A fourth Pond's ad that appeared in 1955 in *Bantu Mirror*, a Southern Rhodesia weekly, targeted black readers and consumers. In contrast to the other Pond's ads, this one focuses on skin color, proclaiming that Pond's Vanishing Cream will make skin "lighter, smoother, softer."[7]

The crucial observation to take away from comparison of these ads is that Pond's and JWT attached different Modern Girl images and attributes to the same product depending on where it was marketed. Whereas Pepsodent apparently tried to create a new "American" standard of white teeth across the globe, JWT marketed Pond's facial creams by appealing to existing standards of beauty among local elites, while at times also stressing the global reach of its products. In all our contexts, we found Modern Girl ads for cosmetics that were produced and marketed by local companies exclusively for national or subnational consumption. For example, in the 1920s and 1930s, women with bobbed or short hair, a telltale sign of the Modern Girl, could be seen in ads for an Indian lightening "emollient," Afghan Snow, and a South African product called Keppels Face Powder (see figure 2.6). Such examples suggest the overlap and intersection among the advertising strategies of multinational and local companies.

The Modern Girl and Technologies of the Self

Comparison of ads produced by both international and local companies has allowed us to discern a Modern Girl aesthetic that cuts across national and imperial boundaries. In the 1920s and into the 1930s, the Modern Girl usually possessed an elongated, wiry, and svelte body. The form first appeared before World War I in cigarette and car advertisements in the United States and Europe,

2.6 Ad from the black South African newspaper *Bantu World* (1939) featuring the products of Keppels, one of the first white-owned South African cosmetics companies to target black consumers.

where it signified the attractions and dangers of androgyny and sexuality outside reproduction (see figure 1.5).[8] The Modern Girl's body is also depicted as excessively refined; individual female body parts are elegantly polished, carefully scrubbed, meticulously sprayed, or, in an astounding variety of ways, cleaned and covered so that lips, teeth, mouth, hair, skin, armpits, legs, and vagina are all stylishly produced. Moreover, the Modern Girl's beauty and youthfulness are often linked to scientific hygiene.

In a series of ads for Odorono, a humorously named antiperspirant and deodorant introduced by a U.S. company and widely distributed in the United States, China, South Africa, India, and Germany, many of these bodily characteristics are evident. In all Odorono ads copy specifies that by applying the product to the armpits, the young, active, trim, and glamorous Modern Girl can prevent unpleasant odors and ensure that social interactions, especially romantic ones, are unspoiled. With references to "sanitary sponge applicators," a "quick-drying formula," and the "doctor" who invented the product and supervised its production, these ads evoke scientific hygiene in rendering an unseemly topic legitimate (see figures 1.3, 1.4, and 2.7). Like many other cosmetics and toiletry ads from the late 1920s and early 1930s, the Odorono ads frequently feature angular drawings of women with long necks and limbs that connote elegance. Graphic designers of ads appearing in all research contexts frequently emphasized diagonal lines to create dynamic images. Often, the proportions used in such drawings suggest "real" women seven or eight feet tall. Heavily indebted to the international art deco movement, such aesthetic exaggeration was employed by international and local companies.[9]

Modern Girl image designers took advantage of the most advanced visual technology available. In the United States, China, Germany, and India, the format of many Modern Girl ads changed from line drawings to lithographic watercolors in the 1920s, and to photographs (often featuring film stars, well-known performers, or socialites) in the late 1920s. In many African periodicals, the shift to photos took place later, during the 1930s and 1940s. Over the decades, influenced by developments in photographic technology and techniques such as the close-up shot in filmmaking, Modern Girl ads in all locales demonstrated changes in the method of representing the female figure, shifting from locating her in the middle of a landscape or room to showing only the portrait of her head, highlighting her hair, eyebrows, eyes, cheeks, lips, or teeth. Occasionally a particular facial feature was emphasized by depicting the Modern Girl's hand touching or caressing it.

Another aesthetic in the U.S. and German cosmetics ads and the early Indian and South African ads that targeted white colonials is what we cautiously describe as the "Asianization" of the Modern Girl. While the term has a negative valence in some contexts, especially those in which ideas of "Asianization" have been used to euphemize the dissemination of Japanese political and military power, we have found the term useful in our exploration of racialized aesthetics. In cosmetic ads that are focused on the body or face, we have found that Asianization involved creation of caricatured, elongated, often slanted eyes. This is especially the case in those ads that employ a modernist art deco style. This stylization is evident in an ad for De Kama facial cream that appeared in 1924 in U.S. *Vogue*, in an ad for Ven-Yusa face cream that appeared in 1930 in the Indian *Statesman*, and in a 1929 German poster for F. Wolff and Sohn's advertising Vogue Perfume (figures 1.2, 2.8, and 14.2). The women drawn in these ads are not clearly identifiable as Caucasian, black, or East Asian, though their eyes are expressly Asianized. In Europe and in the United States, where Orientalism was a venerable tradition and advertising cultures were predisposed to racist graphics, so-called slanted eyes probably denoted Asianness especially during the interwar years, when things "Oriental" gained

2.7 Ad from *Illustrated Weekly of India* (1947) advertising Odorono, a deodorant licensed by a U.S. company that was marketed around the globe.

2.8 An art deco ad from U.S. *Vogue* (1924) for De Kama face cream, featuring abstract "Asianized" eyes.

particular cachet as part of the spread of a worldwide art deco aesthetic that incorporated both chinoiserie and japonisme into its stylized depictions of bodies and faces. Whereas Orientalism is a concept that is typically used to explain the production of the "Orient" and "Oriental" as mysterious, feminine, and unchanging, as well as the consequent construction of the Occidental's superiority and prowess, Asianization, at least for Americans and Europeans, may have expressed an ambition to make the self more "exotic," if only temporarily, and if only from a position of relative privilege.[10]

In addition to the commonalities of body and facial aesthetics, the Modern

2.9 Ad in the *Times of India* (1939) for Palmolive soap featuring the film star Devika Rani.

Girl is most frequently depicted in one of four specific activities or venues: she is figured as a film star; she is represented as an outdoor and sports enthusiast; she is depicted in romantic or intimate poses; and, she is found making up or admiring herself in front of her vanity or in a handheld mirror. Each of these activities or venues suggests a cluster of values and attitudes that contemporaries associated with the Modern Girl.

It appears that the Modern Girl image, in part, reflects observation and adaptation of female bodily practices performed on the silver screen. We know from previous research on *moga* in Japan, flappers in the United States, *modeng xiaojie* in China, and *neue Frauen* in Germany that film watching was a leisure activity routinely associated with the Modern Girl. Contemporaries often viewed Modern Girl postures, hand gestures, and ways of walking and talking as mimicking the movies.[11] Beginning in the late 1920s, in each of our locations, well-known actresses were used to promote products; many ads for cosmetics therefore feature film stars. In a 1939 ad for Palmolive soap in the *Times of India*, for example, the film star Devika Rani is prominently portrayed (see figure 2.9). In linking the Modern Girl and movie watching, this ad enables a British company to capitalize on the glamour and fame of a local celebrity to create nationalist appeal, and also to cast its "beauty soap" as possessing global reach. As the copy explains: Palmolive is used by "millions of women in England, France, Germany, America and 67 other countries." It also specifies that Palmolive "contains no animal fats," thus assuaging potential alarm among Hindu and Muslim consumers. Devika Rani, a globe-trotting local star, ties together the international consumer of Palmolive and the Indian everywoman.

Ads depicting the Modern Girl engaged in outdoor activities invariably valorize her physicality. This trend is apparent in toiletry and cigarette ads from those locales in which the Modern Girl—particularly the white European and American Modern Girl and the Chinese Modern Girl—is depicted swimming, sunbathing, golfing, and, especially, playing tennis (see figures 1.4 and 2.10). By the early 1930s, Indian newspapers and ads also featured the Indian Mod-

2.10 Ad in *Vanity Fair* (1934) for Elizabeth Arden "Sun-pruf Cream" featuring two athletic, beach-going Modern Girls.

ern Girl as an ace tennis player. Although a black tennis-playing Modern Girl did not appear in ads in the African press during the 1930s, she was the subject of written commentary, indicating that tennis was a fashionable pursuit for young, elite African women. By depicting the Modern Girl's athleticism, such ads glorified her strength, her desire for adventure, and her unwillingness to be restricted to the domestic domain. These images may also have been voyeuristically viewed in those contexts in which public displays of female body parts, such as legs and nude shoulders, had previously been eschewed.

No matter where she appears, the Modern Girl is associated with dating, romantic love, and premarital sex. The most interesting cosmetics ads depict the Modern Girl as self-aware of her allure and capable of using it to her advantage. A 1939 ad from South Africa's *Bantu World*, for instance, features a dancing Modern Girl under the slogan "the smartest woman in the hall" (see figure 2.6). In other ads, the Modern Girl's sexuality suggests lesbianism (or, as we will see, autoeroticism). In a 1934 American ad for Elizabeth Arden's Sun-pruf Cream that appeared in *Vanity Fair*, a Modern Girl clad in beach wear proffers a tube of tanning product to her companion in a phallic, erotically charged gesture (see figure 2.10). Most of the time, Modern Girl sexual desire as expressed in cosmetics or toiletry ads was not interracial and thus did not venture to provoke contemporary anxieties about interracial sex and intimacy.

The Modern Girl Around the World   35

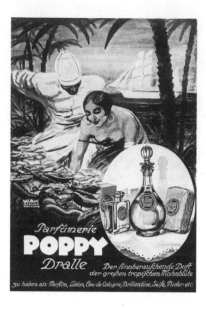

2.11 Ad for perfume in the German *Leipziger Illustrirte Zeitung* (1924) of Modern Girl/Tropical Temptress with suitor.

One 1924 German ad for a perfume with the English name "Poppy," however, depicts a sparsely clad woman — part Modern Girl, part tropical temptress — pursued by a man of color, whose otherness is coded through dress and skin color. This perfume ad appealed to consumers by hinting at multiple transgressions: a smell that "enchanted and intoxicated the senses" and an openly sexualized female body desirous of "otherness" (see figure 2.11). In contrast to ads, filmic and literary representations of the Modern Girl produced in the United States, Africa, and Europe routinely suggest that some contemporaries associated the Modern Girl with transgression of racial boundaries and sexual norms.

When ads represent the Modern Girl at home, she is neither cooking and cleaning nor tending children but rather is caring for her own body in front of her vanity. Instead of being family-minded, the Modern Girl is represented as self-possessed, even self-indulgent. In a 1937 Chinese ad for Richard Hudnut's Three Flowers Dusting Powder that appeared in *Young Companion*, a young woman sits on a stool in a modern, luxurious bathroom and powders herself in front of her mirror (see figure 2.12). She is clad in only a short slip, the kind worn under a *qipao*, a dress popular with Chinese Modern Girls. Our attention is drawn by her partially nude, sleek body, which her self-caressing hand gesture presents as a delicate and precious object.

The literal self-reflection of the Modern Girl in a mirror in numerous cosmetics ads has a dual meaning (see figures 1.1, 1.7, 2.13, 2.14, and 2.15). On

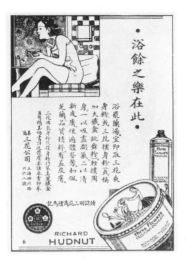

2.12 "The Pleasure of a Bath." Chinese ad for Richard Hudnut products in *Liang Yu* (The Young Companion, 1937) features a young woman wearing a slip in a luxurious modern bathroom.

2.13 In a 1928 ad for Madam C. J. Walker beauty care products that appeared in *The Crisis*, an African American Modern Girl gazes lovingly at her image in her hand mirror.

the one hand, it suggests the possibility of her self-possession. Through hints of a self-touching erotics, it celebrates the Modern Girl's sexuality. On the other hand, mirror gazing also suggests the Modern Girl's constant obligation to judge herself against the beauty and social standards presented in the ads and elsewhere and thus to predict the opinions of others and to adjust accordingly. Though commodities do not necessarily offer the Modern Girl-as-consumer freedom from gendered social constraints or create new social and sexual norms, commodities opened up new possibilities in the realm of self-reflection, self-creation, and self-valuation. This use of commodity culture to create openings for representing a femininity that is self-consciously elected and crafted is a theme that has emerged time and again in our collaboration.

Facial Cosmetics, Skin Color, and Racial Formation

A large proportion of the cosmetics ads that feature the Modern Girl promote products that promise to provide new color or to transform the existing color or quality of the Modern Girl's skin. Such products include makeup and face powders as well as cold, acne, vanishing, bleaching, whitening, and tanning

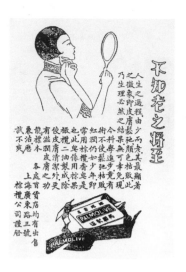 

2.14 Chinese ad for Palmolive soap in *Funü zazhi* (1930)
promises to prevent skin from aging.

2.15 A German ad for Elida cream from *Leipziger Illustrirte Zeitung* (1928)
with a Modern Girl approvingly assessing herself in the mirror.

creams. In our analysis of ads for such products, we seek to elucidate further
how the Modern Girl's bodily self-fashioning is knit into processes of racial
formation. In so doing, we have sought to address two overarching and interrelated questions: How do ads for such cosmetics provide insight into racial
formations, both national and transnational, through which the Modern Girl
emerged? And how do such ads participate in the production and contestation
of these same formations?

We do not take the position that the significance of skin color is similar
everywhere. All over the world, there are deep histories of lightening and darkening; each locale has densely embedded aesthetic regimes and racialized politics of skin color. In tracking the manner in which the Modern Girl participates
in racial formation in a variety of contexts, we thus simultaneously wish to
recognize the singular qualities of each as well as overlap. For although there
may be overlap across regional, national, and subnational contexts, it is never
complete. As we will see, whitening, coloring, and tanning are in most locales
neither equivalent nor opposed processes but rather intimately interlinked
ones. What is most striking is how, in the 1920s and 1930s (and up through the
1960s in some locales), the Modern Girl stood at the center of shifting appeals
to alter skin color made by cosmetic companies and advertising agents, and

how such appeals repeatedly evoked notions of "nature," science, race, social status, refinement, "Americanness," and exoticism.

Cosmetic products aimed at whitening and lightening the skin predate the Modern Girl's first appearance in the 1920s. Pale skin was a beauty ideal for Anglo-American women in the United States throughout the nineteenth century. Possession of lighter and finer complexion was a luxury pursued by those who could afford to stay out of the elements, to pamper themselves, and to enjoy a comfortable life of leisure. Wealthy white women in the United States, Europe, and European colonies used white powders and bleaching creams to achieve the right "white" look. Heavy use of such products, however, could also open these same women to charges of artifice and associate them with both prostitution and the life of the theater. In partial reaction to this taint, by the end of the nineteenth century "looking natural" became a commonplace aesthetic ideal. By the 1920s, ads for thickly applied "lily-white" powders and paints had all but disappeared, while ads promoting products that hygienically augmented "natural" beauty and skin tone became pervasive.[12]

Cosmetic ads featuring the Modern Girl that appeared in the U.S., European, and colonial European press during the 1920s frequently focus on feeding and protecting fair skin. A 1928 German ad published by a Lever subsidiary, Elida, marketed skin creams that healed the skin, made it "even and like alabaster," and "protected it against harsh winds and bright sunlight" (see figure 2.15). As in late-nineteenth and early-twentieth-century ads circulated in the United States, in this German ad fair and refined skin is a sign of upper-class breeding and of white superiority. Unlike earlier European cosmetics ads such as those for British Pears Soap or German *Lilienmilchseife* which presented people of color as dirty and therefore primitive, the Elida ad invokes fairness and whiteness in a distinct way—as linked, if not fully reducible to, racial "phenotype."[13]

Concerns about protecting white skin from the sun and harsh elements of tropical climes often appeared in cosmetic ads in the colonial press in India and Hong Kong. A 1930 ad for Ven-Yusa, "The Oxygen Face Cream," that appeared in the *Times of India* conveys a message similar to that of the Elida ad (see figure 1.2). Other ads, such as an Elizabeth Arden Bleachine ad that appeared in the English-language Chinese press, recommend use of bleaching creams for white women.[14] All these ads expressed an anxious obsession with maintaining whiteness in a world of phenotypic others by claiming to banish what the historian David Arnold has referred to as "fearful tropicality."[15] To stay "natural"—that is, naturally fair—paradoxically one had to evade "nature."

Skin product ads targeting indigenous consumers illustrate the many ways

cosmetic whitening was interpolated into preexisting, precolonial skin preferences. In China, for instance, ads played on the intersection of native skin color
hierarchies and Euro-American ideologies of white racial superiority. Lighter
skin, long a mark of high status, indicated the distance between peasants and
scholar-officials. A light, nontanned complexion also formed an important
element of feminine beauty. Classical literature often likened the ideal woman's
skin color to congealed ointment, white jade, or fresh lichee. Yet in classical
convention "whiteness" never stood as the sole criterion for beauty or ideal
skin; a healthy radiance of rosy color always accompanied clear skin as the
ideal.[16] An illustration of this continuing preference is a 1940 ad, which features products claiming to provide the "natural" whiteness associated with
elite Chinese women. "Why do high class women feel beautiful and pleasant
when they apply Sparrow Face Powder?" the ad inquires; because "it will make
a woman's skin look white and soft in a natural way" (see figure 1.8). While
this ad and others like it mention the color white, they do not explicitly reference European or Euro-American racial whiteness.

In India, the preference for light-colored skin during the 1920s, especially for
women, is undeniable, but the association of light skin with merit or status
more ambiguous. Skin color had social significance in the subcontinent before
European colonialism and prior to the influence of U.S. and European conceptions of race. Indian epics and artifacts are full of references to superior beings
who are dark-skinned.[17] The history of skin color hierarchies in India is further complicated by Turkish and later Mughal conquests of the thirteenth to
mid-nineteenth century, when systems of grading people by skin color — fair,
"wheaten," dark — were used to categorize certain dark-skinned groups as
criminal and rebel. This form of codification passed directly into the British
colonial police records from the mid-nineteenth century on.[18] However, light
skin was not always desirable. Mughal miniature paintings and folk tales of the
seventeenth and eighteenth centuries, while expressing a preference for "trans-
lucent" color, also associated "too white" skin with leprosy. The feminine ideal
was for "translucence," not simply fairness.[19] European colonial ideologies
of racial superiority (from the first Portuguese landings on the west coast of
India in 1498 to the expansion and post-1857 establishment of the British
empire until 1947) thus encountered extant skin color hierarchies and were
themselves reshaped in the process. Colonial anthropological discourses in the
mid-nineteenth century linked Indian aesthetic preferences for whiteness to
caste-based social and economic stratification. Fair skin color, in these accounts, symbolized superiority in a hierarchical social structure and moral
order. Over time, metropolitan outlooks on racial difference and the represen-

tation of whiteness were transformed by discourses on medicine and science that intersected with the preexisting ideas about skin color.[20]

We have found cosmetics ads in China and India where the Modern Girl promotes what appear to be models of beauty that hark back to these older ideologies of whitening by evoking "nature." In China during the 1920s and 1930s ads such as one for Three Flowers Vanishing Cream by the Hudnut Company, which appeared in 1931, promise to improve facial beauty by making skin "smooth," "uniform," and "fresh." The text refers to the product's "secret formula," using an archaic word usually reserved for discussions of Chinese medicine. The ad also represents a Modern Girl body that is expressly Chinese and cast as "naturally" beautiful.[21] A similar 1949 ad for Afghan Snow appearing in the *Times of India* references "nature" in a similar manner: the Indian Modern Girl is depicted with flowers in her hair and exudes "beauty," "charm," and "allure" (see figure 2.16). Notably, these Chinese and Indian ads link fair skin and whitening to "nature."

2.16 Ad for Afghan Snow in *The Times of India* (1949) evokes "natural" beauty by depicting the Indian Modern Girl with flowers in her hair and a floral motif.

Other ads for skin products in India and China combined references to older skin color hierarchies with evocations of scientific authority. For example, an Indian ad for Pearlex that features a white woman declares that scientific progress could make long-standing desires for whiter skin a reality (see figure 2.17). A Chinese ad for Palmolive soap explains that new "scientific developments" can enable one to keep one's skin "rosy and moist" (see figure 2.14). These ads present the ideal skin in a vocabulary loaded with indigenous cultural references, such as "fair" and "pearly-white" in the Indian case, and "rosy" in the Chinese one. At the same time, these ads give preexisting preferences for lighter skin a "scientific," thus modern, twist: they sell the dream that by consuming scientifically produced cosmetics one can assume a cosmopolitan, upper-class look that makes one desirable and modern.

As in the Chinese and Indian contexts, in the African context ads that promised to lighten dark skin appeared beginning in the 1930s. For instance, in 1939 the South African company Keppels ran an ad for its lightening product Freckle

2.17 Ad for Pearlex in the *Illustrated Weekly of India* (1942) that evokes modern science in its promise of whitening.

Wax in *Bantu World*, a paper that targeted a black African readership and published articles and ads in English, Xhosa, Zulu, Sotho, Tswana, Venda, Afrikaans, and Tsonga languages (see figure 2.6). Six years later, Keppels ran an ad in the *Cape Times* promising that products developed by the "famous Keppels laboratories" could combat the harmful effects of South Africa's "cruel" climate by restoring "pristine skin-texture and colour." Although the *Cape Times* was a daily newspaper aimed at white and "coloured" readers, the "avocado"-tinted makeup and dark gray skin color of the ad's primary female image suggest that Keppels was targeting the latter group (see figure 2.18).[22] These Keppels ads show how a South African cosmetics company appealed to a marketplace structured by racial hierarchies through asserting scientific command of local conditions and reconfiguring distinctions of skin color as matters of climate.

In southern Africa, skin color hierarchies were shaped through the long history of European colonialism, dating back to the mid-seventeenth century at the Cape. Under Dutch, and later British, colonial rule, whiteness and light-colored skin became associated with civilization, cleanliness, intelligence, and power.[23] Mid-twentieth-century ethnographies of relatively remote southern African communities mention preferences for "light-skinned girls" or "light brown skin," suggesting a local predilection for light-colored (not white) skin that may not be entirely reducible to colonial racial hierarchies.[24] Within some southern African communities, light brown skin may have been a long-standing beauty attribute for young women.

During the 1930s, colonial racial hierarchies and, perhaps, indigenous preferences for light brown skin became entangled with American racial preferences and dynamics. An ad for Apex products, manufactured by an American, New Jersey–based company, appears to have been the earliest bleach ad to appear in a black South African newspaper. Apex, one of the largest black-owned businesses in the United States during the 1920s and 1930s, was, according to one ad, the first "all Negro Company" in South Africa.[25] The 1933

2.18 Ad from the South African newspaper *Cape Times* (1945) marketing a skin lightener, Freckle Wax, and "avocado"-tinted make-up to black consumers.

Bantu World ad featuring a line drawing of a bobbed-hair and bare-shouldered black Modern Girl gazing into a handheld mirror promises readers an improved appearance through use of Apex hair products and skin bleach (see figure 1.1). During the 1950s and 1960s, particularly in *Drum* magazine, ads for skin lighteners and bleaches manufactured in the United States became more pervasive, despite their often harmful levels of ammoniated mercury and hydroquinone. Many of these ads featured light-skinned black African Modern Girl film stars or beauty queens. Some ads continued to claim the U.S. origins of their product as a point of pride, situating African Americans as role models of racial betterment.[26] These ads suggest that in Anglophone African contexts, at least, colonial ideologies of white racial superiority and scientific improvement were now linked to color-coded hierarchies emanating from the United States. These developments underline that Americanization included a number of complex processes, which at times involved African Americans as capitalist entrepreneurs and racialized role models.

In the black U.S. press, representations of the African American Modern Girl were often strategically deployed to contest Jim Crow racial hierarchies that were buttressed by de jure and de facto racial segregation. Cosmetics ads, especially those run by the C. J. Walker Company in the NAACP's journal *The Crisis,* are a perfect example of a black contrapuntal politicization of advertising. Madam C. J. Walker, one of the most influential and well-known black businesswomen at the turn of the twentieth century, founded a hair treatment and cosmetics company that flourished for several decades by selling hair-care and beauty products to African American women. C. J. Walker's ads (particularly, though not exclusively, those that were produced during Madam C. J. Walker's lifetime) often expressed race pride. Typically, ads proclaimed that the company's products produced "loveliness," "allure," and "charm" as opposed to whiteness or lightness.[27] For instance, a 1928 ad that features a black Modern Girl with bobbed hair looking into a hand-held mirror, promises to bring out the beauty of already existing blackness with treatments that bestow a "transparent tone" as opposed to a lighter or whiter complexion (see figure 2.13). In the case of a product labeled "Egyptian Brown Face Powder" in this ad, the subversive idea of Black Egypt as the archetype of civilization at its most beautiful and advanced (an idea popularized in aesthetics, literature, and pageantry associated with the Harlem Renaissance) is adumbrated. "Egyptian Brown Face Powder," the ad copy explains, does not lighten skin; rather, it embellishes black beauty by invisibly imparting an "olive tint" to "fair complexions" and by harmonizing "bewitchingly with darker skins." This last claim, firmly establishing the beauty of blackness, is consistent with the other advertising markets that we have examined. Such assertions of racial pride speak to the interface between prior, often counterhegemonic traditions of cosmetics use in and outside the hardening conventions of Euro-American racial hierarchies and the scientific racial theories by which such conventions were subtended. In other words, in C. J. Walker ads, as in many others run in the black press, we find a politicized celebration of blackness. At the same time, it is important to note that such ads appealed to black bourgeois ideals of hygiene and deportment that were contoured by elitist, class-marked discourses of "racial uplift."

Within the white U.S. press, Modern Girl cosmetics ads often elaborated taxonomies of ethnicized whiteness. By the mid-1920s, many ads specified and celebrated an array of "beauty types" that were heavily coded according to the various racial and ethnic groups that together constituted the national populace (and thus the U.S. market) in this period. U.S. nativist and restrictionist anxieties about immigration from Southern and Eastern Europe and South and East Asia were expressed in the late nineteenth century and the early twentieth as intensified anti-immigrant animus and were assuaged through implementation of immigration-exclusion laws that reached an apex in the 1924 Immigration Act, which effectively curtailed non-European immigration to the United States for several decades.[28] Instructively, in the mid-1920s the Pompeian company routinely ran powder ads that implicitly invoked racially diverse consumers by

2.19 Ad in U.S. *Ladies Home Journal* (1928) for Pompeian makeup, catering expressly to white ethnics from Southern and Eastern Europe, America's so-called "in-betweens."

referring to skin types ranging from "white," to "olive," to "dusky." In one particularly evocative 1928 ad, the range of acceptable ethnicities and thus ethnic "looks," or "skin types," spans from "Dresden China Blonde" to Spanish "Creole Beauty," while in another Pompeian ad from the same year, recently assimilated white ethnic Americans are celebrated as those truest of Americans, the "in-betweens" (see figure 2.19).[29] Overall, these ads index the history of immigration to the United States through their identification of the multiple types of "American Beauty" and each beauty's particular "shade." In so doing they mobilize the idea of a mixed nation—but one that is mixed within precise racial and ethnic parameters. By buying facial powders and creams, these ads suggest, the immigrant to the United States—she who aspires to full inclusion in the nation—may buy a place in the "melting pot." For although the immigrant's skin shade and hair color may vary from the Anglo ideal, a Modern Girl may become an American among other Americans through commodity consumption. Such ads indicate to consumers which immigrant groups have gained the status of whiteness. Through occlusion or nonrepresentation of other groups they also indicate who is deemed inassimilable within the representational strategies of the advertisements as within the nation at large.

Significantly, Pompeian twisted its ethnicized advertising formula when marketing its powder to Indian and South African consumers. In these contexts, corporate advertisers appealed to color diversity among whites without any reference to "ethnic" differences. In a 1925 issue of the *Statesman* (Calcutta), Pompeian ran an ad featuring Judy, a white brunette Modern Girl. The ad did not disclose the company's Cleveland, Ohio, base; rather, it cast Judy as possessing the characteristics of a British colonial, since, astoundingly, readers are told that she was "sent out to India to have a good time" and to obtain the skin color of "fair 'English peach' Bloom." Like the Pompeian ads that appeared in the U.S. press in the same year, this one delineates a range of beauty types, "Naturelle," "Rachel," "White," and "Rosée," while dropping any mention of "in-betweens." Nearly identical beauty types appeared in a 1925 Pompeian ad that ran in South Africa's *Cape Times*, featuring the story of Modern Girl Dulcie Chetwynd, who was transformed from unmarried "wallflower" to "charming wife" through use of Pompeian.[30] Together, these ads suggest how Pompeian adjusted "beauty types" to British imperial markets by anglicizing copy, narrowing the spectrum of conceivable whiteness, and, in the case of the Indian ad, obscuring the U.S. origins of the product.

One of the most striking features of U.S. and European Modern Girl imagery from the mid-1920s onward is the embrace of tanning. From Miami to the Riviera, upper-class light-skinned Modern Girls tanned. Whereas maintenance of a fair complexion marked upper-class standing in the nineteenth century, starting in the mid-1920s, tanning became an attractive way to distinguish bourgeois and upper-class women from working-class and poor women who toiled indoors and thus wore on their faces the pallor of their confinement in factories or offices. Discussion of the "tan fad" in contemporary U.S. trade magazines like *Advertising and Selling* and *Printers' Ink Monthly* located its origins with flappers and their enthusiasm for outdoor activities and desire for "freedom," "color," and "nothingness in apparel." One marketing man described the tanning "vogue" in the following terms: "[Flappers] flocked to the beaches day after day in bathing suits as close to the ultimate zero as was permitted . . . and return[ed] to their Northern and Eastern haunts to display an expanse of deeply tanned skin that would arouse the envy of an Indian."[31] This quote suggests that contemporaries identified tanning as part of the Modern Girl's panache for outdoor leisure and bodily display and reveals how her pursuit of darker skin unsettled the rigidity of racial distinctions. And at the same time, it also indicates that it was the white Modern Girl's confidence in her racial privilege that made tanning in emulation of an "Indian" both desirable and possible.

By the end of the 1920s, some cosmetics companies in Europe, the United States, and European colonies adjusted their marketing of skin whiteners and

2.20 A 1928 U.S. *Vogue* ad for Helena Rubinstein skin bleach that promises to get rid of summer sun by restoring a light complexion.

bleaches to accommodate the tanning craze. A 1928 Helena Rubinstein ad enjoined the Modern Girl to "Bleach your way to Autumn Beauty" (see figure 2.20). Appealing to an imagined upper-class clientele alleged to spend summers in the country or at the beach, the Rubinstein ad warns: "The loveliest tan soon turns sallow and looks unsightly against city backgrounds." The Pompeian ads earlier discussed had suggested to white Euro-American women that they should either adjust their powder to match their "natural" facial coloring or to alter their facial color by using differently tinted powders. Bleach ads, on the other hand, encouraged white women to seasonally adjust their skin color. For such Modern Girls, skin was evidently another accessory.

Cosmetic companies' segmentation of the market according to the seasons also led to the selling of summer products on the promise of "healthy tanning." In a 1927 German ad for Nivea cream, the Beiersdorf company used a photo of a white, tall, slim, bobbed haired woman wearing a bathing suit; it encouraged consumers to cream themselves before sunbathing in order to become *braungebrannt* (deeply tanned) without burning.[32] Meanwhile, Nivea's winter season ads retooled the message to suggest that the cream protected against wind and rain. References to the exposed tanned bodies of young women remained a staple of cosmetics advertising after 1933 when the Nazis came to power. By 1933, most women featured in Nivea tanning ads are blond, perhaps in line with the ideal of athletic blondness featured in much Nazi propaganda. Nivea's advertising campaigns were explicitly condoned by the National Socialist regime, but Nivea's focus on what one might call a blond "Aryan" ideal was also a response to anti-Semitic campaigns leveled against the Beiersdorf Company, which had Jews among its founders and board members (see figure 2.21). While blonds became more prevalent in cosmetics ads of the Nazi era, depictions of a range of white looks continued, including ads featuring made-up brunettes. Nazi acceptance of such images reveals that certain features of the Modern Girl, such as her tanned athletic body, were acceptable and even desirable for a racist regime, which at times defined itself explicitly in rejection of "*Girlkultur*."[33]

In contrast to Nazi era ads that depicted the tanned female body as white, numerous ads in the United States in the 1930s, in the period after formal enactment of anti-immigration measures, sought to exoticize the Modern Girl's body by depicting it as "not-quite-white." In this period Hollywood joined forces with cosmetics companies such as Max Factor to more directly promote Modern Girl exoticism. Ethnicized Hollywood styles commodified dark "exotic" skin tones and tanned skin as "other" and desirable, a possibility that was precluded in the German Nivea campaign. Makeups that gave the effect of tanning, or simply of dark luxurious beauty, came to be marketed alongside lotions that claimed to enable darkening and tanning. Actresses starring in early Technicolor films were especially selected for their "exotic" skin tones, or were transformed by the studios from blonds into "exotics," a makeup effect marketed to viewers as a commodity that could be purchased and tried on for size like the clothing styles worn by actresses. Stars such as Steffi Dunn, Dolores Del Rio, Tala Birell and Anna May Wong were deemed to have the right type of "colorful beauty" and thus were natural "Technicolor types." Similarly, fair actresses such as Hedy Lamarr, Rita Hayworth, Joan Bennett and Dorothy Lamour could be transformed into dark divas to fit the bill.[34] After all, the studios reasoned, dark beauties allowed them to show off the advantages of the technology, just as the new film technology made the most of dark, "exotic" looks.

Given the eventual celebration of "exotic" darkness, it is not particularly surprising that the fashion for tanning also affected the marketing of skin bleaches to people of color. During the 1920s, "removing a tan" became a euphemism for bleaching in cosmetic ads run in the African American press. A Madam C. J. Walker Company ad that appeared in 1928, nine years after the death of the company's founder, partially eschews the race pride message of other C. J. Walker ads by promoting the suggestively named lightening product Tan-Off. In this ad, an athletic Modern Girl in a natural setting prevents her skin from becoming darkened by protecting it from the sun while she plays sports.[35] Similarly, a 1929 ad for a product named Fan Tan evokes both tanning

2.21 Ad for Nivea in *Leipziger Illustrirte Zeitung* (1936) by German Beiersdorf Company, featuring a blond, "Aryan" Modern Girl, likely to combat anti-Semitic attacks on the company.

and exoticism through discussion of lightening of dark skin. Fan Tan, the ad explains, comes in three shades: " 'Sun Tan' is for very dark complexions and lightens them to a fashionable Sun-Brown"; " 'Ochre' is for medium complexions . . . [and gives them] that flattering Spanish tone"; and " 'Naturelle' is for the girl or man who wishes a creamy ivory skin" (see figure 2.22). The names and descriptions of the first two shades suggest how Fan Tan sought to situate black women's desire for lighter skin *outside* the boundaries of the stark black/white binary held in place by Jim Crow laws by aligning the Modern Girl's desire with an internationally trendy appreciation for tanned skin. The euphemistic evocation of tanning is also found in a 1947 ad for Whitex that appeared in the *Illustrated Weekly of India* and featured headshots of a white-looking Modern Girl. As the copy proclaimed, this skin bleach could turn "Ugly, Sun-Tanned Skin . . . Whiter in 3 minutes." This ad targeted Indian elites by attributing dark skin to sun exposure and casting it as a temporary condition that could be remedied.[36] Cosmetic manufacturers and advertisers deployed the Modern Girl in promoting their racialized marketing appeals.

Conclusion

Our research on cosmetic ads and the contexts in which they appeared shows conclusively that the Modern Girl image became visible in each research locale during the 1920s and 1930s, albeit to varying degrees and in different

2.22 Ad for Fan-Tan skin lightener in *Baltimore Afro-American* (1929) offering a money-back guarantee.

forms. There is no longer any doubt that the Modern Girl was global. The Modern Girl's distinctive bobbed hair, her self-reflexivity, her presumed acquisitiveness, and the commodification of her skin, brows, teeth, body shape, and sexuality — in short the Modern Girl's technologies of self — are recognizable across contexts, whether the cosmetics ads are targeted at consumers in Johannesburg or Shanghai, New York or Bombay, Beijing or Berlin. Cosmetics companies played a central role as global mediators of Modern Girl culture and commodities: advertising budgets for cosmetics were particularly high throughout the interwar years, and cosmetics were understood as products for which needs had to be actively created.

Our analysis further suggests that in all of our research locales, Modern Girl images and cosmetics products were implicated in the production of national racial formation. Through our method of connective comparison, we reveal the multiple ways in which ideas about skin color and race were mobilized and transformed as they were swept up in imperial and international flows. While some companies, such as Pepsodent, promoted a global image of the Modern Girl as white and American, others such as De Kama advertising in the U.S. press, or Apex in the South African press, promoted an image of the Modern Girl with aestheticized "Asian" eyes or brown skin. Still others companies, most notably Pond's, featured drawings and photographs of Modern Girls who shared phenotypic features with the consumers being targeted. In each locale, Modern Girl images were apprehended through long-standing color-coded social hierarchies and racial formations. At the same time, Modern Girl images also contributed to the reworking of such hierarchies and formations. By the mid-twentieth century in all our research locales, discussion of desirable skin color and tone had become entangled with racialized appeals to "nature," science, tanning, and whiteness. These appeals in turn intersected with promises of class mobility that advertisers frequently used to sell products.

Companies based in the United States clearly played an important role in globalizing these appeals. As we have indicated, a large proportion of the Modern Girl ads that we collected are for U.S.-based multinational corporate manufacturers. American advertisers operated with much larger ad budgets than any of their competitors, particularly in the 1920s and 1930s. U.S.-based corporations like Artra, Odorono, Pompeian, and Palmolive aggressively marketed their products by promoting a specifically "American" modernity that was supposedly rational, scientific, efficient, and desirable everywhere. The preponderance of ads for U.S.-based manufacturers also reflects the fact that U.S. capital benefited from linguistic affinities and cultural continuities in the vast imperial markets constructed through centuries of British conquest. The ads for Pompeian face powders that appeared in the Indian and South African press, for instance, suggest how British and American whiteness could easily be blended and conflated, producing an Anglo-American imperial whiteness. Other ads indicate how Americanization could take the form of African Americanization with black Americans appearing as model consumers and entrepreneurs.

In cosmetics and toiletry ads we have found that some of the most intriguing evidence of multidirectional citation — of mutual influences and nonlinear circuits of exchange — is aesthetic. In artistic renderings of the Modern Girl that appeared in the American and German press (and to a lesser degree in the Indian and South African press), we have cautiously noted an Asianized aesthetic. While we recognize that what we have labeled "Asianization" was a product of European and American designers' conception of the "other," we have also noted that Chinese and Japanese aesthetics influenced the representation of the Modern Girl. Conversely, we have found that drawings of the Modern Girl by Chinese illustrators are indebted to French, German, Japanese, and American artistic styles that arrived in advertising and graphic design magazines. In other words, everywhere representations of the Modern Girl can be seen to have actively incorporated aesthetic elements drawn from *multiple* colonial and national contexts.

Research in other sources including press commentary, social science research, fiction, film, photography, and autobiography suggests that what we are calling the Modern Girl's multidirectional citation extended far beyond the realm of advertising. It also involved other discourses, texts, and venues and, as importantly, historical agents living in different parts of the world. Indeed, our research shows that actual Modern Girls traveled within and across colonial and national boundaries. They engaged the latest trends from abroad as they encountered them in magazines, newspapers, and films, and they journeyed or even worked outside their home colonies and countries. The chapters that follow further clarify how the Modern Girl's political significance differed across locales and over time. Although the Modern Girl's provocative fashions and explicit eroticism appear to have animated similar social anxieties about unruly and frivolous behavior across the globe, in each location the political import of these anxieties varied. In some instances the Modern Girl challenged preexisting ideologies of female subservience and self-sacrifice. In others, her desire to select her own sexual partners (male and female) and to delay or avoid marriage transgressed and reworked modern heteronormativity.

Overall, our research has led us to one conclusion above all others: the Modern Girl, perhaps like no other figure of the twentieth century, reveals the complexity of global economic and cultural processes.

Notes

All authors contributed equally to this chapter.

1. Foucault, "Technologies of the Self," 18.
2. See Harootunian, *Overcome by Modernity*; Woodward, "Marketing Modernity"; Peiss, "Educating the Eye of the Beholder."
3. Kathy Peiss and Davarian Baldwin show that black beauty products were also sometimes marketed to white ethnics, especially in the Jewish press. For the purposes of this chapter, however, we have focused on the white and black press only. See Peiss, *Hope in a Jar*, and Baldwin, "Chicago's New Negroes."
4. In the mid-nineteenth century, "coloured" became a common racial designation used to refer to the descendants of mixed marriages and sexual liaisons between Europeans, African peoples indigenous to the Cape region, and enslaved peoples brought from Southeast Asia, South Africa, Madagascar, West Africa, East Africa, and elsewhere during the Dutch colonial period. After 1948, South Africa's apartheid regime deployed "coloured" along with white/European, Bantu/African, and Asian as one of its four racial categories. Beginning in the 1970s, Black Consciousness and some other progressive movements rejected these categories, arguing that all people of color should identify as black.
5. For this chapter, we draw on the pan-Indian English-language press. However, we know from preliminary research and discussion with feminist scholars familiar with popular magazine and newspaper archives in Marathi, Hindi, and Telugu that commodity advertising in these languages varies in its deployment of both "modern" and "traditional" imagery of women.
6. German Pond's ad, Microfilm Collection, reel 41, J. Walter Thompson Collection, Rare Book, Manuscript, and Special Collections Library, Duke University.
7. Ad for Pond's, *Bantu Mirror*, 1955.
8. See especially Roberts, *Civilization without Sexes*; Marchand, *Advertising the American Dream*; and Brumberg, *The Body Project*.
9. On the United States, see Marchand, *Advertising the American Dream*, 140–63; for Germany, see Ward, *Weimar Surfaces*, 81–91.
10. See Steele and Major, eds., *China Chic*; Laurence, *Lily Briscoe's Chinese Eyes*; Yoshi-

hara, *Embracing the East*; Lee, *Orientals*; Meech and Weisberg, eds., *Japonisme Comes to America*.

11. See works cited in note 8 as well as Glenn, *Female Spectacle*; Petro, *Joyless Streets*; Enstad, *Ladies of Labor, Girls of Adventure*; and Stamp, *Movie-Struck Girls*; Bean and Negra, eds., *A Feminist Reader in Early Cinema*; and Zhang, *An Amorous History of the Silver Screen*.

12. Peiss, *Hope in a Jar*, 39–43; Berry, "Hollywood Exoticism," 109.

13. For toiletry ads in the United Kingdom, see Richards, *The Commodity Culture of Victorian England*; McClintock, *Imperial Leather*; for Germany, see Ciarlo, "Rasse konsumieren." For the German example of *Lilienmilchseife*, see Hinz, Patemann, and Meier, eds., *Weiss auf Schwarz*, 57.

14. See ad for Elizabeth Arden Bleachine Cream, *South China Morning Post*, 1937.

15. Arnold, *The Problem of Nature*, 143.

16. For example, see Xueqin and Gao, *Dream of the Red Chamber*, 38, and *The Book of Songs*, 21 and 48.

17. Sumit Guha, "Skin Color Preferences in South Asia," E-post from Friday, 22 March 2002, at http://www.h-net.org/asia/ (visited 25 February 2005).

18. Bayly, *Caste, Society and Politics in India from the Eighteenth Century to the Modern Age*, 104.

19. Guha, "Skin Color Preferences in South Asia."

20. See Harrison, *Climates and Constitutions*.

21. Three Flowers Vanishing Cream ad, *Funü zazhi (Ladies' Journal)*, 1931.

22. Keppels ad, *Cape Times*, 1945.

23. Comaroff, "Medicine, Colonialism, and the Black Body"; Burke, *Lifebuoy Men, Lux Women*, esp. chaps. 1–2.

24. Schapera, *Married Life in an African Tribe*, 46; Hunter, *Reaction to Conquest*, 222.

25. Peiss, *Hope in a Jar*, 92; Apex ad, *Bantu World*, 7 July 1934.

26. On the long and varied history of African Americans serving as potential role models and mentors for black South Africans, see Couzens, "Moralizing Leisure Time"; Erlmann, "A Feeling of Prejudice"; Campbell, *Songs of Zion*; Kemp, " 'Up from Slavery' and Other Narratives."

27. On Madam C. J. Walker, see Robinson, "Class, Race, and Gender"; Rooks, *Hair Raising*, esp. chap. 3; Bundles, *On Her Own Ground*; Peiss, *Hope in a Jar*, 108–14 and 203–37; and Baldwin's chapter in this volume.

28. Jacobsen, *Whiteness of a Different Color*.

29. Pompeian ad, *Ladies Home Journal*, 1928.

30. Pompeian Beauty Powder ads, *Statesman*, 10 April 1925, and *Cape Times*, 4 November 1925.

31. Quote from Cowling, "Will the Vogue for Tan Last?," 31. Also see Du Bois, "What Is Sun-Tan Doing to Cosmetics?," 19–20, 62, and 64; Du Bois, "The Sun-Tan Mode Arrives," 28, 76, 78, and 80; and Berry, "Hollywood Exoticism," 117.

32. *Leipziger Illustrirte*, 5 May 1927, 644.

33. On Nivea and the Nazis, see Gries, *Produkte als Medien*, 467–86. More generally on contradictory Nazi attitudes, see Guenther, *Nazi Chic?*; Herzog, *Sex After Fascism.*

34. Berry, "Hollywood Exoticism," 119–26.

35. Tan-Off ad, *Baltimore Afro-American*, 1928. During the 1920s and 1930s, Tan-Off was, in some markets, the Walker Company's bestseller. Peiss, *Hope in a Jar*, 113.

36. Whitex ad, *Illustrated Weekly of India*, 1947.

3

From the Washtub
to the World

Madam C. J. Walker and the

"Re-creation" of Race Womanhood,

1900–1935

DAVARIAN L. BALDWIN

Surely you are not going to shut the door in my face. I feel that I am in a business that is a credit to the womanhood of our race. I went into a business that is despised, that is criticized and talked about by everybody—the business of growing hair . . . I am a woman who came from the cotton fields of the South. I was promoted there to the washtub. Then I was promoted to the cook kitchen, and from there I *promoted myself* into the business of manufacturing hair goods and preparations.   MADAM C. J. WALKER before the annual convention of the National Negro Business League, 1912

In 1912, Booker T. Washington presided over the three-day annual convention of his National Negro Business League (NNBL) meeting, held that year at Institutional Church on Chicago's South Side. The young upstart "beauty culturist" Madam C. J. Walker also came to Chicago, arriving in a chauffeur-driven Model T convertible touring car, with hopes of addressing this distinguished group of race entrepreneurs about her business accomplishments. However, throughout the conference Washington pointedly denied her any opportunity to speak from the floor or to acknowledge those who attempted to speak on her behalf. After multiple efforts to gain Washington's attention, on the final morning Walker finally seized the floor, proclaiming her right to be there and be heard based on the traditionally masculine narrative of the rise from poverty to wealth. Walker announced she was promoted by others "from the cotton fields of the South" to "the washtub" and finally acquired *self*-promotion in "the business of manufacturing hair goods and preparations." While within the year Walker successfully fought to become a part of this world of "race" entrepreneurs, Washington's initial avoidance of this particular beauty culturist was not surprising. He had long been known to lump together spiritualists, palm readers, and beauty culturists as peddlers of "meaningless stuff." Moreover, his dismissal was part of a growing concern with the black consumption of beauty products — to straighten the hair and lighten the skin — as destructive acts of excessive adornment and white emulation.[1]

The racist ideologies of social Darwinism were quite effectively disseminated through white beauty/cosmetics advertisements, packaging, and procedures. Black women were bombarded with "before and after" ads for products like Black No More and Kink No More, in which a "dark skinned, wooly haired" primitive was transformed into a refined and cultivated "high class" and physically "whiter" lady. For a black woman like Walker to defiantly promote herself in the male-dominated public sphere of race enterprise, as a conscious race woman *and* first and foremost a beauty culturist, was surely disruptive and was considered by some treasonous. There were not many race women like Walker, who had come from the "cotton fields" and the "washtub," defying male authority all along the way, to build a race industry built on the cultural tastes and social practices of working-class black women. Under the veil of race pride and authenticity, struggles over the actual marketing and use of beauty culture begin to reveal an extremely complicated set of meanings and history surrounding adornment practices within black communities.[2]

A highly contested and commanding *black* beauty culture emerged at the intersection of race conscious denouncement, technological innovations, and especially migrant adornment practices. With special attention to Madam C. J. Walker, this essay examines how black working-class women inserted their own visions and desires into beauty culture to enact a gendered politics of black re-creation. I use the term "re-creation" to explain how the industrialized leisure space of adornment was central to new and contested meanings of the modern experience. Jim Crow horrors, migration realities, and urbanizing conditions helped crystallize the social significance of the mass consumer marketplace as an alternative space for literally refashioning the standards of modern woman-hood. The black beauty industry also specifically involved working-class women in political blocs, most notably as part of the wide-ranging New Negro movement of the interwar period. Only six years after Walker took the floor from Washington at the NNBL meeting, an estimated 20,000 agents in the United States and abroad were in her employ and organized into the Walker Hair Culturists' Union that would specifically "protest against" the East St. Louis race riots of 1917 and later even the capitalist business practices of Walker herself.[3] Through the power of their adornment practices and consumption habits, black working-class migrant women transformed an industry of white emulation into a powerful black public sphere of leisure, labor, and politics.

Between Nature and Artifice: Gender, Class, and Black Re-creation

As working-class black women entered urban spaces, an embrace of beauty culture was central to their re-creation. It was embedded in the continuation of prior adornment practices before migration, a desire to construct a particular vision of black modernity, and in the process a challenge to reform and religious prescriptions of bodily temperance and restraint in public behavior and presentation. Competing images of modern race womanhood emerged where a battle line was drawn (yet often transgressed) between, on one hand, excessive public presentations of physical naturalness and, on the other, explicit engagements with excessive adornment and artifice. Much of the black resistance to cosmetics was a reaction to their implicit suggestion that black people required physical (quasi-genetic) alterations to be moral and equal. Race leaders and reformers, at the turn of the twentieth century, responded with a positive and explicitly modest and unadorned image of black womanhood within the confines of Victorian femininity, both as a response to white cosmetics industries and to reinforce their own desires for class and moral distinction. As part of a much broader and more complicated politics of race uplift, clubwomen and race men specifically targeted migrant women's behaviors, styles, and attitudes as obstacles to a respectable black image of thrift, purity, and productive labor. In the elite journal *Voice of the Negro*, the clubwomen reformers Fannie Barrier Williams and Nannie Helen Burroughs argued that "the Colored Girl," must focus on not "Color But Character." Burroughs specifically argued that

This beautiful eyed girl is the result of careful home training and steady schooling. There is an unusual promise of intelligence and character rising out of her strong individuality. A model girl, a college president's daughter, is Lorainetta.

You cannot avoid the motion of this dignified countenance. College training makes her look so.

3.1 "Rough Sketches: A Study of the Features of the New Negro Woman."
Voice of the Negro, August 1904.

black women must be proud of their natural Negro selves and labor at being pure of heart instead of altering external features to look white.[4]

The reform-oriented image of modern race womanhood linked femininity with a physical appearance of "naturalness." Men, elite women, and even working-class sanctified church adherents justifiably protested that black women were naturally virtuous without physical alteration. However, for many working-class migrants, the choice of seemingly excessive adornment practices served as a means to break out of a static state of social existence. Part of women's relegation to a subservient position within the domestic sphere was rationalized through arguments about gendered divisions of natural labor, where women were "products and prisoners" of their physical functions and reproductive capacities, while men seemed to have an innate mastery over their natural surroundings (including women). Therefore, most attempts by women to move from the sacred hearth of home and domesticity, whether through labor or artifice, were interpreted as going against "nature." So when working-class black women began to physically transgress their "natural" social positions through migration, public labor, and leisure, struggles over dress and artifice enacted important "style wars" that were central to larger shifts in re-creating modern race womanhood.[5]

As black women moved from south to north, they were making clear strides in the city but were still constricted in occupation and pay. While Sears and Roebuck and Montgomery Ward selectively hired overqualified black women as temporary wartime help, in a city like Chicago 68 percent of documented black women workers were restricted to domestic service and the overlapping dictates of bodily temperance and subservient restraint. These conditions helped designate the leisure world of beauty culture, a vitally important recreational space for limited alternatives in labor and leisure. In fact the term of the field for entrepreneurs, sales agents, and hair(dressers) — beauty *culturists* — sheds light on the competing meanings of race, artifice, and recreation amid the Great Migration.[6]

The word "culture" generally refers to the cultivation of "natural" or raw materials (from agricultural crops to the mind) through artificial techniques of training and education. The act of cultivation was precisely what race leaders and reformers were claiming to provide for southern working-class migrant women as they entered urban spaces. However, beauty culture, and the specific labor of a beauty culturist, made the same claim while representing a process of cultivation and re-creation more forcefully determined by the tastes and intentions of the migrant women themselves. For example in a *Messenger* article, Louis George, a freelance writer and Walker employee, directly attacked the reformist obsession with naturalness as "fallacious" and contradictory because, in his mind, even "extreme race loyalists artfully avoid the unkempt, unimproved hair and poorly 'attended to skin.' " Using the metaphor of education, he pointed out, "Ignorance, on the contrary, is natural" and natural homes are "dugouts, trees and caves." George finally challenged leaders to forgo the artificial cultivation of homes, clothing, and personal hygiene. In definition, the culture of beauty was in line with the stated intentions of the "better class." But in practice, the seemingly excessive and nonfunctional adornment practices of working-class migrants exposed tensions over who had the right and what social contexts would determine the boundaries of cultivation.[7]

From the start, working-class migrant beauty practices were rooted in a much longer struggle for spaces of personal agency through techniques of physical manipulation and enhancement partially derived from an African past and played out under slave and sharecropping conditions. Men and women treated their hair with earth, lime, vegetable oil, and dyes and wore wigs, tresses, and extensions as part of various Afro-diasporic traditions. These legacies continued where such adornment and leisure practices became a space to create some sense of individuality and self-presentation for the enslaved. Women used whatever was on the plantation, but especially cotton, to "roll" or "wropt" their hair for easier styling. Many also used animal shears to cut and shape their hair. In fact, Madam Walker explained that the process of lengthening the hair was generally termed "pressing" in the business because of its similarity to the labor performed by many black women on plantations: pressing and ironing clothes.[8]

Even after emancipation, the poor condition of one's hair became a material marker of one's social standing. In this context, excessive hair breakage, dry and unhealthy scalps, and skin blemishes converged with the badge of skin color and the material conditions of inequality to further reinforce a status of subservience or even inferiority. The poor health and diet of those surviving Jim Crow did not always allow hair growth for desired styles. The earliest forms of hair relaxing were, in many ways, attempts to stretch the hair out long enough to put it in elaborate styles that were a hybrid of African cultural forms and the emulation, or even parody, of white adornment. Black beauty culture was part of the legacy to reclaim personhood from servitude, a status that had historically derived, in part, from body cultivation. During the Great Migration, urban spaces became prominent battlegrounds among various interest groups over the divergent meanings and practices of beauty culture. What emerged were challenging conceptions of modern race womanhood that included, for many, the use of "artificial" adornment practices.[9]

White Emulation or Black Self-Expression:
Fashioning a Beauty Culture Modernity

It is important to take seriously the charge that beauty culture represents a black desire for whiteness. However, what is rarely asked in such discussions is whether whiteness was the goal or if the desire was really for a new form of black racial consciousness. To be sure, beauty culture was rarely a simple either/or practice but included overlapping realities of white emulation and black resistance and agency. To pose the debate as either white emulation or black self-expression misses the complex and sometimes contradictory nature of the gendered politics of re-creation found within beauty. The beauty salons, kitchens, and porches of urban black communities were important loci where women finalized the process of re-creating themselves through their own visions of sophistication and understandings of modernity.

Working-class black women's engagement in the artifice and recreational leisure of beauty culture signaled both aesthetic and actual breaks from their traditional status as simply and completely mothers, wives, and domestics. Engaging in beauty culture could dangerously link black womanhood to the artificiality of worldly vice or white emulation. However, for others it was precisely beauty culture's artificiality, the collective acts of self-conscious fashioning (waved and dyed hair), that signified black women's growing possibilities for personal liberation from tradition in bodily display, profession, and politics. In this context beauty culture products and practices represented an alternative vision of black modernity. When the southern beauty agent Mamie Garvin Fields saw powerful women like Madam Walker and the educator Mary Church Terrell speak, her evaluation of their modernity included both their abilities and their appearance. Walker's elegant dress represented "a go-ahead, up-to-date black woman" and Terrell's "beautifully done hair" signified "she *was* that Modern Woman." But even beyond the extravagant spectacle of individual black women, letters to the Walker Company reveal that a beauty-culture modernity was most acutely expressed in demands for a complete beauty *system* that could remedy practical or serious problems including scalp disease, skin blemishes, and limited hair growth. At the same time, black *and* white (im)migrants used black beauty products to conform their skin tone, hair texture, and grooming habits to unwritten requirements established by northern industrial and professional industries.[10]

Yet even the majority of black women who remained in domestic jobs reinscribed beauty culture with a meaning of personal autonomy, race pride, and one form of labor-based leisure. In a rare 1932 study of black consumption habits, the economist Paul Edwards confirmed that many black women used beauty culture to separate themselves from an identification with domestic labor and the servitude that aprons and head rags signified. This approach resonated with what black women in Washington aptly called "freedom bags" in which they carried work clothes so they would not have to wear them on the street. In the hands of migrant women, who usually served someone else, the time and space offered through beauty culture was also much less about pure hedonism and more an issue of personal attention and affirmation outside industrialized labor dictates. Concerns with healthy scalps, nonfunctional styles, and time away from domestic drudgery far exceeded the anxieties of trying to be white. Black women's entrée into a commercial beauty culture created new sources of employment, relatively equitable labor/leisure relations, and platforms for political explorations on the local, national, and world stage.[11]

Selling Blackness: Beauty and Enterprise in the Black Metropolis

While the process of black women's re-creation was deeply political it emerged and was facilitated through an intimate relationship with the capitalist marketplace of the World War I era. The rise of Madam C. J. Walker and her amazing network of beauty culturists demonstrates how the consumption habits of working-class women migrants powered a complex network of race markets, consumers, enterprises, and employment. Here the notion of a black beauty industry was both market driven and exceeded a marketplace logic. In many regards, working-class women used the production, distribution, and consumption strategies of black beauty industries to reclaim and develop interpersonal networks among themselves to challenge the very inhumanity of racial-capitalist relations. In fact, it is difficult to disentangle beauty culture's political consciousness from its strategies of marketing and distribution.

Black beauty "culturists" deployed multiple and competing ideologies to nullify the class and gender anxieties of race leaders, while capitalizing on working-class consumption habits. Advertisements and marketing strategies reveal a mass marketplace public sphere of producers, critics, and consumers engaging in an intellectual discourse and debate about the parameters of modern race womanhood. To take a few examples: Anthony Overton highlighted his position as a "race man" and entrepreneur in control of black women's beauty choices. He convincingly argued that white companies were not concerned with refining and uplifting the image of race womanhood but in pushing dangerous products that did not meet the practical needs of black skin and hair. Annie Turnbo Malone presented beauty as a service industry within the race women's sphere of supportive "domesticity." She combined a message of Christian morality and maternal temperance with her own images of African beauty. In response to clubwomen who encouraged "natural" features, Malone argued that African women originated beauty culture, and in fact her company name, "Poro," derived from a West African society committed to "disciplining the body." For Malone, her "Wonderful Hair Grower," beauty schools, and temperance work were not in conflict but in service to the physical cultivation of black women's character.[12]

By contrast with Overton and Malone, Madam C. J. Walker attempted to move black women from the powerful politics of domesticity forthrightly into the public sphere of race enterprise and even race politics. Walker juxtaposed her washerwoman origins with her enormous wealth in an effort to directly locate a female-headed black beauty culture within the male-dominated world of business. She appealed to a wide and varied consumer base and organized a massive network of sales agents and institutions that later challenged her authority. While Malone's stories of African heritage and preslave civilization appealed to Victorian notions of aristocratic discipline and order, Walker's "creation story" combined formal notions of an Africanist race pride with a more "Pentecostal" style of divine dream revelation pulled from the world of her working-class consumer base.

In ads, Walker claimed that the answer to her personal woes as a domestic came in the form of a dream in which "a big black man appeared to me and told me what to mix for my hair. Some of the remedy was from Africa, but I sent for it, mixed it, put it in my scalp and in a few weeks my hair was coming in faster than it had ever fallen out . . . I made up my mind I would begin to sell it." The application of religious signs and symbols and the "African" authority of race pride spoke directly to the social contexts of migrant women. This first-person blending of spirituality and science also offered an alternate narrative of modernity that evoked the more scientific notion of a beauty system without rejecting older rituals of mystical healing. Her reference to the supernatural world also provided Walker with a higher power of authority over disgruntled race men. These stories and their recognition of the worldview of black women migrants are emblematic of the strategies that Walker used to build her beauty culture and help make over modern race womanhood.[13]

Walker's gendered exclusion from traditional commercial spaces forced her, along with other women, to take advantage of and develop alternative strategies of advertising and distribution. From the outset, Walker was conscious of the "hair-straightening stigma." Her earliest ads read "Makes Short Hair Long and Cures Dandruff." She never advocated hair straightening, nor did she elevate glamorous light-skinned or mulatto women with straight hair in her ads (as did Overton) as objects of male desire. Walker offered her own dark-skinned image, the growth and health of her own hair, and the success of her enterprises as the objects of black female desire. Again, with bald patches and overwork as the scarlet letters of poverty for working women in this era, her complete beauty system of relaxation, diet, and adornment recognized that "good" hair was more about general health than straight and stringy hair. Walker showcased herself and her possessions as embodiments of black female agency through slides of her chauffeur-driven car and mink coat, along with well-crafted speeches. She spread the "gospel of beauty" by using the new and urbane technology of glass colored slides in a stereopticon projector, juxtaposing shots of washtubs and irons with photos of her mansion, cars, and growing corps of agents alongside those of respectable race men, including Booker T. Washington. In promotional packets that were tossed from train car windows there were no images of hairstyles but listings of her real estate holdings, personal testimonies, and a picture of her behind the wheel of a Model T, staring defiantly into the camera as a symbol of a modern woman *steering* the direction of race womanhood. She canvassed the United States and the Caribbean selling her products, training agents, and eventually setting up a foreign sales bureau that conducted business in French, Spanish, and Portuguese.[14]

One of her most popular ads, "Learn to Grow Hair and Make Money," was in direct conversation with the aspirations of black women, especially as they migrated to urban centers. Many women were tired of working in someone

3.2 Madam Walker at the wheel of her Model T in front of her Indianapolis home in 1912. Courtesy of A'Lelia Bundles/Walker Family Collection (madamcjwalker.com)

else's kitchen and "going in and out of back doors." Walker persuasively demonstrated that by employing black women, she was making it possible for them to "abandon the washtub for a more pleasant and profitable occupation." She encouraged women "to rise above the laundry and kitchen . . . and to aspire to a place of commerce and trade." By 1916, Walker had employed 20,000 agents in the United States and abroad. While a good factory job could earn a black woman $12 to $18 a week as compared to $4 in southern states, the best Walker agents earned $100 a month (not including 50 percent commission on sales) and the average agent could make $23 dollars a week. But alongside the pay, the Walker agent Lizzie Bryant wrote, "I have all I can do at home and don't have to go out and work for white people in kitchens and factories."[15]

While Walker helped fashion a new race womanhood, she also understood that a relationship with elite "race" organizations would provide some of the most lucrative networks for promoting her products and ideals. Walker knew that her working-class origins, her two divorces, and self-assertion in the world of race (read male) enterprise went against many of the uplift ideals of the "better class." In the face of resistance, Walker used her sheer wealth and celebrity status as a means to boost product visibility and win the seal of

Learn To Grow Hair and Make Money

Complete Course by mail or by personal instructions. A diploma from Leila College of Hair Culture is a passport to prosperity. Is your hair short, breaking off, thin or falling out? Have you tetter, eczema? Does your scalp itch? Have you more than a normal amount of dandruff?

MME. C. J. WALKER'S

Wonderful Hair Grower

Write for booklet which tells of the positive cures of all scalp diseases, stops the hair from falling out and starts it at once to growing. Beware of imitations—all of the Mme. C. J. Walker Preparations are put up in yellow tin boxes. A six weeks' trial treatment sent to any address by mail for $1.50. Make all money orders payable to Mme. C. J. Walker. Send stamps for reply. Agents Wanted. Write for terms.

MADAM C. J. WALKER
President of the Madam C. J. Walker Manufacturing Company and the Leila College, 640 N. West Street, Indianapolis, Ind.

See your nearest Walker Agent or Write

THE MADAM C. J. WALKER MFG. CO.

640 North West Street,   Indianapolis, Ind.

3.3 Madam C. J. Walker Mfg. Co., "Learn to Grow Hair,"
Chicago Defender, 21 October 1916.

respectability from influential race organizations. At the same time, Walker's philanthropic aid "afforded" her the opportunity to make challenging statements on behalf of her working-class female constituency. At the 1914 NNBL annual convention, Walker boldly pronounced, "If the truth were known, there are many women who are responsible for the success of you men." Later she challenged the women of the race "to get in touch with our women in the factory."[16]

Walker's philanthropic power forced elite organizations to accord her the status of racial respectability, yet her previous exclusion from this world kept her suspicious about the terms on which such an elevated social status was achieved. In a letter to her lawyer, Walker remarked, "You should have seen the dictey who did not notice the washerwoman falling on their faces to see her, and everyone wanted to entertain me, but I didn't accept one social call." Even though Walker reportedly made over $1,000 a week, she continued to speak to and not simply for the women who shared her origins, despite her eventual acceptance from the "dictey" class. This is not to argue that Walker was a fully benevolent entrepreneur, but she had to speak in a particular vernacular and address the concerns of her migrant consumer patrons, because it was precisely their tastes and desires that drove the success of her industry. Walker's reliance on a narrative of common origin with consumers encouraged her to redefine modern race womanhood, keeping in mind both her own political desires and those of her agents. In the end, black women used beauty culture networks to catapult themselves into the public sphere of the New Negro movement in the interwar period.[17]

Beauty Culture and the Transformation of the New Negro World

The defiant ascendancy of beauty culturists like Madam C. J. Walker, beauty culture agents, and primarily working-class consumer patrons onto the national and world stage is part of a much larger experience of "black worldliness" that is just beginning to be told. One of the key conceptual rubrics for understanding this early-twentieth-century global experience of cultural renaissance and political resistance is the New Negro. The term "New Negro" in American history and culture has become a conventional way of referring to the literary and visual artists and intellectuals of the Harlem Renaissance. However, this limiting description has divorced the concept from its location within the context of the Great Migration, World War I, race riots, and the combined economic and mass cultural race consciousness that was emerging all over the country and throughout the African diaspora. A shifting and dynamic collection of black entrepreneurs, war veterans, laborers, artists, clergy, political activists, intellectuals, athletes, and entertainers transformed cities and towns in Europe, Africa, the Caribbean, and the Americas into critical parts of an early-twentieth-century black international consciousness.[18]

However, we must also understand how the New Negro movement, and the mostly male intellectuals who defined it, worked within gendered and class exclusions. Both the NNBL's initial rejection of Madam C. J. Walker and aesthetic ideologies of natural femininity fail to acknowledge the powerful and sometimes oppositional ways working-class black women re-created themselves as modern. Nevertheless, the general New Negro stance against the controlling confines of white patriarchy, patronage, and philanthropy resonated with the activities of black women celebrities in the culture industries and in the way migrants practiced adornment.

The modern "New Negro Movement" emerged between 1910 and the midthirties. In the most general terms, the Great Migration of over one million African Americans north and west ignited the movement, and the convergence of Euro-American leftist and black radical visions signaled its decline. World War I specifically brought together the forces of capitalist expansion, migration flows from the colonial poles of Southern and Eastern Europe, Asia, and the Caribbean to global industrial metropoles, and powerful anticolonial resistance struggles. A growing disillusionment with the West was exacerbated by the heightened display of wartime white-on-white violence on the world stage and the social movements of the "Darker Races," including the Great Migration, the Mexican and Bolshevik revolutions, and even Japan's imperial advances. Concurrently, black soldiers quickly returned home fighting alongside newly arriving urban migrants and established residents in struggles against long-standing restrictions on black labor, leisure, and living. White angst about a growing black presence quickly erupted into the "Red Summer" of 1919, in which over forty race-rioting "hot spots" emerged, some as far away as Liverpool, England.[19]

Periodicals as diverse as *Negro World*, the *Chicago Defender*, and *Kansas City Call* expressed a black international and riot-induced New Negro spirit of resistance and critique of white supremacy alongside reconstructed visions of race pride. Their diasporic counterparts, including *Les Continents* in Paris, *Workers Herald* and *African World* in Cape Town, *African Times* and *Orient Review* in London, and *Diario de la Marina* in Havana, all joined the fight. Moreover, race men and race women entered the fray through the mass consumer marketplace of race films, race records, race newspapers, Negro baseball leagues, and black beauty culture to help generate a globalizing New Negro consciousness, traveling and transgressing the very networks of wartime capitalist expansion.[20]

Scholarship on this black modern worldly experience is gradually building. However, few examine the role of black women's resistance against the marker of the "mammy" and its attendant domestic work as part of the larger New Negro militancy against dependency and subservience. Aspects of this militancy encouraged a turn to leisure spaces as sites of re-creation within the mass marketplace. When one Chicago buffet flat prostitute remarked, "When I see the word *maid*—why, girl, let me tell you, it just runs through me. I think I'd sooner starve," she was surely caught within an iron cage of limited capitalist possibilities. However, this woman was also one of many working-class migrants who turned to various forms of commercial leisure to create alternative labor sources, different routes to social mobility within the community, and hence their own New Negro visions of a rapidly changing world. In the arena of moving pictures, Bessie Coleman—the Chicago migrant and beauty culturist turned pilot—was celebrated on film for her exploits in Paris as the race's first "aviatrix," while young migrant girls were chided in those very same theater spaces for their defiant, public explorations of sociability and sexuality in alarmist headlines like "Lip Slobbering in Theaters." Such seemingly contradictory impulses of race celebrity and sexuality coexisted through movie starlets, including the principal actress for Oscar Micheaux films, Evelyn Preer, who bragged in interviews about performing her own stunts. Such a shift from matronly temperance to athletic self-mastery was further captured through women's athletics, including the Chicago Roamers, a championship all-black basketball team.[21]

In the realm of popular music, celebrities including Ma Rainey, Bessie Smith, Arizona Dranes, and Sister Rossetta Tharpe were among the most prominently celebrated arbiters and architects of modern race womanhood. On stages and in recording studios, Rainey and Smith manipulated the objectifying space of female performance to express same-sex desires, to speak out against domestic violence, and to allow stereotypically "mammy"-sized bodies to cut a glamorous figure. Visual displays of furs, sometimes men's suits, and adorned hair brought a new black female sexuality into the public sphere, accompanied by its own soundtrack. In the sacred world, Dranes and Tharpe vehemently eschewed excessive displays of female sexuality but aggressively appropriated "blues" rhythms to make the worldly boogie-woogie piano and blues guitar "talk" as critical instruments in staging an equally dazzling modern religious race womanhood. Finally, the story of Paris-based entertainer Josephine Baker, with her Madam Walker products prominently in hand, further attests to how traveling tours and easily transportable records, films, and beauty aids sent images of New Negro womanhood around the globe.[22]

The Western world's growing fear and fascination with "the Negro" converged with black migrant women's adornment practices to such an extent that even the basic definition of beauty was challenged. In 1921, Frederick Starr, an anthropologist at the University of Chicago, went so far as to claim that "there was no real beauty among white American girls" or within "the blond race" more generally. He argued that "only among Liberian and kindred races is real beauty to be found." While a discussion is beyond the scope of this essay, it is worth mentioning that race radical leftists and nationalists, among others, seized on this link between modern adornment and race pride to stage black beauty contests, pictorial spreads of black women in journals and magazines, and fashion shows and parades. Everyday acts of working women "dressing up" their bodies and hair helped disrupt the carefully cultivated and static image of the masses (or "the folk") as primitively premodern and waiting for literary construction. In fact, interviews from Paul Edwards's study of black consumers concluded that it was precisely in Madam Walker ads that one found the Negro "dignified and made to look as he is striving to look and not as he looked in antebellum days . . . here was the *New Negro*." Adornment practices pushed beyond struggles over cultural representation, and Madam Walker's beauty culture industry became a powerful political bloc whereby working-class women could collectively reimagine the global landscape.[23]

One of Walker's final ads, "A Million Eyes Turned Upon It Daily," directly announced, "We Belt the Globe." This ad asserted more than her aims for global capitalist expansion but also signaled black working-class women's collective re-creation of New Negro experience. The transformative powers of beauty culture were revealed in Walker's organization of an agents union, her support for *Woman's Voice* magazine, and her political affiliations in the World War I era. A primary concern of her agents union was to protect Walker from copyright infringement and competition. But in response to the aforementioned East St. Louis Riots of 1917 the Walker union was converted into a political bloc to protest racial violence. In a powerful telegram to President Woodrow Wilson, the union emphatically stated:

> We, the representatives of the National Convention of the Mme. CJ Walker Agents, in convention assembled, and in a larger sense representing twelve million Negroes, have keenly felt the injustice done our race and country through the recent lynching at Memphis, Tennessee, and the horrible race riot of East St. Louis. Knowing that no people in all the world are more loyal and patriotic than the Colored people of America, we respectfully submit to you this our protest against the continuation of such wrongs and injustices in this "land of the free, and home of the brave" and we further respectfully urge that you as President of these United States use your great influence that congress enact the necessary laws to prevent a recurrence of such disgraceful affairs.

By their 1919 convention, it had become apparent that Walker had roused a political consciousness in agents that could not be fully controlled, even by the Madam herself. Walker's decision to place products in retail stores to counter dwindling wartime profits caused a huge stir within the union. In response to the outrage, she first offered a hollow missive about socializing the business on a "cooperative basis," but then the agents seized the floor: "We . . . do not have the proper protection from you by placing your goods in the drugstore. In this way our sale of goods has been greatly cut down." Protests ensued until Walker finally altered her plans so that agents would not have to fully compete with retail outlets.[24]

By 1916, Walker had also further extended her vision by purchasing *Woman's Voice* magazine, to sell products and offer a forum for her agents and a growing woman-centered race consciousness. Unlike Anthony Overton's *Half-Century*, which contained the traditional and segregated "woman's page,"

3.4 Madam C. J. Walker Mfg. Co., "A Million Eyes," *The Crisis*, March 1919.

Woman's Voice was a fully integrated magazine that contained profiles of black women, a section on the African diaspora, and a current news section that addressed women not only in the home but also in business and politics. Issue covers featured prominent yet provocative female figures such as the blues woman Bessie Smith and the entrepreneur Maggie Lena Walker, who may not be found in more "respectable" black media venues. Such practices, made possible solely because of Walker's wealth, amplify the importance of this forum "For Women, By Women, Of Women." Similarly, Lucille Green Randolph, a Walker agent, owned a beauty shop that subsidized her husband's politically leftist *Messenger* magazine; A. Philip Randolph admitted, "Without her money . . . we couldn't have started *The Messenger*."[25]

Walker remained a strident activist in support of the NAACP's antilynching campaign, among other causes, but like others she grew weary of its white leadership and therefore joined other groups, including William Monroe Trotter's National Equal Rights League (NERL). While W. E. B. Du Bois attempted to lobby the Paris Peace Conference on behalf of the African diaspora, Ida. B. Wells and Walker were chosen as "auxiliary" delegates from the NERL's National Race Conference for World Democracy. At the same time, Walker's New York State mansion was the birthplace of the short-lived International League of Darker Peoples (ILDP) that included the Reverend Adam Clayton Powell Sr., A. Philip Randolph, and Marcus Garvey. Walker met with a Japanese delegation, in the "spirit of race internationalism," as another means to place the "race issue" on the Paris platform. But she also explicitly stated the ILDP was organized to "engage world opinion" far beyond the aims of the Paris Peace Conference. Her more conservative counselors warned against Walker's flirtations with "Bolshevikism" because of the wartime risks of censure, and sure enough she attracted the attention of the War Department's Military Intelligence Division and was added to their list of "Negro Subversives." The State Department denied Walker's request for a passport to France, yet she still put her support behind Du Bois's delegation and, most important, remained open to a variety of options for her black working-class constituency.[26]

Postscript

Walker died in 1919. By the late 1920s and early 1930s, glamorous ads and more strict policies of professionalism signaled a shift in the meaning of black beauty culture. Would the industry serve as a means to the larger goal of female autonomy or would beauty become an end in itself driven by male desire? Heightened professionalization incurred more prominent representations of race pride alongside the declining significance of women-centered entrepreneurship. In most cases, professionalization meant that the pictures of beauty culturists like Malone and Walker were gone, along with their Pentecostal-style testimonials, and in came more centralized market research and mass production strategies, further emphasizing profit margins over personal transformation and political agency. Yet demands that beauty culture remain a viable space for some level of female agency persisted. In the late 1920s the advertising innovator Claude Barnett used his Kashmir Chemical Company to shift focus from images of actual beauty culturists to urbane black models in exotic, even Orientalist settings such as Egypt and the Middle East or the elite cosmopolitan backdrop of the formal ballroom. On the one hand, these ads reinforced the New Negro scholars who argued that the African Nile Valley was the cradle of civilization *and* the birthplace of beauty. On the other hand, the presentation of worldly models in staid and languid poses of glamour focused again on male desire. For example, a Kashmir ad series depicts a cadre of returning World War I soldiers who had been awed by European beauty and for whom, now, only a Kashmir girl could satisfy their new "worldly" outlook. Another ad warned, "THE TIME IS AT HAND! You are just as much a soldier as the husband, brother, son or any that have gone to fight in this great conflict. IT DEPENDS UPON YOU whether he will come back to find you and yours healthy, happy and *pretty* or—sad, discouraged and *homely*" (emphasis added). Kashmir ads succeeded in further professionalizing beauty culture, but black women had been returned to a restrictive modernity where mere beauty qualified one's "race womanhood."[27]

In 1936, only a year after Italy invaded Ethiopia, Madam Walker mentor Annie Malone selected for her graduates a cape fashioned after one worn by Ethiopian emperor Haile Selassie. This choice signaled an important moment of black international solidarity against fascism. But the choice of "African" dress was also meant to assuage any concerns that black men might have about her challenge to their authority in the world of business. She discouraged her students from wearing caps and gowns for graduations, believing that her "contribution to culture and higher learning did not warrant the same symbol as that adopted by great universities." Conversely, Walker's eventual national supervisor, Marjorie Stewart Joyner, attempted to reconcile the push of professionalization with the resilient desire for semiautonomous female labor and leisure. Joyner cultivated relationships with black colleges toward the university certification of beauty culture and lobbied the Illinois state senate for the protection of hair care businesses. These activities helped provide protections for the primarily women-driven personal care and wellness industries that

3.5 Kashmir, "Nile Queen," *The Crisis*, December 1919.

thrive in the present, while also undermining some of the informality, decentralized autonomy, and political organizing found in Walker's era.[28]

Despite limitations, black women's beauty culture in the early twentieth century emerged as an important and dynamic public sphere of race consciousness, which continues to resonate with contemporary debates about competing fashionable and functional meanings of dreadlocks, cornrows, blond hair, and long nails. Such images and imaginations remain a part of ever-shifting discourses of racial authenticity that circulate and take on varied significance within a dynamic Afro-diasporic context. At the beginning of the twentieth century, a refashioning of the hair and body broadened the concerns generally associated with New Negroes by redefining acceptable representations, locations, and occupations for black women. Beauty culture's global imagination and institution building helps to further mark the importance of a black worldly consciousness for the New Negro era, while also providing a race and class specificity that overlaps with the *moga* experience as explored by the Modern Girl Research Group in the opening chapters of this volume. It is important to bear witness to how and why working-class migrant women turned bottles of white emulation into a *black* beauty culture to "make over" racial landscapes as agents, entrepreneurs, chemists, inventors, and political activists in their communities and throughout the world.

Notes

1. See *Report of the Thirteenth Annual Convention of the National Negro Business League* (NNBL) held at Chicago, 21–23 August 1912, 154–55, in Library of Congress (hereinafter LOC); Bundles, *On Her Own Ground*, 152–58; and Washington letter dated 18 December 1911, in Harlan and Smock, eds., *The Booker T. Washington Papers*, 420.

2. See Rooks, *Hair Raising*, 26–40.

3. See "Hair Culturists' First Convention," *New York Age*, 6 September 1917; and *Minutes of the First National Convention of the Mme CJ Walker Hair Culturists' Union of America*, Philadelphia, 30–31 August 1917, 2–3, in Madam Walker Collection, Indiana Historical Society (hereinafter MWC). Also see Gill, "Civic Beauty"; Blackwelder, *Styling Jim Crow*; and Willett, *Permanent Waves*.

4. See Fannie Barrier Williams, "The Colored Girl," *Voice of the Negro*, June 1905; and Nannie H. Burroughs, "Not Color But Character," *Voice of the Negro*, June 1904.

5. See Smith-Rosenberg and Rosenberg, "The Female Animal," 15.

6. See Taylor, "From White Kitchens to White Factories"; and the Chicago Commission on Race Relations, *The Negro in Chicago*, 367, 370, 380–83, 391–92.

7. Louis George, "Beauty Culture and Colored People," *Messenger* 2 (July 1918): 25–26.

8. See Morrow, *400 Years without a Comb*; Robinson, "Race, Class and Gender," 83; and

Madam CJ Walker Beauty Manual, 1st ed. (Indianapolis: Walker Manufacturing Co., 1928), (in MWC).

9. Ibid.

10. See White and White, *Stylin'*, 188–90; Fields, *Lemon Swamp and Other Places*, 187–89; Sarah Armstrong to Walker, 29 April 1918; Marie Alexander Sykes to Walker, 27 April 1918; Annie Dervin to Walker, 4 May 1918; and Bessie Brown to Walker, 28 June 1918; all in MWC. Also see Drake and Cayton, *Black Metropolis*, 499, 501, 503; and Peiss, *Hope in a Jar*, 224.

11. See Edwards, *The Southern Urban Negro as Consumer*; and Clark-Lewis, " 'This Work Had a End.' "

12. See "Anthony Overton," *Journal of Negro History* 32 (July 1947): 394–96; Overton, "The Largest Negro Manufacturing Enterprise in the United States," in 1912 NNBL Annual Convention (in LOC). Also see Mongold, "Annie Minerva Turnbo Malone"; Collier-Thomas, "Anne Turnbo Malone"; and Claude A. Barnett Papers (hereinafter CAB), box 262, folder 3, Chicago Historical Society.

13. See "Queen of Gotham's Colored 400," *Literary Digest* 55 (13 October 1917): 76.

14. For "Makes Short Hair Long and Cures Dandruff," see *Indianapolis Ledger*, 2 May 1906, and the *Freeman*, 16 April 1910. Also see Bundles, *Madam C. J. Walker*, 67; R. W. Thompson, "The Negro Woman in Business," *Freeman*, 20 September 1913.

15. For "Learn to Grow Hair and Make Money," see *Freeman*, 12 April 1913. Also see Chicago Commission on Race Relations, *Negro in Chicago*, 387; 1913 NNBL Annual Report, 211 (in LOC); R.W. Thompson, "The Negro Woman in Business," *Indianapolis Freeman*, 20 September 1913; Robinson, "Class, Race and Gender," 385; Bundles, "Madam CJ Walker — Cosmetics Tycoon," *MS.* magazine, July 1983, 93; and Bundles. *Madam CJ Walker*, 64.

16. See 1914 NNBL Annual Meeting, *Annual Report of the 15th Annual Convention of the National Negro Business League*, Muskogee, Oklahoma, 19–21 August 1914 (Nashville: AME Sunday School Union, 1914), 152–53; and *Minutes of the Eleventh Biennial Convention of the NACW*, 8–13 July 1918 (Washington: NACW, 1918), microfilm, in LOC, 38.

17. See "Over 10,000 in Her Employ," *New York Age* 1916 (no date), Hampton Institute Archives; and MW to FBR, 15 December 1916 (MWC/Indiana Historical Society [IHS])

18. See Locke, *The New Negro*; Gates, *The New Negro*; Edwards, *The Practice of Diaspora*; Foley, *Spectres of 1919*; and Singh, "Culture/Wars."

19. See Moses, *The Golden Age of Black Nationalism*; Gallichio, *The African American Encounter with Japan and China*; and Johnson, *Along This Way*, 341.

20. See Edwards, *The Practice of Diaspora*, and Patterson and Kelley, "Unfinished Migrations."

21. See Drake and Cayton, *Black Metropolis*, 387. Also see Rich, *Queen Bess*; "Lip Slobbering in Theaters is Given the Razz," *Defender*, 16 September 1922; and D. Ireland Thomas, "Motion Picture News," *Defender*, 30 September 1922; "Movie Queen Tells Courier Readers of Her 'Film Thrills,' " *Pittsburgh Courier*, 11 June 1927; and Gems, "Blocked Shot."

22. See Carby, "It Jus Be's Dat Way Sometime"; Davis, *Blues Legacies and Black Feminism*; Oliver, *Songsters and Saints*; Jackson, "Testifying at the Cross"; Rose, *Jazz Cleopatra*; and Archer-Straw, *Negrophilia*.

23. See *Chicago Whip*, 5 November, 19 November, and 17 December, 1921; and Edwards, *Southern Urban Negro as Consumer*, 242.

24. For "A Million Eyes Turned upon It Daily," see *Crisis* magazine in 1919 and *New York Age*, 18 February 1919. Also see MW to Mrs. Smith, 31 August 1917; "Notice to the Agents of the Madam CJ Walker Manufacturing Company, undated; MW to FBR, 15 April 1918; Walker Agents/Chicago to FBR, 22 April 1918; FBR to MW, 26 July 1918 (all in MWC); and "Mme. CJ Walker Holds Second Annual Convention," *Chicago Defender*, 10 August 1918.

25. See Rooks, *Hair Raising*, 105–14, and copies of *Woman's Voice*, December 1919, December 1921, and March 1922, in Moorland Spingarn Collection, Howard University. Also see Anderson, *A. Philip Randolph*, 82.

26. See Bundles, *On Her Own Ground*, 180–83, 257–65, and 270–72; and Skinner, *African Americans and the US Policy Toward Africa*. Also see "Villa Lewaro-on-the-Hudson, Birthplace of the International League of Darker Peoples," *World Forum*, January 1919 (in record group 165, file 10218–296, Records of the War Dept., General and Special Staffs, Correspondence of the Military Intelligence Division Relating to "Negro Subversives," M1440, reel 5); "The Race Issue at the Peace Conference Table," *New York Age*, 30 November 1918; and FBR to MW, 25 January 1919.

27. See Evans, "Claude A. Barnett and the Associated Negro Press," 44–56; "Nile Queen Booklet," 9, and "The Royal Way," Kashmir Press Package, 9; both in box 262, folder 2, CAB. Also see ads in almost every monthly issue of 1918 in *The Crisis*; ads in *Defender*, 22 February 1919; and the World War I ad quoted in Robinson, "Class, Race and Gender," 290.

28. See "Poro College: School of Beauty Culture," box 262, folder 3, 3–4, CAB; Adam Langer, "You Know, I'm 95 and I Know What I'm Talking About," *Chicago Reader*, 11 September 1992, 9; Flug, "Marjorie Stewart Joyner"; and the Marjorie Stewart Joyner Papers (MSJ), Vivian Harsh Research Collection, Chicago Public Library.

4

Making the Modern Girl French

From New Woman to *Éclaireuse*

〜

MARY LOUISE ROBERTS

For French historians, thinking about the Modern Girl brings to mind *la garçonne* — the bobbed-hair, pencil-thin sexpot who smoked cigarettes, drank cocktails, and danced to the rhythms of jazz bands.[1] In the 1920s, the garçonne became a symbol of a new cultural imposition — what came to be called "Americanization." As one contemporary remarked, "The innocent young thing (*l'oie blanche*) of yesterday has given way to la garçonne of today. In this way as well, the war, like a devastating wind, has had an influence. Add to this sports, movies, dancing, cars, the unhealthy need to be always on the move — this entire Americanization of old Europe, and you will have the secret to the complete upheaval of people and things."[2] In this sense, la garçonne was a symbol of the increasingly transnational nature of French gender norms and, more generally, a French culture increasingly patterned by ideas and practices imposed from beyond its borders.

But it would be a mistake to see la garçonne simply as an effect of an American cultural invasion. First of all, while contemporaries deemed la garçonne a product of the war, in fact Anglo-American culture had been insinuating itself into French gender norms for at least a generation. However much the war must be credited for breaking down transatlantic cultural barriers, it was in fact the rise of an urban mass culture in the prewar decades which created a major transnational exchange of ideas concerning gender norms. The origins of the Modern Girl in France date to the 1890s, when such mass cultural forms as journalism and theater brought to French middle-class audiences their first glimpse of an Anglo-American model of womanhood, then called the "New Woman." At first the New Woman was ignored, then she was condemned. By the war's outbreak in 1914, however, largely through the efforts of one extraordinary woman, Marguerite Durand, she had been transformed into something thoroughly French — described by the playwright Maurice Donnay as *"une éclaireuse."* The story of the Modern Girl in France, then, complicates the notion of "Americanization" in still another way: rather than being simply "imposed" from without, the Modern Girl emerged from a uniquely French reiteration of the New Woman. To appreciate la garçonne as a cultural hybrid in this way, we must go back to the prewar decades when a "modern" French femininity began to develop. This evolution was characterized by three processes central to the emergence of the Modern Girl by the 1920s: the creation of a distinctly French version of emancipated womanhood; the crucial role of new forms of mass culture in the production of gender norms; and the striking of a balance between transgressive and conventional behaviors among "modern" girls.

The New Woman

The New Woman emerged in the 1890s, in the context of feminist activism, but also in bohemian artistic circles and the rise of women's colleges.[3] In an article for *North American Review* in 1894, the British journalist Sarah Grand created the neologism "New Woman" to refer to the educated middle-class woman who was trying to break out of her mother's parlor and aim somehow to *matter,* as the historian Christine Stansell has put it.[4] In fact, Grand's neologism had as much to do with race as with gender, as she used it to push for female sexual purity and eugenics as guarantors of the empire's future.[5] In any case, Grand's coinage helped to make the New Woman a popular focus of English magazines like *Punch* and *Yellow Book* and such novels as Thomas Hardy's *Jude the Obscure.* Likewise, her American counterpart began to show up in such journals as *Puck, Judge, Life,* and *Chic* as well as Kate Chopin's *The Awakening* (1899).[6] It was not long before the New Woman became reified in the public imagination, assuming a stock appearance, a fixed set of behaviors, and a cultural weight all her own. Bespectacled, bookish, and austere in dress, the New Woman combined a Jane Eyre–like plainness with dandyish habits such as cigarette smoking. Garbed in bloomers, she was frequently depicted riding a bicycle, the new plaything of the leisured middle classes. Still another important influence for the New Woman was Scandinavian theater. Henrik Ibsen's *A Doll's House* (1879), in particular, became famous for its heroine Nora, a young mother who deserts her condescending, tyrannical husband in order to find moral, personal freedom. Its first commercial production, staged in London in 1889, ignited a firestorm of debate. The play helped to secure the theater as a key site for exploring increasingly embattled Victorian gender norms.[7]

By contrast, the initial French performance of *A Doll's House*, staged April 1894 at the Vaudeville in Paris, was met with a wide yawn. The French saw Nora as a Scandinavian rather than a "Latin" phenomenon—a foreign curiosity, not a threat.[8] The prominent critic Francisque Sarcey noted how uncomfortable it must have been for the celebrated French actress Réjane to play a rebellious, independent woman. "Here's one who is not a Scandinavian," said Sarcey of Réjane. "Ah, and we only love her more for that."[9] The quiet Parisian reception of Ibsen's *A Doll's House* suggests that, at least in 1894, concern over the New Woman had not reached the epic proportions in France that it had attained in England.[10] The feminist demand for equal rights had been squarely in the French public eye for a decade already, as had the spunky young heroines of Gyp and Marcel Prévost—young girls who shared the opinion that "it's horrible for a woman to be dependent on a man."[11] But the specific image of the New Woman—and her symbolic challenge to conventionality—was just coming into view. In his review in 1895 of Sydney Grundy's play about the subject, "The New Woman," the drama critic for *Revue des deux mondes* dealt with the neologism as a British "ghost": much discussed, but never seen.[12]

In 1896, however, the specter made more frequent appearances. In April, Paris played host to an international feminist congress, which attracted advocates of women's rights from all over the world.[13] The event did not go unnoticed by the Parisian press, who sent reporters over to find out what the ladies were up to. On 19 April, the cover of *Le Grelot* followed *La Plume* in featuring a woman dressed in the "New" manner already familiar to the British public. Cigarette in her mouth, sporting a straw boater, plain-Jane blouse, and squat bloomers, she barks to her husband, "I'm going to the feminist Congress," and demands dinner for "precisely" eight o'clock.[14] Bordering the central caricature is a series of other pictures stereotyping the New Woman, including her penchant for nudity and free love. In this way, the New Woman entered France on the tailcoats of the feminist, confusing those two figures in the popular imagination. A flood of literature soon followed. Also in 1896, novels with titles like *L'Eve nouvelle* and *La Femme nouvelle* began to appear in bookstore windows.[15] Readers opening up copies of *La Revue encyclo-*

pédique and *La Revue* found articles and special issues devoted to the topic. There they met with decidedly mixed feelings about the "Anglo-Saxon" New Woman. In *La Revue* of 15 July, for example, Jules Simon, the senator whose midcentury writings on women had been so influential among republican politicians, warned that new educational opportunities for women had gone "too far," and "that the worst thing one can do to a woman is to transform her into a man."[16]

Obviously, *La Revue* was less than keen about Anglo-Saxon prospects for womanhood. Throughout the late 1890s, the New Woman retained a set of physical and moral qualities she acquired in her 1896 premiere. For example, she continued to look, as well as act, like a man. In 1897, the German critic Max Nordau described her as "a hybrid figure, wearing pants, walking in the street with her hands in her pockets and a cigarette on her lips."[17] On the same subject, Maurice Barrès urged his male readers to cheer up, for such women would surely "die sterile." Novels paraded a bleak contingent of virilized man-haters. In Cim's *Les Émancipées,* for example, Katia Mordasz "resembles a graceful young man more than a woman" and is counted among those "women who no longer want to be women."[18] Likewise, in *Les Femmes nouvelles* (1899), the Margueritte brothers' Madame Morchesne is "short-legged, squat, ruddy — a masculine figure, with the shadow of a mustache" — and her American friend Miss Pelboom represents "the third sex in all its horror."[19] The New Woman also continued to be equated with a threat to the well-ordered domestic household. Stunned groups of men gather in Cim's *Émancipées* to note how women "no longer want to do housework, sew, or in particular, cook."[20] Nor did they seem to want children — a rumor that secured their guilt in the depopulation "crisis."[21]

As a French stereotype, the New Woman drew on the old discourse of the *basbleu* or "bluestocking," famously ridiculed by Molière in *Les Femmes savantes.* But at the same time, she continued to be thought of as a foreign import. In contemporary novels, gender trouble invariably arrived from across the Channel, across the Ocean, or from the Slavic East. Pitiful, gnarled travelers with huge chips on their shoulders, the New Women landed in Paris to study medicine, attend feminist congresses, establish women's schools, and above all corrupt the souls of nice French girls. When Romaine Pirnitz of *Les Vierges fortes* arrives in Paris from Hungary in the ill-fated year of 1896, for example, she provides this cryptic explanation for her journey: "The woman who is independent of men is legion in the Anglo-Saxon world, numerous in the Slavic and Scandinavian worlds. And now, we must approach the oldest civilizations."[22] Even those who gave the New Woman a positive reception, like the poet Jules Bois, saw the image as a foreign import. While Bois described himself as a man who had "understood the New Woman's superiority, learned her sublime lessons, and who now inclines towards her, begging to be one of her soldiers," he saw this army as a distinctly foreign lot, including Sarah Grand, inventor of the term "New Woman"; Olive Shreiner, author of *Women and Labor*; the German feminist Hilda Sachs; and the "visionary" heroines of Ibsen.[23] The problem, it seemed, was that the New Woman was hopelessly foreign, even for her ardent fans. If the New Woman was here to stay, how to make her French?

Marguerite Durand's Aesthetic Politics

The solution awaited a young journalist for *Le Figaro* named Marguerite Durand (see figure 4.1). Just as 1896 was a watershed for images of the New Woman in France, so was it a defining moment for Durand. During April of that year, Durand covered the international feminist conference taking place in Paris for *Le Figaro*. It transformed her life. A former actress and a woman who conceived of herself in traditional terms, Durand was hardly a feminist. At the same time, however, she had recently suffered legal discrimination as a woman when she had given birth to a son by a prominent editor at *Le Figaro*, Antonin Périvier. No sooner was the child born than Périvier tried to take him away from Durand, who was forced to enlist the legal help of Georges Clemenceau to get her son back.[24] As an embattled single mother and as a professional woman working outside the home in a male profession, Durand was "surprised" by the "good ideas" of the feminists present at the conference. By the 1890s, the French feminist movement had a long, well-developed agenda of legal and political reforms in such areas as property, divorce, and paternity. But Durand was also impressed by the words of the newcomer Maria Pognon, who allowed the conference to broach such radical issues as suffrage and "free love."[25]

While reporting on the conference, Durand could not help but notice the way in which her male colleagues at *Le Figaro* described the feminists, dwelling on their thick eyeglasses and "resemblance to men, the effect of which was to render their position less interesting."[26] This focus on the New Woman's ugly appearance was no doubt a way for critics to undermine the vision of social and political change with which she was associated. But Durand believed that if she could change the New Woman's appearance, it could hasten her acceptance: "I decided that these women (who admittedly do not always defend their ideas with great skill) were not known by the public, which was getting false ideas concerning them. That is to say, until now the promoters of feminism have been only provocative, somewhat eccentric types."[27] By contrast, Durand herself was a ravishing blond and a former actress. As such, she knew that beauty, in the form of seduction, was power. She had enjoyed first-hand the pleasures and

4.1 Walery, portrait of Marguerite Durand, who famously said, "Feminism owes a great deal to my blond hair." Courtesy Bibliothèque Marguerite Durand.

privileges of being a beautiful woman in French society, and from this experience she developed a new aesthetic politics. Durand dismissed the idea that "while a woman's intelligence is being carefully and completely developed, her sense of the aesthetic alone will be arrested — that is an absurdity."[28] Beauty, she argued, was a political act: "For a feminist, the extreme care of one's person and a studied sense of elegance are not always a diversion, a pleasure, but rather often excess work, a duty that she nevertheless must impose upon herself, if only to deprive shortsighted men of the argument that feminism is the enemy of beauty and of a feminine aesthetic."[29] Durand was careful here to dismantle the traditional linking of beauty to frivolity. Far from being a "diversion" or a "pleasure," beauty was work, a self-imposed duty. If men were "short*sighted*," then in Durand's view, feminism must have a visual component — it must be about *seeing* and being *seen,* as much as behavior or ideas.

Durand recognized that the fate of the New Woman would not be decided at the ballot box. Rather, she realized her future lay in the ever-more powerful urban print culture — the magazines, newspapers, journals, reviews where the New Woman made her first appearances in 1896. Durand's target was middle-class women who had access to such mass-cultural forms, and her real genius

lay in her ability to exploit them for political purposes. One stunning example of her gifts came in 1910 when she ran for municipal office in Paris, stepping out on the stages of well-known theaters in order to make the case for her candidacy and, indirectly, the female vote. Because Durand had no legal chance of winning, advertising for the suffragist cause was her only possible political gain. At some point that year, the governor of West Africa had given her a lioness, which she promptly named "Tiger" and tried to domesticate as a household pet (see figure 4.2). Tiger quickly became a media spectacle and put Durand on the cover of several prominent French journals and newspapers — precisely what she must have intended.[30] The photograph was obviously posed, with Durand, dressed in an ornate, exotic-looking robe, standing regally in her doorway, holding the lioness by a strong rope. But a closer look reveals that a male figure behind the door, perhaps purposely hidden but nevertheless visible, did the real work of controlling Tiger. The picture, then, rested on a deliberate misrepresentation which challenged the equation between seduction and weakness underlying late-nineteenth-century femininity. In Durand's universe, one could both be beautiful and hold a lion at the same time, that is, one could be both elegant and powerful. Here again, Durand was arguing her case that women need not give up beauty or seduction to be strong civic subjects. Her use of Orientalist props to achieve this effect — the lion, the exotic clothing — demonstrates how imperialist tropes of power were used by women to make their own case for authority and control.

Ultimately, then, Durand's feminism was about visibility and *being seen* as much as it was about a set of political ideas. According to Durand, if the New Woman had been lambasted in the press, the only response was for women to create a newspaper of their own, one which produced a more positive image of the New Woman as feminine, elegant, and beautiful as well as powerful and professional. Just seventeen months after Durand walked into the feminist conference in April 1896 she founded a daily newspaper for women, *La Fronde*. Modeled after the daily of the era, *La Fronde* was bourgeois in both content and sensibility. But it differed in one important way from the mainstream bourgeois daily: its staff was entirely female. Women edited, wrote, and even typeset *La Fronde*. Sometimes called "*Le Temps* in skirts," Durand's paper was neither an organ of the feminist movement nor a journal devoted to fashion and the domestic arts. Instead it covered politics, news, sports, and the stock market. To produce it, Durand gathered around her an extraordinary circle of women, including Clémence Royer, the first woman to teach at the Sorbonne; Séverine, the first woman reporter; Jeanne Chauvin, one of the first women admitted to the Paris bar; Pauline Kergomard, the first woman admitted to the Conseil Supérieur de l'Instruction publique; Daniel Lesueur, one of the first women to receive the Légion d'honneur; as well as the first female pharmacist, Blanche Galien, and the first female astronomer to enter the observatory, Melle Klumke. In short, the editorial staff was a virtual hotbed of New Women.[31]

Durand's first goal was to create an exquisite, thoroughly "feminine" aesthetic for *La Fronde* by carefully decorating the paper's offices on the rue St. Georges in Paris. When journalists for *Illustration* arrived there to do a story in January 1898, they gushed over the flowers, the colors, the decor, and the atmosphere. "A feminine paper," one concluded, "is produced exactly like an ordinary paper; only there are many more green plants and flowers, and the furniture is infinitely more elegant."[32] Durand picked blue and green as the predominant tones for the decor because, she felt, they went well with her own coloring. Durand also equipped the office with extensive dressing room facilities. "Because coquetry is far from banished at *La Fronde*," wrote the *Illustration* reporter, "and because by contrast, fingers stained with ink are unmercifully proscribed, a comfortable powder room is at the disposal of these women."[33]

Durand's "feminine" offices were meant to disarm prejudices about ugly, eccentric feminists. But feminists themselves were not always happy. Many socialist and working-class feminists, for example, saw Durand as insincere, shallow, and snobby. For example, Madeleine Pelletier remembered her experience at *La Fronde*'s offices in this way: "I had the idea of going there and naively, I brought an article [to submit]. A woman in a very low cut-dress received me with haughtiness; she took the article and told me that I would see it if it appeared; I would have to buy the paper every day. Evidently I didn't look rich enough in my dress . . . and that was much more important than what was in my article."[34] Pelletier's perception that her appearance meant "much more" than the content of her article roughly transcribes the aims of Durand's feminist aesthetic. But seen through Pelletier's eyes, the notion that a woman's beauty mattered as much to the cause as her ideas was nothing more than bourgeois superficiality. At the heart of Durand's project lay a class snobbery that alienated many working-class feminists.

The offices of *La Fronde* were "feminine" in still another sense, because Durand forbade any man on the premises. Her male colleagues in the press did not approve. In order to smooth ruffled feathers, Durand gave several high profile soirées, which were attended by the most powerful politicians and journalists in Paris (Joseph Reinach, Rene Viviani, Raymond Poincaré, Jules Bois, Jean Lorrain, and Octave Uzanne, to name a few).[35] Invitations specified that women wear a "*toilette de soirée décolletée.*"[36] Although the parties began formally, they somehow evolved into more uninhibited affairs with dancing until the wee hours of the morning. As such, they worked brilliantly to correct "false ideas" concerning the *frondeuses*.[37] One morning-after journalist remarked cozily that although he had arrived at *La Fronde*'s offices "an heir to all . . . common prejudices and cliches" concerning "the proverbial ugliness of the *bas-bleus*," he had discovered women who were well-dressed and warm-hearted.[38] "How pretty they are!" exclaimed another journalist after the same party. "At times, in theory or out of habit, we make fun of the frondeuses without knowing it." But "yesterday's party proved them to be seductive and pretty." He was happy to discover that "speaking of female rights . . . in no way requires renouncing the joys of seduction."[39]

Maurice Donnay's *Les Éclaireuses*

Did Durand succeed in making a distinctly French *femme nouvelle* out of an Anglo-American New Woman? To answer that question, we must jump forward to 1913, and to an important cultural event on the eve of the First World War — one that measures the ways in which the New Woman image had changed since its debut in France two decades before. The occasion is the fiftieth performance of Maurice Donnay's *Les Éclaireuses*, which concerns a group of women trying to construct identities outside marriage and domesticity. A few months earlier, the play had a "brilliant" opening at the newly restored Théâtre-Marigny, one that attracted tout Paris, including President Raymond Poincaré, who went up on stage to say a few words.[40] Hailed by critics and audiences alike as a "triumph," the drama continued to enjoy enormous success."[41] To celebrate its fiftieth performance, the producers organized a panel titled "The Éclaireuses as Explained by Themselves." None other than Marguerite Durand was asked to direct the panel, joined by four other accomplished women—Maria Vérone, Suzanne Grinberg, Nelly Roussel, and Madame Cayrol. The five were also invited to a lunch with the play's actresses, given by Donnay, where they feasted on such dishes as Oeufs Pochés Suffragettes and Salade Féministe as well as Champagne.[42] Durand's panel remarks, preserved in manuscript form, are worth examining in detail, because they can tell us much about French "modern" womanhood on the eve of World War I.

Les Éclaireuses bore cultural traces of the New Woman genre pioneered by Ibsen several decades before. There was the usual restless woman, Jeanne Dureille, as well as the requisite tyrannical husband, Paul—by now both well-established theatrical types in the French as well as the Scandinavian theater. Although A Doll's House had a slow start in France, it was not long before the New Woman was haunting the French fin de siècle stage as well as print culture. Such femme nouvelle plays as Les Tenailles and La Vassale, which followed the basic plot outline of Ibsen's play, were very popular in French theater during the late 1890s and caused much controversy and debate. The first act of Les Éclaireuses recapitulates the plot of such plays. Husband and wife quarrel over the wife's desire to be free, and then the latter, in this case, Jeanne, walks out. But here is the important difference: in the fin de siècle plays, the exit usually occurred in the climactic act of the play. By contrast, in this case, Jeanne walks out at the end of the first act, then has the entire rest of the play to develop a new self beyond the domestic threshold.

And the differences do not stop there. As the curtain rises on the second act, the now-divorced Jeanne is consulting doctor Rose Bernhard about her bad health. Jeanne has recurring dreams in which she suffers from such "obsessions" as cutting her tongue while licking an envelope. "You are scarcely thirty," Rose argues, asking Jeanne when she last had sex, "you have a heart, a brain and a set of hips." When Jeanne is shocked, Rose explains that while she loves her work and independent life, she knows it will suffer if her physical needs aren't answered.[43] In this way, Rose, obviously a role model for Jeanne, establishes herself as a different kind of single woman. In French New Woman plays of the 1890s, single women were largely limited to two types: desiccated old maids or regretful prostitutes. Rose is neither. Unlike an old maid, she loves her freedom. And as someone who makes a respectable living, she is not a prostitute. In short, Rose is neither lonely nor depraved. She is something quite new.

To signal this newer femme nouvelle, Donnay dubbed her the "*éclaireuse.*" The word is a feminization of *éclaireur*, a military term for soldiers who go in advance of the troops for intelligence purposes. According to Donnay, the "éclaireuse" was "a woman who prepares the path for other women to follow in view of a larger movement, in this play, the feminist movement."[44] "The word is brilliant! very French!" exclaimed Durand enthusiastically as she began her comments on 13 March.[45] As a word, it had the advantages of being not easily translatable and coined by Maurice Donnay himself, a member of l'Academie française, the very institution which served as official guardian of the French language. While Anglo-American origins tainted the neologism New Woman, *éclaireuse* insisted on a uniquely French version of the Anglo-American model. At one point, Durand said of the term *éclaireuse:* "When a word perfectly defines the thing that it wants to designate, an immense step is taken towards the exact comprehension of this thing."[46] That exactitude, for Durand, meant a distinctly French version of emancipated womanhood.

As for Durand's commentary on Donnay's female characters in the play, she framed it from the perspective of real referents, that is, flesh-and-blood women sitting beside her on the panel. For example, Durand compared Donnay's Dr. Rose to "one of our youngest and most distinguished doctors," Madame Cayrol, with whom she shared the stage. She then deferred to Cayrol's expertise on the issue of sexual abstinence, informing the audience that the *doctoresse* would be speaking in a few minutes. Commenting on a scene when Jeanne gathers a whole raft of éclaireuses for a rendezvous in her apartment, Durand continued this strategy by identifying one by one their living counterparts. The play's woman lawyer Lucienne David, Durand claimed, was modeled after Maria Vérone, also sitting on the panel. And in the rakish Charlotte Alzette, Durand saw Colette Willy, "one of our greatest contemporary writers."[47] By claiming Donnay's characters for real life, Durand was both arguing for a new kind of woman — the éclaireuse — and claiming her real, live, flesh-and-blood existence.

But the real significance of her strategy can only be appreciated when we note the characters in the play for whom Durand did *not* claim living counterparts. Such disavowals are worth examining, as they clarify Durand's notion of the éclaireuse. Her treatment of "Professor Orpailleur" is a case in point. In Jeanne's apartment, the characters are joined by an uninvited guest, a woman doctor referred to as "Professor Orpailleur." With her brusque manners and masculine, eccentric clothing, she represents, in Durand's view, "the old model, no longer in existence" of the New Woman, "to whom men refer when we are trying to persuade them, and about which they say: 'if this is the type of woman you are preparing for us, no thanks!' "[48] Orpailleur is, of course, "the old model" of the New Woman, who received the predictable response from critics. "Monster, *hommasse*," exclaimed Victor Margueritte, who declared her "of the same species that produced the feminist twenty years ago."[49] To give Orpailleur a real-life counterpart was a political liability for Durand, which is probably why she neglected to do so. In the same way, Durand passed over the radical lesbian feminist character Germaine Luceau, who tries to convert Jeanne to the cause and also falls in love with her. Significantly, Durand also failed to provide referents for any of the foreign women in the play, including the militant English suffragette Edith Schmidt or the American professor Pauline Dabo.

While Orpailleur and Luceau have only minor parts in the play, they nevertheless do perform one crucial role: throwing into positive relief the éclaireuse, the distinctly French modern woman. For instance, Durand was eager to point out the "definite contrast, and a happy one at that" between Orpailleur and the character Blanche Virieu, the elegant leader of the feminist school, also present in Jeanne's living room.[50] Durand's favored characters have all taken on male professions, such as medicine or law, without "virilizing" themselves. They may be mostly single, but none exhibits symptoms of being either an old maid or prostitute, dried-out or depraved. Instead, they keep work and love in healthy balance, managing to shape a personality apart from their relations with men, but without emasculating or alienating them. In other words, the éclaireuse struck a balance between transgressive and conventional behaviors which would also shape the garçonne image after the war. Gone, then, are the cowering husbands of the 1890s. As Durand put it, Jeanne's feminism "neither alienates nor effaces the men in her entourage: on the contrary, they are all in love with her."[51] Far from the ugly, eccentric prudes threatening from the East or over the Channel, the éclaireuses enjoyed beauty and charm, romance and sexual pleasure.

Critics agreed with Durand that the éclaireuses formed a happy contrast to their New Woman predecessors of the 1890s. Donnay's characters "are not the grotesque monsters we could have feared," conceded Abel Hermant.[52] "These women have found a style of life that suits them," wrote Henry Austry of *La Nouvelle revue*. "Charming" was the word Henry Bordeaux chose to describe the éclaireuses: "they have everything it takes to please the amateurs of new ideas."[53] The end of *Les Éclaireuses* is conservative. At the final curtain, Jeanne reneges on her choice and leaves Paris to join her new lover Jacques as his wife.

The denouement pleased both critics and crowds, most of whom saw the play in conservative terms. In the end, Jeanne had given in to her instincts and a higher power. "Love is the force that moves the universe, at least the universe of women" was how one critic interpreted the lovers' ultimate reunion.[54] Another praised Donnay's "sureness of execution" in making the heroine evolve from "ignorance" and "false certainty" to "her veritable vocation."[55] Nor were the so-called real éclaireuses remiss in expressing their approval at the denouement. "We cannot understand feminism without love," said Maria Vérone (supposedly with a "charming smile") at a toast during the special luncheon given by Donnay.[56] "She is such a woman at this moment!" clucked Durand.

As *Les Éclaireuses* demonstrates, Durand had dealt a decisive blow to the public image of the Anglo-American New Woman. If we were to follow Durand's strategy of naming the "real" counterpart of the éclaireuse, it would lead us back to the mistress of the game herself — the frondeuse Durand. For in a very real sense, the frondeuse had become the éclaireuse, the French femme nouvelle. Even a cursory glance at the fiction and drama of these years shows how Durand's vision of the New Woman had triumphed. For example, a stock setting for nouvelle femme fiction became the all-women's community, such as a school or newspaper staff, typically modeled after that of *La Fronde*. Eugène Brieux's *La Femme seule*, which premiered only a few weeks before Donnay's play, featured a female reporter working at an all-female-staffed paper called *La Femme libre*, in which feminist articles combine with "lighter" more conventionally "feminine" features, such as novels, a beauty page, and recipes — precisely the "formula" of *La Fronde*.[57] The roots of the frondeuse / éclaireuse can also be found in such novels as *Les Femmes nouvelles*, in which the heroine Minna, who runs an all-female newspaper called *L'Avenir*, forms a happy contrast to the novel's ugly foreign types. She is strong but feminine, a "person" but not a threat to men — in short, exactly as Durand had imagined her. Striving to balance work and love, Minna illustrates the narrator's argument: "If women truly want to become the equals of men, that will not be accomplished by servile imitation. Above all, they must remain feminine, and not abdicate any of their intimate charm."[58]

That sounds like something Durand herself would say. Similarly, in Marcelle Tinayre's *La Rebelle* (1905), Josanne works in the all-female office of *Monde féminin*. But she refuses to leave behind her womanly side. "You are so feminine!" her boyfriend tells her, "neither the struggle to make a living, nor independence, have destroyed your feminine instincts."[59] Significantly *La Rebelle*'s author, Marcelle Tinayre, was herself a frondeuse who contributed feature articles to Durand's daily. Anyone reading Tinayre's novel would have recognized Durand in the character of Madeleine Foucart, who directs the *Monde féminin* and is considered to be a "great feminist" as well as the "most beautiful woman in Paris."[60]

From *L'éclaireuse* to Modern Girl

The choice of Durand to comment on Donnay's play at the Théâtre-Marigny was no coincidence. She had been shaping the éclaireuse image for two decades already. Durand's feminist aesthetics had a profound impact on how the French imagined being both modern and female. Durand's achievement was to shape the Anglo-American New Woman into something distinctly French by drawing on traditions deeply rooted in her own culture. By 1913, her image of womanhood had reached widespread acceptance, as evidenced by the fact that audiences and critics approved of the characters in Donnay's play. These éclaireuses might have shunned domesticity, lived on their own, and taken pride in their creative accomplishments, but the critics commented only in passing on such radical lifestyles. In part, that silent acceptance resulted from Donnay's happily-ever-after ending for the rebellious Jeanne and her lover. Fictional narratives such as Donnay's play domesticated the modern woman for the masses, neutralizing her threat by confining her to a stage where she was ultimately made traditional once again through plot resolution. At the same time, such women as Marguerite Durand carefully negotiated transgressive and conventional behaviors so as to appear less threatening. The critics' silent acceptance of the éclaireuses had to do with the fact that a new definition of womanhood had taken root in their minds, even without their knowledge.

How did this happen? In part, the answer is individual: Durand's own intuition for what was right for the French at that moment, her own brilliant political instincts. But mass culture also had a central role in shaping the modern woman image: the frondeuse as an image of womanhood would never have arisen had Durand not begun her newspaper — the most popular fin de siècle mass media form — and used it to critique conventional femininity. Nor would the éclaireuse have been possible without a profitable theater industry giving Donnay and other playwrights a bourgeois audience to debate gender roles. The newspaper and the theater — two mass forms of culture widely embraced by the French middle classes at the fin de siècle — mediated the image of the frondeuse/éclaireuse at every step. Among *La Fronde*'s most avid readers were provincial schoolteachers, who praised the paper's ability to educate not only themselves but their male colleagues. One long-time reader, Madame Cadet, wrote Durand that while at first "even very intelligent" gentlemen friends made fun of her for subscribing to the paper, in the end she had gotten her "vengeance" by making them read it: "Because your feminism is made of charm and grace, of goodness and pity, of right and justice, everyone ends by being persuaded and stopping their mockery."[61] The power of Durand's feminist aesthetics depended on the culture industries in which it was staged. Although we can never know how many young bourgeois women mimicked the new images of womanhood they encountered in the press and on the stage, we can say that the material conditions — mass culture industries — now existed for this type of change to take place on a sizable scale. In this new context, one woman's recasting of seduction as feminism was able to have a wide destabilizing effect on middle-class gender norms.

Only a year after Donnay's play was the talk of the boulevard, the Great War brought to an abrupt halt the light-hearted histrionics of *Les Éclaireuses*. Most historians view the war's confusion of gender roles, including the widespread deployment of women in such male occupations as business, civil service, teaching, and medicine, as a decisive turning point in the lives of women. The frondeuse/éclaireuse was soon pushed aside by the postwar garçonne, who took both economic and sexual independence in her stride. A prewar éclaireuse like Jeanne, who ends the play living happily after, looked hopelessly naive in comparison to the postwar garçonne, at once more cynical and aloof. Unlike her predecessor, the garçonne was just as likely to be from the working class as from the middle class; in fact, she made class as a marker of identity increasingly complex after the war. Like the frondeuse, the garçonne became the center of much controversy about changing gender roles. But the failure of liberal beliefs to make sense of the war changed the focus of this preoccupation with female identity. With her fast, loose ways and her short hair, the garçonne embodied, for the French, the war's power to undermine the certainties of nineteenth-century liberal society. As I have argued elsewhere, the garçonne became a privileged symbol of postwar cultural and sexual anxieties — a dominant symbol of change in the postwar cultural landscape.[62]

In light of the differences between the éclaireuse and the garçonne, Durand's attempts to reestablish *La Fronde* again after the war are instructive. In May 1926, Durand reassembled many of the old staff. But the restored paper seems philistine and stodgy in comparison to its prewar counterpart. Durand also took on several men, so that the paper could no longer claim itself an all-female enterprise. In addition, Durand's daily editorials argued in a rote manner for various bourgeois feminist causes. In short, this *La Fronde* lacked both the caginess and the originality of the 1897 version. Its appearance provoked more nostalgia than anything else. "Alas! When the first number appeared in 1897," remembered the journalist Jean-Bernard "we were young, and so were these women!" He hoped Durand would indulge her readers with her memoirs of the long-gone era when she was "blond" and a "model beauty."[63] The paper lasted only weeks before folding. Its fate was a matter of age and timing: Durand was in the last years of her life. More importantly, history had passed her by. Work and play outside the home had become increasingly acceptable for women, and they no longer bothered with such prewar relics as chaperones and whaleboned corsets. While social activism and feminist politics remained important, there were other distractions as well, among them sports, jazz, dancing, automobiles, cigarettes, cocktails, and sexual adventure. If the new woman was eager to read her own daily newspaper, the garçonne was more likely to drive to see a Hollywood movie.

But the garçonne owed two significant debts to Marguerite Durand even if they went largely unacknowledged. The first of these is the garçonne's embrace of mass, consumer culture. The cultural influence of both the newspaper and the theater declined in the postwar decades. But the garçonne continued to be shaped by transnational flows of commodities and ideas concerning gender norms. She became associated with new forms of music, such as jazz, American movies, and international fashion trends. Second, the garçonne inherited Durand's equation of modernity and femininity. This Modern Girl cut her hair, wore deliberately masculine clothes, and deemphasized her hips and breasts. Yet she also strove for a distinctly feminine glamour that was carefree but also charming. Gone forever was the plain-Jane, Anglo-American New Woman. As the Modern Girl collective has written, the Modern Girl image "embodied the paradoxical fantasy that young women could transgress established social codes and conventions by achieving heightened style and elegance through consumption." In this sense, the French garçonnes both threatened and conformed to gender norms. Like their éclaireuse predecessors, they balanced transgressive "masculine" and conventional "feminine" behaviors. Because the Modern Girl was a global phenomenon, this equation of modernity with femininity can hardly be deemed uniquely French. It may, however, be at least partially French in origin.

Notes

1. For a more detailed treatment of the New Woman in France, see Roberts, *Disruptive Acts*, from which this chapter is drawn. The word "garçonne" comes from the novel by Victor Margueritte, *La Garçonne*. The novel, which depicted a modern woman who denounces her bourgeois family in order to lead an independent life in Paris, sold more than a million copies in France before 1929. For an analysis of this novel in the context of 1920s France, see Roberts, " 'This Civilization No Longer Has Sexes,' " and *Civilization without Sexes*, 46–62.

2. "Une Controverse: L'emancipation de la jeune fille moderne est-elle un progrès réel?" *Le Progrès civique*, 13 June 1925, 840.

3. For the New Woman in England, see Brandon, *The New Women and the Old Men*; Showalter, *Sexual Anarchy*; and Walkowitz, *City of Dreadful Delight*. For the American case, see Stansell, *American Moderns*.

4. Stansell, *American Moderns*, 246.

5. Sally Ledger, "The New Woman and the Crisis of Victorianism," in Ledger and Mc-Cracken, eds., *Cultural Politics at the Fin de siècle*, 32.

6. Gardner and Rutherford, eds., *The New Woman and Her Sisters*, 3–4; Marks, *Bicycles, Bangs and Bloomers*, 11, 18–19; Showalter, *Sexual Anarchy*, 41.

7. Sheperd-Barr, *Ibsen and Early Modernist Theatre*, 22–29. Some of the other plays inspired by Ibsen were Arthur Pinero's *The Notorious Mrs. Ebbsmith* (1895), Henry Arthur Jones's *The Case of the Rebellious Susan* (1905), and Bernard Shaw's *Mrs. Warren's Profession* (1902). See Gardner and Rutherford, *The New Woman*, 2–3, 8–9.

8. Sheperd-Barr, *Ibsen and Early Modernist Theatre*, 29–32, and notes 47, 35.

9. Sarcey, *Quarante Ans de théâtre*, 362.

10. In *Art Nouveau in Fin-de-Siècle France*, 63, Silverman argues that the "threat" of the femme nouvelle was most pervasive between 1889, the date of the first International Congress on Women's Rights in Paris, and 1898. Two ways to explain Silverman's different chronology are, first, her close identification of the New Woman with feminism, and second, her looser use of the term "New Woman" (which, as I argue above, did not even exist, technically, until 1894).

11. Gyp, *Autour de mariage*; Prévost, *Les Demi-Vierges*, 27.

12. Augustin Filon, "Le Théâtre anglais contemporain: Dramaturges d'aujourd'hui," *Revue des deux mondes*, 15 September 1895, 320–51; and see also the mention in Henry de Varigny, "Le Cerveau de la femme," *La Revue*, 1 January 1895, 14.

13. On the Congrès, see Klejman and Rochefort, *L'Egalité en marche*, 101–3.

14. *Le Grelot*, 19 April 1896; and Silverman, *Art Nouveau*, 68. For a feminist response to this image, see Séverine, "La Littérature féminine," *Le Journal*, 15 August 1896.

15. Bois, *L'Eve nouvelle*; de Bezobrazow, *La Femme nouvelle*. Bois's *L'Eve nouvelle* was originally published earlier, probably in 1894, then reissued in 1896.

16. Jules Simon, "Il faut rester femme," *La Revue des revues*, 15 July 1896, 135–44.

17. M. Saint-Georges de Bouhelier, "Petite Enquête sur le féminisme," *La Revue naturiste*, July 1897, 228–30.

18. Cim, *Émancipées*, 103, 282, and also 48–49, 117, 282–83.

19. Paul and Victor Margueritte, *Les Femmes nouvelles*, 73–74, 148.

20. Cim, *Émancipées*, 39.

21. Ibid., 40–41.

22. Prévost, *Les Demi-Vierges*, vol. 1, *Frédérique*, 85, 379; vol. 2, *Léa*, 50.

23. Jules Bois, "La Femme nouvelle," *La Revue encyclopédique* 6, no. 169 (October 1896): 832–34, 839.

24. See Mss. 31, *Carnet*, 22 January to 14 December 1897, Bibliothèque Marguerite Durand (hereinafter BMD).

25. On the 1896 conference, see Klejman and Rochefort, *L'Égalité en Marche*, 101–3; Hause, *Women's Suffrage and Social Politics*, 28–29. On nineteenth-century French feminism, see also Moses, *French Feminism in the Nineteenth Century*.

26. Le Passant, "Leur congrès," *Le Figaro*, 12 April 1896.

27. Fogg, "Le Feu à La Fronde," Articles parus sur la *Fronde*, BMD; and also Marguerite Durand, "Les Femmes dans le journalisme," *Manuscrits*, vol. 3, 28–29, BMD.

28. Marguerite Durand, "Un Peu de féminisme," *Le Nouveau siècle*, 27 February 1910, box 2, Dossier Marguerite Durand, BMD.

29. "Confession," *La Fronde*, 1 October 1903.

30. See "Rapide: Agence internationale de reportage photographique," 14 February 1910, folder "Divers," box 3, Dossier Marguerite Durand, BMD.

31. On *La Fronde*, see Welfelé, "*La Fronde*"; Jami, "*La Fronde* (1897–1903) et son rôle dans la défense des femmes salariées"; Scales, "Frivolous Objectives"; and Sylvie Cesbron, "Un Journal féministe en 1900: La Fronde (1897–1903)," *Mémoire dactylographié*, BMD.

32. "Chez les frondeuses," *L'Illustration*, 15 January 1898, box 1, Archives La Fronde, BMD.

33. Ibid.

34. Doctoresse Pelletier, *Mémoire d'une féministe* (ca. 1933), 10–11, Fonds Madeleine Pelletier, Fonds Marie-Louise Bouglé, Bibliothèque historique de la ville de Paris. I thank Joan Scott for bringing this quote to my attention. On Durand's trouble with militant feminists, see Harlor, "Mes Chemins" (1940–44), typed manuscript, 368–69, BMD.

35. See the RSVP notes in *Correspondants to Marguerite Durand*, vols. 1 and 2; Harlor, "Mes Chemins," 368–69; and no author or title, *Le Gil blas*, 11 December 1899, Articles parus sur la *Fronde*, all in BMD.

36. Cesbron, "Un journal féministe," 14.

37. "Jozereau" and Hugues Le Roux, no dates given, *Correspondants to Marguerite Durand*, vol. 2, BMD; Brémontier, "La Fronde."

38. *Le Journal*, 29 June 1898, no author or title, Articles parus sur la *Fronde*, BMD.

39. See also Jean Bernard, "Chez les frondeuses," no periodical or date, Articles parus sur la *Fronde*, BMD.

40. Edouard Saradin, "Théâtres," *Journal des débats politiques et littéraires*, 27 January 1913.

41. Maurice Donnay, "Les Éclaireuses," *La Petite Illustration*, 10, no. 3 (May 1913). For the play's premiere and critical success, see Joseph Galtier, "Propos de Paris," no place, 2 February 1913; and R. D., "M. Poincaré est acclamé à la répétition générale des Éclaireuses," no periodical or date, both in Recueil factice de programmes et articles sur Les Éclaireuses (hereinafter RFPAE), Collection Rondel (hereinafter CR), Bibliothèque Nationale, Département des Arts du spectacle (hereinafter BNDAS).

42. The precise date of the panel is unclear from available documents, but it fell sometime between 12 and 20 March 1913. See Henry Bidou, "Théâtres," *Journal des débats politiques et littéraires*, 20 March 1913; Dossier 840.4 Don, "La Femme dans l'oeuvre

de M. Donnay," BMD; Marguerite Durand, "Les Éclaireuses," *Manuscrits*, vol. 1, BMD. On the luncheon, see particularly A. L., "M. Maurice Donnay traite à déjeuner Éclaireuses et Féministes," *Comoedia*, 27 March 1913.

43. Donnay, "Éclaireuses," 13. On Rose, see Henry Bidou, "La Semaine dramatique," *Journal des débats politiques et littéraires*, 3 February 1913; and Paul Souday, "Les Premières: Théâtre-Marigny," no periodical [l'*Éclair*] or date, RFPAE, CR, BNDAS.

44. Quoted in Monsigny, "Un Mot nouveau," no periodical, 28 January 1913, RFPAE, CR, BNDAS.

45. Durand, "Les Éclaireuses," 4.

46. Ibid.

47. Ibid., 19–20.

48. Ibid., 21–22.

49. Margueritte, "Les Éclaireuses," *Le Figaro*, 15 February 1913; and see also Fernand Vandérem, "Leurs Etapes," no periodical, 29 January 1913, RFPAE, CR, BNDAS.

50. Durand, "Les Éclaireuses," 22.

51. Durand, "Les Éclaireuses," 18. Even the militant suffragette is portrayed as happily married. See Donnay, "Éclaireuses," 17.

52. Abel Hermant, "Les Théâtres," no periodical [*Le Journal*] or date, RFPAE, CR, BNDAS.

53. Henry Bordeaux, *La Vie au théâtre*, 374–75, 377.

54. Ernest-Charles, "La Semaine dramatique"; and H. B., "La Semaine dramatique," *Journal des débats*, 3 February 1913; Léon Blum, "Le féminisme au théâtre," no periodical or date; Félix Duquesnel, "Les Premières," no periodical or date; and Guy Launay, "Répétition générale," no periodical [*Le Matin*] or date; all in RFPAE, CR, BNDAS.

55. No author, "Le Théâtre," RFPAE, CR, BNDAS.

56. A. L., "M. Maurice Donnay traite à déjeuner"; and also Margueritte, "Les Éclaireuses."

57. Eugène Brieux, *La Femme seule*; "Recueil factice, La Femme Seule," CR, BNDAS.

58. Margueritte, *Les Femmes nouvelles*, 246.

59. Tinayre, *La Rebelle*, 134, 166.

60. Ibid., 44.

61. "Enquêtes de *La Fronde*," Archives de la Fronde, box 1, letters of P. Stuart, Marguerite Bodier, Madame Loubirau, C. Pascal, Madame Deleuze, and H. Soulabaille, BMD.

62. Roberts, *Civilization without Sexes*, 9–10, and part 1.

63. Reprinted in "d'Hier et d'aujourd'hui," *La Fronde*, 3 June 1926.

5

The Modern Girl
and Racial Respectability
in 1930s South Africa

LYNN M. THOMAS

During the 1930s, a debate raged in the black South African newspaper *Bantu World* over school-educated young women, often referred to as the "modern girl." Some writers praised African young
women's schooling, professional careers, or cosmopolitan appearances as contributing to "racial uplift." Others accused the African
Modern Girl of "prostituting" her sex and race by imitating white,
coloured, or Indian women, and by avoiding marriage, dressing pro-
vocatively, or engaging in extramarital and interracial sex. Cosmetics
use was one of the most contentious issues surrounding the black
Modern Girl because it drew attention to the phenotypic dimensions
of racial distinctions.

This chapter explores these debates. Previous scholarship has suggested that a black Modern Girl implicated in international circuits of
images, ideologies, and commodities only became visible in southern
Africa in the post–World War II period.[1] Yet analysis of a *Bantu
World* beauty contest together with articles, letters, and advertisements on cosmetics reveals the emergence of such a figure by the early
1930s, suggesting the need for scholars to approach the history of
transnational influences on African women's practices of consump-

tion and self-fashioning as a longer and more complex process. Analysis of these sources also demonstrates how in segregationist South Africa the Modern Girl emerged through and posed challenges to categories of race and respectability.

Bantu World and AmaRespectables

Bantu World was the first newspaper targeting black South Africans to offer women's pages and to feature representations and discussion of the Modern Girl. Bertram Paver, a white advertising salesman, founded *Bantu World* in Johannesburg in 1932. In the midst of the Great Depression, Paver sought to expand the market for white companies by establishing a black newspaper with extensive advertisements and a nationwide circulation. About half of the paper appeared in English, with the rest appearing in the languages of Zulu, Xhosa, Sotho, and Tswana, and, to a lesser extent, Venda, Tsonga, and Afrikaans. Moderate African nationalists like R.V. Selope Thema edited and staffed *Bantu World* and held considerable sway in determining its content. According to Les Switzer, *Bantu World* quickly became "the arbiter of taste in urban African politics and culture and by far the most important medium of mass communication for the literate African community." Although this literate community constituted only 12 percent of the total African population of 6.6 million in 1936, it was a vocal and visible group.[2]

Bantu World embodied the concerns of mission-educated African Christians who worked as clerks, teachers, domestic servants, nurses, and clergy and who struggled, under increasingly difficult circumstances, to achieve middle-class status. Amid the competing ideologies that shaped interwar black politics, *Bantu World* advocated a "progressive yet moderate" agenda.[3] This agenda, in the face of white racism, insisted on the importance of school-educated blacks to South Africa's future. At times, others referred, somewhat derisively, to such Africans as the *AmaRespectables* (respectable people) for their fervent embrace of mission Christianity and their elite ambitions. The English root of the Xhosa-language term *AmaRespectables* suggests the importance of notions of respectability. But what counted as respectable behavior for black South Africans living amid the harsh political realities and shifting cultural terrain of the 1930s was the subject of significant debate. *Bantu World* and particularly its women's pages provide rich material for discerning this debate's gendered dimensions.

Most historians have traced South African notions of respectability back to British colonialism. Vivian Bickford-Smith has argued that respectability emerged as an ideological force in South Africa during the 1870s and 1880s when Cape colonists began to identify the Victorian virtues of "thrift, the sanctity of property, deference to superiors, belief in the moralising efficacy of hard work and cleanliness" with English ethnicity.[4] Black elites from Cape Town to Kimberley soon claimed this ideology as their own, abiding by its tenets and deploying it to counter white racism and promote race pride.[5] John Iliffe has pointed to boarding schools as the key institution through which Africans reworked older "notions of honour . . . [with] their emphasis on rank and prowess" into an ideology of respectability that stressed "virtue and duty."[6] By the 1930s, according to David Goodhew, respectability (defined as faith in Christianity, schooling, and law and order) was so widespread in Johannesburg's townships, and opportunities for class mobility so scarce, that it had become a black working-class ideology.[7] Considering gender politics, Shula Marks has shown how interwar African nationalists and the state deployed respectability to reassert control over unruly women.[8]

This chapter builds on that scholarship by developing the notion of "racial respectability" to explain why the black Modern Girl's cosmopolitan look and use of cosmetics generated both admiration and condemnation among *Bantu World* writers. Racial respectability refers to people's desires and efforts to claim positive recognition in contexts powerfully structured by racism, contexts in which respectability was framed through racial categories and appearances were of the gravest importance. This notion of racial respectability is inspired by African Americanist scholarship that has revealed respectability as a highly malleable ideology. Evelyn Brooks Higginbotham, for instance, has demonstrated how middle-class Baptist women reworked dominant norms of "temperance, industriousness, thrift, refined manners, and Victorian sexual morals" to "counter racist images and structures" that cast black women as immoral and unkempt and to condemn aspects of black working-class life.[9] African Americanist scholarship also reveals how debates over respectability peaked during the interwar years when large numbers of blacks migrated to northern cities where public appearance took on even greater significance, and respectability's emphasis on morals and manners ran headlong into the new consumerism.[10] As we will see, these African American developments both paralleled and influenced processes in interwar South Africa.

Cultivating Women Reader-Consumers and Conceiving Feminine Beauty

Bantu World viewed feminine beauty as key to attracting readers and increasing its early circulation figure of 6,000 copies per week.[11] Six months after its launch, *Bantu World* introduced women's pages. These pages — like the front page and some other sections — appeared in English to ensure an audience that better cut across ethnolinguistic divides. Rolfes Robert Reginald (R. R. R.) Dhlomo, one of the period's most important black male writers, soon became the "editress" of the women's pages.[12] Although some female writers were featured in the women's pages, Dhlomo and a handful of male contributors framed most of the discussion. Together, they promoted an AmaRespectable urban femininity that would distinguish their daughters and wives from the disreputable female figures of the prostitute and beer brewer that black leaders had long associated with South Africa's towns.

R. R. R. Dhlomo's early life provides insight into the social background of these men. Born in Pietermaritzburg in 1901, he attended mission schools. In 1912, the Dhlomo family moved to Johannesburg, where his father worked as a medical dresser on the mines and his mother washed white customers' laundry out of their home. After further schooling, R. R. R. worked as a mine clerk and, in the late 1920s, turned his full attention to writing. Given his expansive commentary on gender relations as *Bantu World*'s editress, it is significant to note that he and his younger brother Herbert, also an accomplished writer, were very close to their mother, Sardinia Mbune Caluza Dhlomo. In his biography of Herbert, Tim Couzens describes how she dominated the Dhlomo household with her storytelling, her Victorian and Christian values, and her keen attention to "appearances."[13]

On its inaugural women's pages, *Bantu World* announced a beauty competition, inviting "All African Ladies" to submit their "best photos" and promising cash prizes. "The Son of Africa," most likely editor Thema, justified the paper's new attention to women by stating, "No nation can rise above its womenfolk," an axiom common to contemporary nationalist discourses. He then explained the multiple motivations behind the beauty competition: to prove that "there are beautiful women and girls in Africa," to promote "diligent perusal of enterprising Bantu newspapers," and to encourage "careless or lazy [ladies] to give a little more attention to their toilet."[14] According to this logic, the competition would foster race pride, a female readership, and conscientious consumption.

Bantu World's competition relied on readers rather than "experts" to select the winner. Beneath each photo entry, the paper printed the name of the town or mission station from which it hailed. Personal names appeared only when the winners were announced. The paper instructed readers to "cut out the three [photos] you think are the best, number them 1, 2, 3, and post them to us."[15] At a time when *Bantu World* was protesting Prime Minister Barry Hertzog's ultimately successful campaign to abolish African men's limited voting rights in the Cape Province, the paper invited all readers to elect "Miss Africa." This beauty competition, like others the world over,[16] drew disparate entrants and reader-voters into new circuits of citizenship by granting voting rights to all consumers and by insisting that what one looked like mattered more than who one was.

Feminine beauty was a long-valued attribute in southern Africa, as in other parts of the continent and world. Nineteenth-century white travelers' and traders' accounts mention that Africans considered "stout" young women with gleaming skin to be the most beautiful. Groups of such women attended the compounds of senior chiefs, demonstrating the chiefs' wealth and sexual prowess.[17] Zulu speakers interviewed by James Stuart around the beginning of the twentieth century testified that Shaka, in particular, amassed large numbers of "good-looking girl[s]" through tribute. When such women "got old and flabby in the cheeks," according to Ndukwana ka Mbengwana, they were married off. Other informants explained how earlier generations made themselves attractive and protected their skin by smearing it with animal fat; they also adorned themselves with beaded ornaments, brass rings, blankets, and skirts and belts made from animal skins. Stuart's informants often described individuals as having particular skin colors including "light-brown," "dark but not black," or "black." Their testimony, however, does not attach explicit and consistent aesthetic preferences to such color distinctions.[18]

In their accounts of Tswana and Xhosa conceptions of beauty from the 1930s, the anthropologists Isaac Schapera and Monica Hunter emphasized the importance of bodily over facial attributes. They noted the appeal of young women with "somewhat heavy build[s]" and prominent and firm breasts, buttocks, hips, and calves. They also described a preference for "light-skinned girl[s]" and those with "thin lips, an aquiline nose, and light brown skin." Unfortunately, Schapera and Hunter shed little light on whether such preferences were rooted in precolonial conceptions of beauty, a product of colonial racial hierarchies, or some entanglement of the two. Xhosa-speaking young men and women used animal fat, butter, and, by this period, Vaseline to make their skin shine. They also enhanced their beauty through facial tattooing, washing daily, plaiting and applying red ochre to their hair, wearing sweet-smelling leaves, and using love medicines. As school-educated Christians abandoned some of these practices, they adopted beauty and hygienic regimes involving store-bought soaps and creams and the wearing of "smart" clothing.[19] Recent scholarship has elucidated how these new bodily routines, most often initiated by Christian missionaries, were an integral part of the cultural and economic colonization of southern Africa.[20]

The advent of beauty contests in South Africa recast such displays and criteria of feminine beauty by linking them to genres of performance rooted in photography, illustrated magazines, newspapers, and film. The American showman P. T. Barnum inaugurated photo-based beauty contests in the 1850s after realizing that "respectable" women would not parade before judges but would submit daguerreotypes. By the end of the century, newspapers throughout the United States had picked up his idea.[21] In other parts of the world, including South Africa, illustrated magazines pioneered beauty contests. According to the German sociologist Siegfried Kracauer, such magazines ranked among the most disorienting media of the interwar period. As part of their effort to reproduce "the world accessible to the photographic apparatus," Kracauer wrote, illustrated magazines filled their pages with film divas and "beautiful girls."[22] Although South African magazines targeted white audiences, the intimacy of the country's racial geographies meant that they were perused and sometimes purchased by blacks. White South Africans documented, often with alarm, how blacks enjoyed foreign magazines like *Modern Romances*, and hung photos of film stars on their walls.[23]

By the early 1920s, South African magazines reported on beauty contests in Britain and the United States to "find" film stars.[24] In 1923, the English-language weekly *South African Pictorial: Stage and Cinema* announced its own contest "open to any girl, woman or child (girls only) residing in Africa south of the Equator." Although this expansive announcement may have caught the attention of some black women and girls, all of the published photos were of entrants who appear white. These carefully crafted studio portraits feature demure young women.[25] By the early 1930s, white beauty contests featured photos of scantily clad bathing beauties, signaling a significant shift in white notions of acceptable female display.[26] *Bantu World*'s 1932–33 competition shared the sensibility of the earlier white contests. In a racist context where most whites and many mission-educated Africans associated black women's partially clothed bodies with "barbarity," *Bantu World*'s staff likely imagined photos of black women in bathing suits as threatening racial respectability. Not until the 1950s did black periodicals publish such photos.

Bantu World's editors also seem to have drawn inspiration for their beauty competition from the African American press. From its defense of black womanhood to its title of "Miss Africa," their competition suggests transatlantic connections. Black journalists in interwar South Africa were deeply influenced by the works of Booker T. Washington, Marcus Garvey, W. E. B. Du Bois, and discussions of the "New Negro."[27] They were also familiar with the African American press. Since the mid-1920s, copies of Garvey's *Negro World* and Du Bois's *The Crisis* circulated in South Africa and occasionally *Bantu World* reprinted articles from them. Black American newspapers had sponsored photo-based beauty contests since the 1890s to boost circulation. What distinguished these contests and *Bantu World*'s from their white counterparts was the additional desire to combat racist denigrations. As this racism entailed disparaging black women's appearances, demonstrating that there were beautiful women in Africa or black America was an antiracist retort.[28] The influence of black American thought can also be seen in *Bantu World*'s decision to crown the winner "Miss Africa" as opposed to "Miss Bantu" or "Miss Native," the latter being terms more widely used in this period for South Africa's indigenous populations. According to James Campbell, black South African writers' use of "Africa" drew on Garveyite notions that linked the term with "an heroic past, an undifferentiated racial identity, an essentially unitary culture."[29] The men behind *Bantu World* viewed attractive and carefully groomed women as contributing to a project of racial uplift that would connect a "heroic past" to a politically progressive and commercially vibrant future.

Portrait Photography and the Beauty Competition Winner

The nearly fifty entries published as part of *Bantu World*'s competition constitute a unique archive of interwar photographs of African young women. Scholars have demonstrated how most nineteenth- and early-twentieth-century photographers sought to frame African women as ethnographic and erotic subjects, often placing them in "sexually suggestive poses." White male photographers created such images for white audiences.[30] *Bantu World*'s beauty competition highlights another photographic tradition involving African women: their own commissioning and sharing of portraits. Some of the earliest extant examples in this vein date to the 1870s, when mission school graduates Tause Soga and Martha Mzimbu had studio portraits taken while studying abroad in Scotland. These photos, given to a former mission school teacher, feature Soga and Mzimbu in high-collared Victorian dress and with short parted hair and dignified countenances.[31]

Most of the entrants to *Bantu World*'s beauty contest resonate with these nineteenth-century figures. They wear blouses and dresses with modest necklines and serenely look toward the photographer without smiling (see figure 5.1). These portraits draw attention to the face and away from bodily attributes that previously dominated some regional conceptions of feminine beauty. Like the photos of well-groomed African converts that often appeared in mission fundraising literature as proof of "success" in the field,[32] these portraits situated their subjects as "civilized." In the 1930s, such photos of African women and men hung on the walls in black homes, were collected in family albums, and enclosed in love letters.[33] Portrait photos had become a medium for expressing and claiming black Christian respectability.

What most readily distinguishes the beauty competition's top two finishers is their rejection of the somber countenance, long a convention of portraiture photography. Mrs. Flora Ndobe of Cape Town, the first-place finisher, and Miss Elizabeth Hlabakoe of Johannesburg, the second-place finisher, sport teeth-revealing smiles (see figure 5.2). The Modern Girl Around the World Research Group has identified this full-smile look as a defining feature of Modern Girl representations the world over. Interwar advertisements for toothpaste and other toiletries, and publicity photos of film stars, promoted this look.[34] In announcing the *Bantu World* competition, "The Son of Africa" had, in fact, encouraged entrants to smile: "Smile sweetly while the camera clicks and post the result to the Editor of this paper ... The trouble with some of our ladies is that they do not know how to smile. Yet what a glorious transformation a smile can give to your features! Practise it in front of your mirror every morning before or after meals it does not matter when."[35] This editorial dismissed any notion that smiling was an immodest gesture for young women. It also linked smiling to another commonplace in Modern Girl representations: mirror gazing.[36] By encouraging entrants to smile before a mirror, "The Son of Africa," like so many contemporary advertisements, claimed that young women could "transform" themselves through careful attention to their appearance.

Contest winner Ndobe further pushed the boundaries of black portraiture and the beauty competition with her glamorous attire and married status. In her cloche hat, string of pearls, drop neckline, and ostrich feather tippet (see figure 5.3), Ndobe appears as a slightly darker version of the white film stars and socialites who featured in *South African Pictorial* and foreign magazines. Her fashionable dress is also reminiscent of photos of African American women that circulated in South Africa through periodicals like *Negro World* and *The Crisis*. Ndobe's light-colored face coincides with some of the beauty preferences documented by contemporary anthropologists. The fact that Ndobe garnered more than twice as many votes as her closest competitor suggests that her appearance strongly appealed to readers. *Bantu World's* staff did not let Ndobe's designation of "Mrs." disqualify her from their "Miss Africa" competition. For readers who recognized Ndobe from her photo, her married status may have even heightened her appeal. The photo reveals how married women could also perform a Modern Girl style. *Bantu World* reader-voters likely appreciated the audacity of Ndobe's photo in enacting a cosmopolitan glamour. In South Africa, as in other contexts structured by white racism, the black Modern Girl caused excitement and anxiety by remaking dominant cultural styles as her own.

Bantu World's staff exhibited their own anxiety as the competition drew to a close. A few weeks before announcing the winners, the paper used the space usually devoted to displaying beauty competition entries to nine photos of "Leading Women of the Race," drawn from T. D. Mweli Skota's fascinating

5.1 (top) Entries to "Miss Africa" beauty competition, demonstrating how most portraits featured somber countenances and modest dress. *Bantu World*, 1932.

5.2 (bottom) Top six finishers in beauty competition as selected by reader-voters. *Bantu World*, 1933.

CAPE TOWN.

5.3 Mrs. Flora Ndobe, winner of the beauty
competition, posing with a teeth-revealing smile
and glamorous attire. *Bantu World*, 1932.

"Who's Who" of black notables, the *African Yearly Register*. The women pictured in these photos shared the modest dress and somber countenances of
most of the beauty competition entrants. They were to be valued for their
contributions to "the Race" rather than their beauty.[37] In the editorial that
accompanied the competition results, Thema claimed that the competition's
purpose had been to promote reading and, by extension, schooling for girls
and women. He insisted that deeds were more important than appearances:
"[While the] Bantu race is certainly proud of its beautiful women . . . it will be
more proud of women who take interest in the welfare of the people."[38] What
ongoing *Bantu World* discussions about the Modern Girl make clear is that the
emergence of a group of school-educated young women committed to racial
betterment could not be disentangled from the cultivation of new looks and
consumptive practices.

The men behind *Bantu World* featured photos of beautiful women to promote race pride and to enhance the commercial success of their newspaper. But
they also worried that excessive attention to appearance could lead to racial
disrepute. It was this ambivalence that suffused their writings on the black

Modern Girl. It also may have been this ambivalence that ensured that this was *Bantu World*'s first and last beauty competition.

Debating Black Women's Use of White Face Powder

In February 1933, as the beauty competition was winding down, a *Bantu World* headline playfully announced "Daughters of Ham Take to Powdering their Faces." The article's author, "Tommy," described how face powder caused him to mistake a young black woman in Cape Town for an Italian. It was not until she inquired in "faultless vernacular" about the beauty competition that he recognized her as nonwhite.[39] This woman may have been Flora Ndobe. Her curiosity about the competition suggested to Tommy that she was an entrant, and Ndobe was one of only two from Cape Town. Moreover, the light-colored face in Ndobe's competition photo may have been powdered. As in other contexts, the rise of portrait photography and a desire to be photogenic may have promoted women's use of face powder.[40]

While Tommy found this woman's ambiguous racial status and powdered face to be charming, most *Bantu World* writers disapproved of black women wearing cosmetics. In his pioneering history of consumption and cleanliness in Zimbabwe, Timothy Burke discusses how African women who wore cosmetics in the 1950s often faced severe condemnation.[41] In South Africa, similar criticism dates to twenty years earlier. In March 1933, a month after Tommy's article, editress Dhlomo launched a campaign against white powder and, to a lesser extent, red lipstick. In many regards, Dhlomo was a strong proponent of women's "advancement." He celebrated black women's educational and professional achievements and advocated companionate marriages. When it came to black women wearing makeup, however, Dhlomo saw nothing redeemable. Many letter writers, particularly men, supported Dhlomo in his anticosmetics campaign.

Their condemnation was part of widespread class concerns about natural versus artificial beauty. Many contemporaries elsewhere in the world would have shared L. T. Baleni's sentiments that "the original meaning of the word 'Beauty' . . . [is] 'Natural Beauty' " and not the "modern meaning of 'artificial beauty' " achieved through "powders and paints."[42] In her history of U.S. beauty culture, Kathy Peiss examines how morally laden class concerns animated discussions of cosmetics from the nineteenth century onward. "Painted woman" was a common euphemism for prostitute as some used powder, rouge, and eye makeup to advertise their trade. Critics of cosmetics associated their use with women's ability to deceive men and take their money. Over the twentieth century, according to Peiss, cosmetics use underwent a remarkable transformation from being "a sign of disrepute" to becoming "the daily routine of millions."[43] Most white South Africans during the 1930s approved of only modest cosmetics. One marketing report found that white and coloured women tended to use face powder, rouge, and lipstick sparingly: "its free use usually draws forth unfavourable comment."[44] Such "unfavourable" remarks likely impugned the woman's sexual morality and class standing. By the mid-1930s, such concerns had reached Fort Hare College, South Africa's premier institution of black higher learning, in the rural Eastern Cape. In her autobiography, Phyllis Ntantala describes how her boyfriend persuaded her to stop wearing makeup with a line from Shakespeare's As You Like It: "good wine needs no bush."[45] Such condemnation of black women's use of cosmetics coincided with broader notions of middle-class respectability in South Africa, the United States, and elsewhere.

In 1930s Johannesburg, where most Africans lived close to poverty, appearances were especially important in defining class differences and claiming respectability. Dhlomo castigated face powder and lipstick for giving "the impression of cheapness."[46] He did not tolerate divergent viewpoints. When S. H. D. Lee Mnyandu wrote that powder and paint made Johannesburg's ladies beautiful and "suitable for marriage," Dhlomo dismissed his letter as naive by appending the following note: "This writer has just arrived in the city from Natal."[47] Dhlomo's concern about urban femininity is evident as early as 1920, when he published An African Tragedy, the first English-language novel by a black South African. Dhlomo's novel chronicles the destruction of a male labor migrant in Johannesburg at the hands of a prostitute, contrasting this domineering urban female figure with the migrant's obedient and Christian wife in rural Zululand.[48] In the decade following the publication of An African Tragedy, black urban populations across South Africa increased dramatically, with the number of Africans resident in Johannesburg nearly doubling. Some female migrants found employment as domestic workers while a few worked as teachers and nurses. In the face of such limited employment opportunities, many washed laundry and sold beer from their homes. Others earned money by providing domestic and sexual services.[49] Poorer women were, in many regards, black South Africa's urban innovators. The social anthropologist Ellen Hellmann documented that young women living in Johannesburg's slums during the early 1930s regularly wore lipstick, rouge, and powder.[50] It is possible that poor and working-class women were the first black women to wear makeup, thereby contributing to Dhlomo's unease about AmaRespectable cosmetics use.

Alongside differentiating women by class, Dhlomo's anticosmetics campaign resonated with interwar efforts by black male leaders to reassert patriarchal control. In the face of some women's increasing social and economic independence, these men promoted gendered policies and conduct that would bolster their authority as fathers and husbands.[51] In *Bantu World*, men charged women who wore makeup with multiple offenses: smoking cigarettes, drinking alcohol, speaking "township languages," wearing trousers, and fixating on romance.[52] As in other Modern Girl contexts, such complaints centered on young women embracing masculine practices and neglecting feminine duties through self-indulgence. Letter writer Walter Nhlapo argued that such habits had turned the "girl" into a "she-man."[53] Another critic wrote that African women would not achieve a "modern and up-to-date" look by wearing powder and lipstick but only by "behav[ing] in a lady like way."[54] Such writers recognized that "modern" conditions demanded new forms of black femininity. But they insisted that they nudge rather than topple the gender norms prevalent in black Christian homes.

Critics of cosmetics intertwined their complaints about class and gender transgression with charges of racial betrayal. As scholars of U.S. beauty culture have argued, concerns about natural versus artificial beauty have taken on a unique salience when directed at black women living in racist contexts. More so than white women, black women's cosmetics use has made them vulnerable to accusations of racial shame. Critics have charged black women who use makeup and hair straightening products of acquiescing to Eurocentric beauty standards.[55] In segregationist South Africa where racist policies privileged light-skinned people deemed of European descent and subjugated, with increasing harshness, those deemed of Indian, "mixed," and African descent, black women's apparent attempts to lighten their faces provoked strong reactions. Dhlomo's condemnation of cosmetics centered, in fact, on racial unsightliness. He argued that powders and lipsticks did "not suit dark skins." Black women, Dhlomo wrote, should abandon their desire "to turn themselves white," recognize "the beauty of their natural coloring," and limit their use of cosmetics to moisturizing creams and hair lotions.[56]

Letter writers similarly accused makeup-wearing black women of foolishly copying white women. M. F. Phala singled out powder use as evidence of how "Bantu people" were not "proud" of their skin color.[57] Another writer noted that black women's "imitative" habits were not reciprocated by "European ladies" as they never wore *imbola*, the ochre used to redden skin, hair, and blankets.[58] At other times, *Bantu World*, with its moderate political agenda, situated white women as appropriate role models. In announcing the beauty competition, "The Son of Africa" had encouraged women: "emulate your white sisters in all that is noble, true and good."[59] For Dhlomo and his allies, wearing makeup was not "noble." Rather, it sullied racial respectability.

Although men authored most of *Bantu World*'s commentary, a few women voiced their opinions. At least one mother agreed that makeup was among the more disagreeable practices that young women had recently adopted.[60] A letter by Sarah Ngcobo of Durban voiced another, more annoyed reaction to men's commentary. Ngcobo wrote that she was "fed up" with reading articles that blamed "women, particularly young girls, for everything . . . [including] for powdering their faces, for going out at night, for snaring other women's husbands, for dressing expensively."[61] Ngcobo's letter suggests how some young women viewed the cosmetics discussion as part of broader efforts to blame them for numerous social ills.

Twice in his weekly column Dhlomo responded to letters that he had received from women who claimed that powder improved their appearances. Dhlomo gave their letters short shrift by not printing them and offering the shrill reply that he did not mind if they "continue[d] to white wash" their faces as long as it was not near him.[62] These women seem to have been insisting that "looking good" could be distinct from "looking white." In their study of African American expressive culture, Shane White and Graham White suggest that during the 1920s young black women wore powder, rouge, and lipstick not to "look white" but to "draw[] attention to their faces" and distinguish themselves from "the 'natural' look of their mothers and grandmothers."[63] Up through the mid-1930s, black South African women who wished to use face powder to even their skin texture, conceal blemishes, or achieve a light brown (not white) complexion had little choice but to use a pale shade. Face powder existed in limited shades ranging from light beige to pink.[64] Cosmetics companies' narrow vision of what skin tones mattered did much to ensure that black women's use of powder was interpreted by some as emulating whites.

Two of the most elaborate female commentaries on cosmetics may have been written by Dhlomo himself. Their use of pseudonyms together with their biting wit and literary sophistication suggest the editress's pen. In testimonial style, "Swanee," a repentant cosmetics user, explained how a male friend had recently convinced her that wearing face powder and lipstick made her look like a "guinea baboon." By comparing herself to a monkey, Swanee drew on racist insults that disparaged Africans as apelike to chide others into abandoning makeup. She warned: "Use a hundred powders and lip-sticks, you'll never change from black to white."[65] "Powdered Face" took a different stance. Expressing frustration with criticism of makeup, she noted that while previously African women wore *imbola*, smoked pipes, and were only "clothed from the waist downwards," today young women are admonished for using powder, smoking cigarettes, and wearing even short sleeves.[66] By identifying older African practices that resonated with a number of Modern Girl practices, "Powdered Face" insinuated that criticism of the latter stemmed more from Christian than "traditional" sensibilities. Such commentaries raise the persistent challenge faced by *Bantu World* and its readers: how to craft "modern" personas that maintained some fidelity to African practices and did not become an unthinking and unsightly imitation of white ways. In seeking a solution, some turned to black people living on the other side of the Atlantic.

African American Beauty Products and South African Business Entrepreneurs

The first makeup advertisements appeared in *Bantu World* in 1933 and featured products manufactured by an African American–owned company, Apex. These were likely the earliest such ads in southern Africa to target black women.[67] Apex marketed a wide range of products including hair strengtheners and straighteners, a deodorant, a skin bleach, and face powder in "all shades." In the early twentieth century, the African American entrepreneur Anthony Overton tackled the problem of inappropriate makeup shades for black women by developing and successfully distributing High-Brown face powder.[68] By the 1920s, some of the largest and most profitable black-owned businesses in the United States manufactured and sold cosmetics. Several of these companies, including Madam C. J. Walker, Poro, and Apex, were women-owned and marketed their products through female agents who sold door-to-door. These companies provided black women with one of their few employment opportunities outside of field, laundry, or domestic work. As White and White have argued, the success of these companies embodied a desire for "personal liberation" through self-improvement: "to an even greater extent than was true of the white beauty industry, black cosmetics were associated with modernity and, most importantly, with progress."[69] African American women's marketing of cosmetics generated wealth and controversy. Although publications like *The Crisis*, the *Afro-American*, and *Negro World* received much of their revenue from advertising cosmetics, some black male leaders denounced the use of certain products, notably hair straighteners and skin bleaches, as racial self-loathing.[70] Among African Americans, the advent of powder in "all shades" did not resolve the cosmetics controversy. It simply shifted the focus to other products.

One *Bantu World* ad declared Apex the first "all Negro Company" in South Africa. While white American capital had been heavily invested in South Africa since the mineral revolution of the late nineteenth century, African American–manufactured goods were a novelty. Apex's agent in Johannesburg was a "European" named "Jolly Jack Bernard."[71] Bernard likely learned of Apex from an

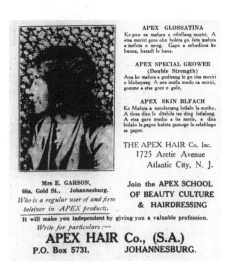

5.4 Cosmetics ad that localized its message for black South African consumers by providing product descriptions in the Sotho language and featuring the photo of a Johannesburg user. *Bantu World,* 1933.

American periodical or while traveling in the United States. As a white man, he was a significant departure from Apex's U.S. marketing strategy of working through black female agents. Barnard, however, was in keeping with *Bantu World*'s founding mission of helping white businessmen to identify and exploit African markets. The fact that Apex's Johannesburg agent was white confirms just how marginalized black South Africans were from commercial opportunities, even ones premised in pan-African affiliations.

The Apex ads downplayed the involvement of a white capitalist by featuring drawings and photographs of black women. The drawings, taken from advertising material developed in the United States, were of young women with gray skin and relaxed hair. In one ad, the central figure appears in a classic Modern Girl pose, seated at her vanity and gazing into a handheld mirror (see figure 1.1). Other ads included photos of Mrs. E. Garson, a light-skinned black woman with relaxed hair. They touted Garson as a "regular user of and firm believer in Apex products" and displayed her photo as evidence of the products' efficacy. By providing Garson's name, photo, and Johannesburg address, such ads cast these U.S.-made products as accessible to South Africans. In a further attempt to localize their message, some ads provided product descriptions in the Sotho language (see figure 5.4).

Several months into this ad campaign, *Bantu World* ran a feature about the founder and president of Apex, Sara Washington. Such features were a common publicity tool used by black beauty companies in the United States.[72] This article positioned Washington as an African American success story, discussing how Apex had created "legitimate business" opportunities for many in the United States. It explained that the company's arrival in South Africa meant that the "Bantu race" could benefit from products "manufactured for them by their brothers and sisters in America."[73] According to the article's logic, cosmetics consumption enabled racial uplift. Such logic discounted criticism of certain beauty products as embodying racial self-loathing and ignored how this particular black diasporic connection required a white middleman.

Apex had a stall at the "Bantu World Trade Exhibition" held in May 1935. Paver, *Bantu World*'s founder and managing director, envisioned this exhibition and others as facilitating the expansion of white capital and improving race relations: "The European business man who participates in it will discover the fact that the Africans are a potential market for his commodities, and, therefore a useful citizen of South Africa. . . . here the two races will meet not as masters and servants but as producers and consumers."[74] Paver provided all *Bantu World* advertisers with a stall and an African translator.[75] As editress, Dhlomo urged women readers to attend the exhibition and purchase products from *Bantu World*'s advertisers.[76] Afterward, Dhlomo noted that the cosmetics stall proved popular with female visitors. Recounting his own visit with his wife and child, Dhlomo described how "sweet smelling fats and oils . . . drew cries and cries of enthusiasm from our fair companions." Such desires, according to Dhlomo, were difficult to fulfill for people like himself who were "not paid a living wage."[77] It was perhaps the expense of Apex products in relation to the meagerness of African earnings that caused Barnard to conclude his advertising campaign just a year after inaugurating it.

Although the Apex campaign was relatively short-lived, it introduced a new set of commercial images and commodities to black South Africans. Paver's multipronged marketing strategy ensured that the Apex ads with their Modern Girl representations reached an audience larger than *Bantu World* readers. In addition to providing advertisers with a stall at the exhibition, Paver gave them 5,000 leaflet-reprints of their ads. These same ads were compiled into a slide show that toured 4,000 miles across the country.[78] It is difficult to know how people interpreted these ads. Dhlomo's criticism of face powder often appeared on the same page as Apex ads. Yet he never commented on them. While he may have welcomed the arrival of face powder in more diverse shades, he likely felt contempt toward Apex's skin bleach. As was the case with much of the African American press, the revenue to be gained from cosmetics advertising probably placed their products beyond reproach. Beginning in 1936, *Bantu World* advertised cosmetics manufactured by another African American company, Valmor Products.[79] During a trip to South Africa in 1938, Ralph Bunche, the African American scholar and activist, visited a dressmaking and hair shop in Johannesburg run by a Mosotho woman who used Valmor products.[80] After World War II, white-owned southern African companies imported and manufactured cosmetics, particularly skin lighteners, on a large scale and aggressively marketed them through black magazines.[81] The history of the Apex campaign reveals how more recent debates over skin lighteners in Africa stretch back to an interwar and transatlantic traffic in cosmetics, visual representations, and concerns about racial respectability.

At least one black South African woman traveled across the Atlantic during the 1930s and gained in-depth knowledge of African American beauty culture. In 1935, Rilda Marta of the Eastern Cape published a series of articles in *Bantu World* describing her adventures in the United States. Marta explained that while she had planned to study medicine or law, she ended up attending a beauty college. When she arrived in New York, she noticed to her surprise that the skin of "the American Negro" was like that of the African — "some are very light, and others are very dark in complexion." Where Africans and African Americans differed, according to Marta, was in their hair: "I was always proud to call myself as African. . . . [but] What really made me feel strange [was] nearly every girl and woman has long hair and I among them looked like a boy dressed in girl's clothes." Marta soon learned that their "long and beautiful" hair was the work of a beautician and, within a year, she "looked just like them[]." To demonstrate her transformation, *Bantu World* published "before" and "after" photos (see figure 5.5). In the before shot, Marta wears a simple white blouse and her hair is cut short. The after photo features a still somber Marta wearing more elaborate clothing and with her straightened hair pulled back.[82] U.S. black beauty culture, these photos suggest, changed Marta from a plain schoolgirl into a sophisticated lady.

Marta added her voice to the ongoing cosmetics discussion. She urged "African ladies" to take the advice of the African American beauty culturist Madam C. J. Walker: "The key to Happiness and Success is a good appearance. You are often judged by how you look." Walker's dictum insisted that black women's attention to their appearance was crucial to achieving respectability in a racist society. Marta agreed that beauty products helped black women respect themselves, win the respect of their menfolk, and contribute to building "a clean, educated nation." Noting that even white women used "powder to make themselves lighter," Marta cautiously endorsed black women's use of makeup: "I do not mean that you should go and use lipstick and rouge because our colour is different to theirs; but if you do want to use some, remember there

Miss Rilda Marta, after her return from America. Note the remarkable change in her appearance. Her interesting article will be continued next week.

Miss Rilda Marta, before her visit to America.

5.5 Before and after photos of Miss Rilda Marta, who traveled from South Africa to the United States, where she attended a beauty college. *Bantu World,* 1935.

is a way of doing everything."[83] According to Walker and Marta, cosmetics enabled rather than undermined racial respectability.

For all the connections that the Apex campaign and Marta's articles drew between South Africa and the United States, profound differences existed in the relationship between cosmetics and racial respectability in these two contexts. Whereas black women in the United States shaped discussions of beauty culture and owned some of the largest cosmetics companies, in South Africa, black men dominated the cosmetics discussion in *Bantu World* and white men owned the companies that imported and, later, manufactured cosmetics for black women. Black beauty culture in the United States, in part, gained its respectability from making individuals like Sara Washington and Madam C. J. Walker into millionaires, and removing thousands of women from back-breaking field, laundry, and domestic work and turning them into sales agents. Such highly successful black businesswomen did not exist in interwar South Africa. Washington and Walker must have appeared as unusual figures to *Bantu World*'s readers. In her study of the "Negro" in interwar South Africa, Amanda Kemp has deftly illustrated that while black South African writers routinely referenced African American male intellectuals and leaders, they rarely evoked African American women. Kemp writes that "when the emancipated, autonomous transnational black subject was gendered female, an ambivalence emerged."[84]

This ambivalence stemmed from a continuing faith in the propriety of patriarchy. For Dhlomo and his allies, "independent" women were not AmaRespectable women.

Conclusion

By analyzing *Bantu World*'s beauty competition and articles, letters, and advertisements on cosmetics, this chapter has explored how new visual media and consumer goods were part of gender struggles in interwar South Africa. The Modern Girl heuristic elucidates how female figures identified by a cosmopolitan look, an explicit eroticism, and the use of specific commodities surfaced in many parts of the globe, and how their near simultaneous emergence was tied to the international circulation of commodity cultures, mass media, and political discourses. The Modern Girl's presence in *Bantu World*'s beauty competition and cosmetics discussions reveals that black South African women were implicated in such circuits earlier than previous scholarship has suggested. Mrs. Flora Ndobe's beauty competition photo and Miss Rilda Marta's diploma from an African American beauty college attest to black women's engagement of transnational forms of self-fashioning and commercial enterprise from at least the 1930s. Given scholars' increasing attention to how globalizing consumer capitalism contributed to the demise of apartheid and has structured social life — particularly among youth — since 1994, it is important to understand the longer history of such processes in South Africa.

Analysis of *Bantu World*'s beauty competition and cosmetics discussions also reveals the introduction of new modes of displaying and assessing feminine beauty. The beauty competition harnessed photos of attractive young women to foster race pride, promote the commercial success of the paper, and encourage women to attend more carefully to their appearance. Photographic portraits drew aesthetic attention away from bodily attributes and focused it on the face. This shift may have encouraged some black women to wear powder and lipstick in order to be photogenic. Cosmetics were small and seemingly intimate commodities that promised to transform one's appearance in a larger public. Almost all of the toiletry and cosmetics ads that appeared in black periodicals during the 1930s concentrated on the upper body by promoting products that cleaned and refined faces, teeth, and hair. In line with these ads, *Bantu World*'s editors viewed smiling as essential to an attractive appearance. Reader-voters agreed. Such aesthetic attention to the upper body and head supported AmaRespectable aspirations by providing a counter to exoticizing and eroticizing representations of black women that focused on sparsely clothed lower halves. But facial beauty regimes could confound racial respectability when they seemed to endorse segregationist South Africa's skin color hierarchy by making black skin look lighter.

More so than other contentious Modern Girl practices like smoking cigarettes, wearing provocative fashions, and fixating on romance, the use of cosmetics emphasized the phenotypic dimensions of racial distinctions. Black women may have worn white face powder to even out their skin texture, conceal blemishes, or highlight their faces. Until the mid-1930s, they had access only to powders in pale shades. Yet for Dhlomo and his fellow critics of cosmetics, such varied intentions and consumer constraints mattered less than the impression that black women were trying to "look white." This impression called into question women's pride in being African and their commitment to racial uplift. Cosmetics use provoked such strong reactions from some *Bantu World* writers and readers because it combined a challenge to middle-class notions of gender propriety with intimations of racial shame. Although all participants in this debate agreed that appearances mattered, they disagreed as to what consumptive practices enabled both a "modern" and respectable look. AmaRespectable women had to walk the very thin line between paying too little and too much attention to their appearance.

Notes

1. Burke, *Lifebuoy Men, Lux Women*. Modern Girls in the form of cover girls, beauty pageant winners, and lovelorn letter-writers proliferated in the pages of the popular magazine *Drum*, founded in Johannesburg in 1951. Throughout this chapter, I use "black" as an umbrella term to refer to South Africans who thought of themselves or were viewed by others, particularly state institutions, as nonwhite, colored, African, Malay, or Indian.

2. Switzer, "*Bantu World* and the Origins of a Captive African Commercial Press," 190–91; Couzens, "A Short History of 'World' (and other Black SA Newspapers)"; J. D. Rheinallt Jones's letter on native newspapers to R. Muir, 16 September 1931, South African Institute of Race Relations papers (hereinafter, SAIRR) AD843 RJ Aa3.3.2 1, Correspondence on the Black Press, University of Witwatersrand.

3. Switzer, "*Bantu World*," 198.

4. Bickford-Smith, *Ethnic Pride and Racial Prejudice in Victorian Cape Town*, 39.

5. Willan, *Sol Plaatje*; Bickford-Smith, *Ethnic Pride and Racial Prejudice in Victorian Cape Town*, 203.

6. Iliffe, *Honour in African History*, 246.

7. Goodhew, "Working-Class Respectability"; idem, *Respectability and Resistance*.

8. Marks, "Patriotism, Patriarchy and Purity."

9. Higginbotham, *Righteous Discontent*, 14 and 187.

10. Ibid., 209–10; Wolcott, *Remaking Respectability*, 1–10.

11. Couzens, "A Short History of 'World,'" 77.

12. Switzer, "*Bantu World*," 190.

13. Couzens, *The New African*, 42–81.

14. The Son of Africa, "Great Progress!" and "Competition," *Bantu World* (hereinafter *BW*), 22 October 1932, 10.

15. "Bantu World Beauty Competition Entrants," *BW*, 18 February 1933, 10.

16. Cohen and Wilk with Stoeltje, Introduction.

17. Isaacs, *Travels and Adventures in Eastern Africa*, 51, 56, 88, 107, 179, 190–91, 221, 265, 289, and 291; Fynn, *The Diary of Henry Francis Fynn*, 73, 164, and 293.

18. Webb and Wright, eds. and trans., *The James Stuart Archive of Recorded Oral Evidence Relating to the History of the Zulu and Neighbouring Peoples*, 3: 151–52 and 4: 339.

19. Schapera, *Married Life in an African Tribe*, 46–48; Hunter, *Reaction to Conquest*, 222–26.

20. Hansen, *African Encounters with Domesticity*; Burke, *Lifebuoy Men, Lux Women*; Comaroff, "The Empire's Old Clothes"; Comaroff and Comaroff, *Of Revelation and Revolution*, vol. 2.

21. Cohen and Wilk with Stoeltje, Introduction, 3–4.

22. Kracauer, "Photography," 57–58.

23. Hellmann, "Native Life in a Johannesburg Slum Yard," 40; Phillips, *The Bantu in the City*, 105; Sachs, *Black Hamlet*, 148–50.

24. *South African Pictorial: Stage and Cinema:* "Found in a Beauty Contest," 5 March 1920, 5; "Searching for 'Stars,'" 24 April 1920, 4; "'Beauty and Talent' Contest," 15 May 1920, 5.

25. "Are You Beautiful?" *South African Pictorial: Stage and Cinema*, 23 June 1923.

26. See *Cape Times*, 13 December 1931 and 25 July 1933, supplement; and *South African Annual Pictorial: A Review of 1933 in Pictures*.

27. Couzens, "'Moralizing Leisure Time'"; Campbell, "T. D. Mweli Skota and the Making and Unmaking of a Black Elite"; Edgar, *An African-American in South Africa*; Kemp, "'Up from Slavery' and Other Narratives."

28. Craig, *Ain't I a Beauty Queen?*, 46–55.

29. Campbell, "T. D. Mweli Skota," 6.

30. Quotes from Stevenson and Graham-Stewart, *Surviving the Lens*, 19–21.

31. Waterston later contributed these photos to the "album of racial types" of the George Grey Collection of the South African library, thereby converting what was likely a personal gift into evidence for "scientific" racial theory. Even these studio portraits commissioned and given by African women could not escape dominant white modes of representing black women. Schoeman, *The Face of the Country*, 68; Grey Ethnological Album 167, INIL 14165 and 14210, Special Collections, National Library of South Africa.

32. Patrick Harries, "Photography and the Rise of Anthropology: Henri-Alexandre Junod and the Thonga of Mozambique and South Africa," Encounters with Photography Workshop, Iziko Museums of Cape Town, 2001, http://www.museums.org.za/sam/ (visited 14 December 2005); Hofmeyr, *The Portable Bunyan*, 185.

33. Mofokeng, "The Black Photo Album"; idem, "Trajectory of a Street-Photographer," 42–45.
34. Modern Girl Around the World Research Group, "Modern Girl Around the World," esp. 251–54.
35. The Son of Africa, "Competition," *BW*, 22 October 1932, 10.
36. Modern Girl Around the World Research Group, "Modern Girl Around the World," 265 and 267–68.
37. *BW*, 25 February 1933, 10. On Skota and the *African Yearly Register*, see Couzens, *The New African*, 3–14; and Campbell, "T. D. Mweli Skota."
38. "Bantu Women and the Community," *BW*, 25 March 1933, 4.
39. Tommy, "Pink-Cheeked Lady and Tom," *BW*, 11 February 1933, 3.
40. Peiss, *Hope in a Jar*, 45–47; Conor, *The Spectacular Modern Woman*, 143.
41. Burke, *Lifebuoy Men, Lux Women*, 193–202.
42. L.T. Baleni, "Unnecessary Expense Incurred by Women Striving for Beauty," *BW*, 30 September 1933, 10.
43. Peiss, *Hope in a Jar*, 4, 26–31, and 53–60.
44. J. Walter Thompson Collection, reel no. 225, Marketing Reports, South Africa, Port Elizabeth, J. Walter Thompson Co. (Pty.) Ltd., "Report for Lehn & Fink,": (September 1931), 2 and 9, Duke University, Rare Book, Manuscript, and Special Collections.
45. Ntantala, *A Life's Mosaic*, 74.
46. The Editress, "Disappointing Make-Ups," *BW*, 23 June 1934, 12; "Over the Tea Cups," *BW*, 3 April 1937, 9.
47. S. H. D. Lee Mnyandu, "Jo'burg Ladies," *BW*, 17 September 1938, 12.
48. Dhlomo, *An African Tragedy*.
49. Mphahlele, *Down Second Avenue*; Bonner, "'Desirable or Undesirable Basotho Women?'"; Bozzoli, *Women of Phokeng*; Coplan, "You Have Left Me Wandering About."
50. Hellmann, "Native Life in a Johannesburg Slum Yard," 40; Hellmann, *Rooiyard*, 78.
51. Bonner, "The Transvaal Native Congress, 1917–1929"; Eales, "Patriarchs, Passes, and Privilege"; Marks, "Patriotism, Patriarchy and Purity"; Ballantine, *Marabi Nights*, 46–50 and 82–83; Kemp, "'Up from Slavery' and Other Narratives," chaps. 2–3; Erlank, "Gender and Masculinity in South African Nationalist Discourse, 1912–1950."
52. Miss Roamer, "Beautiful Bantu Women Need No Lipstick or Powder to Aid Nature," *BW*, 4 March 1933, 10; R. R. R. D., "True Beauty," *BW*, 29 September 1934, 12; Israel Mhlambi, "'Behavior of Girls,'" *BW*, 5 October 1935, 12; The Editress, "Weak Women," *BW*, 20 March 1937, 9; Dimbane, "A Word in Season," *BW*, 27 March 1937, 12; "Over the Tea Cups," *BW*, 3 April 1937, 9; The Editress, "A Terrible Sight!" *BW*, 29 January 1938, 10.
53. Walter M. B. Nhlapo, "Girls Despised By Men," *BW*, 14 September 1935, 12.
54. M. P., "Powder and Lipstick for the Africans?" *BW*, 2 May 1936, 11.
55. Peiss, *Hope in a Jar*, 41–43; Rooks, *Hair Raising*; Banks, *Hair Matters*; Craig, *Ain't I a Beauty Queen?*
56. Quotes from Miss Roamer, "Beautiful Bantu Women Need No Lipstick or Powder to Aid Nature," *BW*, 4 March 1933, 10; R. R. R. D., "True Beauty," *BW*, 29 September

1934, 12; The Editress, "Disappointing Make-Ups," BW, 23 June 1934, 12; "Over the Tea Cups," BW, 3 April 1937, 9.

57. M. F. Phala, O. F. S. Koffiefontein, "The Bantu and Colour," BW, 29 December 1934, 8.

58. Messrs. D. Mogoje and P. J. G. M., "Swanee Should Be Supported," BW, 9 June 1934, 10.

59. The Son of Africa, "Great Progress!" BW, 22 October 1932, 10.

60. L. N. Msimang, " 'Girls Despised By Men,' " BW, 5 October 1935, 12.

61. S. Ngcobo, "Articles on Lipsticks, Dance, Dresses and Love Become Boring," BW, 29 September 1934, 15.

62. "R. Roamer Talks to the People," BW, 9 June 1934, 8, and 4 August 1934, 8.

63. White and White, Stylin', 188–91.

64. "Report for Lehn and Fink," 10.

65. Swanee, "Women Should Not Use Lip-Sticks and Powders as Toilets," BW, 19 May 1934, 12.

66. Powdered Face, "Women Want Good Constructive Advice from Their Critics," BW, 28 June 1934, 10.

67. Examination of other contemporary black South African newspapers revealed no advertisements for makeup.

68. Pciss, Hope in a Jar, 108–9.

69. White and White, Stylin', 189–90.

70. Peiss, Hope in a Jar, 207–13.

71. Apex ad, BW, 15 July 1933, 10; "The Opening of Vast Unexplored Market," BW, 26 May 1934, 1.

72. Rooks, Hair Raising, 81–85.

73. "Remarkable Business Acumen of Negro Woman Shown in Her Work," BW, 11 November 1933, 10.

74. "The Opening of Vast Unexplored Market," BW, 26 May 1934, 1.

75. Couzens, "A History of 'World,' " 77.

76. The Editress, "The Advertisements in Your Paper," BW, 5 May 1934, 11.

77. "R. Roamer Talks to the People," BW, 2 June 1934, 8.

78. Couzens, "A History of 'World,' " 77.

79. Valmor ad, BW, 22 February 1936, 17.

80. Suggesting that Bunche drew distinctions between Valmor and older black cosmetics companies like Madam C. J. Walker, Apex, and Poro that appealed to race pride, he "put her on to Poro." Edgar, The Travel Notes of Ralph J. Bunche, 177.

81. Burke, Lifebuoy Men, Lux Women, 119, 158–61, and 180–202; Modern Girl Around the World Research Group, "The Modern Girl Around the World," 275.

82. Quotes from Rilda Marta, "Miss Rilda Marta's Trip to the United States Full of Excitement," BW, 29 June 1935, 12; "Miss Rilda Marta's Trip to United States of America Full of Interest," BW, 6 July 1935, 12; "Miss Rilda Marta's Trip to America," BW, 13 July 1935, 12.

83. Quotes from "Miss Rilda Marta's Trip to United States of America Full of Interest"; "Miss Rilda Marta's Trip to America."

84. Kemp, " 'Up from Slavery' and Other Narratives," 6.

6

Racial Masquerade

Consumption and Contestation

of American Modernity

ALYS EVE WEINBAUM

The 1920s and early 1930s witnessed a veritable explosion of representations and discourses of masks and masquerade. In the United States motifs, themes, figurations, and literary and visual representations of masks and masquerade pervaded fiction, art photography, Hollywood film, social scientific theory, popular periodicals, and mass advertising. As a display in a 1922 issue of *Vogue* announced, the year marked "The Beginning of the 'Age of Masks'" (see figure 6.1). The masked face embodied the "decline and fall of civilization" that characterized a decadent, modern epoch—one in which "tired survivors . . . erect rococo delicacies . . . on their faces . . . [in] simulation of their former virtues."[1] According to this display, masquerade indexed Jazz Age decadence: to be masked was to be decadent and modern; to be modern and decadent was to be masked. This chapter advances the thesis put forward in *Vogue*, arguing that representations of masks and masquerade were part of a wider cultural process through which modern femininity was produced as a racialized identity, one that could be worn by women like a mask. Because masking and masquerade were intimately linked to dress-up, sartorial display, and cosmetic use, this chapter also argues that the particular form of racialized femininity that was produced through masking and masquerade was made possible by a burgeoning consumer culture in which commodities that enabled masquerade and a new aesthetic of masking circulated both intra-nationally and internationally.

Although consumption was critical to articulation of modern femininity, participation in the new commodity culture was not enough to grant a woman the appelative "Modern Girl." Rather, to achieve the status of "modern" one had to demonstrate control over the consumption process and also, as this chapter argues, control over processes of racial ascription that were intimately bound up with consumption in a period marked by Jim Crow racial segrega-tion, severe immigration restrictions, and anti-immigrant discourses of "yellow peril" and "race suicide." Indeed, it was through an activity that I shorthand as *racial masquerade* — an activity that involved not only *purchasing and putting on* what sociologists of the period dubbed the "racial mask" or "racial uni-form" but also *removal* of the mask and thus the taint of racial "otherness" — that American women became modern. By contrast with Modern Girls, those unable to participate in racial masquerade were perceived as "premodern," "primitive," and/or atavistic members of an outmoded social order that rele-gated them to traditional roles of wife and mother. For to be recognized as "modern" in the context of U.S. racial nationalism entailed sexual liberation and participation in the public sphere (the argument routinely made by histo-rians), as well as an ability to consume, put on, and take off racial "otherness."

Racial Masquerade and the Visual Scene

The form of modern racialized femininity that this chapter limns can be quickly located in several texts — similar to, and thus representative of, hundreds of others — that combine discursive and visual elements in narrating the dynamic of the racial masquerade. In the first, a photo essay on theatrical masks that ap-peared in *Vanity Fair* in 1925, a self-possessed Modern Girl makes a spectacle by demonstrating her control over a series of racialized masks (see figure 6.2). Across a prominent two-page spread, a cluster of photographs depict models sporting masks accompanied by labels such as "Florentine," "Madonna," and "American [Indian]." These are not, however, given equal weight. Rather, one mask dominates, appearing in a cameo photograph directly above the article's title. Significantly, this "Nipponese" mask is not worn by the model but held out in front of her body and below her face. This positioning underscores the model's white visage. As the caption clarifies, this photograph does not depict "[a] cruel case of decapitation." Rather, "the lady who was asked to pose in the Japanese mask . . . [is] *not a Japanese*" and thus has proffered a "polite but

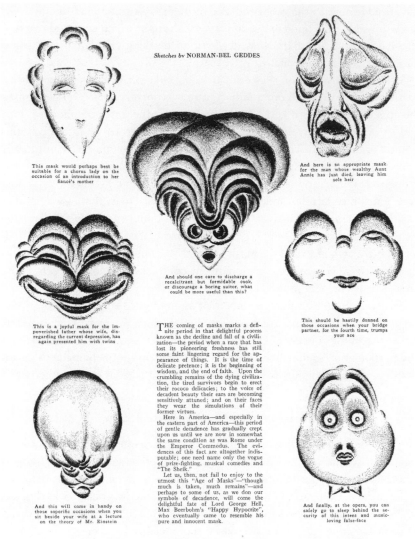

Sketches by NORMAN-BEL GEDDES

This mask would perhaps best be suitable for a chorus lady on the occasion of an introduction to her fiancé's mother

And here is an appropriate mask for the man whose wealthy Aunt Annie has just died, leaving him sole heir

And should one care to discharge a recalcitrant but formidable cook, or discourage a boring suitor, what could be more useful than this?

This is a joyful mask for the impoverished father whose wife, disregarding the current depression, has again presented him with twins

This should be hastily donned on those occasions when your bridge partner, for the fourth time, trumps your ace

THE coming of masks marks a definite period in that delightful process known as the decline and fall of a civilization—the period when a race that has lost its pioneering freshness has still some faint lingering regard for the appearance of things. It is the time of delicate pretence; it is the beginning of wisdom, and the end of faith. Upon the crumbling remains of the dying civilization, the tired survivors begin to erect their rococo delicacies; to the voice of decadent beauty their ears are becoming sensitively attuned; and on their faces they wear the simulations of their former virtues.

Here in America—and especially in the eastern part of America—this period of gentle decadence has gradually crept upon us until we are now in somewhat the same condition as was Rome under the Emperor Commodus. The evidences of this fact are altogether indisputable; one need name only the vogue of prize-fighting, musical comedies and "The Sheik."

Let us, then, not fail to enjoy to the utmost this "Age of Masks"—"though much is taken, much remains"—and perhaps to some of us, as we don our symbols of decadence, will come the delightful fate of Lord George Hell, Max Beerbohm's "Happy Hypocrite", who eventually came to resemble his pure and innocent mask.

And this will come in handy on those soporific occasions when you sit beside your wife at a lecture on the theory of Mr. Einstein

And finally, at the opera, you can safely go to sleep behind the security of this intent and music-loving false-face

1922—The Beginning of the "Age of Masks"

6.1 Masked faces to be worn by a "chorus lady" or wealthy woman when discouraging a "boring suitor" or going to the opera — all are expressive of modern decadence. *Vanity Fair*, 1922.

New Masks by W. T. Benda Revealed in an Outdoor Setting

6.2 a and b Several of Benda's masks with "Nipponese"
in the cameo at center. *Vanity Fair*, 1925.

dignified refusal to pose in it."[2] Here, the racial superiority of the model is equated with her ability to control the "Nipponese" mask — to not only put on Japaneseness but also to take it off to expose her own white modernity.

As historians of blackface performances staged in the 1920s have eloquently demonstrated, modern American whiteness has a long history of production in and through control over the performance of racial otherness.[3] When Jewish blackface performers such as Al Jolson donned blackface, they did so in order to demonstrate an ability to cast off their immigrant otherness, their Old World traditions, and the blackness with which these were associated in the American racial imaginary. In distancing themselves from blackness such performers gained entry into American whiteness. Similarly, in the case of the "Nipponese" mask, the model claims her whiteness by exhibiting control over the denigrated surface of Japaneseness or, put differently, her control over a form of racial masquerade that ultimately announces her American modernity.

Numerous high art photographs, including several by Man Ray that appeared in the 1920s in *Vogue*, exhibit a similar power dynamic (see figure 6.3). In these images, part of a larger collection of Man Ray's lover, Kiki, the whiteness and modernity of the famously flamboyant flapper and bon vivant are produced through juxtaposition of the model's luminous face with the similarly contoured but decisively black and "primitive" face of an African mask. Significantly, as in "Nipponese," "Blanche et Noire," and other similar images, Kiki does not wear the mask; rather, she positions it at a slight distance, as an adornment of the self that embellishes the self by testifying to its whiteness. Photographs by Man Ray's fellow surrealist Claude Cahun also accentuate the distance between white femininity and exotic otherness through photographic representations of racial masquerade. In numerous self-portraits Cahun, whom critics discuss as the Cindy Sherman of her day,[4] dons a Japanese mask not unlike that featured in "Nipponese," or clothes herself in Oriental garb and Asianizes her eyes with the help of kohl. The effect of Cahun's images, like that of Man Ray's, is to testify to power over the racial masquerade — to Cahun's power to put on and take off an exotic, racially distinct identity (see figure 6.4). Foregrounding the centrality of masquerade to her continuous self-production, Cahun wrote beneath one of her images, "Beneath this mask, another mask. I will not stop peeling off all these faces."[5]

While the images introduced thus far expose the dynamic of racial masquerade, they do not yet adequately convey the extent to which racial masquerade was primarily a consumer practice. For the vast majority of women (those who were not artists, actresses, or professional models) it was necessary to consume the clothes, cosmetics, and adornments of the self that enabled successful participation in the racial masquerade in the context of everyday life.

6.3 Man Ray's "Blanche et Noire" underscores the model's
"modern" whiteness through its juxtaposition with the
"primitive" blackness of the mask. *Vogue*, 1926.

6.4 Self-portrait of the surrealist photographer Claude Cahun
sporting "Oriental" garb and seated in a meditative pose.

This commercial aspect of racial masquerade manifests, unsurprisingly, in many advertisements that appeared in U.S. women's magazines throughout the 1920s and 1930s. Such advertisements employ the motif of masking, or suggest that the commodity in question will allow the consumer to purchase and try on racial otherness or exoticness through masquerade. In a fashion spread that appeared in *Vogue* in 1921, for instance, the mark of the consumer's modernity is cast as her ability to purchase clothing and to use her body to exhibit chinoiserie and Japonisme (see figure 6.5). As the caption under a white woman sporting dark bobbed hair, blowing smoke rings, and clad in kimono-inspired "robe d'intérieur" explains: "Not a Yellow peril, but a black one, and the less dangerous in this silken Japanese under-robe decorated with a curious batik design . . . done in Japan [and with] a girdle of white Chinese cord ending in a long tassel."[6] This caption's racial animus resonates with that which accompanies the "Nipponese" mask. The latter appeared one year after and the former a few years before passage of the century's most severe anti-immigration legislation. In the decade prior to 1924, thirty-five million immigrants arrived in the United States; in 1924, the Immigration Act curtailed any further foreign entrance. As is evident in the description for the "under-robe," these texts also appeared in the context of acute racism toward East Asian immigrants expressed as a generalized fear of the so-called yellow peril.[7] Indeed, the 1924 act specifically targeted Japanese in the manner in which Chinese and Indian immigrants had been targeted by previous immigration restrictions in the 1880s and 1890s. And yet, despite this context, the invocation of "yellow peril" in *Vogue* is not intended to dissuade consumption of "Oriental" fabrics and styles but rather to glamorize risqué aesthetic borrowing, nay fraternizing. Highlighting the playfulness and innocence of this performative aspect of racial masquerade for white consumers, another 1921 *Vogue* display offers costume suggestions for "beggar's balls." Two of these instruct readers in how to make an "Oriental" suit out of kitchen implements, flour sacks, and dinner napkins (see figure 6.6). As the caption beneath one such costume quips: "The Chinese Government ought to be told about this chopping bowl, flour bag, and napkin suit."[8] Notably, sharing the page with the "beggar's balls" spread is an advertisement for a new "wrap for evening" by the design house Boué Soeurs. As in other similar advertisements for clothing and cosmetics, an Asianized aesthetic is cast as alluring, desirable, and ultimately transformative of she who is able to procure it, put it on, and, as crucially, remove it at will (see figure 6.7).

It has been argued that elsewhere in the transatlantic world (see Poiger's chapter on Germany in this volume, for example) advertisements for commodities that denote racial "otherness" indicate a liberatory cosmopolitan

IT IS BUT NATURAL THAT ROBES D'INTÉRIEURS

SHOULD BE INSPIRED BY THOSE DISTANT TIMES AND

PLACES WHEN WOMEN LED REALLY SHELTERED LIVES

This colourful example of Turkish delight is a house gown which is, for the most part, of mahogany velvet. The really remarkable feature is, however, the piece of odd Turkish needlework which forms the front. Here burnt orange, dull red, and black predominate and tiny round mirrors lend an amusing note

For all their apparent vagueness of outline, the softest gowns are often the very ones that most urgently require a corset. This one of true elastic confines the hips, but has no suggestion of stiffness; from Franklin Simon

MODELS FROM
WINIFRED WARREN

Women more than a century ago, at Benares, wore the sarong, the oblong shawl of the Hindu woman, from which the panel for this gown was cut. It is of black silk embroidered in red and white stars, edged with peacocks and combined with red and black chiffon

To a slip of orchid velvet is added enough magenta chiffon to make enormous sleeves, one of which becomes a train. An East Indian temple cloth of gold and magenta brocade forms the back panel

Hinting by its glowing colour and straight lines at the glories of mediæval dress, is this narrow slip of orange and silver brocade, which has sleeves and train of orange chiffon and a hood of heavy silver lace

Not a yellow peril, but a black one, and none the less dangerous is this silken Japanese underrobe decorated with a conout batik design in white lined with a clear hard blue. The design was done in Japan. There is a girdle of white Chinese cord ending in a long tassel

6.5 "Robes D'Interieurs" including a so-called Turkish house gown, a Hindu shawl, a robe with back panel of "East Indian temple cloth," and a "Japanese under-robe." *Vogue*, 1921.

6.6 Two "Oriental" costumes suitable for "beggar's balls" made of a chopping bowl, sieve, flour bag, and dinner napkins. *Vogue*, 1921.

PELEAS—Originality and magnificence, typical of the creations of Boué Soeurs, are apparent in this sumptuous wrap for evening. Of Turkish gold brocade in graceful combination with Night blue velvet, ornamented on back and domes with conventional flowers of velvet.

THE splendor of autumn woods, the mystery of purple smoke, the sparkle of frosty stars, the magic of Indian summer—all these find expression in the modes presented for fall and winter by Boué Soeurs. A display is given daily from eleven to one and from three to five.

BOUÉ SOEURS
9 Rue de la Paix,   Paris
NEW YORK, 13 WEST 56th STREET

6.7 An advertisement for a "sumptuous wrap for evening of Turkish gold brocade" that evokes "the splendor of autumn woods" and "the mystery of purple smoke." *Vogue*, 1921.

sensibility, an openness to racial syncretism and racial mixture. By contrast, in the United States such representations play off of anti-immigrant animus, and thus represent patently racist ideas of racial and cultural syncretism. In the United States, the modern consumer's objective was neither to become Asian through purchase of Asian things or an Asian aesthetic, nor to become "primitive" through consumption of "primitive," often African things. Rather, she sought to embrace a cosmopolitan aesthetic so as to distance herself from the racial "otherness" that she had the power to purchase. In this sense representations of racial masquerade suggest that what might aptly be labeled "racist cosmopolitanism" was as constitutive to the production of the Modern Girl's modernity and whiteness, as to forms of racial nationalism pervasive in the period. Indeed, the racially syncretic aesthetic that pervaded U.S. advertisements was a powerful sign of racial supremacy, of white women's control over the racial masquerade, racial ascription, and thus their designation as members of the modern racial nation.

The various forms of masquerade represented in advertisements for fashionable clothing in the 1920s and 1930s also dominated advertisements for cosmetics in the same period. The latter frequently thematized masks and masking and, taken together, suggest that masquerade was a dominant leitmotif in the marketing of these commodities. In numerous ads, the cleansed, moisturized, and made-up face is represented as a mask that can be purchased, put on, and used to transform the self. In an ad for Roger and Gallet soap the copy queries: "Who can be fascinating behind the mask of a poor complexion? . . . It won't be long before this delightful . . . Soap completely washes away your complexion sins and reveals your true complexion at its best" (see figure 6.8). As discussed in the collaborative second chapter of this volume, in the United States, as elsewhere around the globe, many cosmetics advertisements (including those for makeup, tanning potions, skin whiteners and lighteners) took the theme of masquerade one step further, promising buyers the ability to transform not only the quality, tone, and texture of the skin, but also its racial signification. Notably, such appeals to alter skin tone, texture, and color marketed such changes as not only fashionable but also scientific and hygienic and thus decisively modern. (See figures 2.19, 2.20, and 2.22 in chapter 2.)

In a typical U.S. advertisement for Princess Pat brand makeup that appeared in *Photoplay* in 1927 the advertisement's tag line queries "What COLOR do you feel today?" Although it initially appears that this is an advertisement for mood-altering palettes of rouge, the racial resonance of the capitalized term "COLOR" is underscored by the lowercase copy that clarifies that this product's most valuable feature is that its unique shades may be applied and removed to conjure various forms of racial exoticism: "*look the part*," consumers are commanded, "use Princess Pat Rouge Vivid — or the newest shade, Squaw. Watch the mirror . . . you get a complete new thrill from your own reflection in the glass."[9] In a similar ad in 1931 for Elizabeth Arden cosmetics, the advertisement's small print again promises product flexibility so that "the same woman" may use the product to remake her visage differently with each application (see figure 6.9). As in numerous other ads that advertise "palettes" of color, here the "Tri-Color" and "Bi-Color" palettes may be purchased and used to render possible an "infinite variety" of "faces" — or, perhaps more aptly, an "infinite variety" of masks.

The 1931 Elizabeth Arden ad was part of a larger group of advertisements that graphically emphasized the idea of masquerade through use of a turban-wrapped head. This design motif is important in that it renders the face a masklike surface that may be painted upon and transformed with ease. In another Elizabeth Arden advertisement for "Vienna Youth Mask," the model (the same

Let Roger & Gallet Soap reveal your complexion at its best

6.8 An advertisement for soap that represents the face as a mask that can be transformed through cleansing. *Vogue*, 1934.

DEMEYER

"The same woman...
but
with infinite variety"

Women were skeptical about the off-the-face hats...Elizabeth Arden taught them what to do! Then came the new colorings. This seemed an even greater problem, but again Elizabeth Arden has stepped into the breach, and with her fascinating and individual new make-ups has enabled women to face the sun with confidence and assurance. ● Woman now matches her face to her gowns, and colors no longer fill her with fear. She can wear anything and always look beautiful.

"What make-up shall I wear with the new color-contrast fashions?" smart women are asking. Miss Arden's stylist has devised charming make-up ensembles for the contrast effects that are most prevalent. Here are some of them:

First the Tri-Colors

● WITH RED, WHITE AND BLUE...it is smart to harmonize your make-up with all three colors. Use a slightly darker foundation, Rachel or Mat Foncé powder, dark Amoretta cream rouge to contrast with the white of your costume. Have your lipstick duplicate the color of the red in your frock and your Eye-Shado repeat the blue of the dress. Black Eyelash Cosmetique is effective.

● WITH RED, YELLOW AND BLACK...brunettes will remain rather dark-skinned, but avoid sallowness; blondes will choose a make-up with a dash of pink in it. Green Eye-Shado for both blondes and brunettes is most alluring. A lip rouge that matches the red in the costume is suggested.

●WITH LIGHT GREEN, RUST AND DARK GREEN...a clever, new combination that is particularly charming with a tanned skin — use a dark foundation, a

warm tone of rouge, and a lipstick that echoes the red-orange tone of the rust in your ensemble. Green Eye-Shado and brown Cosmetique are suggested for both brunettes and blondes.

Then the Bi-Colors

● WITH BLUE AND WHITE...BLACK AND WHITE...BROWN AND WHITE...your make-up accessories must harmonize with the color nearer your face. If the white area is nearer your face, use a rather dark shade for your powder foundation...a warm shade for your rouge, Poudre d'Illusion in Banana or Rachel ...and a very vivid lipstick, preferably the new indelible "Chariot."

● WITH BLUE the predominating color of the contrast combination, wear a light foundation...a light shade of rouge...powder with a dash of pink in it, and a bright lipstick. Your Eye-Shado must repeat the blue of the dress. For eyes that are blue try finishing the lashes with light blue Cosmetique tipped with black.

● WITH BROWN the principal tone of a bi-color costume, use Rachel foundation and a rouge that will deepen the brown tone in the skin. The Banana shade of Poudre d'Illusion blends well

with brown. Use a bright lipstick...Flame is suggested. For the eyes...light brown Eye-Shado and green or black Cosmetique.

● WITH BLACK, a quite vivid make-up is smart. Blondes with fair skin will keep it so, using a light foundation, Illusion Powder, Light Amoretta Rouge, and a bright lipstick, preferably "Chariot." Blue Eye-Shado and black Cosmetique will add interest to the eyes. Brunettes will intensify the olive tint in their skin by using a rather dark foundation, Dark Amoretta Rouge and a bright lipstick. And for the eyes, try this thrilling make-up...light brown Eye-Shado over the entire eyelid, green Eye-Shado over the iris of the eye, and black Cosmetique on the lashes.

● Miss Arden feels confident that, with these suggestions to guide you, you will be able to create some very interesting make-up ensembles of your own to complement your new clothes.

● Elizabeth Arden's Make-Up Creations are on sale at smart shops everywhere at these prices: Anoretta Cream (foundation for a dry skin) $1, $2. Crème de France (foundation for an average skin) Tube $1.25, Jar, $2.50. Lille Lotion (foundation for an oily skin) $1.50, $2.50. Rouge Amoretta, $2.50. Poudre d'Illusion, $3. Lipsticks, $1.50. Cream Eye-Shado, $1.50. Eyelash Cosmetique, $1.25.

ELIZABETH ARDEN
691 FIFTH AVENUE · NEW YORK

6.9 "Woman now matches her face to her gowns . . . colors no longer fill her with fear" as her makeup is versatile enough to transform her visage for all occasions. *Vogue,* 1931.

one as in the previous advertisement) holds a theatrical mask in her hands, producing a semblance between her own masklike face and the masklike visage that she has purchased and applied (see figure 6.10). In an advertisement for Helena Rubinstein's "much-discussed" "Valaze Face Powder," the model's turban-wrapped head wears its made-up face as a mask, an effect that is enforced by inclusion of a tiny painter, situated atop a scaffold, who applies the finishing touches to the face with a miniscule paint brush (see figure 6.11). Notably, the wrapped heads that were pervasive in cosmetic advertising echo the faces of cloche-clad flappers. As numerous advertisements for these ubiquitous hats reveal, the cloche's close-fitting style, covering the hair and framing the face, rendered the face of the wearer masklike, an abstract surface to be inscribed at will (see figure 6.12). In this sense it may not be far-fetched to suggest that the cloche, a signature Modern Girl adornment, potentially enabled each wearer to become a participant in the racial masquerade.

Before moving on to discussion of treatment of racial masquerade in social theory, three generalizations about the visual scene deserve emphasis. First, racial masquerade involved transformation of the visual surface of the body, rendering it mobile and subject to continuous transfiguration. Second, racial masquerade was a material practice made possible through consumption of the commodities procured in the new mass market. The signature feature of this market was that it created juxtapositions not only of people but also of things, ideas, and aesthetics that had seldom before been as proximate. In this sense racial masquerade brought distant locales nearer and obliterated physical distance through aesthetic syncretism. And, third, within the majority of representations of masking and masquerade in the 1920s and 1930s, race was treated less as a biological posit than as a performance, posture, gesture, façade, or surface appropriable by she who possessed access to consumer culture—she who possessed the power to not only purchase but also to put on and take off the mask. This was a power to engage in consumption so as to exert mastery over racial ascription. In short, this was the power to purchase so as to demonstrate one's possession of American modernity.

Racial Masquerade and Social Theory

In 1929 Joan Riviere, a lay psychoanalyst and key English translator of Freud, made a groundbreaking contribution to the "Great Debate" on the question of female sexuality. In her essay "Womanliness as a Masquerade," she presented a case study of an "American Woman engaged in work of a propagandist nature," who, after virtuoso public presentations, was compelled to coquettishly engage male colleagues.[10] As Riviere explained, through such hyper-feminine

6.10 Advertisement showing turban wrapped head with a masklike face and the product as a mask to be applied and removed. *Vogue*, 1931.

6.11 Advertisement showing turbaned wrapped head and a face undergoing transformation through painting. *Vogue*, 1931.

6.12 Advertisement for a cloche hat that emphasizes the face as a canvas to be made-up for display. *Vogue*, 1930.

performances her patient sought to stave off reprisals for her appropriation of masculine power. For Riviere this woman's masquerade bespoke a wider truth about the nonexistence of an essential female self: "womanliness . . . [can] be assumed and worn as a mask," Riviere averred, "both to hide the possession of masculinity and to avert the reprisals" for possession of the phallus. Anticipating the salient question about the scope of her bold claim, Riviere continued, "The reader may . . . ask . . . where I draw the line between genuine womanliness and the 'masquerade.' My suggestion is not, however, that there is any such difference; whether radical or superficial, *they are the same thing.*"[11]

In the 1970s, Riviere's essay was taken up by feminist scholars developing alternatives to the Freudian account of femininity, and later by those theorizing the performativity of gender (first Luce Irigaray, then Judith Butler). In the 1990s, scholars expanded the discussion to argue that the masquerade of womanliness of which Riviere wrote was racialized — that it was a masquerade of femininity and also, simultaneously, of whiteness.[12] Specifically, several scholars returned to Riviere's account of her patient's sexual fantasy about an American "Negro" who molests her, to critique Riviere's inadequate attention to it. In order to turn her assailant over to "justice," Riviere argued, in fantasy her patient appeased her attacker with sex. In other words, in Riviere's reading the white American woman regarded her black attacker as yet another patriarchal figure. In contrast to Riviere's race-inattentive reading, race-attentive scholars argued that the patient appeased her attacker because she identified with him as someone who, like herself, had reason to fear white men. And yet they also point out that she ultimately turns him in. As one critic explains, whereas the woman "can turn her pockets out and show that she has no penis after all, the black man she fantasizes about cannot do so, and his horrific punishment will be, after all, his literal castration and death."[13] For these reasons the masquerade of "womanliness" of which Riviere wrote should be understood as double and double edged: it is both a feminine masquerade that denies possession of phallic power and a racial masquerade that aligns itself with white racial privilege.

Although race-attentive readings that attempt to mitigate the universalizing tendencies of psychoanalytic theory (particularly the unacknowledged racialization of the analysand as white) are salutary, to fully historicize Riviere's essay it is necessary not only to attend to the fantasy of interracial sex but also to contextualize the essay within a wider discourse on masquerade, especially that which emerged out of the new consumer culture that took root as Riviere wrote. Riviere, a one-time dressmaker, renowned among her colleagues for her fashion sensibility, impeccable sartorial style, and heavy use of cosmetics, elected masquerade as femininity's best metaphor because she, like her patient, was surrounded by ideas, images, and discourses of masquerade.[14] Riviere's central metaphor was part of the cultural milieu in which she participated — one in which not only feminine masks but also racial masks took center stage.[15]

Whereas Riviere unselfconsciously meditated on racial masquerade, other contemporary social scientists directly theorized racial masquerade's connection to modern femininity. Just three years prior to Riviere's essay, Robert Ezra Park, the preeminent sociologist of U.S. race relations between the wars, published a treatise on masquerade titled "Behind Our Masks."[16] Park, a founder of the Chicago School of Sociology, is most famous for work on the figure whom he dubbed "marginal man."[17] This quintessentially modern subject was the product of racial and cultural mixing resulting from increased migration, international travel, and rapid commodity exchange in an emerging world marketplace. He occupied a prominent place in Park's corpus because it was through study of "modern man's" struggle to assimilate the foreign national culture in which he resided that Park believed sociologists could apprehend and measure degrees of cultural contact and conflict. Throughout his writings Park variously refers to such contact and conflict as the "Assimilation Cycle," the "Americanization Cycle," or the "Race Relations Cycle," depending on whether he is studying assimilation by immigrants from Eastern and Southern Europe, East and Southeast Asia, or that by African Americans. As Park specified, "In the mind of the marginal man . . . the moral turmoil which new cultural contacts occasion, manifests itself in the most obvious forms. It is in the mind of the marginal man — where the changes and fusions of culture are going on — that we can best study the processes of civilization and progress."[18]

Although Park's terminology implies a male research subject and suggests a primary focus on "the mind," in many of his writings on immigration, cultural contact, and conflict, female figures — those we might more aptly label "marginal women" — preoccupy him. Moreover, when Park focuses on women his emphasis dramatically shifts to the visible surface of the body. As Henry Yu observes in his study of the Chicago School, Park, like the missionaries before him, was particularly interested in Asian American women (Chinese and Japanese), whose dress and manners indexed their degree of assimilation into Americanness but whose faces appeared as "racial masks" or "racial uniforms" that obscured the assimilated person living beneath the outer shell. Significantly, at least one of the women whom Park wrote about was a flapper, a would-be Modern Girl.[19] According to Park, she revealed her newfound Americanness by casting off the dress and style of her country of origin and replacing it with modern American clothing and etiquette. As he explained, for women immigrants the most important marks of difference are those superficial differences that are manifest "in dress," in "manner," and in "deportment" — those differences that are necessarily elaborated in and through consumption and an individual's participation in consumer culture.

In "Behind Our Masks" Park sought to understand the "position of the Oriental in America" in the 1920s by exploring the extent to which, despite severe anti-Asian and antimiscegenation legislation and sentiment, Asian Americans were becoming "less marginal" to American social life and culture. The central example he uses to illustrate his argument is instructive.

> I recently had the curious experience of talking with a young Japanese woman who was not only born in the United States, but was brought up in an American family, in an American college town, where she had almost no association with members of her own race. I found myself watching her expectantly for some slight accent, some gesture or intonation that would betray her racial origin. When I was not able, by the slightest expression, to detect the oriental mentality behind the oriental mask, I was still not able to escape the impression that I was listening to *an American woman in a Japanese disguise.*[20]

Park next comments that this woman was perceived by other Japanese as having "the appearance of a Japanese woman in *the masquerade* of an American Lady."[21] According to the surface characteristics that mattered most to Park, this woman was completely assimilated. And yet she was marginal to both her culture of origin and to the American culture which she sought to assimilate. In the American context, she felt that the Americans by whom she was surrounded perceived an "oriental mask" rather than the assimilated person beneath its surface. As Park explains, the visual surface of her body (her face as racial mask) blocked accurate recognition of her, giving her the appearance of "a Japanese woman in . . . masquerade" in the eyes of other Japanese and bestowing upon her the appearance of an "American woman in a Japanese disguise" in the eyes of white Americans.

At other points in "Behind Our Masks," Park presages Riviere's generalizations about masquerade, proposing masquerade as a universal human condition in the context of modern consumer culture: "Everyone is always everywhere, more or less consciously, playing a role," he wrote. In the context of mass migration and intensified contact "our very faces are living masks." Further on he observed, "The mask is our truer self . . . In the end, our conception of our role becomes second nature and an integral part of our personality." And yet, even as Park appeared to universalize the condition of masquerade, he also went to great lengths to emphasize the exceptionality of "Orientals [who] live more completely behind the mask than the rest of us [white Americans]."[22] This is at once a racist statement that unselfconsciously draws upon prevalent discourses about reported "Oriental inscrutability" and a theoretical statement about the irreducibility of the primacy of racial visibility in structuring social relationships among people of color and white Americans in the 1920s. As Park conceded, "Physical traits . . . do not change. The Oriental in America experiences a profound transfiguration in sentiment and attitude [when he assimilates], but he cannot change his physical characteristics. He is still constrained to wear his *racial uniform;* he cannot, much as he may sometimes like to do so, cast aside the *racial mask.*"[23]

For the most part Park refused to characterize racial difference as purely biological and in this way anticipated and helped to shape the post–World War II consensus on race as a social construct. Park also complicated the picture offered by other postwar liberals by insisting on the irreducibility of biologized forms of racial ascription as a feature of "race prejudice" in the United States. As he explains in a 1917 article, "Race Prejudice and Japanese-American Relations": "Japanese, Chinese, and Negroes cannot move among us with the same freedom as the members of other races because they bear marks which identify them as members of their race."[24] Though Park was never a race radical (he never let go of mass assimilation into whiteness as an ideal), he was committed to understanding how "prejudice," rather than racialized bodies, constituted the primary obstacle to immigrant assimilation. In the following passage he elaborates his at times contradictory position: "The chief obstacle to the assimilation of the Negro and the Oriental are not mental but physical traits. It is not because the Negro and the Japanese are so differently constituted that they do not assimilate. If they were given an opportunity the Japanese are quite as capable as the Italians . . . of acquiring our culture, and sharing national ideals. The trouble is not with the Japanese mind but with the Japanese skin. The Jap is not the right color."[25] Racial identity, reducible to a visible surface, is an irreducible problem in a nation whose social organization depends upon racial ascription. Put differently, Park understood that because visible racial difference was a problem in the eyes of whites who perceived it, it was an obstacle to those beholden to white perception. Thus he concluded that the racial mask was superficial and, at the same time, nearly impossible to remove.

Whereas Riviere's masquerading white American secures her social position through demonstration of her ability to don and remove her mask at will, Park's masquerading Japanese American flapper is marginalized by white America's perception that she wears a racial mask that cannot be removed. Whereas Riviere never suggests that her patient will or should cease to perform the masquerade — *masquerade is what this woman does in order to survive* in her professional life — Park laments the inability of the Japanese American flapper to remove her racial mask. As he explains in numerous writings on assimilation, including "Behind Our Masks," the end to racial conflict, and thus the possibility for inclusion within the nation, resides in the immigrant's ability to be perceived, first and foremost, as American and only incidentally as Asian. As he comments with perverse optimism, despite the persistence of white perception of the racial mask, "whenever representatives of different races meet and discover in one another — beneath the differences of race — sentiments, tastes, interests, and human qualities . . . that they can understand and respect, racial barriers are undermined and eventually broken down."[26]

The similarities and differences between Riviere's and Park's formulations are instructive. Both agree that control over masquerade guarantees inclusion within the dominant social order. Both insist that in order to procure and maintain power and social position and to escape reprisal for entrance into power and social position, women must masquerade. And yet, while for the white American woman of whom Riviere writes masquerade is readily procured through a combination of consumption and performance, for the Asian American woman the mask fails to function as promised by the advertisements and popular literature that compose the visual and consumer scene in the 1920s. As Park reluctantly concedes, it is only in extremely rare situations that an Asian woman is able to remove her racial mask or racial uniform. She is overdetermined from without in an American racial economy in which racial "otherness" (except in cases in which an individual passes into whiteness) is regarded as an indelible mark.

While "Behind Our Masks" restricts its focus to Asian assimilation, elsewhere Park discusses "Negro" assimilation in Jim Crow America.[27] As in his discussion of "the Oriental," so too in his discussion of "the Negro," race is construed as a visual surface that arrests the white gaze and prevents whites from seeing the assimilated (read "modern" and American) self that lies beneath the visible outer shell. If the racial mask worn by racial "others" in the U.S. context must be pliable in order for the wearer to gain access to "the general flux which we sometimes call democracy,"[28] in the case of African Americans the perpetually deferred promise of racial masquerade is painfully obvious.

Park used a range of sources and experiences, including his time at Tuskegee as Booker T. Washington's right-hand man, to arrive at his conclusions about African American assimilation. And yet, it is noteworthy that in approaching this subject he was especially inclined to turn to what he called "Negro Literature." As others have argued, one of the groundbreaking contributions of Chicago School sociologists, Park included, was the realization that literary texts are "the perfect type of sociological material," and thus recognition of literary and sociological texts as engaged in a mutually transformative dialogue. Put differently, Park and his colleagues found scientific evidence in literature and simultaneously produced themselves as "historically important agents . . . [capable] of turn[ing] cultures into literatures."[29] In "Negro Race Consciousness as Reflected in Race Literature" (1923), Park elaborates on the dialectic between literature and sociology: "My interest in Negro poetry is not that of a student of literature," he writes, but rather that "of a student of human nature. I cannot and shall not attempt to speak in the language of literary criticism. But I am disposed to accept quite literally, not as a figure of speech, but as a matter of fact that a 'people that is producing poetry is not perishing, but astir with . . . life-giving visions,'" and that "Negro poetry" should thus be regarded as "a transcript of Negro Life."[30]

In "Race Literature" Park treats texts ranging from the "sorrow songs" of which W. E. B. Du Bois wrote to "Negro poetry" by Harlem literati including Claude McKay and James Weldon Johnson. In this way he smoothes over the differences between oral and written traditions, and those among song, poetry, fiction, nonfiction prose, and political treatise, grouping all forms and genres together. As this expansive grouping implicitly suggests, Park regarded all texts within his archive as possessing equal value. Of course, it is also this expansive and acquisitive understanding of "Race Literature" that allows him to elevate it "as the perfect type of sociological material." Unsurprisingly, the authors whom Park singles out for discussion include several of his well-known male contemporaries. Surprisingly, given Park's abiding interest in women's use of racial masks, he does not mention any women writers, those who, in the period in which he wrote, commented eloquently on racial masquerade in fiction and nonfiction prose. Indeed, as I explore in this chapter's last section, had Park elected to treat literature by black women — literature by and about those struggling to realize the promise of the racial masquerade — he would have found yet another archival source that not only engaged his theory about the racial mask but also offered a searing critique of the culture of consumption and the false promises it held out to those seeking recognition as "modern" and "American" in a racially segregated nation.

Racial Masquerade and Literary Critique

Although there are several texts that suggest themselves here, Nella Larsen's well-known novel *Quicksand* (1928) warrants careful consideration.[31] As Cheryl Wall has detailed, nearly everything that Larsen wrote is thematically concerned with masking and unmasking. Early writings are themselves masked by the pseudonym "Allen Semi" under which Larsen first published (an anagram that can be transposed to reveal her married name, Nella Imes).[32] Larsen's few short stories deal with cases of mistaken or concealed identity. Her novel *Passing* (1929) treats the masquerade-inflected topic announced by its title. And *Quicksand*, my focus here, details the life of a biracial woman (African American and Dutch) whose experiments with racial masquerade define her and drive the narrative of her life. By contrast to Park, who only implicitly explores consumer culture's role in racial masquerade, Larsen meditates directly, often obsessively, on consumption as a route into American modernity. In creating a protagonist, Helga Crane, who does not elect to pass as white but nevertheless occupies a racially liminal zone that emboldens her fantasies about the promise of racial masquerade, Larsen exposes the false allure of the culture of masquerade by which Helga is enticed.[33]

As Larsen moves Helga through a series of experiments with racial masquerade, she exposes its mechanism and, in so doing, reveals its limits as a strategy for liberation. If, by the novel's end, Helga is revealed to have been deluded in her initial optimistic infatuation with the power of racial masquerade, at its start she is represented as sanguinely captivated by the culture of consumption and the racial masks that it offers for sale.[34] As the novel opens we discover Helga in her lodgings at Naxos, an all-black college created in the image of Booker T. Washington's Tuskegee Institute, surrounded by commodified objects that express her unique sensibility. Larsen writes:

> Only a single reading lamp, dimmed by a great black and red shade, made a pool of light on the blue Chinese carpet, on the bright covers of the books which she had taken down from their long shelves, on the white pages of the opened one selected, on the shining brass bowl crowded with many-colored nasturtiums beside her on the low table, and on the oriental silk which covered the stool at her slim feet. It was a comfortable room, furnished with rare and intensely personal taste . . . Helga sat . . . [in] a small oasis in a desert of darkness.[35]

Helga is surrounded by fine things, many imported from afar; she is also herself positioned as an object among objects. Helga literally blends in with other commodities such that, Larsen wryly notes, "an observer would have thought her well fitted to" the particular "framing of light and shade" that she has created in her stylishly outfitted apartment.[36] In a syntactically evasive and at once instructive sentence that hints at the importance of commodities in Helga's world, Larsen provides a tantalizing glimpse of Helga's clothing before providing us with a look at Helga herself: "In vivid green and gold negligee and glistening brocaded mules, deep sunk in the big high-backed chair, against whose tapestry her sharply cut face, with skin like yellow satin, was distinctly outlined, she was — to use a hackneyed word — attractive."[37] Helga's flesh comes into view in and through the commodity world. Her skin, metaphorized as "yellow satin," is yet another garment to be worn, like negligee and mules.

As the narrative progresses, Helga's masquerade proves less exquisitely perfect than these opening pages suggest and than Helga desires. Helga's difficulties are first foreshadowed through Larsen's juxtaposition of Helga's consumer and sartorial practices and those of her Naxos colleagues. By contrast with fellow faculty whose prim and proper dress, deportment, and commitment to cosmetic practices such as hair straightening and skin lightening enable them to ape white ways, Helga's dress and deportment — nothing less than her racial masquerade — allow her to stand out. Although Helga's "yellow" body and refusal to educate her students to be "mere hewers of wood and drawers of water" set her apart, above all else she is ostracized for her sartorial choices and her unrestrained "craving" for "nice things."[38] As Larsen explains, "Helga loved clothes, elaborate ones." And even though "she had tried not to offend," she had such "small success" that the dean and matrons of Naxos readily detect in Helga's attire "the subtle differences from their own irreproachable conventional garments," noting with disdain that the colors and textures of Helga's clothes "were queer; dark purples, royal blues, rich greens, deep reds, in soft, luxurious woolens, or heavy, clinging silks." Even Helga's "faultless, slim shoes made them uncomfortable" and "her small plain hats seemed to them positively indecent."[39]

If at first Helga smiles "inwardly at the thought that whenever there was an evening affair for the faculty, the dear ladies probably held their breaths until she made her appearance . . . [existing] in constant fear that she might turn out in an evening dress," eventually she finds herself unable to brush off the relentless judgment.[40] Clothes and other "nice things" are not mere adornments; they are Helga's substance. And thus, when Helga finally expresses her rebellion against Naxos, she does so through an explicitly racialized sartorial display that flies in the face of Naxos convention. As Larsen explains, Helga issued a "plea for color" based on "something intuitive, some unanalyzed driving spirit of loyalty to the inherent racial need for gorgeousness [that] told . . . [Helga] that bright colours *were* fitting and that dark-complexioned people *should* wear yellow, green, and red. Black, brown, and gray were ruinous . . . [they] actually destroyed the luminous tones lurking in . . . dusky skins."[41]

Driven from Naxos by an inability to perform the racial masquerade that is required of her, Helga moves to Harlem where she hopes to find kindred souls and a more congenial aesthetic sensibility. And yet, amid a black East Coast elite with whom she shares a critique of the self-abnegation of those at Naxos, Helga ultimately finds Harlem's "Race Men" and "Race Women" no more simpatico. Whereas at Naxos Helga's sartorial and consumer excesses alienated her from her colleagues, in Jazz Age Harlem her inability to control the masquerade leaves her, once again, alone. In her description of Helga's preparations for an evening out, Larsen focuses as meticulously as Helga on getting Helga's outfit just right:

> What should she wear? White? No, everybody would, because it was hot. Green? She shook her head . . . The Blue thing. Reluctantly she decided against it; she loved it, but she had worn it too often. There was that cobwebby black net touched with orange, which she had bought last spring in a fit of extravagance and never worn, because on getting it home both she and Anne had considered it too *décolleté*, and too *outré*. Anne's words: "There's not enough of it, and what there is gives you the air of something about to fly," came back to her, and she smiled as she decided that she would certainly wear the black net.[42]

As she has done previously, in this instance Helga attempts to use clothes to perform the self or, more aptly, to master the racial masquerade. But her efforts fail once again. On the evening in question she wears the black dress not only to the dinner party at which she intended to masquerade as a member of the "Talented Tenth" but also to a "tawdry," "gay," "grotesque" jazz club that she had not intended to visit and where her dress, to her horror, signals not so much a sophisticated black cosmopolitan modernity but rather her "savagery." As "a glare of light" strikes her eyes, and "a blare of jazz splits her ear," Helga finds herself "spinning," enveloped in sight and sound. When she begins to dance she wheels out of control, finding the experience unstoppable, transporting, even orgasmic: "She was drugged, lifted, sustained, by the extraordinary music, blown out, ripped out, beaten out, by the joyous, wild, murky orchestra. The essence of life seemed bodily motion." When suddenly the music stops, Helga is left with a "shameful certainty that *not only had she been in the jungle, but . . . she had enjoyed it*."[43] While the black net dress was meant to enable her masquerade of "uplifted" blackness, Helga finds instead that it has transformed her, against her will, into a member of a black "swirling mass"—into a "primitive" rather than a "modern." For even as Helga reassures herself that she is not a "jungle creature," she finds herself unable to prevent merger with the least desirable members of "this oppressed race of hers."[44]

The failure of Helga's racial masquerade, and particularly her brush with "savagery," compel yet another desperate move in her search for a stage upon which her performance will produce a more convincing, more modern effect. Larsen makes clear, however, that upon Helga's arrival in Denmark, a fetishizing obsession with her "primitive" blackness belies her Danish relative's warm embrace. Almost immediately Helga's Aunt and Uncle Dahl take charge of her consumption habits, rapidly transforming her racial masquerade into an exotic performance that secures and then augments their own social prestige. What begins as an effort to persuade Helga to tailor her clothes revealingly and to dress in bright colors becomes a thorough-going intervention into Helga's self-making. Under the guidance of a famous Danish artist, Axel Olsen, whose modernist penchant for the "primitive" is finely honed,[45] Helga's relatives purchase an astounding array of commodities for her. Larsen provides ample detail in describing these "nice things":

> There were batik dresses in which mingled indigo, orange, green, vermilion, and black, dresses of velvet and chiffon in screaming colors, blood-red, sulphur yellow, sea-green; and one black and white thing in striking combination. There was a black Manila shawl strewn with great scarlet and lemon flowers, a leopard-skin coat, a glittering opera cape. There were turban-like hats of metallic silks, feathers and furs, strange jewelry, enameled or set with odd semi-precious stones, a nauseous Eastern perfume, shoes with dangerously high heels.[46]

Although Larsen suggests that Helga realizes that she is being transformed into an exotic "curio"—a "veritable savage," "a queer dark creature," "a decoration . . . A Peacock," and ultimately "nothing so much as some new and strange species of pet dog"[47]—Larsen depicts her as incapable of divesting herself of the dream, in this foreign land, that she might gain control over the racial masquerade. Indeed, at least initially, in Copenhagen Helga convinces herself that even as she masquerades as "primitive"—perhaps in emulation of the African American performer Josephine Baker, who was then so wildly popular in Europe—she is at once "modern." As Larsen observes, even as Helga perceives the warning signs, she gives "herself up wholly to the fascinating business of being seen, gaped at, desired."[48] And yet, as Park elaborated in the case of the Japanese flapper, in this one, the racial mask can be put on and removed, but only by she whose bodily surface enables racial ascription. Although Europe is free of Jim Crow and lynch mobs, on the one hand, and Race Men and Race Women on the other, Helga remains surrounded by whites who are unable to see anything but a permanently affixed racial mask.

While watching a minstrel performance on a Danish stage, Helga finally recognizes that her entry into modernity is barred in Europe by the failure of her masquerade. As the performers go through their routine she is jolted into awareness of the proximity between her performance as exotic primitive and the one being played out before her eyes. As Larsen explains, as "two black men" danced and sang "an American old ragtime song that Helga remembered hearing as a child," Helga is "filled with a fierce hatred for the cavorting Negroes on the stage" and with the feeling that she has been deeply "shamed" and "betrayed" by the "pale pink and white people among whom she lived." As Helga watches the performance she begins to feel as if these people had "suddenly been invited to look upon something *in her which she had hidden away*."[49] Like Riviere's patient, Helga has "hidden" "something" behind her mask; and yet, unlike Riviere's patient, she is unable to keep this "something" out of view and is thus unable to escape reprisal for possessing it. Betrayed rather than empowered by her racial masquerade, Helga becomes conscious of the false promise held out by the culture of consumption in which she has immersed herself. Confirming the unstated consensus among the Danes among whom she now lives, Axel Olsen remarks to Helga upon her rejection of his proposal of marriage, "You have the warm impulsive nature of the women of Africa, but, my lovely, I fear the soul of a prostitute. You sell yourself to the highest buyer."[50]

Larsen does not conclude her cautionary investigation into racial masquerade in Europe but rather allows readers to witness Helga's helpless struggle in the quicksand that envelops her as she sinks to her figurative, if not literal, death among allegedly "premodern" black Americans. When Helga returns to New York, driven by a desire to be reunited with "her people," she is unable to successfully reintegrate into her elite social circle and thus instead opts to don one last costume, one last racial mask. As a "fallen" woman clad in a clinging red dress, a prostituted, degraded masquerade she has until this point avoided, she elopes with a storefront preacher who carries her off to a small town in Alabama. Once she is removed from the modern city to the rural backwater (in effect reversing the trajectory of the Great Migration), Helga's relegation to "premodern" status is confirmed.

The ironic last sentences of *Quicksand* leave little doubt as to Larsen's critique of the false promise held out to black women by the culture of masquerade. Helga's unsubtly named husband, Mr. Pleasant Green, has delivered her to neither the land of dollars nor the fecund pastures of consumption but rather to a place of living death. At narrative's end, readers find an utterly exhausted Helga confined to her bed, awaiting the birth of a fifth child. As Larsen makes clear, Helga's experiments with consumption and racial masquerade have "ruined her life. Made it impossible ever again to do the things that she wanted, have the things that she loved."[51] At the furthest remove from the luxurious things that surround Helga in the novel's opening passage, in rural Alabama Helga is denuded of the commodified surfaces out of which she hoped to craft her modernity and her sense of belonging in the United States. As she lies upon her (death) bed, her first four children in the care of those whom Larsen labels the preacher's "primitive flock," Helga reflects,

> It was so easy and so pleasant to think about freedom and cities, about clothes and books, about the sweet mingled smell of Houbigant and cigarettes in softly lighted rooms filled with inconsequential chatter and laughter and sophisticated tuneless music. *It was so hard to think out a feasible way of retrieving these agreeable, desired things.*[52]

To be "modern," an American Modern Girl had to have ready access to "desired things." But even more importantly, she had to be able to control the racial masquerade that such commodities enabled. If she failed — if, instead, the racial masquerade controlled her — her credentials as a "modern" were forfeited. From this vantage point, Helga's story is a devastating one about consumption and American modernity that early social scientists attempted to theorize, advertisements of the 1920s and 1930s hid from view, and Larsen narrated for those willing to listen.

Notes

1. "The Beginning of the 'Age of Masks,' " *Vanity Fair,* January 1922, 54. Hereafter *VF.*
2. "New Masks by W. T. Benda Revealed in an Outdoor Setting," *VF,* December 1925, 48.
3. See Michael Rogin's *Blackface, White Noise,* especially his discussion of Al Jolson's blackface performance.
4. See Rice, *Inverted Odysseys.*
5. Ibid.
6. "It Is but Natural That Robes D'Interieurs Should be Inspired by Those Distant Times and Places When Women Led Really Sheltered Lives," *Vogue,* December 1921, 64.
7. See Takaki, *Strangers from a Different Shore,* 209 and passim.
8. "For Beggars' Balls," *Vogue,* October 1921, 114.
9. "What COLOR do you feel today?" *Photoplay,* February 1927, 119.
10. Riviere, "Womanliness as Masquerade," 36.
11. Ibid., 38 (emphasis added).
12. See, for example, Pellegrini, *Performance Anxieties,* 131–43; Walton, *Fair Sex, Savage Dreams,* 17–40; and Bergner, "Who Is That Masked Woman? Or the Role of Gender in Fanon's *Black Skin, White Masks.*"
13. Walton, *Fair Sex, Savage Dreams,* 23.
14. See Heath, "Joan Riviere and the Masquerade," 45–61; Hughes, *The Inner World and Joan Riviere,* 1–44; James Strachey, "Obituary: Joan Riviere (1883–1962)," *International Journal of Psychoanalysis* (hereafter *IJPA*) 44 (1963): 228–30; Paula Heimann, "Obituary," *IJPA* 44 (1963): 230–33; and Lois Munro, "Obituary," *IJPA* 44 (1963): 233–35.

15. On racialization of psychoanalytic universals, see Weinbaum, *Wayward Reproductions*, 145–86.
16. See Park, "Behind Our Masks," 134–39. Notably, when it first appeared in *Survey Graphic* (1926) the essay was illustrated by a series of photographs of Japanese masks that resemble "Nipponese" and the masks in "The Beginning of the 'Age of Masks.' "
17. This figure is more fully developed in Park, "Human Migration and the Marginal Man."
18. Ibid., 893.
19. Yu discusses Park's focus on Flora Belle Jan, a San Francisco flapper, in *Thinking Orientals*; see especially 19–20, 25–26, 29–30, 67–68, 97–98.
20. Park, "Behind Our Masks," 136 (emphasis added).
21. Ibid.
22. All quotes from ibid., 137.
23. Ibid., 138 (emphasis added).
24. Park, "Race Prejudice and Japanese-American Relations," 228.
25. Park, "Racial Assimilation in Secondary Groups with Particular Reference to the Negro," 70.
26. Park, "Behind Our Masks," 139.
27. See, for example, Park, "Racial Assimilation in Secondary Groups with Particular Reference to the Negro," "Mentality of Racial Hybrids," and "Negro Race Consciousness as Reflected in Race Literature."
28. Park, "Behind Our Masks," 254.
29. See Cappetti, *Writing Chicago*, 22, 31.
30. Park, "Negro Race Consciousness," 285.
31. Larsen, *"Quicksand" and "Passing."* Hereafter Larsen.
32. Wall, *Women of the Harlem Renaissance*, 85–138.
33. On the importance of Larsen's and her protagonist's biraciality, see Hutchinson, "Nella Larsen and the Veil of Race," and "Subject to Disappearance."
34. There is much excellent criticism on *Quicksand*. I am especially indebted to that on aesthetics, fashion, and consumption. See Hostetler, "The Aesthetics of Race and Gender in Nella Larsen's *Quicksand*"; Lutes, "Making Up Race"; Roberts, "The Clothes Make the Woman"; Goldsmith, "Shopping to Pass, Passing to Shop"; and Muzak, " 'The Things Which Money Could Give.' "
35. Larsen, 1.
36. Larsen, 2.
37. Ibid.
38. Larsen, 3. With this phrase excerpted from Booker T. Washington's "Atlanta Compromise," a speech often regarded as proof of Washington's acquiescence to the "separate but equal" rhetoric solidified in the U.S. Supreme Court's ruling in *Plessy v. Ferguson* (1896), Larsen directly criticizes Washington's accommodationist posture.
39. Larsen, 18.
40. Ibid.
41. Ibid.

42. Larsen, 56.
43. Larsen, 59 (emphasis added).
44. Ibid. Many critics have focused on Helga's conflicted sexual expression. See, for example, Carby, *Reconstructing Womanhood*, 174.
45. Artists and writers used primitive aesthetics and artifacts to enable modernism. Such (ab)use of primitivism has generated heated debate. See, for example, Torgovnick, *Gone Primitive;* Barkan and Bush, *Prehistories of the Future*, 270–89; and McCabe, "The Multifaceted Politics of Primitivism in Harlem Renaissance Writing," 475–97.
46. Larsen, 74.
47. Larsen, 73, 69, 69, 73, and 70.
48. Larsen, 74. It would have been transparent to contemporary readers that Larsen's portrait of Helga in Copenhagen references the real-life escapades of Baker. Although Baker's masquerade as "savage" enchantress garnered her European fame, she never received a similar reception in the United States. See Wall, *Women of the Harlem Renaissance*, 103–11; and Martin, "Remembering the Jungle."
49. Larsen, 83 (emphasis added).
50. Larsen, 87.
51. Larsen, 133.
52. Larsen, 135 (emphasis added).

7

All-Consuming Nationalism

The Indian Modern Girl in the

1920s and 1930s

PRITI RAMAMURTHY

In the 1920s and 1930s, Sulochana, Queen of the Screen and Star of the Stars, lived life big and boldly as a cinema actress in Bombay, then a cosmopolitan, vibrant, and growing metropolis. A Modern Girl, Sulochana was sexy and provocative; she was long-limbed (or made to look so) and sported bobbed hair, dark lipstick, mascara, and long, painted nails. At times she wore Western-style dresses, pants, hats, and shoes (figure 7.1) and at others she wore saris, Indian-style jewels and braids (figure 7.2). Enormously popular (*lokpriya*), Sulochana was Indian cinema's first "sex symbol," the "girl all men would want to love."[1] Newspapers and film magazines featured photographs and stories about her, especially her passionate on and off screen romance with the actor Dinshaw Bilimoria. Sulochana's name was emblazoned on theater marquees and her image circulated widely via autographed studio shots, postcards, and advertisements for soaps and cosmetics. In 1926, her life story was made into a film, *Telephone ni Taruni* (Telephone Girl), and in 1934 she acted in another film, the eponymous *Sulochana*. She drove around in a white Bentley (and later the slinkiest of Chevrolets) and earned the princely sum of five thousand rupees per month — more than the British colonial governor general of

7.1 Studio portrait of Sulochana dressed in Western suit and hat. National Film Archive of India.

Bombay. Between 1925, when she started acting, and 1937, Sulochana made fifty-two movies, of which many were *bax affice* (box office) hits. Adoring fans lined the streets for hours to get a glimpse of her; they showered her with gifts and pursued her with offers of marriage. Nonetheless, "lonely and forgotten" Sulochana died in relative obscurity in 1983.[2]

There is, to my knowledge, no scholarly study of Sulochana nor of the many other *sitaras*, starlets of the silent movies and early talkies in India who became well-loved symbols of modernity in the 1920s and 1930s. Popular film histories, which usually begin by gesturing to Sulochana and the many other sitaras, contend that they were displaced for quite simple reasons: with the coming of sound in 1931, actresses who couldn't speak Hindustani—a syncretic mixture of Hindi and Urdu which became the most widely used language of film in India—no longer had a role to play.[3] By the late 1930s they were replaced

7.2 Studio portrait of Sulochana dressed in Indian sari, *bindi*, and braids. National Film Archive of India.

by actresses who not only spoke Indian languages as their mother tongues but were more "cultured," educated, and professionally trained, actresses like Devika Rani, the grand-niece of the famous Nobel laureate and Indian nationalist leader Rabindranath Tagore. So convincing is this narrative that in popular film histories it is Devika Rani who is fondly remembered as "the first lady of the Indian screen," even though twelve years prior to her debut in 1933 another sitara, Patience Cooper, had been the first Indian woman to act in an Indian film.[4] What accounts for such profound cultural forgetfulness? Why and how were some women marginalized while others were elevated to the status of national icons? What are the stakes in asking these questions today? What could feminist scholars gain from studies of the Modern Girl in India?

In this chapter I address these questions by studying the Indian Modern Girl, especially the sitaras of early film and the identities of womanhood they inhabited and represented. The Indian Modern Girl of the 1920s and 1930s offers new insights on the relationship between gender, nationalism, and modernity in the crucial years prior to India's freedom from British colonialism in 1947. In the process of nation building, nationalism in India had to define Indianness, represent the nation symbolically and linguistically, and garner ideological support to mobilize large numbers of people for anticolonial political action. Like other nationalisms, it did this by constituting the Indian nation through gender difference and constructing normative notions of femininity (and masculinity) through forms of national belonging.[5] Often, nationalisms appeal to invented "traditions" to assert difference and inspire feelings of belonging, but insofar as nationalism is a form of modernity, nationalism in the colonies had simultaneously to assert its difference from Western modernity, which was, after all, the modernity of the colonizers. In India, the struggle to reconcile the desirable aspects of Western modernity with the need to assert Indian difference was addressed through processes of gendering.[6] The Modern Girl in India is one example of these processes of gendering. Through her identity, women negotiated what it meant to be modern women and Indian in the 1920s and 1930s.

By retrieving the history of sitaras, I trace how the actresses of early film creatively appropriated, engaged with, and challenged Western modernity. This exercise of retrieval simultaneously clarifies how the boundaries of difference — gender and racial difference, in particular — became defined and solidified in the cause of modern nationalism in India. It reveals a struggle over how women could (and could not) be symbolized and represented in the process of enunciating the nation-in-the-making. As we will see, this struggle and the eventual hegemony of nationalism expressed around the Modern Girl came about through the coming together — the articulation — of quite unexpected and contradictory forces.[7]

Furthermore, the chapter deploys the Modern Girl as a heuristic device to question the continuing nationalist bias in the writing of popular history today. Nationalist hegemonies, in common with other hegemonies, are defined in struggle and are always rather fragile; maintaining them takes continuous cultural work which endures into the present. I argue that the historical eclipsing of the Indian Modern Girl is an effect of an all-consuming nationalism in two senses: as a historical process that provided a dynamic space for some Indian women to be modern actors in the 1920s and 1930s but eventually shored up a hegemonic nationalism, and as a continuing tendency in popular film histories to eclipse these alternative and more complex stories about gender, nationalism, and modernity. The chapter concludes with a discussion of the import of these findings for feminists and feminist historiography.

A Note on the Archive

The first cinema show was held in Bombay in 1896, a few months after its introduction in Paris, to packed houses, including special sections for ladies in purdah (domestic seclusion). Shortly thereafter Indian businessmen imported films and set up cinema tents in the major cities; they also sent touring cinemas to small towns and villages. Films started to be produced in India in 1912, and the industry grew rapidly in the 1920s. More than thirteen hundred silent films were produced from 1912 to 1931, when the first talkie was released. Hindustani became the lingua franca of "national" Indian film, in a subcontinent with sixteen major regional languages. During the 1930s, many of the most popular silent movies were remade as talkies. Due to the high cost of converting cinema houses for sound projection, silent movies were shown alongside talkies throughout the 1930s. Unfortunately, only a handful of these early silent films and talkies survived. The bulk of them were "photographed and printed on highly combustible nitrate-based stock and has [sic] either gone up in flames in warehouse fires or crumbled to dust in rusty old cans in forgotten lofts."[8] Nevertheless, synopses of the films have been compiled by film scholars, and I rely on them here.[9]

My research on sitaras focuses on actresses who worked for the major film studios — Imperial, Kohinoor, Madan, Ranjit, and Sharada — in Bombay, Poona, and Calcutta in the 1920s and 1930s. By the late 1920s, in response to the newly created identity of "cinema fan," film stars were photographed for newspapers and magazines, contests were held to judge the most popular film star, and a market for signed studio photos and postcards thrived. The stars themselves were widely gossiped about. They responded in signed and "anonymous" articles and letters.[10] This chapter draws on photographs and secondary materials collected in the National Film Archive of India, Pune, and sitara biographies pieced together from the scholarship of film historians.[11]

A rich primary resource for this chapter was the Indian Cinematographic Committee's report of 1928.[12] The committee was set up by the British colonial government to address its concern about the declining popularity of British films in comparison to Hollywood and with the effect of Hollywood's vulgar depictions of white women on Indian audiences. Based on an extensive survey and interviews with hundreds of fans, actors and actresses, film directors, distributors, journalists, and concerned citizens, some of which are excerpted verbatim, the *ICC Report* provided me with a treasure trove of material on the Modern Girl and early Indian cinema.

I have relied, as well, on primary materials from two of the most widely circulated English newspapers, *The Statesman* and the *Times of India*, and, in particular, a magazine, the *Illustrated Weekly of India*, for the period 1920–42.[13] Although these papers and magazines were mainly read by British and Indian English-educated elites, they contained numerous photographs and film and commodity advertisements which relied heavily on visual cues and thus were probably looked at by those who were not fluent in English. Moreover, the magazines were certainly read aloud to non-English speakers. The *Illustrated Weekly* regularly printed commentaries by and about Indian cinema stars, as well as snippets on Hollywood, European, and other foreign stars. Columns offering fashion, sports, and beauty tips were a regular feature, and the magazine ran cinema, beauty, and photography contests. In fact, the *Illustrated Weekly* was praised by Sulochana for supporting "the cause of the Indian film industry" when "very few other journals of standing have given any such support."[14]

Worldly and Wicked

In the 1920s and 1930s, going to the cinema was a popular activity in India. Working classes in the metropolises and Indian and European elites all viewed films in the cinema halls that proliferated from colonial city centers to the suburbs and to the neighborhoods where industrial workers lived. Indian middle-class women, formally in domestic seclusion, filled the *zenana* or "women only" sections of the growing number of movie halls. Cinema halls were thus places that were shared across the differences of class, race, religion, and gender. How movies were experienced by these diverse audiences may have varied considerably. Anxieties about this open-endedness of film led to the demand for censorship, as we will see.

Cinema audiences had a choice of Hollywood, British, and Indian films. "As regards the relative popularity of Indian and Western films there is no doubt that the great majority of Indian audiences prefer Indian films," the *ICC Report* concluded.[15] The earliest Indian films were "historicals" and "mythologicals": they reworked stories of the past and of gods and goddesses to create a historical and imaginative self-consciousness of something "Indian," native not foreign. By the mid-1920s, however, another genre of films, "socials," had become popular. It is a subsection of socials, movies with "worldly and wicked themes," which I propose to identify as Modern Girl movies.[16] Modern Girl movies included *Cinema ki Rani* (Queen of Cinema), 1925; *Typist Girl* (also called *Why I Became a Christian*), 1925; *Vamp*, 1926; *Telephone ni taruni* (Telephone Girl), 1926; *Bambai ki Bili* (Wildcat of Bombay), 1927; *Indira B.A.*, 1929; *Gunasundari* (also called *Why Husbands Go Astray*), 1934; *Cinema Girl*, 1930; *Daily Mail*, 1930; *The Wronged Wife*, 1930; *The Enchantress*, 1930; *A Woman's Vengeance*, 1930; *Miss 1933*, 1933; *Indira M.A.*, 1934; and *The President*, 1937. Describing how they were different from mythologicals, a commentator in the *Times of India* wrote, "So ancient heroes and serene goddesses are for the future to be replaced by vamps and bucket-shop men, and instead of battle and sudden death there will be beauty and badinage. It is a thoroughly reasonable experiment since battles are tedious things, and if Bombay demands vamps and golden haired home-breakers as a relaxation, it may as well have some homegrown ones."[17]

Indian film historians have failed to recognize how important Modern Girl movies were to representing and recasting the possibilities for modern women in India. In them women were the protagonists who explored the complexities of modernity facing middle-class households by questioning and transgressing gender boundaries. Many featured rebellious, even libidinous wives, who portrayed new relationships with in-laws and husbands, demanding that they share in housework, for instance. Women exercised individual autonomy and the freedom to choose partners; they rejected the authority of older brothers, uncles, and fathers. In the process, they reinvented what it meant to be sister, daughter, wife, and daughter-in-law. "Love" marriages, heterosexual romance, and overt female sexuality were all celebrated in these films. So was kissing, as this exchange between a prominent newspaper editor and the ICC reveals:

Q: With regard to kissing, do Indians not kiss?

A: Not in public anyway.

Q: Most of the scenes shown on the screen are scenes from private lives. If you are going to debar that and love scenes from Indian pictures, are you not taking away the pith of the picture?

A: I do not say take away the love scenes . . . Kissing may be here and there, but not indiscriminate kissing. You have got the long kiss, the prolonged kiss, the hot kiss, the soft kiss, all sorts of kisses.[18]

Kissing in Modern Girl movies is significant in the history of Indian cinema because later, from the 1940s until the 1990s, it was deemed inappropriate and entirely prohibited.

Not only were heterosexual romance and amorous desire commonplace but Modern Girl films featured vamps and prostitutes who were morally ambiguous heroines rather than villains. In others, the fluidity of gender was explored through women masquerading in multiple roles, some of which were traditionally male. In *Wild Cat of Bombay* (1927), for example, Sulochana played a medical student and a mysterious do-gooding criminal who performed eight roles, including those of policeman and European blond. In Modern Girl movies, women accessed modern institutions — educational, juridical, and administrative — to explore the world outside their homes and to demand social justice. College girls (*kallege ladki*) were at the center of several movies, usually enmeshed in complicated love-triangles. "Night clubs . . . Turkish Baths . . . College Life of Girls" reads an ad for *Telephone Girl* that appeared in the *Times of India* in 1927. The Sulochana silent-movie hit *Indira, B.A.* (1929) about a college girl was so popular it was remade as a talkie, *Indira, M.A.* (1934). Several movies were about women who were employed in new urban professions, those of cinema star, telephone operator, typist, teacher, and doctor; one was even the president of a textile mill! In short, in Modern Girl films women were convincingly *modern*, they lived in a metropolitan world, they were members of a cosmopolitan set, and they partook in the institutions and pleasures of modern life, whether commercial employment or heterosexual romance, at college, in the city, or at the cinema. This was so much the case that often the radical disruption caused by women breaking gender codes and transgressing conventional social norms was contained, within the narrative of the films, by having Modern Girl heroines meet a violent end, a common motif in Modern Girl films around the world.

Modern Girl films trafficked in global notions of modern womanhood and so too the sitaras who acted in them. The actresses, particularly their bodies, were a dense node of multidirectional citation.[19] The Indian Modern Girl's predication in English through general terms like "romance ki rani" (romance queen) and "college ladki" (college girl) speaks to this borrowing. Particular stars also acquired English prefixes, as in "Glorious" Gohar, "Sultry" Sultana, "Loveable" Shahzadi, and "Talkie Queen" Zubeida. Many of the photographs of Modern Girl cinema stars in the *Illustrated Weekly* were of them in London,

7.3 "Stars from East and West": Newsphoto of Seeta Devi with Pola Negri in Paris. *Illustrated Weekly of India,* 1930.

7.4 Studio portrait of Patience Cooper with bobbed hair and kiss curl autographed in 1933. National Film Archive of India.

Paris, the United States, Russia, China, and Japan, as, for example, in an image of the actress Seeta Devi with the American movie star Pola Negri (figure 7.3). In another news report covering her trip to Europe in 1929, Seeta Devi was identified as "the brightest star in the Indian cinema world" with "millions" of followers in England, Germany, Poland, and Austria.[20] Patience Cooper even won a beauty contest in England.[21] And Sulochana was extolled as the "Ideal of Womanhood . . . Beauty combined with youth and flavored with Intelligence," comparable to the Venus of Milo, "a universal Ideal of womanhood . . . recognizable by every member of a European, American, or Indian nation."[22]

It was through multidirectional citation that Modern Girl actresses referenced aesthetic regimes from elsewhere. The familiar and global body aesthetics of Modern Girls the world over are recognizable in a studio shot of Patience Cooper, with her bobbed hair, kiss curl, plucked eyebrows, and bold lipstick (figure 7.4). In another image, Patience Cooper was posed lying sexily on a couch, with her arm raised in the angular "Z" reminiscent of depilatory cream ads (figure 7.5).[23] Often, the Modern Girl was depicted romancing in intimate, heterosexual love scenes (figure 7.6), or she appeared in scenes where she gazed deeply into the hero's eyes, her lips close to his. In another still, from the movie *Indira, M.A.,* Sulochana displayed an androgynous look, dressed in

7.5 Studio portrait of Patience Cooper lounging with arm raised in "Z" pose. National Film Archive of India.

7.6 Film still of Sulochana romancing with Dinshaw Billimoria in *Bambai ki Billie* (Wildcat of Bombay, 1936). National Film Archive of India.

a masculine suit and posed in front of that international symbol of modernity, a motor car.

Popular current Indian film histories read these narrative and visual representations as Modern Girl cinema stars mimicking Hollywood "in mannerisms and appearance."[24] B. D. Garga writes, "The imitation of Hollywood permeated most aspects of Indian film production, the star myth included. If in Hollywood, 'America's sweetheart,' Mary Pickford initiated the star era, in India, it began with the beautiful Sulochana . . . With her mercurial charm she could slip under any skin at will, be it that of Theda Bara, Lillian Gish or Pola Negri."[25] However, the "Hollywood look" the Indian Modern Girl was ostensibly imitating was itself global, as aesthetic styles, designers, and commodities crisscrossed the world appropriating and reconfiguring elements from all over.[26] Moreover, the recognizably internationalized image of the Indian Modern Girl existed side by side with representations that were more hybrid. In a studio portrait of Sulochana (figure 7.2), for instance, the plucked eyebrows and painted lips and nails were combined with the bindi (the dot on the forehead that signifies women as Hindu), pearl bangles, and dangling earrings, and the short bobbed hair was replaced by long braids arranged around her head. In a studio shot of "Glorious" Gohar (figure 7.7), her bobbed hair, large eyes, and mascara-laden eyelashes referenced Clara Bow, the famous American movie star widely acknowledged as the "It" girl, but the sari, bindi, and pearls were from a visually Indian cultural palette. Similarly, in a studio shot of the sultry Jahanara Kajjan (see figure 7.8), whose *"spectacular beauty was her wealth,"*[27] the actress wore makeup, mascara, finely shaped lips, and bobbed hair but even though she wore no bindi (her name reveals she is Muslim), her sari and nose ring signified her aesthetic hybridity, neither purely Western nor purely Indian.

The Indian Modern Girl was particularly innovative in the creativity she brought to sari and sari-blouse wear. At a time when most middle-class urban women wore saris that reflected regional specificity (as in figure 7.9), the Modern Girl was innovative and cosmopolitan. In fashioning herself she absorbed, mingled, and transformed several styles — modern and "traditional," Western, East "Asian" and Indian. Her stylish attire cut across religious signifiers as well. Saris were draped, often Parsee style, over the right shoulder not the left and clipped into place with fancy jeweled brooches (see figures 7.4 and 7.5). Sari blouses were sleeveless (see figure 7.2), "cut-outs," or, on occasion, trimmed with frills and flounces, even, sometimes (as in *The President* for the young and unmarried woman who played the tough cotton mill owner) with shirt collars! The material of the saris was sensual, trendy, often imported — see-through georgette, crepe-de-chine, silk-voile, and chiffon with sari blouses in lace (see

7.7 Studio portrait of Gohar with Clara Bow-like mascara, dressed in Indian sari and pearls. National Film Archive of India.

7.8 Studio portrait of Jahanara Kajjan with bobbed hair, nose ring, and lace sari blouse. National Film Archive of India.

figure 7.8), with sequins (see figure 7.2) or embroidery. In yet another display of multidirectional citation, the embroidery was at times reminiscent of chinoiserie. In sum, the Indian Modern Girl was coded and coded herself as a global and Indian modern through the hybrid fashioning of her body, her body language, and her sartorial zest.

The Modern Girl was different from other recastings of modern womanhood in pre-independent India. She was noticeably unlike the *bhadramahila*, a regional prototype of the respectable Indian woman, who, scholars of colonial Bengal argue, inhabited a procreative, middle-class femininity within the terms of heterosexual marriage.[28] The bhadramahila identity selectively adopted bourgeois, Western domestic norms; women were expected to be modern progenitors and companions to their educated husbands, but they were defined against the excesses of Western modernization and Westernized women.[29] The Modern Girl sitara, in contrast, was never photographed with her children or her husband and appropriated, rather than rejected, Western codes of modernity.

Women Picketing Foreign Cloth Shops

Women volunteers parading in the cloth market area in Bombay and urging the boycott of foreign cloth.—"I. W."

7.9 News photo of women in the anticolonial movement picketing foreign cloth shops in Bombay. *Illustrated Weekly of India*, 1930.

As importantly, the Indian Modern Girl was visually distinguishable from another recasting of women in the colonial period, the archetypical New Woman. Iconized as the spiritual, self-sacrificing bearer of a higher capacity to withstand pain, especially that of British aggression, the New Woman fought in the nonviolent, anticolonial struggle. She expressed her agency on the streets protesting foreign consumption, especially of cloth and foreign fashion (see figure 7.9).[30] Conversely, the Modern Girl embraced and reworked fashions from elsewhere.

On the difference between the Modern Girl and the New Woman in India, no less a figure than Mohandas Karamchand Gandhi weighed in. In the progressive paper, the *Harijan*, he wrote: "I have a fear that the modern girl loves to be Juliet to half a dozen Romeos. She loves adventure . . . The modern girl dresses not to protect herself from wind, rain and sun but to attract attention. She improves upon nature by painting herself and looking extraordinary. The nonviolent way is not for such girls."[31]

In Gandhi's view, Modern Girls were girls who were self-fashioned through artifice; they were sexually overt and prone to multiple romantic affairs with members of the opposite sex. After thus characterizing them, he pronounced them unfit for participation in the Indian national movement for independence, with its leitmotif of nonviolence. This is significant because it was Gandhi who had specifically mobilized women for anticolonial protest by suggesting they were more capable of sacrifice and braver than men.

Eleven "English-educated" college girls, to whom Gandhi's missive in the *Harijan* was directed, wrote back: "The modern girl, it seems, has provoked you to the extent that you have disposed of her finally as one playing Juliet to half a dozen Romeos. This remark which betrays your idea about women in general is not very inspiring . . . You yourself have come in contact with quite a number of modern girls and may have been struck by their resolution, sacrifice and other sterling womanly virtues."[32]

The girls challenged Gandhi's restriction of the Modern Girl to the identity of "Juliet." They also questioned his conclusion that girls who were modern could not simultaneously be brave protestors in the independence movement. By suggesting that Gandhi's division of women into those who can and cannot participate in "the non-violent way" is symptomatic of his ideas about "women in general," the girls highlighted how Gandhi's notions of gender were constructed and narrow. Their muddying of the difference between the Modern Girl and the New Woman, and their stinging critique of the "father of the nation" notwithstanding, the question of who could represent the nation as a desirably modern and Indian woman grew increasingly fraught as Indianness came to be a major social identity established through multiple forms of political agitation and cultural production in the 1930s.[33]

The "Homegrown" Sitara

Sulochana's meteoric rise to stardom in the 1920s and 1930s came from seemingly nowhere. The story goes that she was working as a "convent [Christian missionary school] educated" telephone operator when a director spotted her and asked her to act in his film. Film acting was not a "respectable" profession at the time, especially for women from "well-to-do," "good" families, so Sulochana turned him down several times. After he pursued her relentlessly, she gave in, and her first movie, *Birbal* (1925), was a hit. She went on to earn, among other monikers, that of Sulochana the Supreme.[34]

Sulochana was the nom de plume of Ruby Meyers (1907–83). She is identified in most film histories as Anglo-Indian or Eurasian and in others as "a Jewess of European extraction."[35] Not just Sulochana but Patience Cooper, Seeta Devi, and nearly twenty other Modern Girl actresses are all categorized as Anglo-Indian. According to the *ICC Report*: "Indian women of the better class do not take up film-acting as a profession . . . Owing to the difficulty of obtaining suitable Indian actresses some Anglo-Indian girls have adopted the profession and several of them play Indian parts with considerable success and are among the most popular 'stars.' "[36] For Anglo-Indian actresses, racial difference was both the condition for women to enter a disreputable profession and the condition for reworking it.

During British colonialism, "Anglo-Indian" was a fluid term of racial difference. In the nineteenth century it referred to all British people in India; "Eurasian" was the term for people born of relationships between Indian females and British, Armenian, Dutch, French, Flemish, Portuguese, Prussian, Spanish, or Italian males or their descendents. There was a long period, from the mid-seventeenth century until the first anticolonial war in 1791 (the Haitian revolution against French colonizers), during which British and other European men had been encouraged to marry Indian women. It was only in the mid-nineteenth century, with the rescinding of travel restrictions on British women, that these racial intermarriages more or less ceased.[37] Throughout the nineteenth century and until World War I, another form of interracial union took place, the relationships between lower-ranked British soldiers and the Indian women who provided them with sexual services in *lal bazars* (red light districts) set up by the colonial government.[38] In the 1911 census of India, these different genealogies merged when "Anglo-Indian" was generically redefined as any person "formerly known as Eurasian, country-born or half-caste . . . whose father or any other male progenitors in the male line is or was of European descent"; with the same stroke, maternal ancestors, usually Indian, and sometimes going back as far as the seventeenth century, were written out of the definition.[39]

Poor Anglo-Indians were treated as an embarrassment by the British colonial government and, therefore, as a population in need of state support.[40] In the late 1890s, and again in 1920, the government recommended that Anglo-Indian girls be educated to take up service jobs in nursing, teaching, department stores, and domestic service. Hostels, known as working girls' hostels, were set up to provide them with a place to live and to police their morality. Educated and English-speaking, Anglo-Indian women got jobs as nurses and teachers and, in the new commercial establishments of Calcutta and Bombay, as stenographers, secretaries, telephone operators, and department store clerks. They also worked in the entertainment business in itinerant Western-style bands, musical comedy shows, dancing troupes, and revues. "Western dress, work and the freedom to choose whom they wanted to marry" were the self-identified markers of Anglo-Indian difference.[41] These prior histories and transitional labor identities were important antecedents that prepared Anglo-Indian women to become cinema actresses.

While paid employment was an important element of Anglo-Indian women's self-identity, sitaras became popular icons through their malleability. Most Anglo-Indian and Jewish actresses, like Ruby Myers, took on Hindu names. Renee Smith became Seeta Devi, Iris Gasper became Sabita Devi, Beryl Clausen became Madhuri, Marcia Solomon became Vimla, Esther Victoria Abraham became Pramila, and so on. Moreover, they did not just change their names but, as we have seen from the studio portraits and newspaper images, they wore bindis and jewelry which signified that they were Hindu and sometimes they posed as Hindu brides or married women. Patience Cooper, an Anglo-Indian star, dressed in a sari and a Hindu bindi, with her arm raised in the familiar "Z" pose, graced an Eid greetings card replete with the Urdu couplet,

> Since the nights of separation, I long for a glimpse of you.
> It's like the burning sun, this Eid moon.[42]

A second route to cinema acting for women was via the *kothis*, the houses of courtesans where girls were trained to be dancers, singers, and stage actresses. In the early twentieth century, the mostly Muslim courtesans of Lucknow inhabited a transitional class identity, caught between feudal patronage and colonial Victorian values; they were a group whose "immorality" was the grounds for criticism by the new Hindu middle class of upwardly mobile men.[43] Modern Girl actresses who were the daughters of courtesans, in common with Anglo-Indian actresses, carried the baggage of the close connection between their mothers' prior presence in the public eye and their sexualization. The *ICC Report* surmised, "With few exceptions (mostly in Bengal), the actors and actresses are not drawn from the cultured classes. The actresses are mainly recruited from the 'dancing girl' class."[44]

The hybrid images of Gohar (figure 7.7) and Jehanara Kajjan (figure 7.8) demonstrate how Muslim actresses, too, frequently transgressed the religious borders between Western and Indian, Hindu and Muslim, in their attire, body fashioning, and the roles they played.

There is other evidence of the Modern Girl actresses' fluidity between multiple religious and racial identities. One film historian suggests that both Renee Smith and her sister Percy Smith passed for the actress Seeta Devi (see figure 7.3), named after the virtuous wife of the Hindu god Ram.[45] Extolling "her" virtues, a reporter for *Illustrated Weekly* commenting on Seeta Devi's European tour in 1929 wrote: "Rightly she is named Seeta Devi—for Seeta is the sweetest figure in the Indian [i.e., Hindu] Pantheon and has been enshrined

with such notable charm and loveliness in the pages of Indian classical literature."[46] In the same interview, Seeta Devi's own reflection on her Indianness is
less saccharine, more bittersweet. Critiquing the racism of foreign producers,
she writes:

> I have never used either grease paint or water paint in any of my pictures . . . I quite agree
> that I appear much darker on the screen than I actually am. Unfortunately, there is a false
> notion lingering in the minds of the foreign producers that all Indians should and must
> be dark. But then people of North India are very fair — some of them are almost as fair as
> the Westerners themselves. Especially the Mogul princes who hailed from regions of
> Central Asia, and their women-folk are very fair indeed. I do believe, therefore, that
> foreign producers would be well-advised to use more discretion in the matter.[47]

Paradoxically, even as Seeta Devi critiques the racism of foreign producers, she
engages in another kind of racial and gendered mythologizing. She may have
been a Hindu icon of Anglo-Indian descent in India — for, as was also true of
other actresses, her nom de plume was never secret — but abroad she was unequivocally "Indian." At home, this fluidity proved increasingly difficult to
sustain.

By the late 1930s, the Indian Modern Girl cinema icon and Modern Girl film
story lines had faded from popular cinema culture. Many early actresses were
displaced. Patience Cooper acted in sixty-six films between 1920 and 1937 but
just two more after that; Seeta Devi made fifteen films, all between 1922 and
1932; Sulochana acted in fifty-two films between 1925 and 1937 but just
seventeen more in the next nearly forty years. It is possible that they were less in
demand as they aged; however, they were not replaced by look-alikes but by
the new *Bharat nari*, or respectable Indian woman.

Increasingly, film storylines were more didactic and "Indianized," with Indianness signified by woman as a good wife, now in the modern role of companion within the confines of heterosexual, middle-class marriage. Typically, a
heroine's desire for modernity was restricted to serving her modern husband
better, rather than through the assertion of individual choice or autonomy.
The actress Pramila recounted: "The story of *Mother India* was part of an
effort to create a true Indian woman as against a modern westernized one. [In
it I] played the role of the bold, westernized, Indian girl educated abroad
who finally realises the greatness of being a *Bharat nari*."[48] The antiheroine
was more narrowly defined as Westernized and "bad," typically a vamp. This
"gradually institutionalised the hierarchies between mother, wife and vamp."[49]
Western dress, in particular, was symbolically loaded as alien to Indianness and
as colonial. The multidirectional citation or borrowing from global cultural

circuits to visualize "Indian" women's bodies and to tell stories of "Indian" modernity decreased (though in terms of music and dance it continued). The hegemony of a seemingly all-consuming Indian nationalism achieved by the late 1930s was an effect of the articulation of unexpected and contradictory forces.

Imperial Interests and Indian Nationalist Modernity

One of the unexpected and contradictory ways in which the hegemony of Indian nationalism was articulated emerged from British concerns over declining earnings in India. By the end of World War I, over 85 percent of the films imported into India were from the United States. Hollywood established its dominance in movie making because most European countries had to cut down on producing celluloid, which was made from the same material as explosives, during the war. For Indian cinema houses, Hollywood films were also much cheaper to rent than European or even Indian films because their costs were distributed across a by-now global network. Starring silent screen actresses including Mary Pickford, Norma Talmadge, Clara Bow, and Pola Negri, and their male counterparts Douglas Fairbanks and Rudolph Valentino, these films were immensely popular in India (as were the action serials and spectaculars of Charlie Chaplin and Harold Lloyd). In 1918, fearful of heightened competition from Hollywood for British films in India, the British colonial government brought cinema directly under state control. After 1920, when the Indian central administration was financially delinked from London, import tariffs became a major source for raising revenue; an entertainment tax was instituted on cinema, the highest-grossing import industry in India, in 1923. In 1927, still unable to stem the Hollywood tide, and at the behest of the Federation of British Industries, who wanted a protected market, the British colonial government set up the ICC, an advisory committee of bureaucrats and influential citizens.

The ICC was established, as well, out of British imperial concern with Hollywood's depictions of lascivious white women and lurid sex. In the opening pages of the *ICC Report* a well-known bishop "intimately acquainted with India" is quoted from a speech he gave in Britain in 1925: "The majority of films, which are chiefly from America are full of sensational and daring murders, crimes and divorces, and on the whole, degrade the white women in the eyes of Indians."[50]

The pages of *Times of India* in the late 1920s and early 1930s were replete with criticism of the "sex, spectacle and sensationalism" of Hollywood films and how they lowered the prestige of white women and, therefore, the white races in India. "Uneducated" Indians of the "laboring" classes, it was argued in many of these newspaper articles, editorials, and letters, were especially likely to "misinterpret" these overtly sexual images.[51] British imperial feminists, who were members of the British Hygiene Delegation and the National Council of Women in Burma (Burma was part of India until 1937), called to testify before the ICC, were vehement in their criticism and blamed Hollywood for "lowering the standard of sex conduct and thereby increasing the dissemination of disease."[52] In other words, a broad bloc of British colonial business, religious, and women leaders wanted to restrict Hollywood so as to gain an economic advantage or to assert strategies of imperial rule that preserved racial boundaries through the management of sexual desire. Their joint hope was for the ICC to suggest the stringent censorship of Hollywood films. The British desire for film censorship was as much about preventing the use of cinema by Indian directors in the anticolonial cause; actual deletions from Hollywood and Indian films by the Board of Censors were to references to "liberty" and "freedom."

But T. Rangachariar, the Indian lawyer who was put in charge of the ICC by the British to appease Indian nationalist demands for more Indian representation in government, did not comply with this request for censorship. He approvingly quoted an editorial in the *Times of India*, "American films certainly should be fought by British competition but to try and suppress them by hypocritical pleas for Imperial welfare is merely ridiculous"[53] Additionally, he dismissed the British Social Hygiene Council as "ill-informed" and instead endorsed the opposing testimony of Directors of Public Health in India and the Indian Federation of University Women, consisting of Indian academics who held that there was no link between films and an increase of sexually transmitted diseases.[54]

Instead of censoring Hollywood, Rangachariar insisted that Indian filmmakers and Indian audiences were being undermined by Western films, under which he clubbed *both* British and Hollywood imports:

> American civilization is as much Western civilization to them as British civilization. Both are foreign . . . If too much exhibition of American films is a danger to national interest, too much exhibition of other films is as much a danger . . . if, in fact, the exhibition of Western films is doing some mischief in the country the best remedy would seem to be to encourage Indian films to take their place.[55]

Rangachariar recognized film as a potent new medium by which to transmit ideas of modernity in the cause of the Indian nation-in-the-making. Although he was appointed by the British colonial government, in the quotation above he redefined "national interest" to mean Indian nationalist, not British imperial, interest. In addition, he was determined to develop the Indian film industry on economic grounds, arguing, "India has got her own film industry which . . . requires to be protected, guided and encouraged. It is in its infancy and it is vital to the national interest that the indigenous industry should be encouraged in every way."[56] As importantly, Rangachariar wanted to realize the potential of film as a visual, cultural form to educate "the lower classes." He wrote:

> This is art worthy of the attention of cultured men. Moreover, they will be doing national work by propagating Indian ideas and ideals and interpreting Indian literature, history and traditions. But it is not merely as producers that cultured people are required; educated men and women must be induced to act for the film. At present there is a sort of stigma attached to film-acting because the actresses (and to a less extent the actors) are not drawn from the respectable classes.[57]

The putative "Indian" subject, to be instructed through film to be desirably national and modern, could not, in Rangachariar's view, be well served by current actresses. Paradoxically, while Rangachariar rejected the view that Hollywood films led to interracial sex and the spread of disease, he fell back on stereotypical depictions of early actresses as "Anglo-Indian girls" and "dancing girls," unfit for the all-important job of nurturing cultural nationalism. Popular film histories praise Rangachariar as a hero of Indian cinema today, but they do not credit him with laying the ideological grounds for the displacement of Modern Girl actresses in the late 1930s. Their project is as constitutive of an all-consuming nationalism today as Rangachariar's was in the past.

Nationalism Redux

In popular Indian film histories, three reasons are usually put forth to explain the eclipsing of early Indian film sitaras by the late 1930s: First, with the introduction of superior lighting, not the earlier eye-level lighting which reflected off whiter skin more effectively, and with better cameras, the fairer skin of early Indian stars was no longer advantageous. Second, with the coming of sound, being able to speak a native language and to sing became critical, so those actresses who could not speak Hindustani or sing did not transition. Third, "superior" actresses,[58] "educated," Hindu girls from "respectable families" like Devika Rani, Durga Khote, and Shantha Hublikar, all "Brahmin [the highest caste], no less," entered the profession.[59]

All three narratives presume that many early actresses were Anglo-Indian. As one film history puts it, "Most of the stars of the Silent Era had been 'Anglo-Indians' or 'Eurasians' as Europe called them. The community had sent an endless stream of pretty girls into the industry. The introduction of sound literally changed the complexion of Indian screen personalities."[60] Popular histories also claim that Anglo-Indian sitaras only knew what one calls "Kaisa hai" Hindustani and another "atpati-chatpati" Hindi,[61] that is, pidginized Hindi. This ignores the fact that some Anglo-Indian stars like Sulochana took time off to learn or relearn the language. In fact, she made seventeen movies in Hindustani after 1938 until her last one in 1978.[62] Other Anglo-Indian stars, including Madhuri and Sabita Devi, made a number of very popular talkies, all in Hindustani.[63] Pramila proudly remembers a casting session when she "surprised them all by learning her dialogues perfectly."[64] She knew Bengali, Hindi, and other Indian languages and went on to make twenty-three films from 1939 to 1961 (in addition to twelve previously).

The transition story put forth by popular film historians is also complicated by the fact that not only did some Anglo-Indian stars transition well but some Muslim stars, who knew Hindustani and could dance and should therefore have had no difficulty continuing to act, had to drop out. Zubeida, who had created a sensation by acting in the film *Zarina*, with its eighty-five kisses, was edged out by what she called "the increasing conservatism in films"; she left to get married.[65] Despite the suggestion by film histories that Muslim cinema stars transitioned well, in fact the most globally modern and erotic of them were eased out.

The uneven transition of Modern Girl cinema stars through the 1930s reflects in part the growth and economics of the studio system. Studios were organized, Hollywood style, with directors and actors, technicians, and office workers all on their payroll. They bore the entire costs of film production. As the urban, cinema-viewing population increased and the number of studios grew, there was increasing competition for a share of the market. Actresses were much more likely to be cast to type. Sulochana continued to play the glamorous working girl in her silent film hits that were remade as talkies in the mid- to late 1930s and were very popular, but Gohar was increasingly cast more narrowly as a docile wife. With the proliferation of studios and the competition between them that followed, the need for big stars to sell movies increased and the impulse to manufacture the image of the stars became more explicit.[66]

In 1939, the *Illustrated Weekly* ran a series on film personalities that actively reconstructed actresses as good "respectable" national icons, as Bharat naris. In one article, Glorious Gohar, now respectfully called Goharbai Mamajiwala (*bai* is a suffix in Marathi affixed to married women), was represented as a "good" woman character through the assertion that there was "nothing 'actressy' . . . about her; and that she was "doing her bit to making her profession a respected one." Non-"actressy" behavior was described as Gohar's not smoking or drinking and spending her time reading "biographies, fiction and religious literature."[67]

Another feature in the series on the actress Devika Rani traced her antecedents to not only her great-uncle Rabindranath Tagore but also her doctor father, the surgeon general of an important state in the colonial empire.[68] She was celebrated for traveling to London to study art and for acting in plays, highly acclaimed all over Europe. Her success in making Indian movies in English was seen as enhancing the "prestige of the Indian screen in the eyes of foreigner." By 1939, acting had become professional work, which "trailblazing" upper-caste Hindu women had to be educated into and worked extremely hard at. In other words, acting was being recoded as acceptable work.

But for acting to be recoded as respectable, the "private" lives of the stars had to be aligned as properly modern as well. So, unlike Sulochana, whose breakup with her on-screen and off-screen lover was posited as one cause for her decline, Devika Rani was posed gardening at home "at an unpretentious little villa in a Bombay suburb."[69] She was also shown on horseback. In another profile, Shobhana Samarth — a "most cultured Maharashtrian girl" — was similarly constructed as one who had saved acting from being the career of disreputable women.[70] Again, her credentials, like Devika Rani's, rested on her patriline: she was the daughter of a highly educated man, a banker with a Ph.D.; she too had widely traveled since childhood to the United States and Europe and even alone to China and Japan; and she worked hard at her craft of acting. A third actress, Sadhona Bose, was described as "having a well-won reputation as a danseuse," not a dancing girl. She was the daughter of a "barrister of the Calcutta high court, a family well-known for its culture. Her grandfather was the great social and religious reformer, Keshub Chandra Sen, who founded the Brahmo Samaj." Sadhona Bose's dance is portrayed as drawing not from the kothi dances or Muslim courtesan traditions but from the "Hindu" "expressive movements" of Manipuri, Kathakali, and Kathak.[71] Like the others, she was pictured reading a book.

Newspaper profiles were one site where the Modern Girl sitara was recast as a worthy nationalist symbol; advertisements were another. By the late 1930s, multinational and local companies featured photographs and signed endorsements of select actresses in their advertisements for soaps, snows (face creams), and other commodities. One of the first companies to advertise so was Palmolive "beauty soap," which ran four ads featuring Devika Rani in 1939. In figure 2.9, for example, Devika Rani appears with her head modestly covered, an icon of national and modern Indian womanhood of the right kind.

Thus, by the late 1930s the imagination of an "Indian" nation was achieved by symbolically orchestrating a certain kind of respectable modern Indian womanhood. In the popular film history *Looking Back*, the representation of Anglo-Indian sitaras as those who "identified with the ruling British . . . and modeled themselves on the ruling [Hollywood] deities of the day,"[72] or what the film historian B. D. Garga calls their "anglicization," reinscribes a nationalist viewpoint. The national recasting of the sitara is part of a more general forgetfulness about the past that is needed to achieve and sustain a "national" memory. Forgetting, as Renan argues, is crucial in the creation and imagination of nations.[73]

Conclusion

This chapter retrieves the Indian Modern Girl of early cinema for the scholarly record and celebrates her existence as a vibrant social persona. Headily modern, feminine, sexy, and distinctively global in her multidirectional citation, she was enormously popular with directors and fans of all classes, if for a brief time from the mid-1920s to the late 1930s. Through a body language of dress, makeup, deportment, and fashionable accessorizing, and new ways of being and belonging, the Modern Girl of early cinema became a popular icon of gendered modernity in India.

But beyond her retrieval for the historical record, the Modern Girl as a heuristic device brings to light important aspects of Indian nationalism. By connecting her displacement to the articulation of unexpected and contradictory forces, this chapter underscores the interplay between colonial and nationalist intellectuals on moral and market grounds from the late 1920s on. British demands for revenue in India and for moral policing in the face of American hegemony were overwritten by Indian nationalist bureaucrats and Indian film producers trying to expand the Indian market for film and to germinate feelings of Indian national belonging. In the process, the specificity of the Indian nation was constructed by inscribing gender and class through new standards of conduct suited to India, mandating cultured actresses of good reputation for the proper education of the masses.

The Indian Modern Girl draws attention to the racial politics of nationalism. Although India is not usually characterized as an internal racial formation, one in which race is a social feature that ascribes different positions to social groups based on phenotype ascription, the Modern Girl reveals how race was socially loaded. The Indian preference for "fair" skin is one way that perceptual differences between groups in India are hierarchized. The Anglo-Indian Modern Girl, whose whiteness loses luster in nationalist histories of film with the switch to sound, points to the specific conditions which make this form of distinction "socially pertinent, historically active."[74] As racial hybrids, Anglo-Indian actresses mark the recalcitrant difference at the heart of not just colonialism but nationalism, the fragility of binary oppositions at its foundation.

For Indian feminism, which has long had to respond to the charge of Westernization by nationalists, the Modern Girl provides a fresh lens on the cultural politics of gendered modernity in India by offering an account of how nationalist historiography depoliticizes race. The otherwise admirable feminist scholarship on India that pays heed to race has focused on British imperial feminists, on the representation of Indian men's sexual proclivities toward white women, on how Indian women who traveled abroad disrupted racial narratives, and on the articulation of race through familiar discourses of civilization, Christianity, hygiene and science.[75] This chapter adds to this body of research by focusing on the relationship between the conditions under which light-skinned actresses in the 1920s and 1930s entered a new public realm and their depiction in nationalist history and historiography as racially mixed and morally dubious. Instead of blaming the sitaras' poor language skills and more advanced filmmaking technologies, we are now in a position to understand the grounds on which early actresses could be eclipsed in the nationalist construction of the "cultured" upper-caste stars.

The Modern Girl also provokes attention to "sexual economies" in the new urban profession of acting that marginalized women filled. Mary John and Janaki Nair's otherwise path-breaking anthology *A Question of Silence: The Sexual Economies of Modern India* does much to shatter "the conspiracy of silence surrounding sexuality" in India but curiously omits any mention of interracial sexual relations except a passing reference to Indian prostitutes of British soldiers.[76] Similarly, there is mention of mines, mills, plantations, and family farms as sites where new sexual economies emerged but no treatment of the urban occupations that Anglo-Indian women newly filled — as nurses and teachers and as typists, stenographers, office receptionists, telephone operators, and cinema stars. The laboring Modern Girl elucidates how interraciality was one of the conditions for entry into a public domain in new urban spaces which were feminized.

This chapter has traced how the Indian Modern Girl made her flamboyant and very public appearance in the 1920s and 1930s as the cheeky, cosmopolitan, and seductive sitara of early Indian film. By highlighting the fluidity with which the sitara crossed religious and racial boundaries and incorporated aesthetic and performative practices drawn from across the globe and a distinctly Indian cultural palette, a new view of the history of gendered modernity in India emerges. Indian Modern Girl sitaras labored in the new urban economy and actively articulated and reworked what it meant to be Indian and modern women; they were widely embraced by all classes. By the late 1930s, sitaras—in reality and representation—were troublesome to a nationalism that sought to draw boundaries around proper Indian womanhood. In quite unexpected ways, nationalist hegemony regarding what a Bharat nari was and who could represent her was secured by the coming together of British and Indian moral and market interests. Contemporary histories of film, which describe the sitara as a mixed-race fleeting phenomenon, a poor mimic of Hollywood, and an anglicized figure (so implicitly pro-Western and colonial), today continue the cultural work of hegemonic nationalism. By deploying the Indian Modern Girl as a heuristic, one that recapitulates the struggle through which the sitara was displaced, this chapter has questioned contemporary nationalist historiographies as well. The Indian Modern Girl's troublesomeness to hegemonic nationalisms then and now make her not just politically important for Indian feminism but endearing.

Notes

1. Garga, *So Many Cinemas*, 42.
2. Upper Stall Web profile, http://www.upperstall.com/people/sulochana.html (visited on 9 January 2003).
3. *Looking Back*; Tamrakar, *Parade ki Pariya, 1913–1990*; Garga, *So Many Cinemas*; Raheja and Kothari, *Indian Cinema*.
4. Raheja and Kothari, *Indian Cinema*, 35.
5. Sinha, *Gender and Nation*.
6. Chatterjee, "The Nationalist Resolution of the Women's Question."
7. Hall, "Race, Articulation and Societies Structured in Dominance."
8. *Looking Back*, 26.
9. Rajadhyaksha and Willemen, *Encyclopaedia of Indian Cinema*.
10. "The Stars Speak" section in *Indian Cinema*, 101–15.
11. Bhaumik, *The Emergence of the Bombay Film Industry, 1913–36*; *Looking Back*; *Indian Cinema*; Garga, *So Many Cinemas*; *Flashback*; Raheja and Kothari, *Indian Cinema*; Mohan, *Of Wayward Girls and Wicked Women*; Tamrakar, "Film Tarikaon ki Aakaashganga"; Majumdar, *Female Stardom and Cinema in India, 1930s to 1950s*; Rajadhyaksha and Willemen, *Encyclopaedia of Indian Cinema*.
12. *Indian Cinematographic Committee Report, 1927–28* (hereafter *ICC Report*).
13. I could not possibly have done this newspaper and magazine research without the able assistance of Michelle Acupanda, Amy Bhatt, Amanda Berman, Serena Maurer, Sarah McKay, Dipika Nath, Amy Piedalue, and Gazelle Samizay. Thanks are also due the Modern Girl Project research assistants: John Foster, Katrina Hagen, Kristy Leissle, Teresa Mares, Rebecca McColl, and Helen Schneider.

14. "Indian Film Work as a Career," *Illustrated Weekly of India* (hereafter *IW*), 13 October 1929.
15. *ICC Report*, 22.
16. Garga, *So Many Cinemas*, 46.
17. *Times of India*, 8 February 1926.
18. *ICC Report*, quoted in *Looking Back*, 41.
19. Modern Girl Around the World Research Group, Introduction.
20. *IW*, 30 June 1929.
21. "Some Stars in Their Eastern Courses: English Beauty Queen," *IW*, 3 March 1935.
22. Oscar A. Fernandes, "Sulochana," *Filmland*, 11 July 1931, 10–11.
23. Peiss, "On Beauty . . . and the History of Business."
24. *Looking Back*, 21.
25. Garga, *So Many Cinemas*, 55.
26. See chapters 1 and 2 in this volume.
27. Tamrakar, "Film Tarikaon ki Aakaashganga," 16.
28. Chatterjee, *The Nation and Its Fragments*.
29. Sinha, *Gender and Nation*, 22.
30. Kumar, *The History of Doing*; Forbes, *Women in Modern India*.
31. Gandhi, *Women and Social Injustice*, 68.
32. Ibid., 69.
33. Ludden, *India and South Asia*.
34. *Looking Back*, 41.
35. Garga, *So Many Cinemas*, 55.
36. *ICC Report*, 5.
37. Blunt, *Domicile and Diaspora*.
38. Ballhatchet, *Race, Sex, and Class under the Raj*.
39. Blunt, *Domicile and Diaspora*.
40. Hawes, *Poor Relations*.
41. Blunt, *Domicile and Diaspora*, 65.
42. Eid greetings card from Mohan, *Of Wayward Girls and Wicked Women*, 5. My thanks to Cabeiri Robinson for translating the couplet.
43. Joshi, *Fractured Modernity*.
44. *ICC Report*, 5.
45. *Encyclopaedia of Indian Cinema*, 84.
46. "Queen of the Indian Screen," *IW*, 30 June 1929.
47. Ibid.
48. Shahani, *Pramila*, 10. This is the 1938 version of *Mother India*, not the more famous 1957 version starring Nargis.
49. Mohan, *Of Wayward Girls and Wicked Women*, 22.
50. *ICC Report*, 3.
51. "The Cinema and the Child," *Times of India* (hereinafter *TOI*), 17 July 1924; "The Cinema of Crime," *TOI*, 7 February 1925; "Entertainment Tax Not a Real Hindrance," *TOI*, 16 November 1927; "American Films in India: Harmful Effects," *TOI*, 16 October

1927; "Present Censorship of Sex and Crime Films Adequate," *TOI*, 15 November 1927; "The Cinema Inquiry," *TOI*, 12 November 1927; "Indecent Films," *TOI*, 11 July 1934; "Discrimination and the Cinema," *TOI*, 24 November 1934.

52. *ICC Report*, 116.
53. Ibid.
54. Ibid.
55. Ibid., 99.
56. Ibid., 100.
57. Ibid., 47.
58. Raheja and Kothari, *Indian Cinema*, 20.
59. *Looking Back*, 62.
60. Ibid., 41.
61. Raheja and Kothari, *Indian Cinema*, 25; Tamrakar, "Film Tarikaon ki Aakaash-ganga," 19.
62. Rajadhyaksha and Willemen, *Encyclopaedia of Indian Cinema*, 207.
63. Raheja and Kothari, *Indian Cinema*, 30; Tamrakar, "Film Tarikaon ki Aakaashganga," 11, 13.
64. Shahani, *Pramila*, 9.
65. Quoted in Garga, *So Many Cinemas*, 53.
66. Garga, *So Many Cinemas*.
67. "Glorious Gohar," *IW*, 23 July 1939.
68. "Devika Rani Daughter of the Soil," *IW*, 6 August 1939.
69. Ibid.
70. "Sophisticated Shobhana Samarth," *IW*, 20 August 1939.
71. "Her Planet's in the Ascendant," *IW*, 3 September 1939.
72. *Looking Back*, 41.
73. Renan, "What Is a Nation?"
74. Hall, "Race, Articulation and Societies Structured in Dominance," 52.
75. Burton, *Burdens of History*; Sinha, *Colonial Masculinities*; Grewal, *Home and Harem*; Robb, *The Concept of Race in South Asia*.
76. John and Nair, Introduction.

8

The Dance Class
or the Working Class

The Soviet Modern Girl

⌒

ANNE E. GORSUCH

A 1928 cartoon in the Soviet satirical magazine *Bich* (*Rowdy*) showed a young couple dressed in flapper fashions dancing the Charleston (see figure 8.1). "So Vasia, what class do you consider yourself coming from?" one partner asks the other. Vasia responds, "Frankly speaking, — the *dance-class!*"[1] In contrast to rough-and-ready young working-class girls who wore "leather jackets, crumpled skirts, and patched shoes," fashionable young women in revolutionary Russia wore bright red lipstick and narrow-toed high-heel shoes, bobbed their hair, and shortened their skirts.[2] This chapter explores the formation of the Soviet Modern Girl in the particular social and political conditions of revolutionary Russia, her eager adoption of flapper dress and love of popular dance, and official anxieties about her un-Soviet and uncivilized behavior. In the 1920s, a period of great transition and revolutionary construction, dress had more than just symbolic meaning. As Lynn Hunt explains in her history of politics and culture in revolutionary France, clothing, colors, and other outward symbols "did not simply express political positions." Rather they were the "means and ends of power itself," because to have power "meant to have some kind of control, however brief, over the articula-

8.1 The dance class or the working class? *Bich,* 1927.

tion and deployment of outward manifestations of the new nation."[3] Like the
French revolutionaries, the Bolsheviks themselves contributed to the power of
the everyday with their constant efforts to create new signs and symbols for the
Soviet state. But while this preoccupation offered new possibilities, it also
offered unexpected challenges.

A history of the Soviet Modern Girl asks us to reconsider the usual discourse
of difference between authoritarian East and capitalist West as it reveals profound connections and continuities between Russia and the West even under
communism. These connections were especially evident during the New Economic Policy (NEP, 1921–28), a period of relative cultural and economic relaxation when global cultural information about "modern" dress and behavior
crossed even the formidable borders of the new Soviet Union. Indeed, young
lovers of fashion were sometimes called "NEPkas" (NEP girls), a term which
emphasized their connection to the economic extravagances and "decadent"
Western-influenced cultures of NEP. From the early nineteenth century on, Russian upper classes had emulated French and English fashion, and by midcentury journals such as *Moda: Zhurnal dlia svetskikh liudei* (*Fashion: Journal
for Fashionable People*) had contributed to the beginnings of a Russian consumer culture.[4] For this reason, post revolutionary youth were sometimes pe-

joratively described as "aristocratic," as in Vladimir Slepkov's hostile account of Moscow's "golden youth," those "elegant and pensive youth people who can dance the foxtrot so well . . .[who] drink champagne in cut-glass goblets with toasts to all of that is 'elevated and beautiful.' "[5] The bodies of Soviet Modern Girls — the clothes they wore and the exotic dance movements they engaged in — were visible reminders of threats to a healthy communist body politic from both the past and the present. Their behavior was especially contentious in the 1920s when anxious representations of Soviet Modern Girls were part of the struggle to define what a communist ought to be like.

My focus is primarily on representations of Soviet Modern Girls, rather than on what girls said about their own desires and experiences. It is difficult to find more than the occasional example of a Modern Girl's own voice, a common if unfortunate problem for scholars of girl culture, and one exaggerated in the authoritarian Soviet Union. Sources of both representation and experience include fashion magazines, advertisements, popular literature, and travel accounts. Also useful are the publications of Soviet educators, psychiatrists, and criminologists who were energetically engaged in the 1920s in a social science of society (*sotsial'naia nauka*). Party and Communist Youth League (Komsomol) representatives were also involved in this process of observation and instruction. Indeed, the publications and the agitational activities of the Komsomol were particularly important. As the central organization for communist youth, the Komsomol used education and agitation to explain how new social relations were to be structured and how young communists were expected to behave. All of these Soviet "experts" were part of a project to make youth communist in every aspect of their daily lives, and their descriptions of youth culture were usually proscriptive. As they articulated their understanding of the moral, social, and economic causes of improper behavior, experts took an active role in constructing the identities of the youth they described. I have called those involved in this effort to transform behavior and belief "Bolshevik moralists." They were not an organized cohort, however, nor were they were simply presenting a party line. Many were members of the party or Komsomol, but others were not. Most were older than the youth they were describing, but some young people were themselves actively involved in the disciplining process.

Dress and Dance

For communists committed to the revolutionary remaking of everyday life, the playful pleasures of dress were evidence of deviance and even opposition. At issue was the particular meaning pleasure and well-being had in the unsettled and contentious environment of the 1920s. Modern Girls exemplified aspects of NEP (prosperity, material pleasures, even luxury) that made many committed communists uncomfortable. Introduced in March 1921 and ending in 1928 with the introduction of the Stalinist project of collectivization and rapid industrialization, the New Economic Policy was intended to provide a "breathing space" for a Soviet society traumatized by war, revolution, civil war, and famine. The economic disarray stemming from the civil war and the weariness of a war-torn population imposed a new timetable on the transition to Soviet socialism. Socialism was now to be built gradually through cultural work rather than through political and military struggle. As part of this process, and in order to help feed and clothe the population, limitations on private trade were reduced, a highly centralized economic system was replaced by a freer market, and control over state cultural production was lessened. These policies were controversial. Some Bolsheviks supported NEP, either because, like the party theoretician Nikolai Bukharin, they believed that the modern course of NEP was necessary for rebuilding, or because they benefited financially or professionally from the expansion of state bureaucracy under NEP. Others saw the policies of NEP as an unwelcome retreat from the more aggressive and fast-moving policies of the period of War Communism. This was especially true when they were confronted with·the economic contradictions of NEP. Expensive food and clothing stores, flashy nightclubs, gambling casinos, and other manifestations of the changing economic climate resurfaced.[6] At the famous "Eldorado" in Leningrad, Soviet citizens could listen to "the wild caress of a jazz band," and when they finally stumbled from the restaurant at two in the morning, they could hail a cab with a fancy horse-drawn carriage to take them home. According to one angry Bolshevik, some areas of Leningrad were so full of fancy cabarets and cafes that they were starting to resemble New York's Seventh Avenue.[7] With the legalization of private trade came a resurgence of entrepreneurs (NEPmen). Some peddled goods on the street, and others opened small clothing and food stores, cafes, and restaurants. Private traders lined the streets selling everything from furs and velvet dresses to Singer sewing machines and Kodak cameras. Soviet newspapers ran advertisements for corsets, fashion magazines, fancy shoes, and pianos next to notices about the latest books on problems of everyday life and contests for the best enterprise.[8]

These brief advertisements aside, the principal sources of cultural transmission to revolutionary Russia remained different from those in capitalist countries. Multinational corporations, international advertising campaigns, and the mass media did not function in the USSR as they did in many other parts of the global community. If elsewhere advertisements were key sources of transnational ideologies of gender and consumption, in Soviet Russia most advertising in the 1920s was deployed as a political tool to sell state-approved or state-sponsored goods. Advertisements for bourgeois goods and services were printed as a pragmatic, if unwelcome, response to the need during NEP for newspapers to support themselves financially.[9] In Soviet Russia it was foreign visitors, Hollywood movies, and to a lesser extent domestic fashion magazines, that were the most important source of international styles.

Western travelers, including cultural figures, journalists, but also ordinary tourists were welcomed to the Soviet Union as a form of informal diplomacy and ideological promotion. Although the numbers were few, descriptions of their visits — together with photographs — were often prominently depicted in the Soviet media. When American movie star Mary Pickford toured the Soviet Union in 1926, her every move was described in the Soviet screen press.[10] Some fortunate Soviet citizens enjoyed first-hand encounters.[11] As one visitor to Soviet Russia described: "I have had [young people] feel feverishly my foreign clothes, hat, frock, sample the material, stroke the silk, almost pull my underwear from under my blouse in their frenzied hunger."[12] Dance enthusiasts flocked to dance the fox trot and the black bottom to the tunes of traveling American jazz bands. The fox trot was introduced with new vigor to Moscow and Leningrad right after the war by "fifty fox-trotting college boys" working for the American Relief Administration. The Charleston came to Moscow in 1926 (only months after it was introduced in Paris) via a variety revue act called The Chocolate Kiddies.[13] Soviet institutions capitalized on this appeal. The self-financing requirements of NEP forced clubs, restaurants, and movie theaters (as well as other enterprises and industries) to generate their own income rather than relying on state subsidy. Soviet dance acts and jazz bands soon advertised their acts as "American," knowing that this attracted a larger crowd.[14] The Soviet poster artists Vladimir and Georgii Stenberg designed a constructivist montage to advertise the "Negro-operetta" The Chocolate Kiddies, in which a black woman in very short flapper attire and bobbed haircut sat center stage flanked by two "Harlem swells" in tuxedos. "Sam Wooding jazz band, orchestra, chorus [girls] and ballet," the poster reads.[15]

Movies were another way that cultural information traveled across the border between East and West in the 1920s. Self-financing requirements forced the Soviet film studios to rely on the income generated by more popular foreign imports to help support their own nascent efforts. From 1921 to 1931, about 1,700 American, German, and French films were imported into the Soviet Union.[16] The favorites were foreign films with the great early silent film stars: Mary Pickford, Douglas Fairbanks, Harold Lloyd, and Charlie Chaplin. "American films dominate, inundate, glut, overwhelm the Russian motion picture houses today," wrote a troubled (American) observer; "Clara Kimball Young has a theater devoted solely to her in Moscow. In the Arbat, centre of the workers' quarters of the Russian capital, a new building celebrates the glory of Douglas Fairbanks in electric letters three feet high."[17] To attract patrons some commercial theaters resorted to "bourgeois" attractions such as expensive and well-stocked buffets, free coat rooms, and even orchestras that serenaded moviegoers with the latest European and American dance music.[18] Famous costume designers like Adrian of Hollywood created the screen images of innumerable Hollywood stars who then served as role models for young Soviet viewers. Young women "cut back on everything else, so that they can 'look like their screen heroes,'" complained Bolshevik moralist Ivan Bobryshev in 1928.[19] Girls were said to admire Mary Pickford, because she made even rags look like a princess's dress. "She was enchanting . . . although she wasn't especially pretty, she made us believe that she was very beautiful," explained one young Russian woman.[20]

Some of the urban population's information on the latest styles and dances did not come directly from abroad but from Russian-language fashion magazines, which provided European images for the Soviet reader. Two popular magazines were *Mody* (*Fashions*) and *Mody sezona* (*Fashions of the Season*), both of which were published monthly in Moscow.[21] A 1924 issue of *Mody* showed models in soft, full dresses that were very feminine. The young women wore large, wide-brimmed hats, often with feathers or flowers, and leaned languorously against elegant balconies, or strolled in the park holding fancy parasols. Others wore fancy beaded party gowns that were clearly meant for elegant evening parties, not for the neighborhood Komsomol club.[22] By the late 1920s, *Mody sezona* displayed the type of clothing more typically associated with the active and physically fit young Modern Girl (see figure 8.2). The lean, boyish figures wore short dresses that fell just below the knees and their bobbed hair was covered by close-fitting cloches set with ribbon or rhinestones. In the winter issues they were shown in sleek, fur-trimmed coats, and in the summertime in simple dresses with abstract patterns influenced by the artistic avant-garde. As pictured in these pages, the adventurous and independent young woman of the postwar years had a busy social life and needed the right kind of clothing for every occasion. In summer 1928, *Mody sezona* described "the kind of dresses that Parisian women take with them when they go to their summer houses," and the proper outfits for a game of tennis or a drive in the car. The daring young Modern Girl of the modern era might even take an airplane flight, for which she needed a leather aviator's cap and glasses like the ones shown in the spring issue of *Mody sezona*.[23] Soviet fashion magazines were a few years behind their Western counterparts; in the United States and Western Europe, skirts were at their shortest a few years previous.[24] The delay is not surprising; some of the images are exactly the same as those in the Parisian

531. Костюм из светлой шерстяной или бумажной материи. Отделан светлой материей и вышивкой.

532. Пальто из шерстяной материи, кроится прямое, отделано суташем.

533. Пальто из светлого сукна. Отделано клетчатым материалом.

8.2 Flapper fashions in a Soviet fashion magazine. *Mody sezona*, 1928.

émigré journal *Illiustrirovannaia Rossiia* (*Illustrated Russia*) and may have been taken from it. That magazines were published with images—be they domestic or foreign—which were so at odds with the modest, working-class lifestyle advocated by Bolshevik authorities is a vivid example of the kinds of cultural contradictions that NEP enabled.

While young people of means in Paris or London could buy flapper fashions in the latest *grand magasin* or department store, those Soviet youth who could afford to buy clothes were limited to a small number of privately run shops like the popular Moscow stores "Paris Fashions" and "Viennese Chic."[25] The weekly theatrical magazine *Novyi zritel'* (*New Spectator*) published small advertisements for these shops, including one for fancy hats, coats "in the Parisian style," and shoes in the "latest foreign models" (see figure 8.3). Many of the choicest shops in postrevolutionary Russia were to be found in out-of-the-way pri-

8.3 Advertising shoes in the "latest foreign models." *Novyi zritel'*, 1927.

vate apartments whose secretive, backstairs qualities distinguished them from the noise and flamboyance of West European department stores. Advertisements sometimes included apartment numbers, as in the *Novyi zritel'* advertisement for Taranskaia Street, apartment number 15, where one could buy "coats, suits, and items in fur" all in "Parisian styles" (see figure 8.4).

Most young people could not afford to buy the kinds of luxuries sold in private shops or apartments, but they still did their best to imitate them. This was not particular to Russia. One historian of modern fashion notes that the typical chemise dress of the Modern Girl was easier to reproduce at home than earlier fashions had been because it used so little fabric and was so shapeless.[26] Young women in Soviet Russia used fashion magazines to try to reproduce the styles of New York and Paris at home with whatever hard-won materials they could find in public markets or Soviet stores. Journals like *Home Dressmaker* printed clothing patterns "necessary for every family and every woman."[27] The American visitor Dorothy Thompson noted that young women who were unable to afford expensive imported items bought "imitation silk stockings, lip

8.4 Advertising coats "in the Parisian style." *Novyi zritel'*, 1927.

stick and Soviet substitutes for Coty products — made by the Chinese."[28] By the late 1920s, girls could buy inexpensive Russian lipstick, still considered a bourgeois vice but so popular that it was now produced by a government monopoly.[29] Soviet "reproductions" did not always match the originals because of limited materials, but also because of the subtle "Soviet" tweaks sometimes made to them, as seen in the picture of the "young flapper" captured by an American visitor, E. M. Newman, on his trip to the USSR in the 1920s (see figure 8.5). The short coat shows an effort to imitate the basic silhouette of the flapper but the meaning of the kerchief is more ambiguous. The kerchief knotted behind the head may have been the best this young woman could come to a close-fitting cloche. Alternatively it may have symbolized her "Sovietness"; in the revolutionary iconography of the 1920s and 1930s, a kerchief tied in front denoted an unrevolutionary, peasant "baba," while one tied in back signified a revolutionary enthusiast.

As this suggests, interest in flapper fashions and the fox trot was not limited to the children of NEPmen or the Soviet shop girl. It is true that some of the youth drawn to imitate these "decadent" Western fashions were the wealthy children of private entrepreneurs who feverishly shopped and traded, knowing that the right to do so was temporary and subject to increasing restrictions. However, many of the young people who were attracted to the Western fashions pictured in magazines and in Hollywood films were from the working class. In her sketches of working class "womenfolk," Ekaterina Stogova described factory girls as "avid followers of fashion and primpers" wearing "stylish checked caps, and coquettish yellow shoes, and beige stockings."[30] Even those who did not make much money wore "nice dresses specially made for them, and always carefully ironed."[31] Young communist girls were not immune. Some Komsomol girls kept the leather jackets of the civil war period, thinking this demonstrated their revolutionary devotion, but other communist youth succumbed to the lure of fashion and suffered to do so. One young Komsomol woman who made sixty-five rubles a month working in a factory was said by an appalled Bolshevik observer to spend two-thirds of it on "manicures, cosmetics, silk stockings, and dance parties."[32] Komsomol activists in the Red Triangle factory reported that there were many cases of female workers who "literally starved be-

8.5 The homemade style of a Soviet Modern Girl. E. M. Newman, *Seeing Russia*, 1928.

cause they spent all of their wages on silk stockings, makeup, and manicures," while the newspaper *Komsomolskaia pravda* described young women working in another factory who wore "fashionable" low-cut dresses and "scanty shoes that pinched their toes."[33]

Also popular among communist and noncommunist Modern Girls was dancing. To the dismay of Bolshevik moralists, dancing the fox trot and the tango seemed to take place everywhere: in restaurants, in schools, on the street, and in Komsomol clubs. "So far the only place where they don't dance the foxtrot," wrote one worried observer, "is on streetcars and in cemeteries."[34] When allowed (and it was deeply controversial), dancing was one of the most popular activities in factory and young communist clubs. Although a dance hall near Red Square was named after a famous prerevolutionary club for the Moscow elite — the "Yacht Club" — most of the members were tradespeople and many wore "communist pins in their buttonholes." Instead of caviar and champagne, the club served sandwiches and ice cream in the intermissions.[35] Factory clubs even sponsored evening balls for young people, and posters advertising these dances were plastered on the walls of trade union and factory clubs.[36]

Some young people chose to dance away from the watchful eye of communist inspectors. Many of the most exclusive dance clubs met in private apartments. Some were secret hideaways, open only to those who knew the right password. Like jazz music or the sultry rhythms of the tango, these underground places may have had a special kind of appeal due to their vaguely illicit qualities.[37] More commonly, young people danced at small parties held in their apartments or the apartments of friends. They gathered in tiny rooms, pushing the furniture to one side, or simply dancing around the tables and chairs while the latest tangos from Paris played on the gramophone, or, if there was a piano, someone pounded out the fox trot. Popular novels from the 1920s described the lively atmosphere of these parties, where young men and women drank vodka and ate whatever poor appetizers of cabbage salad or cold fish their host could provide. In a small space cleared in the middle of the room, they danced the fox trot or the Charleston.[38]

Imaginative Desires

Although the images shown in American movies presented a lifestyle few if any Soviet citizens could achieve, they encouraged young consumers to buy or make certain kinds of clothing by making an association between clothing and lifestyle, suggesting to young people that wearing the right kind of clothing could lead to a more desirable way of life. As Rosalind Williams has argued about the capitalist West, magazines, movies, and department stores make a link between "imaginative desires and material ones," between "dreams and commerce."[39] The question is how to understand and interpret the persistence of such desires in a postrevolutionary Soviet environment.

For some young women, the light-hearted qualities of "bourgeois" amusements appear to have been antidotes to the traumas of war and revolution and the postrevolutionary problems of poor housing, hunger, and juvenile unemployment. The political and economic retreat signaled by the introduction of NEP was accompanied by an emotional retreat from the challenges of revolutionary upheaval. As one young woman told the journalist Edwin Hullinger in the early 1920s, "I am trying to live on the surface of life . . . I have been in the depths for five years. Now I am going to be superficial. It hurts less."[40] For this young woman, silk stockings and red lipstick were a manifestation of her desire for easy and enjoyable forms of everyday life. On another level, however, imitation of Western styles can be seen not only as a type of release from the difficult realities of working-class life but as a devaluation of certain "traditional" forms of working-class culture. It seems that fashion-conscious factory youth had internalized the message implicit in some commercial culture that suggested that their own forms of dress, behavior, and language were not as good as those of the middle and upper classes. By imitating the dance and dress of North Americans and Europeans, even as they toiled away in the heat and dust of the factory floor, some young women hoped to appropriate some of the modern independence, chic, and sophistication they associated with shorter dresses and bobbed haircuts. For a minority, this participation in non-Bolshevik culture may even have had more obvious political intent as they insisted on carrying out their lives as closely as possible to what they imagined the prerevolutionary or Western bourgeois experience to be. In the popular novel *The Diary of a Communist Undergraduate,* a young Modern Girl who is challenged by the communist student Kostya defends her interest in dancing in just these terms:

> "So you believe in Communism?" said the Zizi girl. "It's a silly question," said [Kostya] getting up. "I'm a student and a young communist." "Very well! But remember that I believe in God and the foxtrot!" she cried. "And no one — do you hear? — no one can stop me. Do you hear, Young Communist?"[41]

We should not overemphasize the purposefulness of this emulation of the urban classes or the upper classes, however. As Kathy Peiss argues in her history of working-class leisure in turn-of-the-century New York, dress can be a "potent" way to "play" with the "culture of the elite."[42] The notion of play is essential as it reminds us of the pleasure some youth received from dressing up, a pleasure that may have had little deliberate political signification. As the historian Diane Koenker has argued: "Some women defined their class culture differently from party norms: why should not the fox-trot and cosmetics — living freely and looking good — mean 'modern,' not bourgeois?"[43] In other words, "modern" may have had different meaning for those who were wearing the clothes and those watching them being worn: for Modern Girls they signified "up-to-date," for Bolshevik moralists they signified just the opposite.

The Abandonment of Civilized Restraint

Although only a minority of girls may have purposefully used the language and gesture of Modern Girl culture to disrupt the fragile boundaries of Bolshevik desires, young people did not need to be consciously resistant to have a political effect. The politicization of daily life meant that dress and behavior contrary to Bolshevik moralists' own preferences were often seen by anxious observers as alternative articulations not only of the everyday but of the nature of the new state. For committed communists, Modern Girl dance and dress violated cultural and political ideals: they signaled a rampant individualism of personal and cultural expression; they represented the threat of the feminine to the revolutionary project; and they were "immoral" and erotic, sparking fears of sexual excess and uncontrollability.

In contrast to the socially aware young communist who was supposed to sublimate her own desires for pleasure to the wider concerns of society, the behavior of the Soviet Modern Girl seemed to emphasize her rejection of the socialist agenda. Bolshevik moralists worried that for some youth the "culture of clothing" had become "more important than any other question."[44] They condemned the sacrifice of Soviet women to the altar of fashion and they warned girls to protect themselves against its dangers. Indeed, some stories about youth and fashion might best be understood as "cautionary moral tales."[45] In one such story, the protagonist, a young Komsomol worker named Olga P., is said to be "consumed" with clothing. As the moralist Ivan Bobryshev described it, "Class, revolution, construction — these ideas didn't exist; there was a different 'sun' — a skirt." When Olga discovered one day that her favorite velvet skirt was missing, she cried to a friend: "I have no life . . . they stole my skirt . . . In my velvet skirt I looked like the daughter of a nobleman."[46] Olga then committed suicide by drinking a bottle of vinegar essence.

In contrast to Olga, the dedicated young communist of the early 1920s was supposed to be a lover of books, not of fashion (and the books she read were to concern technical topics rather than love affairs). According to the Soviet commissar of health, Nikolai Semashko, the simple, hygienic dress of the revolutionary should be functional (allowing for the proper regulation of body temperature), neat, and clean.[47] Of course, these attributes could themselves be seen as "bourgeois." The key for Semashko was moderation — adopting the clean and cultured culture of the middle classes without, at the same time, expressing too much interest in clothing or good manners. Not everyone agreed. Some Komsomol enthusiasts went to the opposite extreme, advocating a severe cultural asceticism that criticized even the most minimal adherence to traditional standards of cleanliness and neatness, such as a necktie or clean blouse, as unrevolutionary. Indeed, the young female communist enthusiast of early NEP developed a reputation for "dressing like a slob" in order to "show everyone" that she was a communist and not a young woman who adopted the latest feminine fashions.[48] For many enthusiastic young women "outward symbols of masculinity," such as wearing shirts and ties and trimming one's hair like a man's, were associated with women's emancipation and thus "were replete with positive value."[49] While elsewhere the Modern Girl was often seen as a symbol of liberation, to prominent Bolshevik activists like Alexandra Kollontai Modern Girls recalled the dependent, unrevolutionary, and unequal female of the prerevolutionary period.[50]

Not everyone was comfortable with the "masculinization" of communist women, however. Semashko complained about young women with "disheveled, often dirty hair; a cigarette hanging from their mouth (like a man); a deliberately gruff manner (like a man); deliberately rude speech (like a man)."[51] This "vulgar 'equality of the sexes'" was not right, he argued, because women are naturally different from men and have "their own social functions and their own particular characteristics."[52] On the other hand, the feminine excesses of the Modern Girl were also undesirable. For some moralists, what was most dangerous about the Modern Girl was not her supposed lack of revolutionary commitment or dependence but a shocking independence and proclivity toward eroticism. Cosmetics, which were still associated with a kind of moral ambiguity, the new shorter dresses, and bobbed hair suggested degrees of sexual liberation which made some Bolshevik moralists uncomfortable. In a discussion of the meaning of the new style in interwar France, Mary Louise Roberts argues that the short hair of the "femme moderne" was interpreted by many French critics as "evidence of a refusal among women to pursue traditional gender roles."[53] In revolutionary Russia, such a "blurring of sexual difference" might have been thought to be a good one, given the ostensible focus on gender equality. But many Bolsheviks, Komsomol members, and noncommunists alike were still uncomfortable with women's full and equal participation in the cultural sphere, the political sphere, or the sexual sphere.[54] For these individuals, the provocative postwar fashion of the Modern Girl may have played much the same role as it did in France, where it was seen as a threat to "traditional notions of female identity."[55]

The eroticism of the female flapper was especially dangerous because it was thought to distract men from the serious tasks of communist construction. It is true that some young men were also thought to be victims of Western culture and preoccupation with style (they wore tight double-breasted jackets, trousers in the "Oxford" style, and boots called "Jims" ("sapogi Dzhim").[56] But boys were thought to be not victims just of Western culture but of girls who too often used their feminine charms, sometimes augmented by flapper fashion, to distract boys from more important revolutionary tasks. Komsomol newspapers complained about young communists who preferred to go out with "the made-up daughters of NEPmen," rather than the supposedly less attractive, but more communist, Komsomol women.[57] If in real life communist women often complained to Komsomol committees that they were regularly and humiliatingly treated as nothing but sexual objects by young men, in popular novels from the

1920s it was often young women who were held to blame for "sexual hooliganism." In Goomilevsky's novel *Dog Lane*, it is the female protagonist Vera who has multiple sexual partners, sleeping with four different men a week. The "feelings, thoughts, and desires" of these young men were said to be "caught in the web of the huge, white, smug [female] spider called sex."[58]

Dance was thought particularly dangerous in this respect. The tango and other popular new dances rejected the distant and formalized steps of figure dances such as the mazurka in favor of expressive movements and closer contact between men and women.[59] The very nature of the fox trot and tango, their close physical contact and strange, jerky movements were said by some Bolshevik moralists to embody a loss of control and "the abandonment of civilized restraint."[60] The Soviet author Vladimir Lidin described the Charleston as a kind of uncontrollable seizure: "The two girls, linked together, began to twitch their legs as though palsied, and to stamp convulsively in one spot, their knees knocking, and their calves slanting outwards."[61] Anxiety about eroticism, and about overly sexualized youth, was a common trope during NEP when sexual consumption served as a metaphor for social corruption. Like an excessive attention to dress and dance, sexual activity suggested that the individual was out of control (just as the cultural and economic liberalism of NEP threatened to get out of control) and was operating from personal desire rather than collective interest.[62] According to the psychologist Aron Zalkind and the party leader Emel'ian Iaroslavskii, a good communist was to lead a spartan existence, rejecting the opulent pleasures of NEP and abstaining from sexual intercourse.[63] Party and Komsomol disciplinarians argued that instead of dancing, the Komsomol should encourage healthy diversions such as going to the theater and to museums and inspecting factories, all of which would presumably protect youths' physical and ideological "cleanliness." If, despite everything, young people insisted on dancing, then the Komsomol should come up with "dances for the masses" as a healthy form of relaxation that developed physical ability and encouraged a sense of the collective.[64]

Again, not everyone agreed with this assessment. Early Soviet jazz was extremely popular, as was dancing, and not only among noncommunists. The disciplined and sober activities proposed by Bolshevik moralists often led to empty Komsomol club rooms. In a survey in the mid-1920s of over three hundred young people living in Leningrad, A. G. Kagan found that most complained that the Komsomol did "nothing" (of interest) to organize their leisure time. When Kagan made the rounds of Komsomol clubs to see what they offered, he was distressed by how limited their programs were, and by how few young people attended. In the Karl Marx club he found a handful of young people listening to a lecture on the health of women and infants, while the

Red Beacon had an evening program devoted to Chekov that was "boring" and required tickets. Only a club holding a dance was full of young people.[65] Over two-thirds of those surveyed by Kagan said they liked dancing and danced whenever possible, and 11 percent admitted that they had taken dance classes.[66] Pragmatic communists understood that the youth league (and indeed the party as a whole) needed to provide more in the way of "popular" leisure activities if they were not to lose the attentions of the majority of young people. In 1925 the general secretary of the Komsomol, Nikolai Chaplin, condemned what he labeled "absurd communist asceticism," blaming it on militant enthusiasms left over from the civil war. There have been times, he said, "when a guy buys an accordion, plays it and is expelled from the Komsomol, or when a girl who dances is also expelled. This goes too far, comrades. We have to understand that the economic situation of youth is improving, that young people don't just want to sit in meetings and listen to dry lectures about every kind of international and national issue, but want to enjoy themselves, to have fun."[67]

Chaplin's pragmatic approach is a good example of the ways in which popular desires could influence official Bolshevik culture. It is also an example of how in a state in the process of making itself, there remained debates about how best to transform culture just as there were debates about how best to transform politics. Communist youth themselves often remained confused, torn between belief in a stringent revolutionary asceticism and a longing for pleasure. The tension between official proscriptions and the temptations of the popular was captured in another popular novel, *Diary of a Communist Schoolboy*. In the novel, the young hero Kostya asks his friend Sylvia whether she can dance. She says she knows how but claims she does not like to, and yet "her eyes all sparkled, and her face was flushed and her bow hopped up and down to the music." Sylvia then asks to leave, commenting on her way out, "There are all kinds of things one would like to do; but if one did them, where would our ideology come in?"[68]

Anxiety and the Modernizing Project

While the history of the Soviet Union, and indeed of prerevolutionary Russia, has often been portrayed as distinct (read "backwards") from the modernizing trajectories of Western Europe and North America, recent work has begun to challenge this interpretation, arguing that although Russia did not follow the same course to liberal democracy and industrial capitalism, it shared many of the preoccupations common to the modernizing project elsewhere. This included the attempted restructuring of society by the state along scientific, aesthetic, and ideological lines, as well as mass mobilization for political, industrial, and military needs.[69] My work suggests that it was not only the urge to remake society that was shared between the Soviet Union and other modernizing countries but the anxiety provoked when this did not happen easily or uniformly. While many anxieties about Modern Girls were specific to the ideological and cultural challenges of revolutionary Russia, Bolshevik moralists had much in common with their modernizing counterparts in North America and Europe who also worried about the "decadent" behavior of their youth.[70] To adults in both East and West, jazz and the flapper dress that often accompanied it appeared uncivilized, challenging standards of mature, self-controlled, and sober behavior. That many Bolsheviks held standards for public behavior that were similar to those held by Western capitalists suggests that some of their fears were not always specific to socialism but reflected a general anxiety about the meaning of youthful behaviors, styles, and attitudes in the uncertain postwar period. The international reach of the Modern Girl project is an opportunity to explore not only global commodity and cultural flows but the anxiety such global modernization sometimes leads to.

However, a history of the Soviet Modern Girl is also representative of the limits of the economic and cultural integration of the Soviet Union into global processes of modernization and commercialization. The Soviet economy was largely noncapitalist and the ideology focused on the advancement of the collective rather than the satisfaction of individual desire. Many Soviet Bolsheviks strongly objected to those elements of commercialization that did exist, arguing that it was both degrading and immoral.[71] Indeed, the relative openness of the New Economic Policy to the popular cultures of the West only deepened Bolshevik preoccupation with ideological and cultural purity and contributed to the ending of NEP in 1928.[72] In the 1930s and 1940s, the Stalin regime would find different ways to address and contain popular desire by, on the one hand, redefining certain aspects of Western bourgeois culture as acceptably "Soviet," and on the other, forbidding through propaganda and physical force the more provocative aspects of Modern Girl culture, including its associations with autonomy, eroticism, and political opposition.[73]

Notes

1. "Sotsial'noe polozhenie," *Bich* 5 (February 1928): 7.
2. Strogova, "Womenfolk," 282. Also see Grigorov and Shkotov, *Staryi i novyi byt*, 52; Lebina, "Molodezh' i NEP," 12; and Strikhenova, *Iz istorii sovetskogo kostiuma*.
3. Hunt, *Politics, Culture, and Class in the French Revolution*, 3–54.
4. See Goscilo, "Keeping A-Breast of the Waist-Land"; Ruane, "Clothes Shopping in Imperial Russia."

5. Slepkov, "Rytsari skorbi i pechali," 84.

6. See the descriptions in Reswick, *I Dreamt Revolution*, 52, 55; Duranty, *Duranty Reports Russia*, 105–6. Although most of the descriptions of NEP life I discuss here refer to Moscow and Leningrad, other cities in the Soviet Union experienced some of the same changes. In his memoirs, a Komsomol activist sent to work in Rostov-on-Don remembered the busy restaurants with bright signs, the "dissolute variety shows," and the vulgar films of that city in the 1920s. See Mil'chkov, *Pervoe desiatiletie*, 73–74.

7. Tramp, "Pod fonarem El'dorado," 28, 30.

8. Ball, *Russia's Last Capitalists*; Bower, " 'The City in Danger," *Izvestiia* 58–62 (March 1928); Ehrenburg, *Memoirs*, 68.

9. Cox, "NEP Without Nepmen!," 122–125.

10. Youngblood, *Movies for the Masses*, 54.

11. David-Fox, "The Fellow Travelers Revisited," 300–335.

12. Winter, *Red Virtue*, 48.

13. Starr, *Red and Hot*, 55–56.

14. Ibid., 69.

15. See a copy of the poster at http://www.all posters.com/ (visited 10 March 2008).

16. Youngblood, *Movies for the Masses*, 51; Kenez, *Cinema and Soviet Society, 1917–1953*, 39; Youngblood, "The Fate of Soviet Popular Cinema during the Stalin Revolution," 153; Stanichinskaia-Rozenberg, "Vliianie kino na skhol'nika."

17. Paxton Hibben, "The Movies in Russia" *Nation*, 11 November 1925, as cited in Leyda, *Kino*, 185.

18. *Pionerskaia Pravda*, 3 March 1928, as cited in Latsis and Keilina, *Deti i Kino*, 13.

19. Bobryshev, *Melkoburzhuaznye vliianiia sredi molodezhi*, 105.

20. Rubenshtein, *Iunost.' Podnevnikam i avtobiograficheskim zapisiam*, 222.

21. *Mody*, which appeared between 1924 and 1929, had a circulation of close to 14,000. *Mody sezona* was even more popular; circulation figures reached 25,000 copies in 1928.

22. See for example, *Mody* 1 (1924), *Mody* 3 (1924).

23. *Mody sezona* 3–4 (1928): 4, 22; *Mody sezona* 5–6 (1928).

24. Maltby, *Dreams for Sale*, 79.

25. Kolesnikov, *Litso klassovogo vraga*, 35.

26. Ewing, *History of Twentieth Century Fashion*, 96. See Thompson, *The New Russia*, 46; and Wicksteed, *Life under the Soviets*, 12, for a description of young women making their clothing at home. For a similar effort by young working women in interwar Britain to make copies of fashionable clothing "with material a few pence a yard," see Alexander, "Becoming a Woman in London in the 1920's and 1930's," 263–64.

27. Advertisement from the back page of *Mody* 7 (1925).

28. Thompson, *The New Russia*, 46.

29. Ibid., 30.

30. Strogova, "Womenfolk," 282. Getting "dressed up" for work was common in later periods as well and was similarly condemned as unsuitable and immodest. See Vainstein, "Female Fashion, Soviet Style," 69.

31. Strogova, "Womenfolk," 282.

32. Rafail, *Za novogo cheloveka*, 50, 51.

33. Ibid.; Bobryshev, *Melkoburzhuaznye vliianiia*, 68.

34. Tramp, "Pod fonarem 'El'dorado,'" 31.

35. Ibid., 323–24.

36. Ibid., 31.

37. See the description in Hullinger, *The Reforging*, 326–27.

38. Lidin, *The Price of Life*, 122; Ognyov, *The Diary of a Communist Undergraduate*, 118–24. A nonfiction account can be found in Kagan, *Molodezh' posle gudka*.

39. Williams, "The Dream World of Mass Consumption," 203.

40. Hullinger, *The Reforging*, 323.

41. Ognyov, *The Diary of a Communist Undergraduate*, 122–23.

42. Peiss, *Cheap Amusements*, 65.

43. Koenker, "Men against Women on the Shop Floor in Early Soviet Russia," 1463.

44. T. Kostrov, "Kul'tura i meshchantsvo," *Revoliutsiia i kul'tura* 3–4 (1927): 27.

45. This is Stephen Frank's term for a similar phenomenon in the prerevolutionary period among peasants. See Frank, "Simple Folk."

46. Bobryshev, *Melkoburzhuaznye vliianiia sredi molodezhi*, 104–6. This story bears a notable similarity to prerevolutionary "moral tales" told to and about young peasants who were also condemned for "striving to be like the petty bourgeois." In one story from 1910, a young woman goes without food to save money to buy a dress in the shop window. Like Olga, she too dies because of her "unhealthy strivings." Frank, "Simple Folk," 87.

47. Semashko, *Iskusstvo odevat'sia*, 3. For a discussion of the artistic and often utopian arena of Soviet fashion and textile design, see Bowlt, "Constructivism and Early Soviet Fashion Design."

48. Petrova, "Iz stenogrammy soveshchaniia devushek-rabotnits moskovskikh fabric," 27–29.

49. Healey, *Homosexual Desire in Revolutionary Russia*, 62.

50. See, for example, the description of the decadent NEPwomen in Kollontai's fiction as described by Stites, *The Women's Liberation Movement in Russia*, 356–57.

51. N. Semashko, "Nuzhna li' zhenstvennost,'" *Molodaia gvardiia* 6 (1924): 205–6.

52. Ibid.

53. Roberts, "Samson and Delilah Revisited," 661.

54. See Gorsuch, "'A Woman Is Not a Man.'"

55. Roberts, "Samson and Delilah Revisited," 683.

56. Grigorov and Shkotov, *Staryi i novyi byt*, 52, and Lebina, "Molodezh' i NEP," 12. Also see Strikhenova, *Iz istorii sovetskogo kostiuma*.

57. See, for example, Kostrov, "Kul'tura i meshchanstvo," 27. In his famous play *The Bedbug*, Vladimir Mayakovsky satirizes this drive to find a wealthy NEPman or woman to marry. Mechanic: "I'm no deserter. You think I like wearing these lousy rags? Like hell I do! There are lots of us, you know, and there just aren't enough Nepmen's

daughters to go around . . . We'll build houses for everybody! But we won't creep out of this foxhole with a white flag." Mayakovsky, *The Bedbug and Selected Poetry*, 256.

58. Goomilevsky, *Dog Lane*, 68, 102.

59. See Ketlinskaia, "Zdravstvui, molodost'!," *Novyi mir* 11 (November 1975): 77; *Russkaia sovetskaia estrada, 1917–1929*, 249; and Starr, *Red and Hot*, 60–61. On popular music, including dance music, see Rothstein, "The Quiet Rehabilitation of the Brick Factory," 376; and Rothstein, "Popular Song in the NEP Era."

60. My argument here has been influenced by Erenberg's description of the same dances in prewar New York. See *Steppin' Out*, 81.

61. Lidin, *The Price of Life*, 121–22.

62. See the discussion in Naiman, "Revolutionary Anorexia (NEP as Female Complaint)."

63. Ibid., 306.

64. Zelenko, *Massovye narodnye tantsy*, 3; *Iunyi proletarii* 1 (January 1924): 6; Lunacharsky, "Proletarskii muzykant" 4 (1929), as cited in *Dovesti do kontsa bor'bu s nepmanskoi muzykoi*, 30.

65. Kagan, *Molodezh' posle gudka*, 77–79.

66. Ibid., 39, 44.

67. Rossiiskii gosudarstvennyi arkhiv sotsial'no-politicheskoi istorii (RGASPI), f. M-1, d. 2, op. 19, 1. 105.

68. Ognyov, *Diary of a Communist Schoolboy*, 90–91.

69. See, for example, Hoffmann and Kotsonis, *Russian Modernity*, and Hoffmann, *Stalinist Values*.

70. See the discussion, for example, in Maltby, *Dreams for Sale*. See also Wickham, "Working-Class Movement and Working-Class Life," 336. On American anxieties, see Latham, *Posing a Threat*.

71. See Kelly and Volkov, "Directed Desires," 291.

72. Gorsuch, *Youth in Revolutionary Russia*, chap. 8 and epilogue.

73. See, for example, the discussion of Molotov and other Soviet leaders learning to dance the tango in the 1930s in Gronow, *Caviar with Champagne*, 10. See also Cox, "All This Can Be Yours!"

9

Who Is Afraid of the Chinese Modern Girl?

MADELEINE Y. DONG

In Zhang Henshui's novel *Shanghai Express* (1935), the young protagonist Xuchun, on board the Beijing-Shanghai express, at first appears to be an ideal modern woman. Her tasteful dress, charming smile, graceful gestures, skillful handling of complicated situations, her eloquence, her independence, and her ability to read English, quickly catch the attention of Mr. Hu, an older, married businessman. Although Hu is attracted to Xuchun's modern appearance, it is her willingness to become a concubinelike secret lover and submit her life to his control that convinces him to enter a relationship with her. As the train dashes toward Shanghai, Hu falls asleep fantasizing that Xuchun will belong to him, but he wakes up only to find that she has disappeared with all his money and stocks. Now penniless in the big city Shanghai, Hu sees Xuchun in every modern-looking woman on the station platform and cries out warnings to all men.[1]

Zhang's story is a quintessential cautionary tale of the modern told through the figure of the Modern Girl. Its crux, the anxiety caused by a combination of attraction to and fear of the unknowable Modern Girl, was shared widely by her representations in news reports, literature, and visual culture.[2] While the Modern Girl was represented in advertisements as a beguiling icon of the glamour of modern life and happiness ostensibly achievable through consumption of industrial commodities, she also often appeared as a mystery and was seen as a threatening figure.[3] Modern Girl Xuchun, for example, is nothing but artifice or performance. By the end of the novel, the reader learns nothing about this woman except her modern appearance. Her name is false, and all her history is bogus. She is the perfect con artist whose true identity is impossible to know, a woman as baffling as the modern city Shanghai itself. In addition, guarding against this Modern Girl also means fighting against one's own desires. Hu's warning about the Modern Girl, therefore, is also one against men's own fantasies toward the modern. In this sense, her attractiveness and men's inability to resist it conceal the real threat of the Modern Girl.

The prevalence of themes and plots such as those in *Shanghai Express* indicated the angst and titillation among the elite caused by the Modern Girl. In the first two sections of this chapter, I examine how the "Modern Girl look" facilitated the crossing of class boundaries and how the elite tried to salvage this look to defend its privilege to be modern. In a third section I discuss how the Modern Girl upset social conventions in her relations with her male counterpart, the modern man. Historically, the "superficiality" of the Modern Girl has been the focus of her criticisms from all sides. The last section of the chapter considers the historical and historiographical effects of such a focus.

In order to understand the Modern Girl figure, it is necessary to confront the issue of the dominance of male perspectives in her representations. Major changes in Republican-era Chinese social practices — such as the establishment of the nuclear family as the norm; young men and women receiving education or joining in the work force in integrated public spaces away from their parents' homes; and the emergence of an urban culture targeting the young — opened up potential spaces for single young women to play new roles in society. These public roles for women involved unprecedented visibility and shifts in representation, including Modern Girl fashions, attitudes, and images. The forms and meanings of these representations gave rise to a host of disputes, anxieties, and marketing schemes. The representations of the Modern Girl in stories, cartoons, and pictures were a major staging ground shaping these images and people's actions in relation to them. Though women were key actors in the social changes, this world of image production and interpretation was controlled and shaped mainly by men and capitalist forces. Hence, the main focus became the male issues of desire and fear and an all–or–nothing vision of the Modern Girl as emasculating or confirming modern masculinity. This chapter treats the bias in such male perspectives as an entry point to unravel how, through the figure of the Modern Girl, the desires, fantasies, and disillusionments of young women and men of the post–May Fourth period were not separated, but deeply entangled.

Who Were These Modern-looking Women?

The Modern Girl look, with its painted face, bobbed or permed hair, fashionable *qipao*, and high-heel shoes, was so widely adopted by women of diverse social groups, including high school and college students, professionals, young wives of the upper and middle classes, and prostitutes, that by the 1930s it had become a passport to opportunity and a dress code of necessity for young female city dwellers. In an article written in 1933, Yunshang argued that the Modern Girl phenomenon had spread from the "leisure class" to the "middle class" and then led to the emergence of dance girls, masseuses, waitresses, saleswomen, all of whom were seen as prostitutes in disguise.[4] If a woman's appearance is often the first quality used to identify her in the modern city, the Modern Girl look was nonetheless often considered as veiling more than it revealed. While they reflected the new urban anonymity, representations of the Modern Girl as a mysterious figure also indicated anxiety over her blurring of class and status lines.

The magazine *Young Companion* (*Liang Yu*) stood out in featuring images of modern-looking women. Established in 1926, this popular pictorial was set apart from contemporary magazines through high-quality printing and avoidance of tabloid-style content. Reports on international news and eminent figures on the national stage, fiction, advertisements for cosmetics, cigarettes, fabrics, and other "modern" commodities filled its pages. The magazine juxtaposed photos of real women with advertising images and fashion sketches and created a space for imagining the modern by blending reality, desire, and fantasy.

After featuring female movie stars and two young female students on the covers of its first few issues, the magazine received the following response from a reader, which it published in its eleventh issue: "The magazine focuses on women visually and uses them as ornaments, but the texts treat them as subjects for jokes. Does this elevate women's status, or does it treat them as playthings?" The editors defended the magazine by arguing that it was the deteriorating social conditions that distorted the meaning of women's physical beauty. But the editors admitted that they once offended a high school student by publishing her picture without her consent. The editors observed, "Her attitude is typical of the mentality of the majority of people who consider all females whose pictures appear in magazines, except old ladies with white hair and wrinkled skin, cheap women of low moral quality."[5]

This mentality changed by the end of 1927 when a Chinese "high society" took form following the reunification of China and the establishment of the Nationalist government in Nanjing. The magazine developed its high-class reputation, and it became acceptable, even honorable, for young women to have their pictures published in *Young Companion*. A column named "Women's Page" (*Funü zhi ye*) featured images of modern Chinese women around the world. Appearing in hairstyles, fashions, and makeup identical to those of Modern Girls in ads, the women in *Young Companion* were graduates of elite high schools, college students from around the country, daughters of eminent families in China and overseas Chinese communities, or young wives of famous men. The word "debutante" often accompanied the photos. In some cases, the young women in the pictures were attached to well-known families, but most of the time they were identified only by their own names. In other words, they were not defined in relationship to patrilineal families but as free and available young women in a public space. The only guarantee that they were "respectable," "good," and "high-class" was the highbrow medium in which their pictures were displayed. In contrast, newspapers and magazines published during the same period targeting a relatively lower-class audience, such as *Shanghai huabao* (*Shanghai Pictorial*, published in 1925), *Fu'ermosi* (*Sherlock Holmes*, published in 1926), and *Jingbao* (*Crystal*, published in 1929) displayed no such photos of young women.

While the magazine apparently intended its covers and the Women's Page to showcase debutantes and high-class women, those whose images were chosen sometimes turned out to possess surprising qualities or even scandalous associations. The cover of *Young Companion*'s issue no. 130, published in July 1937, the month when Japan officially began its invasion of China, featured a charming and confident young woman. The magazine identified her as Ms. Zheng.[6] Zheng appeared in the perfect Modern Girl look: permed hair, careful makeup, bright smile, and form-fitting floral qipao. She could have been just another debutante, except that three years later, instead of marrying an eminent man, she was executed by Chinese collaborators with the Japanese occupation army for being a spy for the nationalists. Zheng's Modern Girl appearance played a major role in her disarming of Ding Mocun, who headed the intelligence agency of the collaboration force and was a target of assassination by the nationalists, but that appearance belied a political commitment for which she was ready to sacrifice her life. Contemporary reports, expectedly, stressed her love affair with Ding, and it was widely rumored that she was executed at the urging of officials' wives who considered her and women like her a major threat to their families.[7]

If the Modern Girl on the cover of *Young Companion* could be a national hero but also a "threat to families," Ms. Peiying, whose photos appeared in the magazine's Women's Page in 1929, became an example of all that had gone wrong with "women's liberation movement." In this case, under the Modern

9.1 Zheng Pingru on the cover of *Young Companion*, no. 130, 1937.

Girl look was a college student who descended into a cabaret dancer and was "forced by a dance partner to drink poison." An editorial in the same issue commented: "There is no longer any doubt that we have to break the old moral codes; but what is the solution for women after their liberation? Some have indeed achieved happiness through liberation, but opposite cases are abundant . . . For example, one woman eloped with a janitor; some left school and became prostitutes. They would claim that they had done it out of love and were breaking vulgar social codes."[8] The lesson the magazine's readers were expected to draw from the story was that the wrong kind of "liberation" could be dangerous. The editor clearly made a connection between "women's libera-

9.2 "Sir . . . I am here to interview for the position for a woman clerk," by Lu Shaofei. *Shidai Manhua*, 1934.

tion" and achieving a higher class status; careless Modern Girls could easily slip down the social ladder, and "they will become excuses for the conservatives and turn into barriers to women's liberation."[9]

For women who worked in government institutions, schools, companies, and stores as teachers, clerks, secretaries, saleswomen and typists, the Modern Girl look was a necessity. Yang Gonghuai noted the difficulty for women to find jobs and explained that their employment often resulted from an employer's desire to use the women to "improve the atmosphere of the office." When interviewing female applicants, employers paid much less attention to their knowledge and abilities than to their "look" (*maixiang*, literally "selling appearance"), as shown in a cartoon printed in 1931 (see figure 9.2). Consequently, working women uniformly wore permed hair, fashionable clothes, high heels, as well as powder, rouge, and lipstick. Yang is critical of these women and of the social environment. He recognizes that the women had to endure harassments from both their bosses and the customers. On the other hand, he criticized the women for preferring to spend their leisure time shopping, in movie theaters, or dining in restaurants but not doing housework or studying, which he considered an indication of their flawed moral character.[10]

The Modern Girl look also reached women workers living along the heavily polluted Suzhou Creek, an area of shacks housing the city's poorest labor forces. While spending little on food, these workers invested their money in dressing up. In the mid-1930s, it became popular in schools to elect "queens" and "school flowers." Following this example, factory workers elected as factory flowers women who displayed three attributes: pretty faces, good relationships with co-workers, and talent in singing, dancing, and the art of conversation. As a folk song puts it, "Her fragrance wafts three miles, and so white is her face powder." When participating in social events, factory flowers dressed up in a "modern" (*modeng*) style, donning qipao or Western suits and leather shoes and wearing permed hair. They looked like high-class "young ladies [*xiaojie*] at aristocratic schools" and "people could not tell that they came from factory worker backgrounds at all." "Factory workers" then were transformed into "modern metropolitan girls" (*dushi modeng nülang*). In one case, a teacher allegedly fell in love with a factory flower, but she dumped him and became a dance hall girl and "made very good money."[11]

Stories about rural women's transformations into urban Modern Girls also frequently appeared in major Chinese-language newspapers such as *Shenbao*. One article described a married woman from Suzhou who worked as a maid in Shanghai. She spent all her income on clothes and jewelry until she "did not look like a country woman at all." She attracted a man working at the customs and moved in with him, bluntly telling her husband, who came to Shanghai to look for her, that she no longer loved him.[12] Another report, titled "Country Girl Suddenly Became Fashionable," told the story of a nineteen-year-old country girl who went to work in a Shanghai silk textile factory and became an outstanding worker. Having been promoted and making a decent income, she began dating a young man in her neighborhood and spending all her wages on clothing. One day, she bought a pink qipao and Western-style shoes and had a perm at a hair studio in the concessions. About her new look her aunt commented, "A country girl should not dress like this." Enraged, she left the house she shared with her uncle and aunt.[13]

What made these cases scandalous and newsworthy was that these women

9.3 "When permed hair became popular," by Zhang Guangyu. *Manhua daguan,* 1931. The women's clothes indicate that they are of the lower class.

were using the Modern Girl look to enter the society to which they did not belong, disturbing the social order. There was no sure way to tell the class of a young woman sporting the Modern Girl look, nor was there any guarantee of her high moral standing. Even *Young Companion,* among the most elitist magazines at the time, juxtaposed pictures of famous wives and debutantes with those of movie stars and Peiying, the college student who deteriorated into a dance hall girl. Young unmarried women within the elite class were disturbing marriages as they enjoyed their "provisional space." "Low-class" women workers and rural migrant women dressed up as Modern Girls to "seduce" respectable young men of higher class. While "bad women" of lower classes were sneaking into the elite marriage market, good women could fall out of it because the Modern Girl look led them down a path toward disreputable actions or dangers. Both were class slippages based on the inability of women and men to see beyond the artifice of the Modern Girl look to the reality of a woman's character. The Modern Girl look, then, blurred class and status lines and threatened the purity of the elite marriage market. The life path prescribed for young women in *Young Companion* aimed at securing the patrilineal family within the status quo: attending school, coming out as a debutante, marrying a successful man, and enjoying children as a young mother. But in reality, this ideal was hard to maintain and social boundaries were difficult to police.

Molding the Ideal Modern Woman

The role the Modern Girl look played in blurring class boundaries and its serving as a means for female upward social mobility made it an object of scrutiny by the social and cultural elites, who considered it their privilege and duty to define the meaning of being modern. Their efforts at crafting a more skilled reading of appearances to distinguish "true" from "false" modern involved two not necessarily harmonious, and at times even conflicting, goals. Fighting to maintain their privilege to be the "truly" modern, "cosmopolitan elites" took it upon themselves to separate "high-class" modern women from the rest. The scrutiny applied to the Modern Girl, in this sense, indicated a struggle between the attempt to cross the class boundaries and the need to establish and maintain them. Meanwhile, through commercial publications, the social and cultural elites were also molding the "modern women" according to their own aesthetic and moral criteria.

Furen huabao (*Women's Pictorial*), published from 1933 to 1935, offered a complete manual on how to be a "real" modern woman. Guo Jianying served as the chief editor. Interested in Japanese modernist literature, and a close friend of the New Perceptionist writer Liu Naou, Guo published a fair number of translations as well as his own writings in the literature journal *Xin wenyi* (*New Literature*, 1929). His drawings of modern urban life began to appear in Shanghai's newspapers and magazines in 1931 and were published as a collection in 1934. Shunning the politicized terms for women at the time, *funü* or *nüxing*, Guo chose the more neutral *furen* for the title of his magazine. At the peak of its publication, in contrast to most contemporary popular magazines, which used photographs of Chinese beauties on their covers, *Furen huabao* featured line drawings to achieve a more cosmopolitan look (see figure 9.4). Complaining about the rarity of "ideal modern women" in Shanghai, Guo designed the magazine to teach Chinese women to distinguish "high-class" (*gaoguide*) from "native and vulgar" (*xiangtuqide*) modernity. The magazine presented a plethora of information on fashion, makeup, fragrance, foreign and Chinese movie stars, fiction, poetry, essays, and cartoons by the most eminent modernist artists. As a finishing school on paper, it provided the knowledge for the "truly modern woman."[14]

The magazine paid close attention to details of women's appearance and behavior. Many articles and images instructed the readers how to care for their facial skin, eyebrows, hair and hands, and how to apply cosmetics. A large portion of the magazine was devoted to pointing out fashion mistakes made by the Chinese Modern Girl and how to correct those following Western role models. Readers were encouraged to pay attention to European and American

9.4 Guo Jianying's line drawing for the
cover of *Furen huabao*, no. 22, 1934.

fashion magazines such as *Vogue*, for inspiration on what kinds of dress and shoes to wear for different occasions. Every issue of the magazine featured articles and images informing readers of the latest fashion trends in Europe and the United States, especially Paris, so that they would not be confused by any "low-class taste."[15] Guo's special column, "Modeng shenghuo xue jiangzuo" (Forum on modern life), took references from *Vanity Fair*, *College Humor*, and Japanese women's magazines to teach the proper etiquette in various social situations such as dating, dancing, dining, walking in the street, or riding the bus.[16] The "ideal modern woman" was one "without any trace of modern," a standard hard to meet by just any woman who, often out of necessity, wore a qipao, a pair of high heels, and lipstick.[17]

The colonial worship of things foreign (including foreign women) had a strong impact on the modernity of the Chinese Modern Girl. *Furen huabao* clearly defined the ideal modern Chinese woman as authentically or properly Westernized in her appearance, behavior, education, and mentality. Using her Western counterparts as role models, the Chinese Modern Girl was expected to be beautiful, healthy, energetic, cheerful, and lively. A number of articles in the magazine concurred that traditional Chinese standard of beauty — oval face, willow leaf eyebrows, long thin eyes, small cherry-like mouth, and slim fragile-looking body — had been replaced by one featuring big eyes, long thin eyebrows, broad mouth with fine white teeth, and an agile, energetic body.[18] Ten contemporary Hollywood actresses were presented as examples of ideal feminine beauty.[19]

The modernist writer Ouwai Ou scrutinized the faces and bodies of Chinese women in great detail. Their faces, in contrast to those of Caucasian women, lacked shadow due to the flatness of their noses and eye sockets. The only way for them to compensate for this flaw was to learn from Western movie actresses how to make their faces more expressive. The author noted approvingly that Chinese women had in fact gleaned from movie close-ups how to improve their expressions by presenting a "Hollywood screen face." "Urban women's faces are no longer authentically Chinese," he wrote. "It is not an exaggeration to say that they now reflect international beauty beyond national boundaries."[20] Ouwai also suggested that all Chinese women needed the help of surgical measures to reshape their eyebrows and make them similar to those of Caucasian women. On the other hand, he praised straight black hair and "yellow" skin color as the special advantages of East Asian and Chinese women. Ouwai's comments exemplify the numerous contemporary critiques of the appearance of the Chinese Modern Girl and of Chinese women in general. Although not always espousing conventional Western racial schemes, these critiques are nonetheless racial. The creation of the ideal "look" for the Chinese Modern Girl thus involved both class and racial discourses — being high-class meant being properly Westernized, socially and physically.

In addition to the correct "modern look," the magazine also inculcated its readers with the idea that a truly modern woman was expected to develop her "internal qualities by attaining a certain level of taste for modern life." Specifically, she needed to have sufficient knowledge in film, sports, readings (weighted equally among modern literature, classical literature, self-development, the domestic arts, and contemporary magazines), social dancing (but not at dance halls that hired commercial dancing girls), music (the ability to play an instrument, and an album collection made up of 40 percent jazz and 60 percent classical), and handicrafts (such as knitting).[21]

The new meaning of "morality," apparently, settled heavily on domesticity. Women readers were admonished not to forget the ultimate purpose of all this self-polishing — to attract men and to become their worthy companions.[22] The magazine warned that indulgence in youthful fun might divert attention from marriage until it was too late. Letters from "old maidens" regretting their missed opportunities in marriage were published as warning lessons for young women.[23] An article written in 1934 by Xu Xinqin in *Shidai manhua* (Times Cartoon), a popular Shanghai magazine, confirmed that marriage was considered the proper destiny for the Modern Girl. Xu observed, "The first concern on people's minds for the future of a *shidai xiaojie* [modern young lady/Modern Girl] is her marriage . . . In the way this world is still organized, a woman always belongs to a family . . . Society considers being a wife the proper destiny for a *xiaojie* . . . It is commonly recognized that it is difficult for a *xiaojie* to avoid becoming a *taitai* [wife]." The author admitted that there were young women who did not want to become "slaves of the family" but pointed out that it was extremely difficult for them to make a living on their own.[24]

One purpose of creating the "real modern woman," then, was to prepare her for marrying the modern man. The ubiquitous appearance of young, unmarried women in the city was preceded and accompanied by the urban influx of young men for education and work, away from their extended families. As Susan Glosser argues, in spite of the radicalism of the May Fourth moment, young, educated urban men still defined themselves through marriage and family. Glosser points out that socioeconomic issues, rather than nationalism or individualism, drove the young urban man to challenge traditional family structure and authority and to be "passionately involved in redefining himself as a member of an industrializing economy and a modernizing state."[25]

> Because it was so important to a man's identity as a modern, enlightened individual to make a freely chosen love-marriage, the quality of his marriage and his wife became absolutely essential to his self-image. Consequently, despite the rhetoric about women's rights to independence and full personhood, these men were most interested in creating women who met male demands for educated, enlightened companionship. And men complained bitterly when women failed to meet their husbands' expectations.[26]

Thus, the primary motivation of marrying a "modern woman" was to achieve and maintain social status. It was not new to preserve the status quo through marriage. As Susan Mann points out in her study of texts and practices on marriage in eighteenth-century China, discourses on preparing young women for marriage were often "metonymic comment on larger social issues of mobility and class."[27] Mann argues that through protecting the purity of the marriage market, elites "sought to fix the fluidity of social change that threatened to erode the boundaries defining their own respectability."[28] Since wives and daughters carried forward the status of elite families and the honor of their class, the elites were always "discovering ways to valorize the status of brides and wives in their class and to emphasize the differences that separated marriageable women from concubine and women of lower rank."[29]

Like their eighteenth-century counterparts, the twentieth-century elites also attempted to control the marriage market; the difference lay in the new tensions and means in defining class boundaries. One quality *Furen huabao* considered important for modern Chinese women to develop was openness in their interaction with men. American college students — healthy, energetic, lively, and sexy — were presented as their role models.[30] Modern women should not be constrained by traditional cultural codes. But this was considered a privilege reserved for elite women. Xu Xinqin distinguished between "modern young ladies" (*modeng xiaojie*) and "old style young ladies" (*jiushi xiaojie*). Modern young ladies determined their own marriage; parents and family could only play the role of consultants. "Girls of modest and working class families" had adopted some ideas from the "*modeng xiaojie*" and "put on some love tragedies." But they never ended up well: eventually, they were either taken home by their parents to be disciplined or sold to brothels in far-away cities.[31] While elite women should be "modern" and practice free love, women of lower classes needed to adhere to more traditional standards with trenchant (and dull) fervor. Again, as with the Modern Girl look, the correct practice of love also had to be class specific. In the Republican period, free love was a luxury to be enjoyed only by the elites. Without the scrutiny by the extended family and arranged marriage as the first line of defense, and as elite men were beginning to make their own choices and decisions in marriage, the pool of candidates for "free love" must be kept pure. Elites such as the editors of *Furen huabao* were fighting to take control of the double-edged sword of the Modern Girl look that served as the new status marker in the city but could also slash open class lines.

The Modern Girl and the Modern Man

Although the Modern Girl phenomenon touched upon a wide social milieu, it involved most directly urban upper-class and middle-class women and men. The modern urban men expressed paradoxical feelings toward the Modern Girl: both longing and fear. Such an attitude was most clearly expressed in their anxieties over the Modern Girl as lover and wife. In this section, I discuss the representation of the Modern Girl in love and marriage in social cartoons by a group of modernist artists.[32]

Manhua (satirical image, caricature, and cartoon) emerged in China at the end of the nineteenth century, following the development of lithograph printing, newspapers, and pictorials. An emergent and ever-growing middle class provided a willing market for stereotypical images in which it recognized itself. By the 1920s and 1930s, caricature had become a staple item in almost all newspapers and magazines across China. From 1934 to 1937, the number of cartoon magazines increased dramatically—Shanghai alone had nineteen.[33] Representative of this trend was *Shanghai manhua* (*Shanghai Sketch*), a large-size color lithographic cartoon magazine founded and financed by Shao Xun-mei, the modernist poet and quintessential modern boy who earned himself the name "Shanghai dandy."[34] It was first published from 1928 to 1930, during which time each of its more than one hundred issues sold about 3,000 copies. It was then folded into *Shidai manhua* and continued to be published for three more years in the early 1930s.[35]

Unlike earlier cartoons that focused on national politics, a large number of social caricatures appeared in these magazines through which the artists hoped to observe and express "the richness of Shanghai life."[36] Relationships between the sexes constituted a major theme for these social cartoons on urban life; in particular, the artists focused on the Modern Girl and her relationship with the modern man in both the public and private realms of city life. These caricatures, as interpretations of gender relations with an attitude, provide unique lenses for examining the role of the Modern Girl in creating new gender relations.

Most of the pieces in the magazines were by young male cartoonists who also worked for advertising agencies. Ding Song was employed by the advertising department of the British American Tobacco Company (BAT) in Shanghai, whose calendar posters featuring the Modern Girl created a new genre of commercial art in China.[37] Dan Duyu painted the Modern Girl in his advertisements and calendar posters, as did Lu Shaofei.[38] Ye Qianyu contributed his fashion drawings to *Young Companion*, while Guo Jianying's appeared in *Furen huabao*. These artists simultaneously created an idealized image of the Modern Girl in their advertisements, fashion drawings, and film while at the same time they critiqued her in their cartoons. From their constant shifting of position emerged a complex image of the Modern Girl, to her male counterpart, as a source of both fantasy and fear. The caricatures reflected ambivalence between desire for and resistance to the Modern Girl and incited self-recognition in their satirical depictions of flawed fellow beings. In so doing, the caricatures provoked humorous laughter that reflected a new kind of male identity created through the Modern Girl. As Ainslie McLees points out, "Social caricature is thematically affiliated with genre painting, which by definition portrays types rather than individuals, and modest, often domestic, situations rather than the exalted personages of history painting."[39] The caricatures thus created stereotypical images of modern urban women and communicated the artists' attitude toward them through the Modern Girl, an attitude that they believed would echo the sentiments of their audience.

The Modern Girl was seen as part of the scenery of the modern city. Guo Jianying claimed: "The youth of Shanghai women is endowed with energy and creativity. How boring and bleak Shanghai streets would be without the youthfulness of the women."[40] Much of Guo's work depicted the Modern Girl as spectacle. His artistic style reflects the influence of Aubrey Beardsley, who was himself impacted by Japanese erotic prints and in turn inspired Chinese artists with his black and white pen and ink drawings. His illustrations for *Salome*, which was translated and staged by the Southern Society together with *Pan Jinlian* and *A Doll's House* in 1926, became familiar to Chinese intellectuals. Beardsley's depictions of women are often grotesque; his influence on Chinese artists, however, led to the creation of a very soft genre, *shuqing hua* (lyrical drawings), of which Guo was a practitioner. In figure 9.5, a cartoon of a scene on a bus, although the Modern Girls are making the man nervous, they are depicted in a way that is decorative, feminine, and not austere. Guo apparently intended to depict women and modern urban life as "lively, vigorous, and refreshing."[41]

In these male depictions of the Modern Girl, the man's desire for her is apparent, but so is hers for him. Many of the caricatures show the male gaze at her. In public and private spaces — at work, in the streets, on balconies, on the bus, in the classroom, in front of the camera, and in men's fantasies — the Modern Girl is always being looked at. While she is represented as an object of desire, fetishism, and voyeurism, she often does not appear to be passive but a desiring subject instead. She rarely shuns such gazes but instead blatantly ignores them, enjoys them, gazes back, or even purposely provokes and attracts them. She also gazes at herself: she is narcissistic and consciously makes herself sexually attractive. She is aware of the value of her charm and uses it in her relationship with men. What these caricatures say, essentially, is that the Modern Girl solicits male attention. In the male's projection of his desire through the Modern Girl, the young woman becomes a powerful figure because she, while an object of the gaze, also possesses the gaze and thus is capable of objectifying those who would objectify her.

When the Modern Girl is depicted as interacting closely with men instead of as a distant spectacle, the caricatures reveal a critical attitude in general: she appears to be calculating, flirtatious, venal, and greedy. She is a gold digger; the first thing she looks for in a relationship is the man's money.[42] She is a consumer who uses her checkbook compulsively.[43] Her conspicuous consumption of commodities, including cosmetics, leads to spousal tensions. The crisis caused by transformation of the Chinese family from principally a unit of

9.5 "Brutal torture . . . A shy young man stepped on the trolley bus,"
by Guo Jianying. *Jianying manhua ji*, 1934.

9.6 "The photographer thinks that these are his best lenses,"
by Lu Shaofei. *Manhua daguan*, 1931.

學校裏新請了一位女教師

汪振慧作

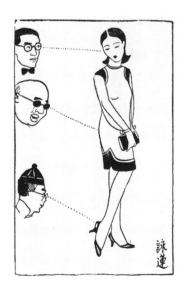

詠蓮

9.7 "A new teacher has come to the school," by Wang Zhenhui. *Manhua daguan*, 1931.

9.8 "Three stages of the gaze," by Yonglian. *Manhua daguan*, 1931.

9.9 "Memos of love," by Guo Jianying. *Manhua daguan*, 1931.

production to one of consumption is narrated through the spending habits of the Modern Girl. She does not know how to do housework or take care of a baby.[44] She is treacherous, entertaining her husband's friends when he is on a trip.[45] She is unchaste; premarital sex and simultaneous relationships with multiple men are normal for her. In Guo Jianying's "Memos of Love," a Modern Girl keeps information about men—names, ages, looks, physiques, wealth—and assigns a grade to each item under each name. When she wants a man who knows how to have fun, she calls Wang and extracts "unlimited pleasure from this handsome young man." When she needs money, she writes Shen because "this old man's wallet is always full." When she wants to take a walk, she calls Lin; and if she needs someone with strength, she turns to Chen.[46]

In these cartoons, men's experience with urban life appears to be totally different from the Modern Girl's. The cartoon images of the Modern Girl are highly dramatic and dramatized—these young women are always in public or places of entertainment: coffee shops, shoe stores, university campuses, dance halls, parks, beaches, and city streets. In contrast, quotidian and mundane themes are reserved for the male figures, who are often depicted as trapped in domestic, private spaces. The men are the ones who have to worry about the responsibilities of family and domestic life: mending socks, taking care of babies, bringing home the bread, and, as shown in figure 9.11, paying for the wife's expenditures to keep up her "modern" look.

9.10 "Mama is not home," by
Zhang Guangyu. *Manhua
daguan*, 1931.

9.11 "Clothing, food, and housing,"
by Zhang Guangyu. *Manhua daguan*,
1931. Inside the house, a woman with
the Modern Girl look is gazing
at herself in a mirror.

住　食　衣

The Modern Girl's aura of romance provokes male longing, but also fears. Just like Mr. Hu in *Shanghai Express*, the male figures in the caricatures appear to be trapped between their desire for the charming femininity of the Modern Girl and the danger of that charm. They are often overwhelmed by fears: of contracting sexually transmitted diseases; of competing with other men for women's attention; of dysfunctional relationships; and of rejection, emotional pain and loneliness. For men, urban life means both anxiety resulting from their own desires and fears caused by the constant presence of temptation. Men appear in these cartoons to be the victims in this new gender relation. In contrast to the confident Modern Girl who is totally at ease with and in command of modern urban life, her male counterpart seems to have difficulty living up to her challenge.

A reversal of power relations between the sexes and the contrast between powerful women and powerless men are clearly evident in these cartoons. The men do not assume the usual postures that signal power; for example, they do

9.12 "Playthings of different times," by Shen Baohui. *Manhua daguan*, 1931.

not stand in the conventional male stance, with legs apart and feet parallel. When their arms are outstretched from their bodies, their gesture does not signal power and authority but petty meanness or surprise. The body language of the women also reflects a break with traditional roles. They occupy no less, and very often even more, space than men, and their stance is neither modest nor less affected than that of men. Women are rarely shown with feet together or arms held close to their torsos — except where the artists depict ideal types. Female gestures are not responsive; instead, women often initiate actions and interactions with men. Their facial expressions are more individualized and articulated than those of men. The Modern Girl does not keep to herself. She gazes directly and smiles flirtatiously. With her slender waist, polished nails, painted red lips, plucked eyebrows, careful makeup, fashionable attire, and delicate high heels, the Modern Girl is a perfect image of seductive aggressiveness. She is always romantically involved with men but turns a deaf ear to male professions of love and is a threat to the patrilineal household — she does not cook, clean, sew, or have babies. In these cartoons, women conquer men; women, no male playthings, treat men as their playthings; husbands take on what should have been wives' work; men follow women; and women's images loom larger than men's. If the young, educated urban men sought their version of ideal marriage in modern women, then the Modern Girl figure was used to stand in for these women who, in reality, often turned out to be "imperfect" companions in the eyes of their male counterparts.

In these cartoons, the social imbalances with which the hapless men have to cope make them, instead of the women, objects of laughter. Caricatures speak in coded language whose deciphering releases recognition and understanding in the audience. The resulting laughter reveals that the observer recognizes in the image before him his own imperfection and despairs over it while triumphing over it aesthetically.[47] The cartoonists apparently believed that their audience would understand and identify with the images and captions. The expected, knowing chuckles of the male readers thus indicate a common understanding of male identity that would not have existed without the image of the Modern Girl. She might have been comfortingly fictional, but she played a central role in defining modern masculinity.

The "Superficiality" of the Modern Girl

The Chinese Modern Girl was criticized fiercely by many of her contemporaries, including the leftists, nationalists, and different strands of feminists. All the criticisms of her, however, share a common vocabulary, focusing on her "superficiality." She was "degenerated" (*duoluo*), "indulgent" (*xiangle*), "comfort-seeking" (*anyi*), "parasitic" (*jisheng*), "decadent" (*tuifei*), "vain" (*xurong*), "extravagant" (*shechi*), "impetuous" (*ganqingyongshi*), and "slavish to foreign (products)." Her sexuality was commodified (*xing shangpin hua*), which made her a prostitute in disguise (*changji bianxing*). Four aspects of the Modern Girl, in particular, were singled out by her critics. First of all, her appearance solicits male attention. She wears qipao, high heel shoes, and permed hair. She applies face powder, rouge, and lipstick. She chases after new fashions. Her behavior was also scrutinized. She dances, frequents cinemas, enters men's rooms, and makes appearances in public gatherings. Her marriage, love, and sexuality received condemnation. She prefers to stay single, feels negative about family life, and refuses to have children. Or, otherwise, she is flirtatious, cohabits with men without getting married, and becomes pregnant out of wedlock. Sometimes the Modern Girl even practices homosexuality. She openly seeks sexual pleasure, plays emotional games with men, and pays too much attention to their appearance. She was also denounced for her consuming imported clothes and cosmetics and indulging in good food and wine.[48]

To the leftists, the Modern Girl and her male counterparts such as Shao Xunmei were products of colonial culture. As Louise Edwards argues, the Modern Girl was a site where leftist intellectuals attempted to define women's modernity by rescuing the New Woman from her shallow counterpart. The Modern Girl, to them, usurped personal style as a political tool and depoliticized it. Challenging conventional dress codes had been a radical act for youth of the May Fourth period; choosing to have natural feet and bobbed hair and wearing the short skirt adopted by students could make a young woman a social outcast or even cost her life. Edwards argues that the May Fourth modern woman was conceived as "politically aware, patriotic, independent, and educated." In contrast,

> By the late 1920s and early 1930s, big Shanghai companies used the modern woman as an enticement to purchase and consume "modern" goods and services. In this commercial framework, the modern woman was glamorous, fashionable, desirable, and available. Thus, two decades after their first appearance in 1918, the modern woman became a symbol of a national modernity that was commercially rather than politically centered. Commercial power usurped the reformist intellectual's guardianship of the modern woman.[49]

In distinguishing a real from a pseudomodern woman, intellectuals in the post–May Fourth era dismissed external manifestations of modernity such as clothing, hairstyles, and shoe styles as superficial trappings. A truly modern woman, they argued, had inner qualities centering on an abiding concern for China's national welfare. This preoccupation with the moral attributes of the modern woman, Edwards argues, was an attempt by some reformist intellectuals to reclaim their role as enlightened moral guardians and therefore leading advisers for the nation.[50] Sarah Stevens also points out that women's bodies were used to enact the struggle between conflicting aspects of modernity. The Modern Girl and the New Woman serve different functions in literary texts. The New Woman is always linked to the positive aspects of modernity. She symbolizes the vision of a future strong nation and her character highlights the revolutionary qualities of the modern women (*nüxing*). As Stevens puts it, "The contrasts between the figures of the New Woman and the Modern Girl illustrate the tensions inherent within the very construction of modernity itself."[51]

The Nationalists and leftists, although political rivals, shared commonalities in their criticisms of the Modern Girl. The heyday of the Chinese Modern Girl roughly overlapped with the "Nanjing Decade" from the Nationalist government's reunification of China in 1927 to the Japanese invasion in 1937. In addition to purging radical intellectuals and silencing the left, the new nationalist government began to regulate daily life as soon as it took control of the cities. "Cloth demons" — women in "Westernized" fashions — were to be banned from public spaces.[52] Many cities, including Beijing, Shanghai, Nanjing, Tianjin, and Hankou, organized "Brigades of Destroyers of the Modern"

(*Modeng pohui tuan*), whose members patrolled the streets and cut women's clothes if they appeared too "modern" and "strange."[53] The government also enforced the regulation by policing public spaces and arresting women in "strange clothes."[54]

The policing of women's fashion reached a peak during the New Life Movement in 1934. Inspired by German and Italian Fascism, this was an attempt to mobilize the masses during a time of national crisis by fostering in them qualities such as frugality, self discipline, and a spirit of self-sacrifice. During the New Life Movement, the Modern Girl look was considered un-Chinese, and her consumerism once again became an object of criticism and reform.[55] Song Meiling, wife of Nationalist leader Chiang Kai-shek, claimed that Chinese women should not wear permed hair, which was banned, together with nail polish, especially among professional women.[56] Women were required to abide by dress codes that limited the length of dress, jacket, and skirt, and to abandon "modern" (*modeng*) fashions.[57] These bans and codes, however, were not very effective and rarely followed. Public morality and national mobilization were excuses for these restrictions, and the national economy was another. The Modern Girl's consumption of imported luxury goods allegedly hurt China's economy. Men and women were told to wear plain clothes made of China's own fabric.[58] The year 1935 was designated "Year of National Products for Women" and the Modern Girl image, including photos of movie stars like Hu Die (Butterfly Wu), was widely mobilized to promote Chinese products. Here, the Nationalist government apparently attempted to recruit the Modern Girl as citizen, albeit still through consumption.

Unlike what had been historically considered models for women's liberation — the good wife and wise mother of the late Qing, the radical Nora, the professional women, and the working-class women — the Modern Girl was seen by most feminists as pulling the movement a step back. The May Fourth and New Culture Movement encouraged young women to venture into the public realm, to pursue modern education, to break away from the patriarchal family, and to struggle for free love and marriage. The Modern Girl appeared to be fulfilling most of these conditions. But what the Chinese Nora left was her father's house, and from there she was expected to walk into the "small family" of her husband. The Chinese Modern Girl did not revolutionize or abolish marriage but rather sought to negotiate "a better marriage," which was the main trend during this time. To Lu Xun's answer to his own question, "What happens after Nora leaves home?" — that she would either return, or become a prostitute — the Chinese Modern Girl provided an alternative. She undermined the patrilineal household from inside and brought changes to gender relations in everyday interactions with men and through new expectations for marital relations.

In this way, the romance she offered posed a major threat to the patrilineal family. As Sally Mitchell points out, "Girl's culture suggested new ways of being, new modes of behavior, and new attitudes that were not yet acceptable for adult women. It authorized a change in outlook and supported inner transformations that had promise for transmuting women's 'nature.' "[59]

The Modern Girl and the modern man, the next generation of the May Fourth youth, together created new gender relations and entangled interests, as well as hopes and disillusionment for the urban nuclear family. The Modern Girl's aura of romance, together with the modern man's attraction to it, destabilized the patrilineal family. Beneath her consumerist façade, the ebullient, uncontainable Modern Girl challenged, historically and historiographically, male-centered conceptions of "youth" and commandeered societal expectations of the "girl-wife-mother" life cycle. The Modern Girl herself rarely voiced protest against criticism, but her having fun in the modern city with a smile on her face definitively caused plenty of fear.

Notes

I am indebted to Susan Fernsebner, Joshua Goldstein, and the Modern Girl Around the World Research Group at the University of Washington for their comments and suggestions.

1. Zhang, *Shanghai Express.*
2. Shih, *The Lure of the Modern.*
3. Laing, *Selling Happiness.*
4. Yunshang, "Lun Modeng nülang zhi suo you chansheng" in *Funü gongming,* June 1933, 2–6.
5. *Young Companion,* no. 11, 1.
6. Ma, *Liangyou yi jiu,* 236–37.
7. Lo, "Historical Narrative and Literary Representation," 47–98.
8. Liang Desuo, "Bianhou yu" in *Young Companion,* no. 50, 2.
9. Ibid.
10. Yang Gonghuai, "Shanghai zhiyejie de nüzhiyuan," *Shanghai shenghuo,* no. 4 (1939): 20–21. Goodman, "The Vocational Woman and the Elusiveness of 'Personhood' in Early Republican China," 265–86.
11. Xu Xing, "Shanghai de nügong," *Shanghai shenghuo,* no. 4 (1939): 24–25.
12. *Shenbao,* 23 January 1930, 15.
13. *Shenbao,* 13 January 1930, 15.
14. "Opening remarks" in *Furen huabao* 1, no. 1.
15. Zhang Lilan, "Liuxing jie de bei xi ju," *Furen huabao* 25 (1935): 9–10.
16. Jianying, "Modeng shenghuo xue jiangzuo," *Furen huabao* 1, no. 1 (1933): 16.
17. Ms. Zhao Lianlian, "Ruguo wo shi ge nanzi," *Furen huabao* 16 (1934): 17.

18. Hu Kao, "Zhongguo nüxing de zhizhuo mei" and Moran, "Wairen muzhong zhi Zhongguo nüxing mei" in *Furen huabao* 1, no. 4 (1933), special issue on beauty of Chinese women, 10–12.

19. "Biaozhun meiren," *Furen huabao* 1, no. 1 (1933): 18.

20. Ouwai Ou, "Zhonghua ernü mei zhi gebie shenpan," *Furen huabao* 1, no. 4 (1933), special issue on beauty of Chinese women, 12–16.

21. Zhang Lilan, "Nide xiandai shenghuo quwei yingyou zenyang de chengdu ne?"*Furen huabao*, 25 (1935): 13.

22. Ma Guoliang, "Shidai nüxing shenghuo zhi jiepou,"*Furen huabao* 15 (1934): 9–11.

23. Huang Jiade, "Lao chunü de houhui," *Furen huabao* 27 (1935): 6–7.

24. Xu Xinqin, "Shidai xiaojie de jianglai," *Shidai manhua* 1, inaugural issue (1934).

25. Glosser, " 'The Truth I Have Learned," 121.

26. Ibid., 139.

27. Mann, "Grooming a Daughter for Marriage," 94.

28. Ibid.

29. Ibid., 101.

30. Huang Jiade, "1934 nian de Meiguo nu daxue sheng," *Furen huabao* 14, special issue for the New Year (1934), 25–26.

31. Xu Xinqin, "Shidai xiaojie de jianglai," 6.

32. The discussion in this section is based mostly on cartoons collected in Ye Qianyu, ed., *Manhua daguan*, published in Shanghai in 1931, unless otherwise referenced.

33. Bi and Huang, *Zhongguo manhua shi*, 93.

34. Hutt, "La Maison D'or," 111–42.

35. Bi and Huang, *Zhongguo manhua shi*, 86.

36. Ibid.

37. Ibid., 43.

38. Ibid., 56–57, 116.

39. McLees, *Baudelaire's "Argot Plastique,"* 15.

40. Guo, *Modeng Shanghai*, 16.

41. Chen Zishan, "Modeng Shanghai de xiantiao ban: Guo Jianying qiren qihua," in Guo, *Modeng Shanghai* (no page).

42. Lu Zhixiang, "Her Hope," in Ye, *Manhua daguan*, 64.

43. Lu Shaofei, "Woman's Checkbook: To Save or Not to Save?" in Ye, *Manhua daguan*, insert, 4.

44. Guo, "No Need to Worry," in Guo, *Modeng Shanghai*, 20.

45. Lu Shaofei, "Jihui," in Ye, *Manhua daguan*, 75.

46. Guo, "Ai de beiwang lu," in Ye, *Manhua daguan*, 71.

47. McLees, *Baudelaire's "Argot Plastique,"* 33–40.

48. Yunshang, "Lun Modeng nulang zhi suo you chansheng," 2–6. Also see Sachiko Egami, "Xiandai Zhongguo de 'xin funü' huayu yu zuowei 'modeng nülang' daiyanren de Ding Ling," *Zhongguo xiandai wenxue yanjiu congkan*, no. 2 (2006): 66–88.

49. Edwards, "Policing the Modern Woman in Republican China," 116.

50. Ibid., 115.

51. Stevens, "Figuring Modernity," 86.
52. Beiping Municipal Government, *Jingshi jingcha gongbao*, 25 June 1927 (no page number).
53. Beiping Municipal Government, *Shizheng pinglun*, 1 June 1934, 58–59.
54. *Jingshi jingcha gongbao*, 16 July 1927.
55. Gao Long, "Tantan funü biaozhun fuzhuang," *Funü yuebao* 1, no. 5 (June 1936): 9–10.
56. "Shi Jiaoju jinzhi nü jiaoyuan tangfa tuzhi," *Funü yuebao* 2, no. 8 (September 1936): 20.
57. "Bang Xinyunhui qudi funü qizhuang yifu," *Funü yuebao* 1, no. 3 (April 1935): 53–54; and "Guangzhou qiangzhi zhixing qudi qizhuang yifu," *Funü yuebao* 1, no. 9 (October 1935): 31–33.
58. "Shi Shanghui chengqing qudi qizhung yifu," *Funü yuebao* 1, no. 7 (August 1935): 35.
59. Mitchell, *The New Girl*, 3.

10

"Blackfella Missus Too Much Proud"

Techniques of Appearing, Femininity,

and Race in Australian Modernity

⌒

LIZ CONOR

Topsy, a sixteen-year-old "Abo. Maid," was reputed to have "a wild imagination" by her Missus, a contributor to the *Australian Women's Mirror* in 1925 who signed herself as "Country Mother." Topsy appeared "as a real live golliwog" to Country Mother's "idolising" children, and yet she also wrote that Topsy "has little vanities like the white girl, using face-cream, powder, and even lip-salve with weird results." She remarked that Topsy — a "full-blooded abo." — was made to wear a hat by her own mother "to prevent freckles!"[1] Country Mother thought this native mother's advice on preventing a darkening complexion reached "the limit," as indeed it did. White Australia had strict limits around the enactment of Aboriginal femininity. These limits included the notion that Aboriginal women were unable to approximate modern white women in appearance and, as insinuated here, that they did not make good mothers.

In this chapter I'm interested in how limits of acceptable behavior for Aboriginal and white women were articulated through what I will call "techniques of appearing" — the manner and means of the execution of one's visual effects and status.[2] During the 1920s, industrialized image production wrought a new relationship between femininity, race, and visibility. Modern identity was increasingly enacted through street presence, self-fashioning, and dress. Skin color, self-adornment, cosmetics, and ready-to-wear fashion were all under scrutiny in Australian popular culture. By having her own vanities, Topsy "appears as" an American-derived golliwog—a blackface minstrel-inspired children's character doll[3]—and "like" a white girl. Australian popular culture produced by whites, including newspapers, magazines, and postcards that assumed a white readership, repeatedly invoked the liminal status of Aboriginal femininity by elaborating on the "weird results" of Aboriginal women's attempts to appear as Modern Girls. It is this account of Aboriginal modern femininity, as it was circulated within Australian white popular culture and as it shaped images of white Australian modernity, that this chapter will consider.

I will also trace how representations of Aboriginal girls and young women intersected with the Modern Girl during the 1920s when their lives were governed by the various Aborigine state protection boards. In the interwar years, state policies pursued the policy of "assimilating" Aboriginal peoples—principally through widespread child removal, the closing of many of the reserves and missions into which surviving groups had been displaced, and the placement of Aboriginal girls in training institutions, in white homes, and pastoral stations as domestic servants. Popular images of Aboriginal girls in the white press circulated alongside commentary extolling "dying race" theory, evolutionary racial hierarchy, and racial destiny. Racialized accounts of techniques of appearing powerfully shaped these representations. While keeping the particular difficulties of accessing Aboriginal experiences in mind, the chapter also speculates on the meanings of "modern" interwar photos of Aboriginal women, photos that rarely entered the popular press.

Cosmopolitan Looks and National Politics

As Angela Woollacott has argued, late-colonial Australian women's modernity was derived from a sense of "global connectedness." In Woollacott's study, it was the internationalism of the feminist movement, also written about by Marilyn Lake, that enabled women's travel between metropolitan London and its far-flung dominions. White Australian women won the federal vote in 1902, before British or American women. This newfound citizenship impacted on their sense of modernity, which "depended on a comparative international perspective."[4] Unmarked whiteness or the pervasive assumption that whiteness constituted the norm of Australian identity also lay at the heart of late-colonial

Australian women's modernity and was facilitated through the consumption of international cultural forms. Cosmopolitan consumption integrated Australian women into the clientele of globalizing markets. London was perceived as the center of national origin and culture while the colonies were reliant on the imperial center for manufactured goods and seen as merely the source of raw materials. But the metropolitan and discriminatory idea of Australian women settlers as "fictive Europeans" and "Brash Colonials" was challenged by their presence in cosmopolitan political and consumer circuits.[5]

Significantly, cosmopolitan products enabled modern techniques of appearing. The Flapper, for instance, was a type of Modern Girl imported from the United States and Britain.[6] Her techniques of appearing were scrutinized for their internationalism. One tram traveler contributing to the popular magazine *Aussie* "studied" the "amazing geographical array" evident in the Flapper's dress, remarking on her French gloves, American shoes and silk stockings, Italian hat, German handbag, and Swiss handkerchief.[7] Through her visual style, the Flapper spanned modernity's global commercial and representational networks, while her presence in public space simultaneously situated her before a local and scrutinizing gaze. Similarly, the Screen-Struck Girl, a controversial type of Modern Girl that appeared in Australian print media during the 1920s, was mesmerised by American movies and was thus said to be turning her back on the Australian character. White Australian young women constituted 70 percent of Australian film theater audiences and were "eager for entertainment." One advertising campaign that American Paramount Studios ran in the film trade journal *Everyone's* recognized the Modern Girl's consumer power by proclaiming her "Miss 1928." According to the campaign, the Screen-Struck Girl was the "pacemaker of to-day," who could "dictate motion picture styles to-day just as she does clothes and cars." The up-to-the-minute visual style of "Miss 1928" — with her "bobbed hair and knee high skirts" — identified her as an exemplar of modernity.[8] As a self-possessed consumer and spectator, the Modern Girl went about her daily life and leisure with a catalog of international products before her eyes.

It was, however, a delimited cosmopolitanism. Australian types of the Modern Girl were unmarked as white through a prior restriction of non-British immigration that situated whiteness as integral to Australian national identity. The Immigration Restriction Act was the "first major question of policy to come before parliament" after the federation of Australia in 1901.[9] The White Australia policy, as it came to be popularly known, restricted immigration on the basis of race, identified principally by skin color, country of origin, and language. In his work on the spread of European settlers from coastal townships into the Northern tropics, Warwick Anderson finds that whiteness was a persistent category in medical discourse as national hygienists attempted to ameliorate a sense of "racial displacement" and physiological incompatibility with climate and land. He writes that after the 1880s whiteness referred simply to British ancestry.[10] By the 1920s, media references to "native-born" had long assumed whiteness as Australia was the natal home of most white Australians. Where it was conceded to be the home of black Australians, it was a home they had not settled, nor cultivated, but wandered aimlessly over within huge unbounded tracts.

The unresolved paradox of the White Australia Policy was the presence of Australia's original inhabitants and traditional land-owners, the diverse and numerous nations of Australian Aborigines. Aborigines — even if classified racially as "dark Caucasians" or "archaic whites" — were thought to be the last surviving examples of Palaeolithic man, "living fossils" isolated from the inexorable forces of evolutionary selection. They died on contact with modernity because they were its antithesis. As "primitives" they were logically a "dying race" within the hierarchy of racial destiny established by social Darwinism. Aboriginal girls were thus seen to be an anomaly within the Australian modern scene.[11]

The impact of white "settlement" on Aboriginal communities was catastrophic. In the state of Victoria alone, where a permanent settlement commenced at Port Phillip in 1834, it is estimated the Aboriginal population had suffered losses of over 90 percent by 1850.[12] The doctrine of *terra nullius*, which assumed the Australian land mass had been "waste and uncultivated" and that the native inhabitants had no concept of property, enabled a wholesale "revolutionary expropriation of property" from Aborigines.[13] The process of dispossession and the manifest impoverishment and suffering of Aboriginal peoples was rationalized through the discourse of social Darwinism as a "law of nature that where two races whose stages of progression differ greatly are brought into contact, the inferior race is doomed to whither and disappear."[14] By the 1920s, despite the loss of land, kinship ties, and food sources — not to mention the loss of culture through displacement and the deaths of elder custodians of law, ceremony, and language — population decline had been arrested. Aborigines accounted for an estimated less than 2 percent of the nationwide population.[15] The evident growth of "part-Aboriginal" offspring challenged the assumptions of "dying race" theory and inaugurated the assimilationist policies of the 1930s that aimed at the biological and cultural absorption of Aborigines.

As anxiety about the "half-caste problem" grew and Aboriginal girls and young women came under increasing surveillance, 70–80 percent of Aboriginal children removed from their homelands and families to training homes and domestic employment were girls.[16] Aboriginal lives were highly regulated by the state protection boards: from forced settlement on reserves, child removal, employment permits, and marriage laws to the consumption of alcohol, the restriction of education until a maximum of Grade 3, and the disposing of property.[17] As the historian David Hollinsworth writes, "Aborigines were to be controlled in such a way as to exclude them almost completely from the social, cultural and political life of Australian society."[18]

In the training homes, the girls' environment and identity were made to conform to an idealized notion of white female domesticity promoted by the government and its agencies as key to the "successful assimilation" of Aboriginal people.[19] Domestic training in modern techniques of appearing, dress, and, particularly, hygiene aimed to expunge the dirtiness associated with blackness and reorder the identity of Aboriginal girls as servants who enabled and assisted white women's modernity. When the girls were sent into service as apprenticed Aboriginal domestics, their wages were set by protection boards and paid into trust accounts. Sometimes small amounts of pocket money were given to apprentices. Large numbers never saw their accumulated wages.[20] As Jackie Huggins's research into the lives of Aboriginal domestic apprentices in Queensland reveals, women placed into white homes lived under the strictures of the Queensland Master and Servant Act of 1845. They were not allowed to move outside the places of their employment and required a permit to see family. One woman recalled being locked in a cell when her employers went away for weekends. Girls worked on average fifteen-hour days in manual labor that could include digging fence posts, mustering cattle, droving, butchering bullocks, drawing water, and cleaning. Only two of Huggins's research subjects were allowed to handle or prepare food.[21] In addition, physical, sexual, and emotional abuse was commonplace with large numbers of Aboriginal girls becoming pregnant during employment.[22]

There were, of course, significant variations in indigenous modernities in the 1920s. However, in the main, Aboriginal Australians were a population excessively administered and institutionalized.[23] As the indigenous scholar Gordon Briscoe describes, a dual process of segregation of "full-bloods" and assimilation of "half-castes" was well under way in the 1920s and the structural contradiction of these twin colonizing strategies — of exclusion and absorption — created ambivalence in white responses to diversifying Aboriginal identities.[24] In-as-much as the 1920s was a transitional decade in women's relation to modern visual culture, it was a period of change in the administration of Aboriginal populations. These oppressive circumstances dissuaded the social presence of Aboriginal Modern Girls. For Aboriginal young women, participation in Modern Girl styles meant negotiating white policies of assimilation and, perhaps, their own desire to claim "civility" and self-determination.

Modern Girl Types

Australian print media featured the Modern Girl — presumed to be white — in a number of different types. The Business Girl type exemplified that the entrance of women into the Australian public and, specifically, urban space had assumed an ordinariness by the 1920s. And yet Business Girl imagery was suffused by anxieties that still accompanied women through the city's thoroughfares. This figure was represented as misusing her sexual capital by attracting visual attention on the street, associating her with the street whore. She disrupted the flow of looks on which the regulated metropolis depended but was herself seen to be at risk through this exposure. This type embodied Australian women's modernity as manifest in capital exchange, urban mobility, economic independence, and unspoken whiteness.

In a survey of Australian 1920s print media, nonwhite women do not appear as Business Girls. While the public visibility of the Business Girl depended on mobility through the city's thoroughfares, Aboriginal girls lived under a permit system that prohibited their freedom of movement. In addition, Aboriginal populations had been removed to rural reserves where Aboriginal girls were placed as domestic servants in white homes. As with other types of Modern Girl, a virtual white-out occurred in Australia over the Business Girl. As late as 1981 in Darwin, Aboriginal women amounted to only 0.35 percent of the private-sector workforce.[25]

As the Hollywood-derived Screen Star gained prominence in cinema, commentators construed this type of Modern Girl as emblematic of the visual deception of mechanically reproduced spectacle. Questions surrounding the legitimacy of her fame and wealth and the truth of her images recurred. Did the Screen Star hide behind a cosmetic and celebrity mask of her own making, or was she, as a spectacle, being true to her feminine nature? The Screen Star was seen to be representative of an essential aspect of modern feminine identity — the desire to be publicly visible and visually appealing. Commentators viewed the Screen-Struck Girl's proximity to modern spectacle as causing her moral disorientation. She was as easily tricked by unscrupulous "movie sharks" as she was by the reproduced image, leading to an immodest and immoderate desire to appear as a spectacle herself.

The Screen-Struck Girl assumed the burden of social othering through class distinctions. A slum-dwelling type, who did domestic and menial labor, she was never depicted as nonwhite. Personal biographies, however, reveal that some Aboriginal young women relished the cinema, a quintessentially modern experience.[26] Along with dress, engagement with modern technologies was a key marker of racial difference. In 1927, a royal commission into the moving picture industry recommended that Aborigines only attend film screenings that were specially classified as suitable since "with native races the same equanimity is not preserved, vivid and lasting impressions are retained by the natives, and frequently their imagination is riotously aroused."[27] Aboriginal spectators, according to the commission, did not "dictate motion-picture styles" as did "Miss 1928." Instead, their perceived "strong dramatic sense,"[28] facility for ceremonial mime, and acute perceptual faculties as hunters and trackers led them to be overwhelmed by the modern image. An Aboriginal young woman did not appear as a lead in a feature film until 1955 when Ngarla Kunoth-Monks starred in Charles Chauvels's *Jedda*. It had taken Chauvel and his wife, Elsa, two years to cast this Arrernte (Arunta) girl, "one of the most beautiful specimens of her race." Chauvel wrote of the two-year search that spanned 20,000 miles, "We were trying to make women, who had been hopelessly suppressed for thousands of years, 'emote' freely before the camera."[29] This sense of "primitive" anomaly before the modern lens also informed the earlier absence of Aboriginal young women as Screen Stars or Screen-Struck Modern Girls in Australian print media.

During the 1920s, display mannequins expanded from featureless dressmakers' dummies to full-body replicas of white feminine elegance. The display mannequin heralded, from her department store pedestal, that modern feminine beauty was exclusively white, for her skin design was carefully toned as fair and she was mostly blond and only occasionally brunette. The newfound disposable income of Modern Girls was the raison d'être for the mannequin. While Aboriginal young women saw fashions on display and, sometimes, were able to access them through their white mistresses, to the best of my knowledge, a display mannequin has still never been modeled from Aboriginal women in Australia. Since their wages as domestic servants were paid to the state, they hardly had the means to carve out a niche as consumers, mirrored back to them in shop windows in the form of Aboriginal mannequins.[30] Instead, they struck another ornamental pose in Australian cultural life in the decades following the 1920s. They were adopted within Australian domestic and touristic iconography as figurines or as motifs on dishes, ashtrays, souvenir ceramics, and tea towels. They became domestic rather than commercial icons. Aboriginal femininity became a souvenir of racial exile. Often purchasing them while on vacation, whites placed these domestic relics among their knickknacks and in their gardens when they returned home, evoking the

ABORIGINAL BEAUTY
This young lady of the Bush dresses her hair with grass and ochre, and adorns her body with curious designs done in pipeclay. She is a member of the Arunta tribe, from Central Australia.

10.1 White Australian publication depicts Aboriginal beauty as natural unselfconscious yet entailing the universal feminine trait of self-decoration. *Modern Pictorial Atlas*, ca. 1938.

presence of an absented, segregated peoples who nevertheless ornamentally figured a home nation distinct in origin.[31]

A rash of beauty competitions emerged in the Australian print media in the 1920s as refinements in printing techniques and industrialized image production made the use of photographs in newspapers and magazines commonplace. The print beauty competitions inaugurated the twentieth-century habit of judging beauty from reproduced images. The definition of beauty was revised from being the manifestation of inner virtue, particularly modesty, to a purely visual, surface effect. Commodified beauty culture capitalized on the proximate appraisal instituted by the photographs in print beauty competitions. Modern girls were admonished to attend to minute facial imperfections and to "measure up" to celebrity beauties.[32]

Whiteness appeared as a corollary of modern beauty in the print beauty competitions of the 1920s. No photos of Aboriginal young women featured in these competitions, although one Maori entrant's portrait was reprinted from an earlier competition in New Zealand. The photographic representation of indigenous beauty emerged in entirely different media in which Aboriginal women were not assumed as readers or possessors of their own portraits. They were pictured unnamed in ethnographic studies popularized in pictorial atlases, magazines, and travelogues (see figure 10.1).[33] This image appeared in a pictorial atlas around 1938. It also appeared in the nature writer Charles Barrett's booklet *Blackfellows of Australia*.[34] Elaborate techniques of appearing are noted as "curious designs" rather than as insignia of self-mastery or as self-positioning within community-held ceremonial law and traditions. This Arrernte young woman is marked as "primitive" by being naked. The omission of her name from the caption suggests that she did not consciously return the gaze of the camera.

The Flapper was a figure of scandal who excited an enormous amount of popular attention and commentary not only because she associated agency with visibility but because she asserted *sexual* agency through constituting herself as spectacle. The Flapper was perceived to be both naive and calculating about her public exposure as spectacle. As a Modern Girl type, she was associated with mass spectacle as an ardent cinema patron. She symbolized feminized mass culture, modern youth, and modernity as youthful, full of spasmodic movement, and in perpetual flux.

The freedom of movement, disposable income, and sexual self-determination required to enact this type was largely denied Aboriginal women. In addition, their vulnerability to rape was so widespread that it informed the policy of their removal to reserves for protection from marauding white men. Unlike Flappers, Aboriginal young women did not accrue modernity by making themselves visually appealing to, flirting with, or exchanging sexual favors with men. The view voiced in 1884 by the Queensland colonial secretary, A. H. Palmer, that it was impossible to rape Aboriginal women as "they had no idea of chastity" still prevailed among some in the 1920s.[35] When five men from the Victorian town of Sale pleaded guilty to sexual offenses against a "half-caste" girl, under sixteen years of age, from the Lake Tyers Aboriginal Reserve, the defense exonerated them as "easily tempted" and the police denounced the girl as "just like an animal" and "a 'throw back' to the 'primitive' without any idea of morals or restraint."[36] While the Flapper cast "the glad-eye" at men, soliciting them into a relay of looks over which she purportedly had control, the Aboriginal young woman risked sexual assault with such behavior.

It was difficult for Aboriginal young women — as white mistresses' servants and custodians of the state — to inhabit Modern Girl styles and modes of being. They were denied mobility, disposable income, and sexual autonomy, as well as access to media, leisure forms, and urban life. Yet these could be "porous" restrictions as white employers and the state construed Aboriginal young women as both an anomaly to the Australian modern scene and its necessary recruit to meet the aims of assimilation.[37]

Like White

In popular images and narratives about Aboriginal women's engagement with modernity, white Australians were preoccupied with the question of likeness between women of different races. Amid assimilationist policies, likeness was specifically like-white. The longest serving matron at the Cootamundra Training Home for Aboriginal Girls was Ella Hiscocks.[38] One of the so-called ex-inmates has a memory of Matron Hiscocks, a white woman, sitting with her before she went to sleep each night, from the age of three (she was removed from her family and placed in the home when only a few months old), making her pull her nose while Hiscocks stroked it to make it straight.[39]

Anxiety surfaced over whether white girls' self-decoration made them like "primitive" women. If the Modern Girl was unmarked as white in Australia, she was nevertheless seen to be engaging in a kind of cultural miscegenation through her engagement with exoticism. Much humor was derived in popular magazines from identifying the undress of white Modern Girls or their wearing of animal skins and feathers with "primitive" femininity. In one cartoon in *Aussie,* a white girl poses before her mirror in an abbreviated tunic and exaggerated headdress. She asks her friend: "Do you think that my costume is rather original, Peggy?" "Oh my dear, yes! Almost Aboriginal!" Peggy replies.[40] According to this cartoon and other commentary, indigenous and European girls shared "the same decorative instinct."[41] The fad of sunbathing was further proof that modern emancipation was simply a throwback to the uncivilized. One magazine commentator wrote that young women who tanned were "reverting to primitive man's belief that a bronzed skin adds considerably to beauty." This "desire for colour" was seen as "an amazing anomaly . . . in this white Australia of ours."[42]

In a black-and-white drawing by Victoria Ethel Cowdroy (1908–94), the "primitive" and Modern Girl eye each other in a vaudeville club, occupying the same social and significatory space (see figure 10.2).[43] This drawing graced a 1927 cover of *The Triad,* a Sydney art periodical that featured modernist cultural forms in literature, art, theater, and music. While it is unclear whether they are performers backstage or part of the audience, their leafy surrounds and the comparison made between "primitive" and modern dress allude to the essentially primordial nature of modern femininity. Importantly, it was as spectacle that the "primitive" and Modern Girl mirrored each other. Such imagery was influenced by African and Oriental motifs in modernist art and art deco design. The uncovering of the Luxor caves sparked a rash of Egyptian-derived designs in fashion while the popular impact of American jazz was immense. Cartoonist Cowdroy, who also provided illustrations for more popular magazines, positions an African rather than Aboriginal woman to signify jazz's ambiguity as a modern albeit primitive form.[44] In Australia, jazz was perceived as "the revenge of the jungle on civilisation" and "a nigger shuffle" provoking "tottering ape-like convulsions which express the primitive savage."[45] Both as a dance craze, and as a widespread entertainment form in revues and vaudeville minstrels, jazz challenged racial and gender norms.[46]

The modern compulsion to be visible extended to Aboriginal young women at this time but under racially specific conditions. They appeared before a late-colonial administration that aimed to assimilate them not so much as modern subjects but in service to white women's modernity. When girls were placed in white homes their employers were required by law to supply them with clothing.[47] Yet Aboriginal women's appropriation of their employers' techniques of appearing elicited a decidedly ambivalent response from whites. Aboriginal

6d The Triad 6d

VAUDEVILLE—AN IMPRESSION BY VIC COWDROY.

From a Sydney Notebook—See page 2

JUNE 8th, 1927

PUBLISHED BY ART IN AUSTRALIA LTD. 24 BOND ST., SYDNEY.

10.2 Australian jazz positions modern and "primitive" women as mirror images. *The Triad*, 1927.

women's self-mastery in visual appearance was required around white home-steads because white women did not want to be exposed to nakedness and indecency, not because they thought their servants should look fashionable or glamorous. Whites interpreted Aboriginal women's "comic" misappropriation of modern dress as demonstrating their childlike primitiveness and fumbling grasp of modernity.

Significantly, it was the liminal figure of the "station black" who predominated within popular cartoons of the 1920s. This was because the station black negotiated the contradictory imperial imperatives of segregation and absorption by living in separate camps but working either in houses or alongside whites as domestics and stockmen. The jest of a Hugh MacLean cartoon in *Aussie* in 1928, turns around their liminal status (see figure 10.3).[48] It follows that the "detribalised" young woman is semidressed, as her negligee is confused with bridal attire. The "flash pflapper's'" mother, it is suggested, would aspire to the racial uplift signified by "so much" clothing and the joke is on her, I think, as the "naked savage." While the young woman in the cartoon has

"Hooray! Close up get it married quickly now, mine tinkit."
"Py cripes, flash pflapper that one!   Poor ol' mother never had that much clothes in 'er plurry life!"

10.3 Aboriginal women missed the visual cues of the Modern Girl. *Aussie,* 1928.

techniques of appearing in common with the Flapper type, she misses visual cues essential for the correct occupation of Modern Girl style. She wears her "smalls" out of doors. In spite of all these missteps, the ragged pair look on with envy at the smartly dressed girl. White media lampooned Aboriginal responses to modern visual culture and techniques to contain the possibilities of Aboriginal modernities.

The state records of New South Wales (NSW) contain dozens of images of Aboriginal young women dressed in fashionable 1920s attire, including starched white domestic uniforms, street wear and, in one image, a bathing suit. These photos testify to Aboriginal young women's engagement of Modern Girl styles. Yet the circumstances under which these photos were produced highlight the fraught nature of that engagement. These portraits did not appear in white popular media. Recently, they have become important to descendents tracing family members lost through child removal policies. They are, therefore, too sensitive to publish in the context of this chapter.[49] Some of the images

10.4 Hyllus Briggs SNR and Maude Morgan (nee Ross) of Maloga,
Cummeragunga. Photographer unknown, ca. 1920s. From the collection
of A. Jackomos. Reproduced courtesy of the Museum of Victoria.

appeared in an exhibition titled "In Living Memory: Surviving Photographs
from the Records of the Aborigines Welfare Board from 1919 to 1966."[50] This
studio portrait of Hyllus Briggs and Maude Morgan that belongs to the Jack-
amos archive with the Museum of Victoria collections is very similar to the
studio portraits found in the NSW state records (see figure 10.4).

The girl wards of the NSW Aboriginal Welfare Board were photographed in
studios or on city streets in contemporary fashions, uniforms, and, sometimes,
with white child charges. Yet, as the exhibition curator, Susan Charlton, has
written, the images are compromised in that the "very context of their creation
casts doubt on ever being able to reconstruct the complete picture."[51] It is
difficult to ascertain whether the pictures were taken by the board for "in-
mates" to send back to their families or for use in placing them in employment.
Descendents are unsure as to whether the clothes were borrowed or belonged
to the wards. Archivists at the NSW State Records believe the portraits may
have been sent back to Cootamundra by the girls, though the photographs

were originally taken for employers.[52] The portraits clearly had significance to the girls themselves as many of them are signed and dedicated to loved ones. The fact that the portraits remained with the NSW Welfare Board possibly indicate that they were not sent on to families as the girls had perhaps requested. These photos are representations of modern Aboriginal elegance that never circulated in the press. They suggest an engagement with Modern Girl styles that transgressed the racial boundaries signified in the above-discussed black-and-white cartoons while negotiating state policies of assimilation.

The photos also seem at odds with research done into Cootamundra and Aboriginal female domestics. While some of the Huggins's interviewees recall being dressed by their mistresses, who sent away to stores in Brisbane, other Aboriginal women recall wearing their employers' castoffs, sometimes stitching together articles from scraps.[53] Forty girls at Cootamundra, aged from a few months to sixteen years, were supplied with clothing by the Prisons Department that Matron Hiscocks deemed "inappropriate."[54] She repeatedly complained to the Protection Board that shoes supplied were too big and sometimes didn't match up. She reported that she was able to get anything she asked from women's and church charity organizations. Huggins also found that when the girls were placed in white homes, those who received pocket money often spent it on clothes. One of Huggins's interviewees, Mrs. Bond, recalled older girls returning to the mission clad in beautiful clothes. She remembered wanting to earn wages in order to "dress up" in and afford such lavish outfits.[55]

The difficulty in reading these images is highlighted in the response to Diane E. Barwick's article "And the Lubras Are Ladies Now" (1978). Barwick argued that the proficiency of women residents at Victorian government stations between 1860 and 1886 at sewing, crochet, dress, and housekeeping demonstrated their "new emancipation" from authoritarian and patriarchal tribal structures. She claimed white women reserve managers treated them as "friends and equals and because of this they were extremely effective exemplars."[56] Other scholars have refuted the idea that traditional Aboriginal women had little tribal agency and authority and have argued that the coercive hierarchy of white custodian to black "charge" meant that "the missionaries had perfect conditions for creating Black clones of themselves."[57]

The voices of Aboriginal women are essential to resolving the question of their experience of and negotiation of Modern Girl styles. The representational scene in which Aboriginal women occupied Modern Girl imagery in common with white Australian young women was striated by contradictory discourses of assimilation and primitivism. With this in mind, consider what another "abo.maid" named "Amelia" and described by her mistress in the *Australian Woman's Mirror* in 1926 does with the possibilities produced under these conditions. We only have her Missus's word to go by but the Missus's description of Amelia's actions reveals, in the words of Antoinette Burton, "the ways in which women's bodies signalled the instability of cultural difference":[58] "Amelia, who is six feet tall, came in to wait on the table one night dressed in a cerise petticoat and light-blue striped shirt with the tail hanging out all around. A red handkerchief tied over her head and elastic-side boots two sizes too large completed the ensemble."[59] Not lost on this white Missus is the significance of correct appearance in assigning modern feminine identity. She depends on racial abjection to cast Amelia's visual effects as confused, childish, and lacking self-mastery. Lost on Missus, however, is the possibility, perhaps intended by Amelia, of dressing down racial and visual hierarchies.

A photo of the Merry Singers and Dancers of Cummeragunga, taken around 1930 and used in their promotional material to Aboriginal audiences, points to the failure of white popular culture to exclude Indigenous women from the subject position the Modern Girl (see figure 10.5).[60] The Dancers of the Cummeragunga embrace Modern Girl modes of dressing and performing and have presence within the cultural institutions and visual apparati of modernity. Here, a Modern Girl style provides livelihood through its performance as spectacle on the Aboriginal vaudeville touring circuit.

Each of the modalities of Aboriginality discussed above underscore the indigenous scholar Aileen Moreton-Robinson's discussion of "the complexities Indigenous women face in a world under conditions not of their choosing, where they must translate and interpret whiteness, while being 'Other.' " She adds,

> Learning to speak English and mimicking the customs of the coloniser does not fundamentally transform subjectivities that have been socialised within Indigenous social domains. Individuals learn to acquire new knowledges in order to act and function in contexts not of their choosing or control within the dominant culture. Indigenous women have had to gather knowledge about white people and use it in order to survive in the white Australian society. The accumulation of such knowledges does not mean that we have become assimilated. Instead, what it points to is that Indigenous subjectivity is multiple because of the conditions under which it has been shaped. However, multiple subjectivities do not preclude the existence of a core subject position that has the ability to acquire, interpret and create different subject positions in order to participate in society.[61]

This intersubjectivity was visually inscribed within modern culture, facilitating the occupation of Modern Girl types, often with uncertain political effects. The differing occasions of Aboriginal young women's engagement of Modern Girl styles and representations suggest an irregular and uneven process of racial

10.5 Merry Singers and Dancers of the Cummeragunga, Iris Atkinson (nee Nelson), Nona Tye (nee James), and Clare Mouton (nee Murray). Photographer unknown, ca. 1930. From the collection of V. Heap. Permission to scan from *Daughters of the Dreaming* provided by the Museum of Victoria.

distinction that was at play, confounding any dichotomy between agency and racial oppression. These engagements evidently fascinated whites because they simultaneously articulated and broached the visual signifiers of modernity.

Notes

Aboriginal and Torres Strait Islander readers are advised that this chapter contains photographs of people who are deceased. I consulted unpublished writing based on the experiences of Susan Charlton and colleagues at State Records NSW while working with photographs from the records of the former New South Wales Aborigines Welfare Board.

1. "An Abo. Maid," *Australian Woman's Mirror*, 24 November 1925, 42. This mistress wrote unselfconsciously of her charge as having "been in my possession" for six months, and claimed Topsy only needed "warm garments, plain food and kind words, the wages being very small." Another contributor wrote of Aboriginal maids who were spoilt by white influence — "the civilised lubra" knew her "worth too well to be a really satisfactory servant." Wingella, "The Abo. as a Servant," *Australian Women's Mirror*, 3 August 1926, 32.

2. Conor, *The Spectacular Modern Woman*, 2.

3. The golliwog figure appeared as a character in English children's literature. It was derived from American blackface minstrel vaudeville. For instance, see Upton, *The Adventure of Two Dutch Dolls and a Golliwogg*; and Blyton, *The Three Golliwogs*.

4. Woollacott, "White Colonialism and Sexual Modernity," 50; Lake, *Getting Equal*. Each of the then-existing colonies granted women suffrage separately: South Australia in 1894, Western Australia in 1899, New South Wales in 1902, Tasmania in 1903, Queensland in 1904, and Victoria in 1908. The federal franchise was granted to white women in 1902.

5. Maxwell, *Colonial Photography and Exhibitions*, 4.

6. For a discussion of the flapper's origins, see Conor, *The Spectacular Modern Woman*, 213–16.

7. Sally Forth, "The Flapper in the Tram," *Aussie: The Flapper Edition*, 15 April 1929, 66. *Aussie* began as a magazine for Australian diggers (soldiers) in the French trenches in 1918 and continued after the war as a Melbourne-based humor magazine until 1931.

8. "Have You Booked Miss 1928?" *Everyone's*, 4 January 1928, 17–19.

9. La Nauze, *Alfred Deakin*, 277.

10. Anderson, *The Cultivation of Whiteness*, 2.

11. Maxwell, *Colonial Photography and Exhibitions*, 40; Lott, *The Invention of Race*, 7–13.

12. Broome, *Arriving*, 32. In Van Diemen's Land, now Tasmania, an estimated population of 5,000 in 1803 had diminished to 500 on the arrival of Governor Arthur in 1824. Auchmuty, "1810–1830," 53.

13. Reynolds, *Frontier*, quotes from 167 and 194.

14. Editorial from *The Age* (1888) quoted in Hollinsworth, *Race and Racism in Australia*, 91–92.
15. Hollinsworth, *Race and Racism in Australia*, 122.
16. Ibid.
17. Robinson, " 'We do not want one who is too old,' " 167; Cole, "Unwitting Soldiers," 146; Ellinghaus, "Absorbing the 'Aboriginal Problem,' " 196.
18. Hollinsworth, *Race and Racism in Australia*, 97.
19. Cole, "Unwitting Soldiers," 153.
20. Huggins interviewed one Queensland child employed as a domestic worker who reported receiving token amounts such as six pence per week pocket money and a postal check of eight pounds six pence for seven years work. Some received rations such as a new dress every six weeks, flour, tea, and sugar. Others reported receiving no wages whatsoever. Huggins, " 'Firing on in the Mind,' " 14. Also see Cole, "Unwitting Soldiers," 158, n. 73.
21. Huggins, " 'Firing on in the Mind,' " 15–16.
22. Haskins, " 'A Better Chance?' " 34.
23. First contact with Western Desert peoples continued from 1932 to 1984. See Batty, ed., *Colliding Worlds*.
24. Gordon Briscoe, "Aborigines between the Wars: 1920–1944," http://histrsss.anu.edu.au/projecton.html (visited 15 June 2004).
25. Bradley, "A Change in Status for Aboriginal Women?" 147.
26. For instance, see Langford, *Don't Take Your Love to Town*, 6.
27. The 33rd recommendation of the 1927–28 Royal Commission regarding the Moving Picture Industry stated under the heading "The Film and Native Races": "That no moving picture film shall be screened before audiences of Aborigines or natives of the Mandated Territories unless such film has been passed by the Censorship Board for such exhibition." The recommendation to classify films especially for Aboriginal audiences was not realized in legislation. Bertrand, *Cinema in Australia*, 119; "Film Commission's Report," *Everyone's*, 25 April 1928, 6.
28. Duncan-Kemp, *Where Strange Paths Go Down*, 39.
29. "Eve in Ebony . . . the story of *Jedda*," *ScreenSound* (1954). *ScreenSound* was a promotional magazine published by Columbia Pictures of Sydney. This issue examined at the National Film and Sound Archives, Canberra.
30. The clothing fashion chain Bardot featured an Aboriginal model ("Samantha") in its winter 2005 season. Australian media reacted positively and other Aboriginal models are now discussed as up-and-coming models in websites.
31. See Marcus, *A Dark Smudge upon the Sand*, 187–96.
32. Smart, "Feminists, Flappers and Miss Australia"; Conor, "The Beauty Contest in the Photographic Scene."
33. "Aboriginal Beauty," 82.
34. Barrett, *Blackfellows of Australia*, 10.
35. Quoted in Hollinsworth, *Race and Racism in Australia*, 83.

36. "Half-Caste Girl Menace," *Truth*, 6 December 1924, 9. The girl was detained by the court and then committed to the Salvation Army Home at Riddell's Creek, Victoria.

37. See Burton's discussion of "the porousness of colonialism" in her Introduction, 2.

38. Cootamundra Girls Training Home was 380 kilometers southwest of Sydney, established in 1911. Cole, "Unwitting Soldiers."

39. Ibid., 148.

40. *Aussie*, 15 October 1930, 51.

41. "Like White Feller Missus!" *Adam and Eve*, 1 January 1927, 45.

42. "Effect of Sun-Bathing: Beneficial in Moderation—Dangerous in Excess," *Adam and Eve*, 1 September 1929, 15.

43. *The Triad*, 8 June 1927, 1.

44. Kerr, ed., "Vic Cowdroy," 148.

45. Quotes from "Jazz Music," *Gossip*, 10 December 1924, 31; "That Is—The Charleston Craze," *Adam and Eve*, 1 September 1928, 34; and Isadora Duncan, "My Life," *Herself*, 20 January 1931, 32.

46. *Truth* (16 January 1926, 9) reported that "nigger minstrels" were at the "height of a boom in Australian vaudeville." Australia was "one step in the large Pacific vaudeville circuit" and minstrel shows had toured there since the *Argus* advertised "Rainer's Original Ethiopian Serenaders" in January 1853. See Bisset, *Black Roots and White Flowers*, 4.

47. See Chauvel, *Walkabout*, 190.

48. "Flash Phlapper," in *Aussie*, 15 February 1928, 61. MacLean's black-and-white drawings of Aboriginal Australians appeared in major newspapers. Along with notable early-century Australian artists, MacLean was an original member of the Prehistoric Order of Cannibals Club. Lindsay, *Drawing from Life*, 91.

49. Photographs of the Aborigines, Welfare Board, ca. 1924–61, New South Wales State Records.

50. See special exhibition issue of *Vital Signs* 9 (September 2006). My thanks to the curator, Susan Charlton, for informing me of this exhibition. I urge readers to access the website at http://www.records.nsw.gov.au/exhibition/ using the password "exhibition."

51. Charlton, "In Living Memory," 36.

52. Personal communication with Kirsten Thorpe, Archivist-Aboriginal Liaison Public Access, State Records NSW, April 2005. See also Cooper, "The Aboriginal Welfare Board Photographs," 65–69.

53. Robinson, " 'We do not want one who is too old,' " 173.

54. Cole, "Unwitting Soldiers," 150.

55. Huggins, " 'Firing on in the Mind.' "

56. Barwick, "And the Lubras Are Ladies Now," 51–63.

57. "Little tribal agency": see Bradley, "A Change in Status for Aboriginal Women?" 151–54; "Black clones of themselves": see Tonkinson, "Sisterhood or Aboriginal Servitude?" 28.

58. Burton, Introduction, 5.

59. The contributor also describes Dinnah and Mary as comic in domestic ineptitude: Mary

picked up the carcass of the chicken from the serving platter and left the room with it in her hands; Dinnah took five weeks to learn to set the table. "The Ways of the Abo. Servant," *Australian Woman's Mirror*, 16 November 1926, 11.

60. The Museum of Victoria, *Daughters of the Dreaming*, 41. This image also appeared in an exhibition at the Museum of Victoria in 1990. I have been given permission to reproduce this image from Mary Morris, Collection Manager for Indigenous Photographs, Ethno-Historical Collection, the Museum of Victoria.

61. Moreton-Robinson, *Talkin' Up to the White Woman*, 89.

11

The "Modern Girl" Question in the Periphery of Empire

Colonial Modernity and Mobility

among Okinawan Women

in the 1920s and 1930s

RURI ITO

In Japan the Modern Girl, or *moga*, appeared in the aftermath of the Great Kantō Earthquake of 1923. While the term "New Women" (*atarashii onna*) had been widely attributed in the years following 1910 to intellectuals involved with the journal *Seitō*, it was generally said to symbolize autonomous personhood, a belief in the freedom of love, and the pursuit of a distinctive women's culture. Moga, on the other hand, was intricately related to the rise of mass consumer culture.[1] Without drawing a rigid distinction between these two representations of modern Japanese women in the early twentieth century, it is important at the same time and for the purpose of this chapter to confirm some of the traits that were attached to moga. These included a drive toward gendered consumer culture, conspicuous consumption, defiance against patriarchal control over women's body and sexuality,[2] and cosmopolitan urban taste, all leading to a new sense of femininity.

Tracing the Silhouette of Modern Girl in Okinawa

This chapter approaches the Modern Girl question from the vantage point of Okinawa, a prefecture of islands that was integrated to Japan in 1879, eleven years after the Meiji Restoration. The question of whether or not there ever was a Modern Girl phenomenon in these poverty-stricken islands seems not to have attracted researchers' attention. This may be because in the prewar period, the main island of Okinawa remained a heavily agrarian society, as did the smaller, more remote islands. In the 1920s and 1930s, the population of Naha, prefectural Okinawa's largest city, fluctuated at around 60,000 inhabitants. Tokyo, on the other hand, had already exceeded a population of two million. Indeed in the mid-1920s, when urban mass culture was flourishing in Tokyo or in Kobe during the rise of Taisho democracy, the Okinawan economy was taking a drastic turn for the worse due to the fall of the price of sugar on which much of the countryside depended. This period was remembered as *sotetsu jigoku* or the "sago palm hell," because people in the rural area had so little food they were forced to subsist on the scarcely edible inner part of sago palm. Okinawa, thus, was not only located far from the center of the Japanese empire, at the southern periphery of its "*naichi* (inner territory); it was also a distance from the centers of capitalist growth. The urban culture and consumerism, usually considered prerequisites for the moga phenomenon, were still very weak.

Yet, significantly, Makiminato Tokuzō (1912–2004), an Okinawan journalist and poet, recalling his youth in the early 1930s, states that he met a bobbed hair woman coming out of the street of Kaminokura-dori, a quarter where well-to-do families of Naha lived.

> In the old days of Naha, with a background of *bayan* and *fukugi* trees, roofs covered with red clay tiles and stacked up stone walls, I remember having met a thrillingly beautiful woman walking down the lane. She wore a short hair, a so-called Brookes type haircut. Dressed in Japanese kimono matching strangely well with her bob hair, the woman had big eyes, rich and dark eyelashes, a feature rather common among Okinawan people. Her somewhat round countenance as well as her bare feet, wearing a pair of *geta* without *tabi*, left me a strong impression.[3]

Makiminato's nostalgic description is a rare source that explicitly refers to the existence of the Modern Girl phenomenon in Okinawa.

The significance of the Okinawan case in the cross-national study of Modern Girls is twofold. First there is the obvious question of how a Modern Girl could emerge at all in a provincial city with limited urban infrastructure and still

11.1 "Louise Brooks was in Naha as well." Sketch drawn by Makiminato Tokuzō. Makiminato, *Gensō no Machi*, 1986.

poorly developed consumer culture. A second issue to be addressed here is the question of "colonial modernity,"[4] and the dynamics of assimilation in Okinawa under the Japanese empire. This context gives a totally different perspective to the Modern Girl question viewed hitherto from the imperial capital city. Since the late fourteenth century, Okinawa, known then as the kingdom of Ryukyu, held tributary ties with various Chinese empires. This arrangement continued even after Satsuma *han* invaded in 1609 and forcibly made it a de facto protectorate of the Tokugawa Shogunate. This history of *nisshi-ryōzoku* (dual subordination to Japan and China) was officially ended through territorial integration to the modern Japanese state. But it was not until 1895, when China lost the Sino-Japanese war, that the remaining hope among pro-China Okinawan leaders that they might be able to remain a Chinese protectorate was abandoned.

Within the Japanese colonial empire, Okinawa's experience of *dōka*, or assimilation to Japanese culture and way of life, had commonalities with other Japanese colonies such as Taiwan or Korea.[5] However, the integration of Okinawa into Japan took place in the initial phase of nation-state building, before the promulgation of the imperial constitution of 1889. This made Okinawa juridically part of *naichi* rather than *gaichi* (outer territory) or "colony" in a formal sense. Also, according to Oguma Eiji, since the interest the Meiji government held in Okinawa was mainly focused on territorial security and southern expansion, the government did not invest in Okinawa's economic development as much as it did in the case of Taiwan or Korea.[6]

What characterized colonial policy in Okinawa then was its emphasis on assimilation. As soon as the first governor of Okinawa arrived in Naha in 1880, *kaiwa denshūjo* (conversation school) was founded to teach Okinawan elites the "Japanese language," which in fact was the Tokyo language since at that time the very concept of "*kokugo*" (national language) had yet to be established. By the turn of the century, the emergent Okinawan new leaders, such as Ōta Chōfu, were promoting a wholesale "*yamatoka*" or Japanization, in terms of language, dress, manners, and customs, and boosted it as the road to civilization and modernity. In the endeavor, women, especially young women of the upper classes, were expected to play a crucial role as enlightened "wives" and "mothers" of the future.

The point is that "modern" and the stakes involved in the Modern Girl question were sensibly different in Okinawa. Whereas in Tokyo, the representation of modernity was necessarily linked to the West, in Okinawa, the frame of reference was *tafuken* or "other prefectures," and mostly importantly, Tokyo.[7] For Okinawa Japanization overlapped with modernization and the latter with the standardization of Japanese national culture. The dynamics of this colonial modernity also meant that in response to the assimilationist pressure of the new Japanese nation-state, the identity of Okinawan people came to be forged through the intellectual movement of what was later called *Okinawagaku* or Okinawan studies.

This chapter is divided into three sections, followed by a short conclusion. First, I discuss the creation of modern schoolgirl culture in early-twentieth-century Okinawa, as a prerequisite for the emergence of both New Women and Modern Girls. Schools, a core institution of assimilation policy, also stimulated the desire for upward mobility. They constituted a "contact zone,"[8] where mainland-educated teachers, many from the former Satsuma han, and themselves migrants, came into contact with girl students, who, in their turn, would travel in various ways and to diverse destinations in the Japanese colonial empire. *Yūgaku*, or pursuing studies on the mainland, was particularly popular among the daughters of upper classes.

Section two deals with another site of modernity, Iha Fuyū's intellectual circle. Known as the founder of Okinawan studies, Iha played a central role in efforts to develop a group of so-called New Women educated at Okinawa's girls' higher schools.[9] After looking at the traits distinguishing these New Women, I examine in the third section a series of portraits of young women, daughters of the rising new Okinawan elite, published in the newspaper *Ryūkyū Shimpō* in 1934. This section focuses on the effort among new elite families to reconfigure gender and it relocates Modern Girls within a class dynamics. My discussion throughout draws heavily on the biographies and autobiographies of women, who lived their youth in the 1920s and 1930s. Evidence from essays compiled by the alumni association of prefectural girls' higher schools will also be offered to illustrate my arguments.

Girls' School Culture: Negotiating Assimilation and the Modern

Girls' education in Okinawa was launched in 1885, five years after the institution of public boy's education. This marked a tremendous change in the history of Okinawa, since female illiteracy was universal even among the upper classes.

Hokama Yoneko's anthology of eighty "notable women" includes striking stories about girls and women born of *noro* or priestesses families, a traditionally privileged status for women, who, with the Japanization, made a dramatic shift from their traditional religious roles to active participants of the modern "good wife, wise mother" project disseminated in the modern school curriculum.[10]

Modernization through Japanization for Okinawan women was thus abrupt, condensed, and accelerated. It was accelerated not only because of the assimilationist policy that intensified in the late 1930s with the general social and military mobilization but also because of the internal pressure that male leaders in Okinawa placed on the women of Okinawa to Japanize.

Komagome Takeshi points out that in the case of Japanese imperialism, public schools played an important role in cultural integration, comparable to missionary schools in Western imperialism.[11] As in more distant colonies, schools provided the entry points for tennoism or emperorism disseminated through the Imperial Rescript on Education and the imperial portrait. Schools were a privileged site of Japanization, a place to "improve the manners and customs" (*fūzoku kairyō*). This was a particularly important aspect of girls' education. Beginning with the campaign to learn *futsūgo* or standard language,[12] girl students had to switch from *ryūsō* (Okinawan-style clothes) to *wasō* (Japanese-style clothes) and, once graduated, they were to promote the campaign to do away with local ways of life in the community.[13]

In this respect, two institutions merit particular attention: Prefectural Girls' Higher School and Prefectural Women's Normal School, known respectively as Ichikōjo and Joshi-shihan.[14] Ichikōjo was the first girls' higher school (*kōto jogakkō*) to be established in Okinawa and provided a four-year program for girls aged thirteen to sixteen.[15] Founded as a private school in 1900, it soon obtained the status of prefectural school in 1903.[16] On the other hand, Joshi-shihan, whose mission was to train future schoolteachers, originated first as Joshi Kōshuka (a two-year program) in 1896. After becoming a division of the Prefectural Normal School in 1910, it finally obtained its independence as the Girls' Normal School in 1915. Ichikōjo and Joshi-shihan maintained a close relation — indeed a rivalry — since they were located for the most part on the same campus. While Joshi-shihan recruited students from different parts of Okinawa and its students lived in dormitories, the students of Ichikōjo came mostly from Naha and Shuri and hence were said to be more urban and sophisticated in their taste.

Higa Kame, herself from Ginowan and one of the twenty girls to have entered Private Girls' Higher School (former Ichikōjo) in 1900 with the first batch of students, recalls that her classmates — except for one — were either daughters of Ryūkyū aristocrats or daughters of merchants coming from mainland Japan, known as "*kiryū shōnin*."[17] Higa switched to the Joshi Kōshūka program immediately because Okinawa lacked teachers for primary schools at that time. Soon, students from different parts of Okinawa increasingly joined Joshi-shihan. In its dormitory, students encountered for the first time the different dialects and customs of Okinawa at the same time as they were learning Japanese language and manners. Schools were also a place where teachers educated on the mainland brought new knowledge and information from the outer world.

In this newly created contact zone, a different sense of social distinction grew rapidly to replace the previous hierarchy of feudal statuses. A new type of cultural capital linked directly to the urban culture of Tokyo and other big cities infiltrated schoolgirl culture. Higa notes, for instance, that already in 1900 she felt that the daughters of Japanese merchants living in Naha were more fashionable because they knew how to use cosmetics. Apparently in Naha, wearing makeup — using face powder or rouge — was considered indecent, a courtesans' practice from the district of Tsuji, and not part of "respectable" women's culture.[18] Obviously, then, a new sense of femininity was clearly being constructed at school and in the dormitories, a girls' aesthetic distinct from that of their mothers' generation. The competition for fashion seems to have rapidly grown, because six years after its inauguration, Prefectural Girls' Higher School (Ichikōjo) established a dress code. It prescribed that students could spend no more than three yen when making new *hakama*, a pleated long culotte, or buying a new pair of shoes. The school regulation also banned the use of silk for making clothes or Western umbrellas; and students were commanded to refrain from buying any kind of luxury or unnecessary commodities.[19]

Kinjō Yoshiko also notes that by the time she reached Ichikōjo in 1914, the girl students were competing over matters of taste and style in language. While she spoke Okinawan language with her classmates at school, when it came to talking to teachers or speaking in public, she used standard Japanese. Indeed, the girls considered a Tokyo accent particularly fashionable and "*modan.*" Understandably, a strong rivalry existed between the Naha children (*nahakko*) and *yamatunchu*, or Japanese girls studying in the same class.

> "We cannot allow ourselves to fail in front of those people," was our feeling, but there was a variety of *yamatunchu*. For example, the daughter of the Director of Education unit at the prefecture, or of a judge. These children stayed only a short time, just during their father's stay. When his term was over, they left. Sometimes, children from the Tōhoku area, with a heavy dialect came too and we could make fun of them. They were not our rivals.

Our rivals were those who were living in the same area as us. These people had economic power and sometimes their cultural level was also superior to Okinawan people. By and large, their children got good grades. In the past, it seems that their manner had been quite arrogant, but by the Taisho period, their status was beginning to erode, so our feelings toward them were [softening, too]. So we did not consider them to be enemies but rivals.

. . . Since at school, Japanization was top priority, the Japanese descendants were our suitable target of competition. We did not "sneeze as the people of other prefectures do" but when those *yamatunchu* sneezed with a Kagoshima accent, we would sneeze back with a Tokyo accent. That was the kind of spirit we had.[20]

The "rivals," as Kinjō calls them, were descendants of merchants, doctors, and junior high school teachers who had come for the most part from Kagoshima Prefecture, the former Satsuma domain. The statement made by Ōta Chōfu in 1900 had urged high school girls to imitate the Japanese in everything, even in sneezing. Kinjō recounts how one of her best Okinawan friends would visit Tokyo during the holidays and come back with the newest fashion, such as "chignon à la Louise."[21] To excel in fashion and in language vis-à-vis daughters of *yamatunchu* was the same logic that built Modern Girls' culture through competition.

Around 1901, girl students at the two-year teacher training program found themselves obliged to wear a Japanese style kimono with a tight *obi*, a sash. The students started complaining that tight Japanese clothes were not suitable for climbing the steep slopes of Shuri to school. They asked for changes in the regulations so they could wear hakama, which was much more practical and starting to become a fashion in Tokyo. The principal of the normal school, Andō Kiichirō, refused, stating: "The traditional Okinawan clothes are of bad taste and it is not good to maintain such weird looking clothes now that we are part of Japan . . . From a practical point of view, it is true that the traditional clothes are more convenient. If it were only a matter of practicality, we need not wear those inconvenient '*naichi fuku*' [clothes of inner territory]. As we have opted for '*naichi fuku*,' we are adopting a viewpoint not of practicality but the 'necessary unity of customs and manners.'"[22] This somewhat esoteric interpretation of dress code policy was abandoned with an unexpected ease when a new teacher arrived from the mainland, dressed in hakama. Immediately students learned how to make the garment and afterwards hakama was adopted as the symbol of modern professional Okinawan women.[23]

Westernized clothes, the other gateway to modernity that Hani Motoko (1872–1957) was advocating in Tokyo through the mainland women's journal *Fujin no Tomo*, reached Okinawa girls' higher schools in the mid-1920s.[24]

After debates among students on whether they should wear Japanese style clothes or Western-style clothes, Ichikōjo decided to adopt a "sailor type" uniform, which was considered both Western and the height of schoolgirl fashion in 1926.[25] At that time Naha was in an incipient phase of urban culture that included the opening of the department store Yamagataya in 1923, the transition to automobile transportation, and the introduction of tramways.

Anecdotes like these are abundant and illustrate how the dynamics of Japanization unfolded at the micro level of girls' everyday life at school. Not only was assimilation not unilateral; the evidence suggests that women and girls contested and negotiated the content of what would count as modern at the various schools.

A Desire for Freedom: Iha's Enlightenment Project and the New Women

In 1916, the year *Seitō* stopped publication, Iha Fuyū along with Higa Seikan and others founded Okinawa Kumiai Kyōkai (Okinawa Congregational Church). A group of young women female graduates from Ichikōjo came to join the church. Among them were Tomihara Hatsuko (1888–1974), Macda Fuyuko (1897–1975), Tamaki Oto (1897–1993), Kinjō Yoshiko (1901–91), and Arakaki Mitoko (1901–96).[26] Soon local conservatives were mocking them as the New Women of Okinawa.[27] According to Tamaki, because of her classmate Maeda's passion for Japanese tanka and novels, Tamaki had learned about the journal *Seitō* and read some of the issues, although the movement led by Japanese New Women had relatively little impact on the local girl culture.[28] Rather it was Iha's erudition and the enthusiasm for the enlightenment of Okinawan women that drew them to his circle.

By this time, Iha was already a well-known linguist and folklorist. After graduating from Imperial University of Tokyo in 1906, Iha was appointed the first director of the Prefectural Library, and he played a central intellectual role before universities existed in Okinawa. Most commentators concur that in his role as spiritual leader of the Congregational Church he spent less time preaching religious dogma and more time exposing Okinawan students to a wide range of knowledge deriving from the Western world.[29] Iha's insistence that they read as many books as they could in the library led his young female disciples to Tolstoy, Dostoyevsky, and Shakespeare, and to theories in philosophy and social sciences, including August Bebel's *Women and Socialism*, the work of Kawakami Hajime, linguistics, art history, and classes in Esperanto.[30] Importantly Iha's circle involved a transnational network of Okinawan pastors, scholars, students, and transmigrants, who traveled back and forth between Naha and points abroad, including the United States and South America. Such

11.2 Iha Fuyū and the New Women of Okinawa, ca. 1916. Back row at far left is Kinjō, a bearded Iha standing beside her. Front row, second from the left is Maeda. Naha City Museum of History.

travel brought first-hand information about Western lifestyles back to the is-lands and expanded broadly what modern could mean beyond Japanization.

Another feature of Iha's lectures was his profound interest in the folklore and the history of Okinawan people. *Koryūkyū*, his first book on ancient Ryūkyū, published in 1911, made him the most prominent scholar of Okinawa and inspired important folklorists like Yanagita Kunio and Origuchi Shinobu. Eight years later, he and Majikina Ankō published *Okinawa Joseishi* (Oki-nawan Women's History), in which, on the basis of an analysis of women's status in ancient Ryūkyū, he concluded with a plea for the education of Oki-nawan women, declaring it the most urgent issue facing Okinawa's develop-ment. For young Okinawan men to satisfy their ambition for social mobility, in which, incidentally, he included *ijyūyoku* or "the desire to migrate," it was important that they be blessed with educated wives.[31] In a transitional period such as this, Iha wrote, many of his friends were suffering "unhappy, or to be more precise, unbalanced marriages" because there were not enough suffi-ciently well-educated women available for marriage. Behind Iha's enlightenment project for island women, then, it is possible to read an acute anxiety regarding the "underdevelopment" of Okinawa.[32]

Viewed from the perspective of the New Women, however, Iha's circle did provide a space for independent thought beyond Japanization. This is not to say that Iha rejected assimilation. Like his contemporary Ōta, Iha was keen to educate women, even when this meant their Japanization. In this respect, Iha exhibits his own limitations.[33] That said, Iha's circle offered an alternative site of modernity where, in contrast to the girls' higher schools, women could cultivate their knowledge of Western thought and be introduced to Okinawan culture and history, denied them under the Japanese policy of assimilation. New Women accompanied Iha, who made multiple visits to remote islands and villages in Okinawa, lecturing on what he called "*minzoku eisei*" or the "hygiene of people." These lectures, influenced by eugenicist ideas and given in Okinawan dialect, aimed at the improvement of Okinawan people and were mostly addressed to local women.

Although the New Women were not exactly an intellectually homogenous group, they held a common belief in the kind of humanism Iha was professing, particularly the freedom of love and marriage. Almost all of them challenged the traditional norms of family and marriage in one way or another. In the case of Tamaki, her participation in Iha's circle led her to join a socialist study group organized by Yamada Yūkan, a leading theorist of Bolshevism. Yamada, then married, and Tamaki established a romantic relationship. This extramarital affair provoked such strong criticism that Tamaki had to resign from the primary school where she had been teaching. She later married Yamada and gave birth to a son, whom she named "Lenin." After her son Lenin's death, she divorced Yamada and emigrated to Brazil in 1927.[34] Romantic love and the freedom to love is also a feature in the case of Maeda Fuyuko, who, after divorcing her first husband, struck up a love relation with Iha himself and as a consequence had to leave Naha for Tokyo in 1924.[35]

In Kinjō's case, her mother had chosen to affiance her when she was attending Ichikōjo.[36] As a result of frequenting Iha's circle, Kinjō began to question this arrangement and eventually fell in love with Yamada Yūkō, Yamada Yūkan's brother and also a socialist thinker, who was married and already had one child. After her romance with Yūkō ended, Kinjō eventually moved to Tokyo in 1925, where she married Kinjō Chōei, one of Iha's disciples, and settled down. She worked for a time at Kaizōsha, one of the era's major publishers, and after confronting many difficulties finding a stable job, she ultimately made her career as a social worker.

Iha's enlightenment project in Okinawa came to an end in 1925 when he himself left Naha to join Maeda. As if in a cultural exodus, many in Iha's circle came to resettle in Tokyo, perhaps to transplant the intellectual network of Iha's Okinawa studies to a place less subject to Naha social pressures. Although most of these people had come from upper-class families in and around Naha, the worsening impoverishment of Okinawa, especially in the rural areas, and the higher cost of life in Tokyo meant that means were extremely limited. Mutual aid through the network of Okinawan relatives and friends proved crucial to daily survival in the emerging ethnic networks of Tokyo. Significantly, Kinjō recalls that despite severe economic hardship, life in Tokyo during the second half of the 1920s was exciting in terms of intellectual and cultural life.[37] This indeed was the period of flourishing urban mass culture symbolized by mogas and *mobos*, or modern boys. Okinawan poets, artists, novelists, and scholars participated in the various movements that characterized Taishō modernism.

Unlike the Japanese New Women of *Seitō*, then, these Okinawan women did not organize themselves as a group and were not defined by a specific project. Between 1910 and 1925 it was their passionate commitment to new knowledge and their pursuit of modernity, expressed most eloquently through their romances with the new generation of Okinawan male intellectuals, that characterized them as a cohort. In their defiance against traditional patriarchal control over women's bodies, and their taste for cosmopolitan aesthetics, they shared some of the traits of Modern Girls. Due to Iha's own cosmopolitan taste for coffee, cigarettes, Western delicacies, and rare commodities that travelers brought from abroad, New Women in his circle found themselves exposed to imported goods that most people in Naha would never have seen.[38] The famous picture of the members of the Congregational Church, taken circa 1916, illustrates this relation between the men intellectuals, dressed in elegant Western suits, and the women of Okinawa gorgeously wearing *sokuhatsu*, a modernized Japanese hairstyle, kimono, and tabi (see figure 11.2).

The Ambivalent Look: Daughters of the New Elite and the Reconfiguring of Gender

Among these New Women, Arakaki was the only one able to pursue her professional career as a writer and a novelist. She did this in a unique way. After a passionate romance with Ikemiyagusuku Sekihō, a well-known Okinawan novelist, during her student years in Tokyo, Arakaki decided to raise her son by herself in Naha, where she obtained a job at the Prefectural Office. But pregnant with her second child and hoping to earn a better living, she returned again to Tokyo in 1928, where she studied at Marie Louise School of Beauty Treatment, a pioneer in the beauty salon industry. Then, in 1930, Arakaki set up a salon of her own in Naha, in the house that Iha had used for his seminars.

Her shop soon became popular for permanent waves and is reputed to have been the fashion leader of its time in Naha. The income from this salon enabled Arakaki to pursue her own writing.[39]

The bob-haired Modern Girl that Makiminato reported seeing in the early days of Shōwa coincides precisely with the time that Arakaki opened her beauty salon. Also in 1930, Yamagataya opened a new department store branch in Ufujōme dori, the main street of Naha, and initially recruited for the first time twenty *depāto girls* (department store sales girls). The announcement said that depāto girls were required to be "good looking and clear-headed." One hundred and thirty candidates showed up; twenty of them, all graduates of girls' higher school, were selected for employment. The depāto girls dressed in kimono and wore makeup. Ōmine Katsuko, who was among the twenty hired, recalls that she was in charge of the necktie section. In 1934, Yamagataya changed the shop girls' uniform from kimono to Western-type dress. Along with schoolteachers, bus conductors, nurses, bank employees, and telephone operators, department store clerks represented the emergence of new female professions and the advent of *shokugyō fujin* (professional women).

"Portraits of Beauties," published in 1934 by *Ryūkyu Shimpō*,[40] is one of the rare remnants of visual information remaining in the archives which portrays these elegant modern young women of the early Shōwa period and includes some description of their background. The series shows thirty-eight young women, daughters of the new elite class born between 1910 and 1916, thus ranging between eighteen and twenty-four years of age. All but eight were of Okinawan origin. Among their fathers' professions, medicine was by far the most prevalent (44 percent), followed by business (24 percent), politics (14 percent), and others including law, civil service, and journalism. Eighteen of them were declared to be *kaji tetsudai*, domestic work helpers.

From the viewpoint of Modern Girl studies, two elements attract our attention. The first is how these young women are dressed. At this point, none is dressed in Ryūkyū-style clothes.[41] Twenty-eight are dressed in formal Japanese-style kimono, two in hakama, five in sailor-style school uniform, and eight in Western dress. Among the latter, four have short permed hair and a clear Modern Girl look. All were born in Naha. Two, Ōkubo Mutsuko and Kiguchi Chieko, come from settler families. Ōkubo's father, a Christian and a doctor by profession, came originally from Tokushima prefecture and settled down in Naha in 1896. Kiguchi's father came from Kagoshima and settled in Naha in 1885 as a doctor as well. Both Ōkubo and Kiguchi studied in Ichikōjo; following her graduation, Ōkubo studied in Tokyo, and Kiguchi worked in Naha as a dentist, a new profession for women. The other two originated from Okinawa. Nakayoshi Toshiko's father was a doctor. After graduating from

11.3 Yamagataya in Naha. Naha City Museum of History.

11.4 Marume Market and Maruyamagō in Naha. The signboards on the left read "Lion hamigaki" (Lion toothpaste) and "Lait Keshohin" (Lait Cosmetics). Naha Shuppansha.

11.5 Ufujōme Street, the main street of Naha in the early 1930s. In the right-hand corner is a bob-haired woman. Naha City Museum of History.

primary school, Nakayoshi was sent to Tokyo, where she completed her studies at a girls' higher school and then majored in gymnastics and modern dance. She signed her portrait using roman letters, a mark of cosmopolitan taste. Agena Chieko's father, a lawyer, saw his daughter graduate from Ichikōjo and go on to Tokyo Women's Academy of Fine Arts, where she learned Japanese embroidery, which she described as "an art that is not yet well known to people."

The second element of interest concerns the hobbies these young women were said to pursue. In general, there is a strong emphasis on *shūyō*, or moral cultivation, which is related to their future role as housewife.

Miss Minami Yoshiko is the daughter of Mr. Minami Yoshijiro, a business leader. Currently 22 years old. Miss Yoshiko has many hobbies. She is knowledgeable in classical Japanese hobbies, such as *naga'uta, koto*, and sewing and is now striving to cultivate herself as a young woman . . .

On the left is the elder sister Akiko (22 years old) and on the right younger sister

Setsuko (20 years old). Both graduated Girls' Higher School No. 2 in the spring of 1932. Both are getting trained by their mother to become housewives capable of fostering healthy and good families. Under the influence of their father, they are cultivating themselves not to be self-centered but to be home-centered and always cheerful.

Miss Tanaka Chiyoko is 20 years old. She is the eldest daughter of Dr. Tanaka Otokichi of Nishihonmachi. After having graduated Girls' Higher School No. 2 in 1932, Miss Tanaka enrolled in the one year specialized course of Osaka Girls' Higher School, where she majored in Japanese sewing . . . As the eldest of four sisters, Miss Tanaka is presently at home helping out with the housework, and cultivating herself as a Japanese woman through lessons in *koto* and flower arrangement.

"Moral cultivation to be acquired as a [Japanese] woman" is an expression that appears in almost all of the descriptions. Hobbies such as flower arrangement, Japanese traditional music (*koto, naga'uta*), or tea ceremony are perceived as the kind of culture young women of "good families" are expected to acquire before marriage. The three most popular hobbies listed in these short biographies are flower arrangement, Japanese traditional music, and sewing.

There are, however, strikingly obvious hobbies that do not really fit into this more conventional model. These less predictable ones include watching movies, reading books, photography, and social dance. Among the four Modern Girls in the series, Nakayoshi declares her hobby to be "dancing," which she learned studying with Nikaidō Tokuyo, founder of Japan Women's College of Physical Education in Tokyo. Kiguchi's hobbies are photography and cinema. She is described as a woman who "owns her favorite camera with which she loves to take snap shots." Others, although dressed in kimono, talk of cinema, social dance, or tennis as their hobbies. These new activities and the cultural propensity for urban taste, symptomatic of Modern Girls, are likely to have been acquired in their experiences of "*yūgaku*." Among the thirty-eight women, fourteen, or 37 percent, of them pursued their studies outside Okinawa: eleven in Tokyo, two in Osaka, and still another in Taipei.

What the analysis of these thirty-eight portraits of young women reveals is a reconfiguring of gender relations among the new Okinawan elite families. In the context of traditional Naha work culture, it was common for women — even among *shizoku*, the upper class — to practice commerce or work as artisans and to sustain the household economy.[42] Kinjō recounts that when she was a child, her mother trained her to sell matches or firecrackers in the street with a melodious cry, and that this kind of training was considered part of cultivation for girls even from upper-class families.[43] The new urban work style of *shokugyō fujin*, which gradually penetrated the ascending new middle class, was based on a different assumption according to which "home" was to be

11.6 Ōkubo Mutsuko, age eighteen. *Ryūkyū Shimpō*, 1934.

11.7 Kiguchi Chieko, age twenty-four. *Ryūkyū Shimpō*, 1934.

11.8 Nakayoshi Toshiko, age twenty. *Ryūkyū Shimpō*, 1934.

11.9 Agena Chieko, age nineteen. *Ryūkyū Shimpō*, 1934.

distinguished as the privileged space of *shufu*, or housewife, and that employment for women was to be of a temporary nature before marriage. This Japanization of work style for Naha women and the change in gender roles and power relations are clearly reflected in the hobbies and expectations documented by *Ryūkyū Shimpō* journalists in their portraits of these thirty-eight future housewives.[44]

Viewed from this perspective, the hobbies that the Modern Girls opted for were at odds with their gradual incorporation into the emerging gender order of the new elite families. It is also in this light that we can see the dual aspect of yūgaku. On the one hand, the opportunity of pursuing studies in the mainland was perceived by schoolgirls as a means of self-fulfillment, an escape from the shackles of patriarchal authority, and an adventure in the "outer world" for which they had long competed. On the other hand, by the early Shōwa period, these new elites seem to have begun to see the acquisition of shūyō in mainland schools as an investment required to maintain their status. It is possible that the fashion and hobbies that Modern Girls brought back seemed "excessive" to their parents. From the Modern Girls' point of view, however, they may have been expressions of cultural autonomy vis-à-vis the new moral cultivation that their parents were imposing.

Modern Girl, Mobility, and Colonial Modernity

The conundrum of the Modern Girl question in the remote island of Okinawa sheds light on the importance of young women's mobility. In the absence of an overwhelming growth of urban consumer culture such as occurred in New York, Paris, Tokyo, or Shanghai, girls' higher schools played a crucial role in incubating a girl culture that motivated schoolgirls to identify themselves with role models in distant cities. The constant coming and going of teachers from different parts of Japan, the mingling of daughters of *kiryū-shōnin* and other Japanese settlers with those of old Okinawan families of Naha, the competition among them, the eventual participation of graduates, classmates, sisters, and nieces in the migratory network of the grown-ups through yūgaku or through job-seeking — all ignited the "desire of migration" among schoolgirls. The desire for modernity — via or beyond Japanization — among New Men who assembled in the intellectual circles — the missionaries, journalists, scholars, activists, and students — synchronized with the desires of New Women who sought freedom of love and marriage, putting into question both customary marriage and the logic of traditional patriarchy. This desire for modernity in its turn produced the cultural exodus of the New Women and New Men of Okinawa to Tokyo.

The Modern Girl phenomenon in Okinawa, however, was short-lived, since, in 1937, only three years after the *Ryūkyū Shimpo* series was published, Japan directly attacked all points on the China mainland and initiated the sustained and bitter military conflict that would continue until the decisive and worldwide defeat of Japanese militarism in 1945. With war, the assimilationist movement intensified and was classified under the general mobilization order. This tightening of assimilation policy is reflected in the fact that in 1941, Ichikōjo instituted a new code determining students' hairstyle by grade level: bobbed hair for first-graders, short hair parted at the side for the second-grade girls, hair parted and done up for the third grade, and tightly braided hair for the fourth grade.[45] Ichikōjo and Joshi-shihan were merged in 1944, and in March of the following year, the schoolgirls were mobilized in a troop named *himeyuri* (star lily). The overwhelmingly tragic end of himeyuri unit, decimated in war by the exorbitant demands of militarism and nationalism, makes it almost impossible to imagine the Modern Girls of early Shōwa in this group of sacrificial maidens.[46] Nevertheless, as we have seen, the Modern Girl question is in fact connected to this very same cohort of girls, the daughters of the rising new elite of modern Okinawa.

Notes

I am particularly indebted to Miyagi Harumi at Naha City Museum of History for guiding me through the archives and finding some most interesting images related to the question of modernity and women in Okinawa. Without her generous help, this research could not have been possible. I benefited also from the inspiring discussions that took place at the workshop "Modern Girl, Asia and Beyond" (Tokyo, 22–25 September 2004), co-organized by the Modern Girl and Colonial Modernity in East Asia Research Group at the Institute for Gender Studies, Ochanomizu University and the Modern Girl Around the World Research Group at the University of Washington. My thanks go to all those who have given me comments to the earlier version of this chapter, and particularly to Tani Barlow, Lynn Thomas, and Priti Ramamurthy, for their insightful suggestions and encouragement. Last, I am grateful to Naha City Museum of History, Makiminato Jōichi, and Naha Shuppansha for their permission to use the images.

1. Sato, *The New Japanese Woman*, chap. 2.
2. It is said that both New Women and moga defied the dominant values imposed under "*ie*," a patriarchal family system that was legally implemented under Meiji civil law in 1898 after much polemics. However, their respective positions in this sort of defiance may have not been congruous. While in the case of New Women, sexuality was important as part of their personhood and as expression of their autonomy, for moga, or at least in the multiple representations of moga, what was emphasized was not so much

sexuality in itself but flirtation, or the frivolous and somewhat decadent modality in which sexual desire was to be consumed in the new urban environment. See Muta, " 'Ryosai Kenbo' Shisō no Hyori," and Kataoka, *Modan Gāru no Kenkyū*.

3. Makiminato, *Gensō no Machi, Naha*, 110. "*Geta*" is a wooden clog, *tabi* are socks.

4. The significance of the concept of "colonial modernity" is defined by T. Barlow in her research on women in Chinese intellectual history. See Barlow, *The Question of Women in Chinese Feminism*, 87–91, and Barlow, ed., *Formations of Colonial Modernity in East Asia*. I am using this term fundamentally for its destabilizing effects on any pre-established idea of modernity. It is particularly useful in understanding the complex conditions in which "modernity" was imagined, sought, and negotiated among diverse actors involved in the "modernization" of Okinawa. What I wish to illuminate in this chapter are the ways in which migratory movements by the agents of colonial modernity had impact on Okinawan women to imagine "modernity" in their process of growth from girlhood to adulthood, nourishing in themselves a "desire to migrate" and to construct a new sense of femininity.

5. The concept of *dōka* or assimilation as part of colonial policy was defined as follows: "to Japanize not only on the surface but also to the very psychology of the people, and to cultivate thoughts and emotions of harmony and friendship (*yūwa shinzen*) toward Japan" (Yanaihara, 1937, as quoted by Komagome, *Shokuminchi Teikoku Nihon no Bunka Tōgo*, 20–21).

6. Oguma, *Nihonjin no Kyōkai*, 54, 57.

7. The islands of Okinawa prefecture are spread over 1,000 km east to west, and 400km north to south. Depending on which part of the prefecture one came from, the frame of reference for modernity could have been different even among inhabitants of Okinawa. For example, for those in Yaeyama islands, Taipei was much closer than Tokyo or even Naha as a place to find employment or to pursue studies.

8. According to Mary Louise Pratt, "contact zone" refers to "social spaces where cultures meet, clash, and grapple with each other, often in contexts of highly asymmetrical relations of power." See Pratt, *Imperial Eyes*.

9. Established as a secondary school for girls in 1899, "girls' higher school" provided a four-year or five-year curriculum aiming to produce "good wives, wise mothers."

10. There are cases of women, such as Higa Toru, who having encountered at their middle age an opportunity to read and write in Christian churches, decided to leave their status as priestess despite vehement opposition from their family members, to be converted as Christian. See Hokhama and Shimpōsha, eds., *Jidai wo Irodotta Onnatachi*, 35–40.

11. Komagome, *Shokuminchi Teikoku Nihon no Bunka Tōgo*.

12. According to Hokama Shuzen, standard Japanese was mostly referred to as "Tokyo no kotoba" or the language spoken in Tokyo from 1880 to 1897. From 1897 to 1935 it was called "Futsugo" or the standard Japanese. See Hokama, *Okinawa no Gengoshi*, 51–63.

13. These included traditional hand tattoo for women (*hajichi*), group socializing among boys and girls (*mōashibi*), consulting traditional shamans (*yuta*), and other various cus-

toms. See Nahashi Joseishi, Henshu Iinkai, and Nahashi Sōmubu Joseishitsu, eds., *Naha, Onna no Ashiato, Naha Joseishi (Kindai hen)*, 328–64; Horiba, "Inaguya Nanabachi."

14. These two schools have changed their formal names over the years. However, to avoid confusing readers, I will mostly use here their abbreviated names, *Ichikōjo* and *Joshi-shihan*.

15. Instituted in 1899, girls' higher schools offered a four-year course (ages thirteen to sixteen), and after 1920 a five-year course. They spearheaded *"ryōsai kenbo"* (good wife, wise mother) education.

16. By 1930 there were in total three prefectural girls' higher schools in Okinawa.

17. Okinawaken Joshi et al., eds., *Himeyuri*, 67.

18. Nahashi Kikakubu Shishi Henshushitsu, ed., *Naha Shishi Shiryōhen*, 159–60, 185.

19. Kawabata et al., eds., *Himeyuri no Kaori*, 38.

20. Kinjō, *Naha Onna Ichidaiki*, 134, 138.

21. Probably named after a Japanese-born, half-British half-Japanese hairdresser, Aihara Mine (1875–1957), alias Marie Louise, who had come back from Paris in 1912 to become a beauty advisor to the imperial family and the aristocrats. See Hayase, *Marie Louise*. She opened a school to train hairdressers where, as will be discussed later, Arakaki Mitoko probably studied in 1928.

22. Quoted in Kinjō, *Naha Onna Ichidaiki*, 133.

23. Ibid.

24. Kabira Chōrei, principal of Ichikojo in the early twenties, was particularly interested in the management of Jiyū Gakuen, founded by Hani Motoko. Following the example of Jiyū Gakuen, Kabira introduced the principle of self-sufficiency and autonomy of the students — growing vegetables in the school garden, learning how to shop in the markets, etc., — in the new program of home economics (*kaseika*) established in 1932. See Okinawaken Joshi-Ichikojo Dosokai, *Himeyuri*, 165–66. On the campaign for Westernization of clothes by Hani Motoko, see Kohiyama, "Not Imitation but Practicality."

25. In Kunigami Girls Higher School, located in the northern area of the main Okinawan island, which became Prefectural Girls' Higher School No. 3 in 1930, the uniform was already Western by 1925. See Nagoran Dosokai, ed., *Nagoran, Gojunen Kinenshi*.

26. Okinawan women of this period had traditional names taken from common objects of the life world, such as *Ushi* (cow), *Kame* (jar or turtle), or *Kamado* (oven). Many of the New Women changed names in the course of their studies, particularly at the moment of *yūgakū*, to Japanese-style names. Born Higa Moushi, Tomihara Hatsuko first changed her first name to Hatsuko during her trip to study in Tokyo and later married to Tomihira Morikiyo, one of the pastors of the Congregational Church. Maeda Fuyuko was born Maeda Kamado. Maeda changed her first name to Fuyuko and later married Iha Fuyū. Nintō was her pen name with which she wrote *tanka*. Kinjō Yoshiko was born Chinen Mazuru. She changed her first name to a more Japanese-style Yoshiko, and later married Kinjō Chōei.

27. Governor Takahashi Takuya depicted the phenomenon of New Women to be a "perver-

sion" (*hentai*) with nothing "new" in it and called them "tomboys" (*otenba*). See Kawabata et al., eds., *Himeyuri no Kaori*, 113.

28. Hokama and Shimpōsha, eds., *Jidai wo Irodotta Onnatachi*, 113–14; Maezato, "Yabu no naka no Kanaria," 33.

29. As a junior high school student, Iha participated in a strike organized with his friends against their principal's decision to abolish English classes. Principal Kodama Kihachi justified his decision by saying that it was not useful for Okinawan students to learn a foreign language when even their Japanese was not good enough. However, this meant that the students would be deprived of pursuing their studies in advanced schools on the mainland. The strike took place from November 1895 to March 1896. For having participated in this strike, Iha was dismissed from school with his companions. See Iha Fuyu Seitan Hyakunen Kinenkai, *Seitan Hyakunen Kinen Arubamu Iha Fuyū*, 10.

30. Kinjō, *Naha Onna Ichidaiki*.

31. Iha with Majikina, *Okinawa Joseishi*, 82–84.

32. This indeed was a problem Iha himself had to face in his personal life. His first marriage, which was arranged by his parents, was to an illiterate woman of upper-class family. Iha suffered from this "unbalanced marriage" and for this reason was strongly against early-age marriage and advocated for freedom of love and marriage. See Iha Fuyu Seitan Hyakunen Kinenkai, *Seitan Hyakunen Kinen Arubamu Iha Fuyū*; Kinjō and Takara, *Iha Fuyū*.

33. Yakabi, "Kindai Okinawa ni okeru Mainoritî Ishiki no Hensen."

34. Hokama and Shimpōsha, eds., *Jidai wo Irodotta Onnatachi*.

35. Ibid.; Kinjō, *Naha Onna Ichidaiki*; Kinjō, *Okinawa wo Kataru*; Higa, *Sugao no Iha Fuyū*.

36. Kinjō, *Naha Onna Ichidaiki*.

37. Ibid., 302–7.

38. For example, Kinjō recalls that it was with Iha that she first saw Colgate toothpaste or ate cornflakes. See Kinjō, *Naha Onna Ichidaiki*, 41; Kinjō, *Okinawa wo Kataru*, 85; Higa, *Sugao no Iha Fuyū*.

39. Miki, ed., *Naha Onna no Kiseki*.

40. The first Okinawan newspaper, founded in 1893.

41. The absence of Ryūkyū style clothes among the daughters of new elite marks a significant contrast with the situation in colonial Taiwan studied by Ko Ikujo (Ko, "Shokuminchi Taiwan ni okeru Fashion to Kenryoku"). While in Okinawa traditional clothes were completely abandoned by young women of this class, Ko points out that women in Taiwan followed the boom of the China dress (qipao) in 1920s Shanghai which, in turn, brought about a revival of "tsunsa," a Taiwanese version of China dress, in the 1930s.

42. Nahashi Joseishi Henshu Iinkai et al., eds., *Naha Joseishi Shōgenshu*, 70–142.

43. Kinjō, *Naha Onna Ichidaiki*, 51.

44. Nahashi Joseishi Henshu Iinkai et al., eds., *Naha Joseishi Shōgenshu*, 118.

45. Okinawaken Joshi, ed., *Himeyuri*, 730.

46. Himeyuri gakutotai ("star lily students' unit"), named after the alumni association's

journal title for Ichikōjo and Joshi-shihan, was a group of 240 students and teachers mobilized in the last phase of the battle of Okinawa as nurses, of whom 136 were killed. The figure of himeyuri came to be known nationwide through books and other media, including four films, two of which were directed by Imai Tadashi. In addition, in 1989, to commemorate their tragic death, a Himeyuri Peace Museum was inaugurated in Haebaru, where the field hospital was located. It is to be remembered, however, that himeyuri was not exceptional. Other girls' higher schools, such as Prefectural Girls' Higher Schools Nos. 2 and 3, and private schools such as Sekitoku-kōjo or Shōwa-kōjo were also mobilized at the ultimate stage of the battle.

12

Contesting Consumerisms in Mass Women's Magazines

BARBARA SATO

Generally, mass women's magazines are considered to have been the bastion of an expanding middle class in Japan during the interwar years. Under scrutiny a more complex and multifaceted picture emerges, of a readership encompassing a much broader segment of women than those ostensibly targeted. While education and jobs would seem to have positioned ordinary lower middle-class and working-class women on the outskirts of the "middle class" and consumerism, the complexity of everyday lives turns out to have been, as Raymond Williams sagely noted, far more complex than the analytical *category* of class would imply.[1] Mass magazines for women were not the only media diffusing consumer culture, but they were one of the affordable commodities that connected less privileged women to those of the middle class, and hence to the culture of consumerism.

Consumerism in 1920s Japan was not monolithic. Located in the experience of the everyday, it appeared in surprisingly diverse cultural manifestations. The Modern Girl is a powerful symbol of transnational modernity, no doubt even the quintessential icon of modern consumerism. But it was a conspicuously urban-centered and middle-class consumerism. Given that the 1903 Japanese National Income Tax records found that only 2.3 percent of the nation's total population fitted the category "middle" class, having an annual income of between 500 and 5,000 yen, this conspicuous urbanity had limited purchase. This was the case in the 1918 records, which noted a percentage climb to 6.5 and the rise, in 1921, to a stellar 10 percent.[2] This chapter investigates another kind of consumerism, by considering the discursive quality of the category "class" and adding a new perspective to the consumer practices of less privileged women as they, too, were pulled into the forefront of a modernity bound up with mass magazines and the unsettling figure of the Modern Girl.

When the writer Kitazawa Shūichi introduced the term "Modern Girl" to Japanese readers in 1923, his point of reference was the young working woman in England, an idealized version of whom he anticipated would soon appear in Japan.[3] Within a year, the outward displays that were to characterize the Modern Girl in Japan had surfaced and crystallized. Despite Kitazawa's prediction, most Marxist, socialist, and conservative intellectuals put aside their ideological differences and joined the general public in denouncing what they deemed an outright imitation of tainted Western styles with American roots. Often interspersed in intellectual discourses were the words "decadent" (*taihaiteki*) and "hedonistic" (*kyōrakuteki*). Both terms conveyed the intellectuals' misgivings about this so-called by-product (*sanbutsu*) of the conspicuous articulations of a middle-class consumerism, which followed on the heels of the white-collared salaried workers who had flocked to the cities in the wake of the Great War.[4]

The concerted attacks on the Modern Girl in Japan reflected an attack on commodification and the spread of capitalism, which most Marxists linked to the degenerative aspects of America's consumer culture. Any social change impacted even in part by *amerikanizumu* (Americanism) was suspect. By contrast, in Berlin consumerism pervaded everyday practices from the early 1900s. As George Simmel concludes in an essay written in 1903, "Only by screening out the complex stimuli that stemmed from the rush of modern life could the extremes be tolerated."[5] The historian Detlev Peukert, an expert on the Weimar Republic, asserts: "In the twenties Americanism became a catchword for untrammeled modernity in Germany."[6] The cultural and social historian Irene Guenther addresses the notion of "fascination" and "fear" that Americanism evoked. From Guenther's perspective, the fear emanated from "the dilemma modernity posed for the preservation of traditional Germany society and culture (Kulture)," although she goes on to say that intellectuals leveled their most strident criticism at France, not America.[7]

To speak of consumer culture as a static American construct is hardly commensurate with a consumerism that transformed the landscape in the United States, Europe, Asia, and elsewhere at approximately the same time. Invectives by intellectuals, though central to an analysis of the Modern Girl, are not enough to explain the extent of the dislocations of consumerism and the discredited (albeit defining) role that consumerism played in negotiating the lifestyles of less-privileged women.

Less-Privileged Women as Consumers

Let me begin then with an exploration of the role of mass women's magazines in the "massification" of publishing, which accounts for the encoding of consumerism as feminine. As the growth of industrial capitalism was coterminous with the search for new profit-making markets, magazine editors and publishers quickly identified an untapped segment of consumers: women. Conscious of the connection between marketing and the consumer potential occasioned by a new reading public, publishers sought the status of mass magazines. Since the price of *Shufu no tomo* (*Housewife's Companion*, 1917), *Fujokai* (*Woman's Sphere*, 1910), and *Fujin sekai* (*Women's World*, 1906) amounted to approximately 0.5–1 percent of the average monthly salary of a middle-class working woman with a higher-school degree, and 0.3–1 percent of the wages of a working-class woman with basic literacy, less privileged women could also presumably purchase a single copy.

"Michiyo," a pseudonym for a young woman who lived and worked on a farm north of Tokyo, exemplifies the latter: "I am a poor uneducated country girl. Still, for four years I scraped together the funds to purchase *Shufu no tomo* (*Housewife's Companion*), which saved me from my isolation. Unfortunately, the cost became more than I could manage on my meager salary. I want you to know my joy at having saved enough money to renew my subscription."[8] Astute editors and publishers soon recognized that if they attached phonetic symbols to the Chinese characters, women with the equivalent of an elementary school education could negotiate the magazines. They wasted no time in courting women like Michiyo as consumers.

According to a survey published in 1924 by the Ministry of Social Affairs (Shakai-kyoku), young factory women housed in dormitories in western Japan (Kansai), none of whom received fixed monthly salaries (*nikyū*), allotted approximately 0.6 percent of their 1 yen per day earnings (or 30 yen per month) for entertainment. "Lower-level" typists, proficient only on the Japanese keyboard, appropriated 3 percent of their monthly salaries for amusement, office clerks allocated 5 percent, and department store sales-girls spent approximately 7 percent on leisure activities.[9] Many factory women spoke of pooling their resources and purchasing joint subscriptions to mass women's magazines. Often ten to twenty women shared one magazine, which they read in their limited free time.

Together with middle-class women, the mainstay of readership, a second tier of readers comprising lower-middle-class and working-class women became conspicuous in the 1920s. These women worked in small offices and department stores, held jobs as low-level bank clerks, became bus conductors, domestics in private homes, cleaning women, and factory workers.[10]

Magazine editors and executives recognized the need for flexibility and set about to diversify their content. Most publishers adopted similar marketing and promotional strategies to meet the needs of this new reading class. Careful not to alienate conservative subscribers, women educators like Umeda Utako, Miwata Masako, Hatoyama Haruko, and Hani Motoko continued to contribute articles that embellished the domestic ideals of the "good wife" and "wise mother" (ryōsaikenbo) ideology which, in spite of its repressive impact on women, remained the cornerstone of middle-class and higher education from the late 1890s until after the Asia-Pacific War. In addition, new trademarks of production appeared, including a new genre of sophisticated family articles (katei kiji) that looked beyond the status quo to bring larger society into the home; trendy articles (ryūkō kiji) that featured the latest beauty tips and fashions as well as news about suitable employment possibilities; and confessional articles (kokuhaku kiji) in which readers exchanged private thoughts with women they knew only by pen names and locale but with whom they bonded and formed a readers' forum.[11]

Confessional articles encouraged women readers to articulate the problematic relationships between their dreams and the realities of their positions. Although they were not openly antithetical to the ideals of the official ideology of the "good wife and wise mother," these articles revealed alternative thought patterns. Women who were legally forced to remain within the parameters of the Meiji Civil Code (1898–1946) infused their lives with a sense of personal importance.

While confessional articles could not resolve women's struggles with their parents, in-laws, or unfaithful husbands, the dialogues helped relieve these strains and demonstrated that something was wrong. If more confessional articles addressed the mundane, that is because the mundane formed the core of a woman's everyday space. Lower-middle-class women submitted fewer confessional articles than middle-class readers, but their letters indicated similar desires for greater autonomy from family pressures. This is a documented phenomenon in many journal cultures. For instance, in 1889 the middle-class American publication Ladies Home Journal launched the column "Side Talks with Girls," which became a regular feature for the next sixteen years. From the late 1890s, the middle-class English journal Women at Home (1893–1920) also added a section for readers' letters.

Fiction also found its place in mass women's magazines. Serialized novels and short stories had delighted Japanese readers from the mid-nineteenth century, when magazines initially targeted intellectual women. A marked feature of less-privileged readers' letters is the enthusiasm they voiced for romantic fiction. "Shigeko" was a pseudonym for a young woman who lived and worked in the metropolis. "Tomiko," also a pseudonym, came from a rural village in Okayama prefecture in western Japan. Both young women were from disparate backgrounds, but they conveyed relief at being able to identify with the characters in popular writer Kikuchi Kan's melodramatic novel *Shinju* (The Pearl) written in monthly installments for *Fujokai* (*Women's Sphere*) in 1924. "Toyoko," a pseudonym for a young woman from Nagasaki struggling to make ends meet, joined other readers in expressing empathy for the protagonist featured in Kikuchi Kan's novel *Aijin* (The Lover).[12] Whether or not this can be read as a commonly "shared" pleasure for lower-middle-class and working-class women readers is open to debate. Janice Radway's analysis that "women are reading not out of contentment but out of dissatisfaction, longing and protest" merits consideration here. She continues: "Romance reading buys time and privacy for women even as it addresses the corollary consequence of their situation, the physical exhaustion and emotional depletion brought about by the fact that no one within the patriarchal family is charged with *their* care."[13]

Although compulsory education, regardless of gender, was established in 1872, formal education for women, and particularly less-privileged women, was treated lightly.[14] According to a 1911 survey, out of 3.5 million girls enrolled in elementary school, 90 percent ended their formal schooling at the elementary level and took jobs in factories or as domestics. Of that number, approximately 7,000 went on to higher school, middle school not being an option for young women until after the Asia-Pacific War.[15] Statistics for 1923 and 1928 confirm that only about 10 percent of all elementary school graduates went on to higher school.[16] Some girls unable to attend elementary school acquired rudimentary literacy skills at home.

Takai Toshio, a precocious youngster from a poor farming family in a mountainous hamlet of Gifu prefecture in central Japan, mastered the phonetic language on her own at the age of eight. Hustled off to a spinning mill in 1913 shortly after her eleventh birthday, she worked under exploitative conditions until 1921.[17] Factories often promised parents they would educate children in classrooms established on the premises. Elite textile concerns like Kanebo and Gunze that had their pick of employees actually made good on their promises. But young girls who worked twelve and more hours a day often found it easier to endure their fates in intimidating workplaces and forgo "lessons."[18] Based on figures from the Tokyo City Office Survey for 1931, 86.1 percent of factory women worked to supplement the family income.[19]

Graduates of women's higher schools, granted middle-class status by virtue of their education, dominated the readership of mass women's magazines. Higher education also made them privy to the new salaried occupations that opened up before and after World War I and defined their work as "intellectual" (chinōteki, chiteki).[20] Known as "professional working woman" (shokugyō fujin), they garnered coveted jobs as office girls (gāru) in modern buildings like the Marunouchi building (Maru biru) located in the heart of Tokyo's business districts, became shop girls (shoppu gāru) in lavish department stores like Takashimaya and Mitsukoshi in Tokyo or Daimaru and Hankyu in Osaka, nurses in large reputable hospitals, elementary and higher-school teachers, telephone operators, and high-level typists with a mastery of the Japanese character and English language keyboards.[21] For middle-class parents in need of extra income, who were yet wary of the stigma of outside employment, the classification "intellectual" lent an aura of respectability to daughters working outside the home.

In addition to professional working women, other middle-class readers included higher-school graduates, who spent their days working toward the accomplishments that were essential for any would-be bride (like flower arrangement and letter writing), and stay-at-home housewives with the wherewithal to mold their identities around domestic values after marriage. Since marriage marked a natural end to paid work for these women, supervising the household (which involved directing and managing the help), balancing the monthly budget, and satisfying the wants of husbands, children, and recalcitrant in-laws accounted for their tasks. Class markers, determined more by modes of education than salary, imbued the upper strata of women readers with the "respected" prerequisites that separated them from women who engaged in manual labor (rōdō fujin), toiled in factories (jokō), or worked as maids (jochū).[22] Figures from the Japanese National Census Bureau reveal that in 1918, women factory workers and domestics totaled 534,348. In 1930, the Census Bureau reported 697,116 women held manual labor jobs, evidence of the class-based nature of women's work.[23]

Personal accounts written in magazines in conjunction with government-sponsored and private surveys bear witness to less-privileged women's reading practices. Even if we momentarily accept Richard Hoggart's analysis that "the mass of talented commercial writers ensures that most people are kept at a level in reading at which they can respond only to the crudely imprecise," the assumption that less-privileged women are unable to articulate their identities by means of consumerism is a significant element of consumer history.[24] Contrary to expectation, working-class women trapped in a cycle of jobs that offered few options for agency also were turning their gaze to mass women's magazines.[25]

One woman, whose family's fortune declined and who was forced to work in a spinning mill on the outskirts of Okayama after elementary school, reflected: "Reading was my favorite subject in school. For over ten years I've worked in this factory. I'm overjoyed that at last the practice of sharing magazines is commonplace in the dormitory. In our free time we take turns reading and rereading old issues. We practically memorize the [monthly] installments of popular fiction." This reader was well-acquainted with the popular magazines *Jogaku sekai* and *Fujokai*, but she praised *Shufu no tomo* for lowering its subscription price by 10 percent for people who took out company subscriptions. She added: "I especially like the recipes because I can learn about new foods, and I also follow the fashion trends. Recently I spent several months in the factory infirmary and a kind nurse lent me her monthly copy of *Shufu no tomo*. That was my only joy. The issue devoted to marriage preparation filled me with so much hope I dreamed about it at night."[26] This factory worker envisioned upward mobility through marriage, which meant finding a marriage partner whose socioeconomic position would help raise her social status. Higher education was beyond her reach, but she envisioned it as the birthright of her children.

"Michiko," a pseudonym for a young housewife with basic literacy, took in sewing to make ends meet. She described the self-confidence she gained from reading *Fujokai*, which apprised her about middle-class lifestyles. Michiko yearned to purchase fancy sweets sold at department stores for her four children. Unable to do so, she compromised by reproducing the "modern" recipes found in the magazines in her own kitchen.[27] Department store shopping epitomized middle-class living for Michiko, but it was off-limits to her. Instead she, and others like her, accessed modern lifestyles through print. Although these young women could not participate equally in consumer activities with middle-class readers and responded only in their imaginations, that did not prevent them from trying to gain a better grasp of their own situations.

Neither of the women described above fits the label of professional working woman or elite housewife. Both lacked higher educations. Mass women's magazines as instruments of consumer capitalism gave their lives unfamiliar dimensions. Rather than resisting the dominant culture, the media was both a vehicle for the spread of consumption and the production of the desire for new things and a new way of life. Helen Damon-Moore, a specialist on women's magazines in the United States, argues that from the perspective of "agency and constraint," assessing how reading was used by particular readers is not an easy task. Damon-Moore's view parallels that of Carl F. Kaestle, who postulated

12.1 Factory workers in a spinning mill in western Japan show off their Western-style uniforms and modern hairstyles, extremely rare dress for factory women. All the women are smiling broadly, but like any image, there is more than one level of meaning. Approximately 1930. Reprinted with permission of *Mainichi shinbun* (newspaper).

12.2 Factory women in a western Japan thread mill. Conventional white aprons (*kapogi*) protect their simple kimono and their hair is done up in the old-fashioned hair comb. Approximately 1930. Reprinted with the permission of *Mainichi shinbun*.

that, in the early 1900s, readers acted alone "to develop identities, choose allegiances, form beliefs, and conduct their day-today lives, but they [did] so within the constraints of cultural inheritances and economic hardships." Damon-Moore praised Kaestle's model because it represents "both agency and constraint in the world of reading."[28] Less-privileged women's earnings could not guarantee a secure standard of living, yet access to consumerism did not necessarily imply a trade-off between class identities and material aspirations.

Tensions existed between ways that less-privileged women were seen and represented and ways they sought to appropriate consumer culture for their own ends. The factory workers pictured in figure 12.1 were employed at a spinning mill in Osaka. The owner probably found Western clothing charming and chose the uniforms himself. From the look on the young women's faces, they delighted in being among the few factory women to sport fashionable short haircuts, wear Western-styled uniforms gussied up by belts, and don silk stockings and leather shoes. But, as Georg Simmel also wondered, to what extent is fashion a response to our desire to modulate the tension between the expression of the individual self and the sense of belonging to a larger collectivity? Indeed, the image of the women in the Osaka mill differs from most visuals that capture women factory workers at work. The young women portrayed in figure 12.2 are laboring in a thread mill. They are dressed in simple kimono covered by conventional white aprons and their hair is done up in a bun.

Mass women's magazines offered middle-class culture as a model for less-privileged women who sought to grasp the rungs of a ladder that they, too, longed to climb, even if that lifestyle bound them up in an imagined relation to modernity and consumerism. For women raised in a rigid patriarchal society, physical and moral constraints added to their social stratification and the status hierarchy. Nevertheless, the desire for a happy family life and material goods became part of their yardstick for measuring changes in social status. The following section addresses the multifaceted character of consumerism that led readers to construe the content of mass magazines in their own distinct ways and consume selectively.

Early Stages of Consumerism for Less-Privileged Women

As the quality of mass market journal illustrations improved, the visual aroused women's daydreams. Even if readers had no direct link to department store shopping, the do-it-yourself patterns and plethora of diagrams that filled the pages of all mass women's magazines instructed readers on sewing and knitting techniques for making modern fashions at home. The January 1924 issue of *Fujokai* carried detailed explanations on reforming "old-fashioned" kimono into "modern" Western dress suitable for the "new" (*shin*) age. Articles like "The Secret of Restyling a Haori [a short coat worn over a *kimono*] that Would Be the Pride of Any Woman"; "Secrets for Sewing the Latest Fashions," ranging from undergarments to fancy hats; "Seven Different Styles of Over-Coats and Hats," suitable for women and children; and "Seven Patterns for Knitting the Latest Knit Bags" introduced the ultimate in fashion to a growing audience.[29] Conflating consumerism, however, with the acquisition of goods bought in department stores and thus with middle-class shoppers exaggerates the amount of control middle-class women had over the larger process of consumption in Japan. Judith Giles and Tim Middleton, who elaborated on Stuart Hall's analysis (1980) regarding the process of encoding and decoding, point out: "A woman who decodes from a negotiated position may enjoy looking at the femininity offered in advertisements and magazines but may, quite happily, spend very little time or money in her daily life attempting to emulate these."[30] In reckoning with the less conspicuous form of consumerism from its place in changing consumption and marketing patterns, images of the Modern Girl scattered throughout mass magazines cannot be measured against a given typology.

Unraveling the threads of the Modern Girl's significance for less-privileged women does not hinge on whether she was a substantive entity who paraded the streets of Tokyo's Ginza or Osaka's Shinsaibashi in knee-length skirts and silk stockings, sported cloche hats, and favored red lipstick (see figure 12.3). Nor does it hinge on whether she was clad in Japanese kimono like the young woman who worked in the tie department at a boutique in the ultramodern Marunouchi building (see figure 12.4), dubbed a notorious site for promiscuous escapades between professional working women and their male cohorts. The salesgirl exhibited no visible "modern" accessories, except for her meticulously made-up "face," but as a higher-school graduate, she bore the identity professional working woman.

For some middle-class and upper-class women, consumerism meant combining the old with the new. One woman favors the kimono, but she chooses to accent her attire with a trendy fake fur shawl, and permanent-waved hair covers her ears (*mimi kakushi*) (see figure 12.5). Seated around marble-topped tables in art deco–styled coffee shops surrounded by foreign fauna, they sipped coffee.

In keeping with the image of a woman engaging in consumption, the Modern Girl stood for the propensity of all women to consume. Consequently, the Modern Girl lacked a clear social referent. She could have been a cafe hostess or dancer who stood out as a sign of desire in the form of sexual liberation, the young woman who sold flowers in a modest shop on the Ginza instead of a

12.3 Two modern girls browse on the Ginza probably during their lunch break. Late 1920s. Courtesy of Endo Noriaki.

12.4 A professional working woman (*shokugyō fujin*) sells ties in a boutique located in the ultra-modern Marunouchi building, in the center of Tokyo's business district. Only her carefully made-up face smacks of the "modern." Late 1920s. Courtesy of the *Mainichi shinbun*.

12.5 An example of "conspicuous consumption" associated with
the image of the Modern Girl.

fancy establishment with a modern façade, or the aristocratic young daughter of the tycoon who drove a fancy car dressed in Japanese attire.[31] Depending on the context, the Modern Girl moniker fit all these women. Working-class women no doubt were anxious to shed the label of second-rate "citizen," but in determining the coherence of the Modern Girl phenomenon for these women, it would be unfair to assume that a radical self-transformation occurred. Rather, less-privileged women turned to mass women's magazines as a location where they might participate in their own way in consumption. The publication of mass women's magazines did not link this process with political liberation, but neither did magazines dismiss less privileged women's ambitions as misguided.

Don Slater's analysis that "consumer culture moves in two contradictory, but interrelated directions" is pertinent. In one sense, "consumer culture seems to emerge from the production of public spectacle, from the enervated and over stimulated world of urban experience so powerfully captured in Baudelaire's image of the *flaneur*: in modernity all the world is a consumable experience." But Slater also opines that "much debate on consumer culture was carried out in terms not of the consumption of goods, but of *time*."[32] In 1920s Japan, the literary and social critic Hirabayashi Hatsunosuke and the journalist Chiba Kameo were among the few intellectuals to evaluate consumerism and its particular relationship to women positively. Most intellectuals could not recognize that the discourses on women's everyday lives taken up in mass women's magazines constructed a new notion of gender.

Surveying Readers

The socialist feminist Yamakawa Kikue, a staunch advocate of gender equality, located women factory workers at the heart of the proletarian movement. Situated in highly politicized leftist circles, she advocated a reorganization of society where a causal relationship between the dictatorship of the proletariat and social change would precipitate a new world over. Yamakawa counted on factory women to read politically charged articles, but instead she expressed shock and dismay when she saw young women poring over advertisements for cosmetics in "bourgeois" mass women's magazines at lunch.[33] A self-satisfied factory worker from the Sumida area of Tokyo put it this way: "Contrary to opinion, modern factories like mine provide good pay and excellent working conditions. I'm proud of my work and my salary. If you ask me my favorite pastime, it's reading *Shufu no tomo*."[34]

The women workers in a rubber factory adored modern dancing and staged their own rendition of a modern revue at a factory festival (see figure 12.6). Dressed in short skirts, with legs outstretched, they danced uninhibitedly on a stage in front of enraptured employees. This image denotes a sense of liberation, however short-lived, from the strains of their daily experiences. To fabricate a woman's life around the contents of mass magazines is unrealistic, but as sources of information, magazines served as a gauge for testing change. The factory workers shown in figure 12.6 may never have visited a bustling emporium nor seen ready-made clothing on display. But advertisements produced yearnings, and images worked on the imagination and had the power to sway readers' tastes.

The media studies scholar Nagamine' Shigetoshi's detailed analyses of readers' backgrounds and reading preferences confirm Yamakawa Kikue's fears. In 1920, before the conspicuous aspects of consumerism were firmly in place in Japan, the Tokyo Metropolitan Police Department conducted four different surveys of women factory workers in the Tokyo area. One question that appeared on every survey concerned working-class women's reading preferences, which were broken down into newspapers, magazines, and books. Over 2,350 women who worked in a spinning mill, 631 women who worked for a

12.6 Young women employees in a rubber factory stage a modern revue
at a factory festival. Mid-1920s. Courtesy of Endo Noriaki.

cosmetics' factory, 231 women who worked in a factory that produced fabric
dye, and 1,054 women who worked in a printing factory participated in the
interviews in Tokyo. All listed mass women's magazines as their first choice of
reading.[35] Another survey taken in the same year targeted 390 women from
a rural spinning factory in Gunma prefecture in northwestern Japan. Once
again, mass women's magazines took first place, with *Shufu no tomo* the overwhelming favorite.[36]

   In 1927, 1,812 women in a Himeiji textile factory located in Hyōgo prefecture in western Japan discussed their reading habits. A similar survey taken in
1928 indicates that among 4,543 women textile workers surveyed in Miyazaki
prefecture, another outpost for women factory workers in southern Japan,
2,813 listed women's mass magazines as their favorite reading. *Fujokai* topped
the list. In the same year in the western Japan city of Kobe, out of 330 women
factory workers whose reading habits were surveyed, 169 women endorsed the
general entertainment magazine *Kingu* (*King*). But 161 women claimed that
women's mass magazines offered emotional support. In order of their preferences, 50 women read *Fujokai*, 43 *Shufu no tomo*, 18 *Shojo kurabu* (*Young
Women's Club*), 16 *Fujin sekai*, and 14 *Fujin kurabu* (*Woman's Club*).[37]

Nagamine's findings clarify that the women interviewed lived in factory belt areas located on the fringes of urban centers as well as provincial areas as far north as Hokkaido and Akita, Gunma to the east, and Kagoshima to the west.[38] Some readers responded to inducements from editors and publishers who promoted reading as a means of self-improvement (shūyō). For others, the magazines' contents, supported by phrases like "something for everyone," captured their interest.[39] Articles afforded more than comforting words that acknowledged readers' conflicting desires and vulnerability. The selections contained various levels of "hidden" meaning that appealed to different classes of women readers and even some men. "Hanako," who went to Korea (Chosen) with her husband in the 1920s as part of the state's early farm colonization program, said: "I would rather read Shufu no tomo than eat. My husband feels the same way. He confided in me that Shufu no tomo has helped him overcome his loneliness."[40]

Less-privileged women and elite middle-class readers alike drew on insights from publisher/editors like Tsugawa Masashi (Fujokai) and Ishikawa Taketoshi (Takemi) (Shufu no tomo) and novelists such as Kikuchi Kan and Tanizaki Junichirō. A former prostitute turned journalist, Yamada Waka, well-known for her advice columns, became a role model women could identify with and turn to for advice. The tenuous links that less-privileged women shared with women's higher-school graduates did not deter them from experimenting with new values and novel ideas. When women realized they could enjoy some forms of consumerism without accepting it all, magazines became a site of expectation where transitions were visible, demonstrating another side to the fashionable modernity conveyed by the image of the Modern Girl.

Different social experiences reflect different responses to modernity. Lower-middle- and working-class women negotiating the challenges posed by consumerism were acutely aware of their lack of skills. Possibilities for participating in the more beguiling sectors of the economy were limited. At its inception Fujin koron (Women's Review) vowed to serve the interests of "intellectual" professional working women. Unable to compete with other mass women's magazines, in the 1920s the magazine altered its format to appeal to a wider readership. A survey in the April 1925 issue clarified that over 5,400 women nationwide had vied for positions as typists, which, together with department store salesgirls, represented the ultimate in "modern" jobs for women's higher-school graduates. Even so, a devoted reader with only an elementary school education, determined to overcome the adverse odds and become a typist, sought advice. She was told that by perfecting her skills on the Japanese keyboard and not seeking work that entailed using the English alphabet, she might become a "lower-level" typist in spite of her education. Her thirty-to-forty-yen monthly salary would amount to less than a higher-school graduate, whose chances of moving up on the wage scale were better, but her job would afford some economic independence and the realization of her dream.[41]

Another elementary school graduate lamented her inability to become a salesgirl in a department store. Instructed to face reality, she was encouraged to apply for a position behind the scenes — perhaps in the dining room, which better suited her educational qualifications. Even if the job definition differed, she, too, could enjoy the benefits and glitter of working in a bustling emporium, but from a different perspective. A third young woman longed to work in a "modern" beauty salon. She was advised to forget higher education. Working for one or two years as a beautician's apprentice provided a far more practical solution. The invaluable experience of on-the-job training could lead to a job in a fancy salon and a salary of forty-five yen a month, and possibly more. To improve her work status, she was instructed to research new cosmetics so she could advise her customers on the latest beauty techniques and commodities being marketed.[42] At the same time mass women's magazines were in the process of redefining their readers, women from different backgrounds were in the process of redefining themselves.

Mark Liechty expressed it like this: "The more closely one looks at a class group, the more its boundaries dissolve and its supposedly distinguishing features blur into a haze of contrasting and conflicting detail."[43] Housewives on a tight budget, for example, were in the precarious position of having to balance household desires fostered by mechanization and rationalization with a limited ability to purchase new time-saving goods. On the one hand, they learned to internalize their dreams. On the other hand, because of the triumphant success of installment buying, some of their dreams materialized quicker than before. This crossover of readers' identities questions issues of class and culture and is more complicated than the stereotype of imitation would lead us to believe, a point that also requires further research.

Firmly embedded in the culture of consumerism, mass women's magazines were not simply a counterpart to magazines that addressed men. To label them mere repositories of established routines and gender conventions downplays the intricacies, ideological and economic, involved in their production.

The Site of Contesting Consumerisms

Three aspects of consumer culture help explore the character of consumerism in mass women's magazines and further our understanding of the relationship of lower-middle- and working-class women to the Modern Girl: (1) advertisements, (2) mail order catalogs, and (3) the content of articles. Mass women's magazines ministered to a national reading audience. Magazines were launched by publishing companies on the basis of their marketability and profitability, and women's magazines were no exception. General advertisements formed an essential part of the magazine's contents and revenue. From the early twentieth century, drugs and cosmetics accounted for the biggest percentage of all advertisements. A large portion of advertisements focused on practical commodities like books and household items, ranging from light bulbs to canned foods, that did not require men to join in the decision making. These advertisements echoed the keywords "convenient" (*benri*) and "rational" (*goriteki)* and promised quality modern goods.

In a more glamorous vein, the line drawing of a Western woman clad in a form-fitting gown and seated on a silk-striped upholstered stool (see figure 12.7) legitimized the elitism of the Shiseido trademark. Similar advertisements appeared in several mass women's magazines, a factor that helped boost the popularity of brand name products. But it is improbable that any but upper-middle-class women could have reaped the benefits of Shiseido's handsomely packaged and priced perfumes and toiletries. At a glance, Shiseido's advertisement offers an illusory image, but if we focus our gaze on the Japanese and English text, the image begins to evoke meaning.[44] The allure of prioritized representations underlay the images of the Modern Girl and conspicuous consumerism, but magazines could not confer special privileges on readers. Marketing a product required not only a relationship between product and market but also knowledge of the people in its market. More likely women readers forwent Shiseido's perfumes and toiletries and settled for lower-priced cosmetics like Maddo (see figure 12.8) sold in ordinary apothecaries and through mail-order catalogs.

Particularly revealing are advertisements placed in mass women's magazines by department stores that catered to buyers nationwide (see figure 12.9). Unlike newspaper advertisements, department store advertisements contained no mention of bargain sales that affected one branch store and not another. Instead, advertisements of imposing images of buildings that depended on architectural imagery to help sell their names and evoke a sense of trust appeared month after month. The purpose of shopping changed. Year-end gifts wrapped in department store paper helped establish the store's reputation and also created an awareness for national brands. Frequenting fashionable emporiums like Mitsukoshi just to window shop was open to all classes of women. Department stores offered escapism.

Paul Glennie observes that "department stores were pivotal sites of cultural appropriation and identity construction, through their ability to create the

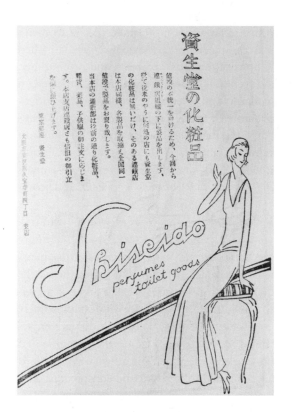

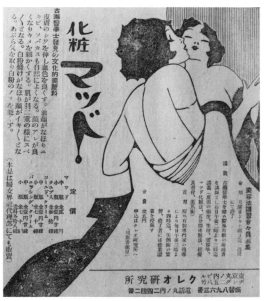

12.7 Line drawing of Western woman perched on an upholstered stool wearing a tight-fitting gown advertises top brand Shiseido perfume and toiletries. *Fujokai,* 1924.

12.8 Maddo, a popular brand of lower-priced cosmetics, promotes its face cream. *Fujokai,* 1924.

12.9 Illustrations similar to this advertisement for Mitsukoshi Department Store appeared in all mass magazines for women.

meanings of commodities and consumers."[45] In writing about early-twentieth-century America, Richard Ohmann notes that "the products and their auras resided not only in proper social space but in the system of symbols," through which people perceived "their affinities, their place in the world, and their historical agency." Ohmann cautions that "to grasp consumption as the same meaning across class lines is to falsify the reality of the time."[46] From the standpoint of less-privileged women, more important was the role mass women's magazines played in supporting a form of consumerism that provided an innovative concept of buying for an unlikely class of consumers.

Not all women experienced commodification as an external force, and without question they relied on their own potential for imagining and building new worlds. Inasmuch as mass women's magazines exposed women to commodities for personal and household use, they incited some uneasiness in women. But they very likely offered simultaneously the hope and opportunity for a satisfactory form of release from the desire for material goods, which had until then been largely repressed. In Japan, and other parts of the world, cumulative social changes were disrupting life in city and country alike. The pull to maintain the ties of family existed, but signs of instability sent tremors through the domestic community and society as a whole.

A second factor in grasping the character of consumerism is mail-order shopping. At the back of most mass women's magazines was a substantial section devoted to mail-order shopping that acquainted readers with various commodities. Magazines served in the capacity of agents and decided which products to promote; in turn, they received a percentage of the profits, which offset operating costs. Understanding the psyche of their readership was essential for the success of this type of selling, a feature of mass women's magazines. Among the items advertised were cosmetics, clothing, and children's toys in addition to practical commodities like cleaning products, sewing materials, and medical supplies. The key word for mail-order consumers was "choice" (erabu). Since the practice of offering samples for sale at a reduced price did not exist, for readers with some wherewithal, the incentive to buy was the discounted prices of the products offered. Less fortunate readers without disposable incomes and unable to make any purchases continued to be courted by publishers, but in the context of future consumers.

Mass women's magazines, replete with gossip columns that targeted film stars and printed pictures of noble families, clearly capitalized on urban tastes and interests. Mail-order selling, however, connected the urban to the rural and intensified an interest in consumer commodities for women who lived on the periphery. The woman factory worker outside Osaka and the housewife tucked away in a rural hamlet outside Hiroshima accessed information about "mod-

ern" lifestyles different from their own, a factor that contributed to the diffu-
sion of new female images. Judging from readers' letters, some women who
lived far from urban centers actually believed that even they were not socially
isolated but part of a larger family. Harry Harootunian stresses that "the state
momentarily tried to prevent consumers from being interpellated by the commodity," but he goes on to say that "all these new commodities pointed to the
acquisition of new identities that often traversed class, gender, and sexuality,
even though 'cultured living' was at first limited to the urban middle class."[47]

Third, evidence that editors and publishers perceived some obligation to
less-privileged women, both as consumers and readers, is apparent in the ad-
mixture of articles, which indicates a dual standard continued to govern editorial policies.[48] *Fujokai*'s series "Competitive Buying" illustrates how editors
involved women readers to push consumer commodities and assess which standards would determine less privileged readers' buying practices. Beginning in
October 1922, a male and female staff writer received twenty yen per month
for six months to spend on products they deemed valuable to readers.[49] The
reporters stated what prompted their choices, while readers, in turn, sent in
their evaluations of the products to the magazine.

One Tokyo housewife explained her criteria for buying: "I am well aware of
changing modern lifestyles [*bunka seikatsu*], and my purchases reflect the new
way of life. But quality is a major concern. Foremost in my mind is my family's
needs." Unlike the conspicuous consumerism symbolized by the image of the
Modern Girl, this reader wanted to avoid false pleasure. "Useless [*muda*] products have no place in my budget. Of ultimate importance is how the product
will improve our standard of living." She admitted, however, that eye-catching
"consumer products influenced her choices." A young clerk from Kyoto on a
limited budget voiced similar concerns. "Price, quality, and trends govern my
choices." She, too, stressed "new" (*shin, atarashii*) commodities, but she insisted on quality at the cheapest price. She added that shopping in a department
store was particularly exciting and marveled that department stores sold standardized goods at standard prices, which made shopping convenient.[50] However, she relied on the less expensive mail-order shopping to fill her needs.

Together with the different styles of magazine advertisements that manipulated what was appealing and useful, the diversity of articles apprised urban
and rural women of new practices both inside and outside the home. Tony
Bennett's analysis of Louis Althusser's *Ideology and Ideological State Appara-
tuses* (1971) is compelling: "When, for example, I am told by an advertisement
that 'people like you' are turning to this product, I am being interpellated as a
member of a group, but more importantly, as an individual 'you' of that group.
I can recognize myself in the imaginary space opened up by the pronoun 'you.'

Thus I am invited to become the 'you' spoken to in the advertisement."[51] Women readers were not homogeneous. Editors and publishers could not impose their standards on all women. Less privileged women's letters conveyed a sense of the hardships they endured. But they also spoke of hope. Still, for the growing segment of less privileged women readers, reality was more complicated than the ideals they embraced.

Conclusion

Two tendencies dominate these seemingly contesting consumerisms. Because mass women's magazines became a site for a less conspicuous form of consumerism, women struggling to appropriate a balance between the pleasures of consumerism and the reality of their lifestyles could legitimize their would-be purchases as rational (*goriteki*) and "modern" (*bunkateki*). Second, unlike the conspicuous consumerism embodied in the image of the Modern Girl, this was a consumerism firmly planted in the everyday. The products advanced were rooted in the temper of the changing times, but they were geared to women's budgets and pocketbooks. This opened up a possibility for a different dynamic of consumption where a second tier of lower-middle- and working-class women could identify their subjectivity with consumer potential, however slight.

Social class needs to be read carefully. Cultural variations within classes differ as do boundary patterns. The debut of the Modern Girl does not represent the full repertoire of interpretations for clarifying the implications of the social and cultural changes that this image of consumerism represented for lower-middle-class and working-class women readers. Articles in mass women's magazines that focused on the Modern Girl in Japan from after the Great Kanto Earthquake (*Kantō daishinsai*) of 1923 may have whetted the imagination, but they did little to revamp less privileged women's everyday lives. This draws attention to the blurring of class lines in the debate over the shifting complexities of the modern as it relates to the commodification of the everyday. For Antonio Gramsci, working-class women were not totally distracted by the prevailing hegemony but rather caught in the process of groping for a language that described their own perceptions of reality. While the "modern" that identified the Modern Girl clearly was inconsistent with prevalent female norms, Miriam Silverberg convincingly stresses that the Modern Girl stood for the "willful determination" that "posed a challenge to reigning social practices" and the "defiance" of a lifestyle presumed impossible to transcend.[52] Images of the Modern Girl burst on the scene around the world in the midst of the consumerism boom and challenged the myth of a fixed definition of femininity.

Notes

1. Williams, *Marxism and Literature*, 112.
2. Yamakawa Kikue, "Chūryū fujin to rōdō mondai," *Warera*, January 1919.
3. Kitazawa Chōgo (Shūichi), "Modan gāru no hyōgen-Nihon no imoto ni okuru tegami," *Josei kaizō*, April 1923, 69.
4. Takada Giichirō, "Modan gāru no honke to honmoto," *Josei*, February 1927, 285–95; Sakurai Heigorō, "Modan gāru to shokugyō fujin," *Josei*, August 1927, 169–74; Kaetsu Ko, "Modān gāru zakkan: chishiki no henjō to shinnen no busoku," *Fujin kōron*, January 1927, 59–60; Hayashi Fusao, "Kakuteru no koseibun," *Chūō kōron*, October 1929, 150–51; Kurahara Korehito, speech delivered 12 February 1930, "Teikokushugi to geijutsu," *Kurahara Korehito hyō ronshū* (Tokyo: Shin Nippon Shuppansha, 1967), 50–52.
5. Simmel, "The Metropolis and Mental Life."
6. Peukert, *The Weimar Republic*, 181.
7. Guenther, *Nazi Chic?*, 70, 74.
8. Michiyo, "Reader's Letter," *Shufu no tomo*, April 1925, 378.
9. *Shokugyō fujin ni kansuru chōsa [1922]* (Tokyo: Tokyo-shi shakaikyoku, 1924); reprinted as *Fujin jiritsu no michi* in *Kindai fujin mondai meicho senshū zokuhen*, vol. 7 (Tokyo: Nihon tosho sentā, 1982), 81, and *Shufu no tomosha gojyūnen* (Tokyo: Shufu no tomosha, 1967), 39.
10. *Fujin nenkan* (Tokyo: Nihon fujo tsūshinsha, 1920); reprinted in *Fujin nenkan*, vol. 2.
11. Sato, *The New Japanese Woman*, 80–82.
12. Shigeko, "Readers' Letters," *Fujokai*, June 1924, 287–88; Tomiko, "Readers' Letters," *Fujokai*, June 1924. Regarding the novel *Aijin*, see "Readers' Letters," *Fujokai*, March 1927, 334.
13. Radway, *Reading the Romance*, 214.
14. See "Joshi shōgakkō shūgaku ritsu," in *Meiji ikō kyōiku bunka tōkei* (Tokyo: Kokuritsu kokkai toshokan chōsa rippō kōsakyoku hen, 1957); reprinted in Ōhama Tetsuya and Kumakura Isao, *Kindai Nihon no seikatsu to shakkai* (Tokyo: Hōsō daigaku kyōiku shinkōkai, 1989), 72–73. Also see *Kōtō jogakkō shiryō shūsei — kōtō jogakkō no kenkyū*, vol. 2, ed. Fukuda Sumiko et al. (Tokyo: Ōzorasha, 1990), appendix, 29.
15. *Meiji ikō kyōiku bunka tōkei*; reprinted in Ōhama and Kumakura, *Kindai Nihon no seikatsu to shakai*, 72–73.
16. *Meiji Taishō kokumu sōran* (Tokyo: Tōyō keizai shinpōsha, 1927), 677–78.
17. Takai, *Watashi no jokō aishi*, 5–7.
18. Japan's first factory law (*kōjō hō*) went into effect in 1911, stipulating that children under twelve years of age could not work, and women and children under sixteen years of age were prohibited from doing night work. The workday was fixed at twelve hours by law.
19. *Fujin shokugyō sensen no tonbō* (Tokyo City Office Survey of 1931) (Tokyo: Tokyo shiyaksusho, 1932), 32–35.
20. Ōbayashi Munestsugu, "Jokyū no shakaiteki kōsatsu," *Chūō kōron*, April 1932, 153.

21. Murakami Nobuhiko, *Meiji joseishi—onna no shokugyō*, vol. 2 (Tokyo: Rironsha, 1973), 315–17. Also see *Shokugyō ni kansuru chōsa [1922]*, in *Tokyo-shi shakai-kyoku*, 1924. This survey was published in 1925 under the name *Fujin jiritsu no naichi* and reprinted in *Kindai fujin mondai meichō senshū zokuhen*, vol. 7 (Tokyo: Nihon tosho sentā, 1982), 107.

22. Honda Tōru, "Shokugyō fujin to shūshoku nan," *Fujin kōron*, March 1930, 97.

23. Yamakawa, "Gendai shokugyō fujin ron," 334–35; Okuda, "Shokugyō fujin no tanjō," 239; see also Oku Mumeo, "Fujin rōdō kumiai undō" (1925); reprinted in *Kindai fujin mondai meicho senshū*, vol. 6 (Tokyo: Nihon tosho sentā, 1982), 463–66.

24. Hoggart, *The Uses of Literacy*, 197.

25. Ōkōchi, *Nihonteki chūsan kaikyū*.

26. "Reader's Letter," *Shufu no tomo*, April 1925, 56.

27. Michiko, "Reader's Letter," *Fujokai*, August 1926, 348.

28. Damon-Moore, *Magazines for Millions*, 9–10; Kaestle, "The History of Reading," 51.

29. Fujokai, "Onna bakari wo kakou yoku shitateru himitsu," "Fujin yōfuku wo shincho nasaru katagata no tamen ni."

30. Giles and Middleton, *Studying Culture*, 65; Hall, "Encoding and Decoding."

31. As in, for example, the film *Tokyo Rhapsody* (1936).

32. Slater, *Consumer Culture and Modernity*, 15.

33. Yamakawa Kikue, *Yamakawa Kikue shū*, vol. 5 (Tokyo: Iwanami shoten, 1982), 290.

34. *Shufu no tomo*, April 1925, 26.

35. Nagamine, *Zasshi to dokusha no kindai*, 197–98.

36. Ibid., 200.

37. Ibid., 201–10.

38. Nagamine classified women's magazines into general magazines like *Fujin kōron* (*Women's Review*) which initially catered to "intellectual women"; *Katei zasshi* (*Home*), which recognized the potential of targeting housewives; literary magazines like *Fujin geijutsu* (*Women and Art*); and ideologically inclined magazines like *Fujin kaizō* (*Women's Reform*) that targeted socialist women. See Nagamine, *Zasshi to dokusha no kindai*, 176.

39. Noma, *Watashi no hansei*.

40. "Reader's article," *Fujin kōron*, June 1927, 326.

41. *Fujin kōron*, April 1925, 232–40.

42. Ibid. Elementary school graduates hopeful of becoming nurses and midwives, who did not fit the definition of professional working woman, also sought advice.

43. Liechty, *Suitably Modern*, 64.

44. Advertisement in *Fujokai*, February 1924. The average middle-class family living on a monthly budget of seventy to a hundred yen would not have been described as affluent.

45. Glennie, "Consumption within Historical Studies," 185.

46. Ohmann, *Selling Culture*, 172.

47. Harootunian, *History's Disquiet*, 117–18.

48. Katayama, *Kindai Nihon no joshi kyōiku*, chaps. 1–3.

49. This was a substantial sum, considering that an elementary school teacher's salary was approximately forty yen. See Shūkan, *Zoku-nedan no Meiji, Taisho, Showa fūzoku shi*, 19.

50. "Kaimono kyōsō," *Fujokai*, January 1922, 172, 217.

51. Bennett, "Introduction, Structuralism and Post Structuralism," 97.

52. Silverberg, "The Modern Girl as Militant, 1600–1945," 239–66.

13

Buying In

Advertising and the

Sexy Modern Girl Icon in

Shanghai in the 1920s and 1930s

TANI E. BARLOW

> To discover the various use of things is the work of
> history. MARX, "Commodities," *Capital*

This chapter concerns trite, black-and-white drawings like figure 13.1, which depicts a sexy Modern Girl icon exterminating bedbugs using a DDT-loaded Flit gun. The scene transfers an intangible promise of carnal pleasure, a girl, onto a seemingly tangible object, the transnational, corporate, commercial commodity. Sexualized Modern Girls embody the promised pleasures of industrial society. Visual icons are line drawings of real persons, the movie star Hu Die, for instance, or imaginary ones, like Betty Boop, stylized, widely reproducible, and immediately identifiable. During the interwar years, 1919–37, renditions of the sexy Modern Girl icon acting out imaginary social scenes connoted Shanghai's economic primacy and fantasy, high-society fashions.

At the same time, media in which sexy girl iconography appeared were also promoting cutting-edge vernacular sociology (popular, authoritative ideas about subjectivity and the relation of individuals in society). This widespread social philosophy was vernacular in relation to the classical conventions of Qing dynasty (1644–1911) norms, in relation to U.S.–financed, academic social science in the interwar years of the twentieth century, and in relation to European philosophy, because it claimed to establish a Chinese expression of universal modernity. Read in the same glance, vernacular theories about social life and advertising iconography sutured modern personhood to visual fantasies about commodity use in an imminent future via the sexy Modern Girl icon.

Neither vernacular sociology nor cartoon advertising media "represented" contemporary social truth. They did not reflect an existing reality. The iconic girl and her pretend activities opens to historical analysis the fantasy of modern social life in a colonial modern arena. While advertising cold cream or chemical fertilizer using a girl image aims to increase sales and thus add to the company's profit, advertisements actually put into play fantasies in the social world that do not index the realities of exchange value. "A use-value," may indeed be a "property that satisfies some human need, such that someone might want to purchase the commodity." But once the advertising industry on the China mainland had placed into circulation these banal and effective images, the scenes and figurative women that condensed into iconic form took on a career of their own. One cannot exhaust the meaning of these banalized popular images solely in economic terms which is why I define these ads as "other scenes of use value."[1]

Žižek and Balibar defined the other scene to be a way of thinking that inhabits consciousness, is neither consciousness nor the unconscious, but which nonetheless shapes everyday thinking.[2] Balibar, for instance, proposes an "other scene of politics" as the moment when destructive passions shaping catastrophic political behavior flicker into visibility inside rationalized practices like genocide.[3] For me, the other scene of use value is the moment when knowing how to use modern commodities and modern erotic or bodily pleasure is manifested in a commercial advertising scene that visually encourages consumers to fantasize that they, too, are using the sexy commodity.

The first section of this chapter examines the advertiser Carl Crow's role in developing the prototypical Shanghai sexy Modern Girl icon. Section two sketches out core ideas in vernacular sociology. Section three closely examines a long-running set of Cutex hand-care products ads, which explicitly linked industrial commodities and their uses to vignettes of everyday life in the futuristic new society. The concluding section puts under the microscope a series of sexy Modern Girl icon advertising images that explicitly fuse erotic pleasure, imaginary use values, and the experience of being a subject.

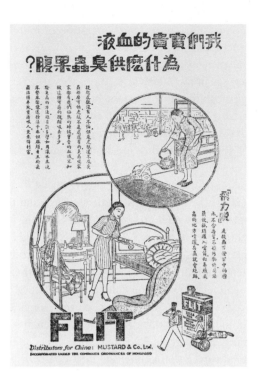

13.1 "Sexy modern girl icon with her Flit gun."
Fünu zazhi 17, no. 4 (April 1931).

In 1931 when the ad for insect spray appeared in the *Ladies' Journal* (*Funü zazhi*, hereafter FNZZ), the Shanghai Modern Girl icon already stood at the "confluence of commerce and desire" typical of international commodity culture during the interwar years.[4] The figure in the first cell in figure 13.1, her tiny face anxious and frustrated, highlights the other scene of modern use value. There the iconic girl pumps her DDT gun in a bedroom flush with European-style vanity table and chair, electric lamp, perfume and cream bottles, and princess bed. While the advertising copy introduces frightening ideas about blood, dirt, and dangerous old methods for controlling household pests, hygiene theory takes a back seat to the image of a delighted girl.

The Shanghai Advertising Industry and the Early Modern Girl Image

On 7 March 1920, the visionary Shanghai advertising agent Carl Crow took out a full page in the Chinese language paper *Shenbao* to place his first ad for

Pond's Vanishing Cream (see figure 13.2). This image retooled a progressive icon already familiar from the covers of *Funü shibao* (1911–17), early *Funü zazhi* (1915–31), and other early-twentieth-century publications, a curious girl (see figure 13.3). Putting the image to use selling industrial commodities was not conventional, however, and Crow says in his memoir that, to his surprise, the business made money for years to come from the Pond's account on the strength of this one composite commercial image.[5]

The Carl Crow Inc. advertising agency was part of an industry that had apparently originated in Hong Kong but mushroomed in Shanghai during the interwar years.[6] Native or not, directly and indirectly, Shanghai advertisers operated on business principles just coalescing into the U.S. social science of advertising. Together with the Australian, British, Italian, Japanese, Hong Kong, U.S., and local entrepreneurs like Huang Chujiu, Jin Xuechen, and Ni Gaofeng, foreign advertisers including Carl Crow formed a self-conscious community of interest. Between 1918 and 1923, the Advertising Club of China met regularly in Shanghai to hear lectures on the science of advertising.[7] Tipper's *Advertising, its Principles and Practice* was available in Shanghai bookstores.[8] Additionally, all of the larger agencies, not just the British, Japanese, or American-owned firms, handled international accounts. The Chinese-owned Dongya Advertising Agency had the Osaka-based Nakayama Taiyodo soap and cosmetics company account, for instance. C. P. Ling (Lin Zhenbin), a U.S. university-educated, Shanghai-born advertiser who established his agency in 1926, had the Ford, General Motors, Coca-Cola, Philip Morris Cigarettes, ASPRO (an Australian branded aspirin), KLIM milk powder, Horliks, Parker Pen, and Pan American World Airlines accounts.[9] The point is that Crow and his Crow agency belonged to a large transnational community of interested, profit-seeking, colonial entrepreneurs.[10]

The Shanghai advertising agency was a modern, business administrative innovation that took two basic forms: the in-house department of a larger concern like Chinese Commercial Press or British American Tobacco, and independent, proprietor-centered entities like Lang Jinshan's Jinshan guanggao she or Crow's Carl Crow Inc. Both count as agencies by virtue of the three defining services they provided. First, they all employed or organized professional artists, often, but by no means exclusively, Chinese trained in the *Shanghaipai* style. Second, from one-man or one-woman outfits to Millington's Agency, which had a staff of seventeen named executives in one 1930 *Directory*, all advertisers bought space.[11] They placed ads in the various print media, newspapers, journals, and supplements, as well as selling outdoor venues like billboards and posters.[12] Third, advertisers gathered information. Crow was convinced that he succeeded because he was able to shape advertising messages

13.2 Carl Crow's first Pond's Advertisement. *Shenbao*, 7 March 1920.

13.3 "A typical curious girl image." *Min'guo ribao*, 9 March, 1917.

around already existing consumer preferences. "We make market surveys," Crow said, "speculate on what articles they [Chinese consumers] will buy, how the article should be packed, how advertised, and what merchandising methods should be followed."[13] He surveyed consumers in part to teach them about products, how to procure and use them. Particularly agencies handling corporate accounts sold directly to retail consumers in the Shanghai region and by mail order to readers all over China and Southeast Asia.

The sexy Modern Girl icon cannot be extricated from these embryonic, interlocked, and international commercial practices.

Fabricating the Sexy Modern Girl Icon

The primary challenge of the 1920s was to shift from an already lucrative business advertising wholesale commodities to a postwar, retail market aimed at the new professional middle class.[14] In this regard, there was nothing singular about advertising in Shanghai.[15] Two advertisements for oil will illustrate this point. In 1921, Devoe's Brilliant Oil advertised its usefulness to commercial consumers in Shanghai. This company, a New York–based kerosene producer, was already a significant transcontinental player by 1876 (see figure 13.4).[16] There is nothing distinctive about this ad. It meets international standards for commodity advertising of the time, simply establishes a trademark image, alleges its useful and patented packaging, and extols the product's virtues. *Millard's Review,* the Shanghai English-language news-weekly like the British-owned, Chinese-language daily *Shenbao,* had generated revenue from this sort of ad (in the case of *Shenbao,* since the late nineteenth century). A mere ten years later, in 1931, Ditmar Brunner Bros., a Vienna-based company, put a sexy Modern Girl image into a complex, educative mise-en-scène (see figure 13.5). She is caught in the process of enjoying her domestic goods. The scene is socially complex. It mirrors hundreds of similar advertising mise-en-scènes.[17]

The example of Carl Crow is a good way to show how the innovation worked because he appears to have had a decisive hand in creating the Shanghai sexy Modern Girl icon. Crow established his agency in 1919, and by 1929 he was handling "25 accounts — American, British, German, Japanese and Chinese — including some of the heaviest advertisers known."[18] Apparently Crow operated the Pond's account at the behest of J. Walter Thompson, the giant U.S.–based international advertising firm. Crow acknowledged on record, "We always *redraw* the pictures in China,"[19] and JWT iconography was clearly the prototype for his innovative advertising image (see figure 13.6). To sell cold cream, however, commodity adverts had to teach potential consumers the proper uses of the new cosmetic cream. In line with Pond's general,

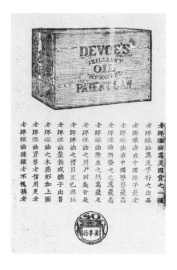 

13.4 "Simple commodity ad for Devoe Brilliant advertising."
Dongfang zazhi, 25 June 1921.

13.5 "Ditmar Brunner girl entertains en famille."
Funü zazhi 17, no. 9 (September 1931).

probably global strategy, Crow decided that his best bet was to merge cosmetics with soap advertising and accelerate the number of soap ads in "all the leading newspapers and magazines" to create repetitive, instructional copy.

It was Crow's opinion that Chinese women of all but the poorest classes already used rouge and talcum powder, so his cold cream copy chose to emphasize two modernist aspects of cosmetic use: hygienic preparation of the skin and social liberation. He targeted the "small pored" Asian woman who could afford trademarked goods because she was middle class, married, and employed servants for household labor. "The net result of all this publicity on the subject of beauty," Crow believed,

> was to change the attitude and, to a certain extent the psychology, of the Chinese women. Before this all beauty aids had been a feminine mystery, like midwifery, but as soon as they were given publicity they became genteel and respectable. Chinese girls, for the first time, began to powder their noses in public with no sense of shame, and their horizons immediately broadened. They had been kept in seclusion for several thousand centuries, but as soon as they discovered [modern cosmetics] . . . there was no holding them back.[20]

Encouraged by response to his 1920 *Shen-bao* ad, Crow continued redrawing and by December 1925 there were major new iterations. Crow's artists added narrative content, placing the girl in a modified bathroom, for instance, but without altering the key elements — the mirror or vanity mirror, the iconic girl, and a commodity image (see figure 13.7). In another variant the girl with the braid appears, seated inside a mirror frame, gazing outward toward the Eclat bottle pictured at the bottom of the ad in its attractive package.[21] Colgate's Eclat, the "Gold headed perfume," was a Crow product. While I have no proof that Crow's agency is responsible for a 1921 Sunlight ad, whoever drew it lifted the curious commodity girl out of Crow's ad and placed her into a highly complex scene of two figures in a dressing room (see figure 13.8). This image helps establish two points related to the theme. First, the cliché of girl, mirror, and product moved rapidly into a general lexicon of girl-fetishizing advertising images. Second, when the fashionable girl is placed in a commodity advertisement, the drawing is invitingly complex and easily draws attention to the new product and its modern use value.

13.6 "Pond's Extract Company's Vanishing Cream," n.p., 1910. Courtesy of Database #P0038, Emergence of Advertising On-Line Project, John W. Hartman Center for Sales, Advertising and Marketing History, Duke University Rare Book, Manuscript, and Special Collections Library, http://scriptorium.lib.duke.edu/eaa/.

A central element of the Sunlight soap image is the imported vanity table. Crow's agency was responsible for a remarkable 1921 Colgate ad of a sinic-looking woman sitting in front of a European vanity.[22] As Ellen Laing has pointed out, not only was the image distinctive in the context of existing advertising art but the local knock-off product, Three Stars face cream, instantly imitated key elements — girl, boudoir, and mirror — and used them to transform its own outdated product image.[23] Crow's 1925 "Shanghainese" version of the sexy girl icon ad retained girl, vanity mirror, and product but dressed the icon in local fashions and portrayed her as giving a sexy shrug (see figure 13.9). The rapidly stylized signifier of colonial modern femininity, the European vanity, continued to appear regularly in formulaic ads for Pepsodent and Palmolive over the thirties with minor changes of style, though increasingly the icon gazed

13.7 "A Shanghai Pond's girl and her mirror."
Dongfang zazhi 22 (25 December 1925).

13.8 "Mistress and curious girl launder with Sunlight soap."
Dongfang zazhi 22, no. 11 (25 November 1925).

13.9 "Sexy Shanghai girl at European vanity table."
Funü zazhi 11, no. 4 (April 1925).

directly into a commodity, rather than the mirror.[24] Eventually Crow's sexy Modern Girl icon drifted out of commodity ads for cosmetics and into black and white fantasy mise-en-scènes across the board.

Self-Love of the Modern Girl and Core Concepts of Vernacular Sociology

In contrast to identifiable girl icons elsewhere in China, the sexy Shanghai Modern Girl signified everyday life in the most advanced sector.[25] If, as Marx demonstrated, the usefulness of a thing or commodity rests on what you need, then, as Donald M. Lowe has shown, advertising is a major venue for explaining the ways commodities work, how they can be used, why we need them, what is desirable about them.[26] These Shanghai images are typical of thousands of similar drawings. Collectively they suggest how repetition of the sexy Modern Girl icon contributed to restructuring femininity, as well as linking erotic modernity to clichés about everyday modern use values. Of course these cartoons intimate that Vanishing Cream, Colgate perfume, Nanyang Bros. machine-rolled cigarettes, Ditmar Brunner kerosene, Flit insect spray, and so on are proofs of a luscious, new, modern, scientific femininity. What they do as well is to ingratiate a way of seeing *as if* scientifically and objectively. If your body used to belong to your parents, but applying modern, scientific Cutex manicure products puts *you* in charge of your own hands, then Carl Crow and Giorgio Agamben have a good point: commodity culture does make bodies tangible in new ways.[27] Your body belongs to you now, these interwar years' scenes of use value seem to say, in the same ways your cold cream or your education or your erotic choices do (or ought to) belong to you. This reiterates a point Henri Lefebvre made decades ago, that in a capitalist society "subjectivization and objectivization go hand in hand, inseparably."[28]

"Subjectivization," or personhood, in Shanghai's colonial modern years had many sources of inspiration. The point to stress is that these ads did not cause personhood, nor did they represent subjects already existing in the world. Emotional, happy iconic girls appear to inhabit a world of commercial commodities and to know all about their use values. Sunlight brand soap, Staycomb Hair Cream, and Kodak film and camera advertising show a future possibility of modern femininity via knowledge of commodity use. Because the sexy Chinese Modern Girl icon is intimately linked to knowing how goods work and how they make one modern, her desire is a mirror of modern self-recognition. The increasingly explicit anatomical references to her breasts, legs, lips, feet, and so on open her up as a modernist erotic object, and emotions such as we see in the Flit advertisement depict the joy of an icon who knows how to exterminate vermin. In other scenes of use value featuring the sexy

Modern Girl's savoir faire, the elements combine in a sensual appreciation, perhaps suggesting to hopeful consumers of imported commodities how use value works, how in modern society it improves the self, and thus why self-love is good for society and social relations as such.

Vernacular sociology, a kind of thinking and writing which explained everyday life in terms of Chinese enlightened social theory and legitimated the ascendant elite's new social relations (small families, companionate marriage, possessive individualism, and so on), and social practices (scientific birth control, domestic hygiene, professional training and so on), suffuses advertising copy, particularly in mise-en-scènes where the Shanghai sexy Modern Girl icon appears. Sociology is globally the science of modernity. Chinese vernacular sociology preceded and then encompassed professional and university styles of sociological reasoning, which, in China at least, were, as Yung-cheng Chiang has established, largely funded through ongoing, U.S.–based Rockefeller Foundation grants.[29] Contemporary readers of vernacular (as opposed to professional) social theory had an acute interest in the question of subjectivity, and from its inception, Chinese vernacular sociological writing focused on the problem of how individuals are created and why the psychodynamic processes of identification and self-forming should, in the natural course of things, produce healthy, individual persons. Endo Ryukichi's *Sociology in Modern Times* (1903), for instance, summed up international sociology's contents, materials, and methods, as well as its major problematics and typologies or systems. Endo stressed how humans had emerged out of general mammal culture into an assertive, self-evolving, self-willing, individuated social species with a perceivable, traceable evolutionary timeline. Like most vernacularists, Endo theorized that the constituent parts of individual subjectivity were will, desire, spirit, and self-consciousness. Drawing heavily on the American sociologist Lester Ward's speculative ontology, Endo spent a lot of energy elaborating on philosophies of human will and particularly Ward's notorious belief in the capacity of human beings to control their own evolution as a species. Endo assumed that theory captured social realities and historical evolutionary movements such that when an educated person consumed a précis of modern thought, the reader like the theorist was grasping real social processes.[30]

Vernacular sociological thinking came in the interwar years to form a preserve where educated Chinese people, like their peers elsewhere in the world, read key social theories in modernist journals of opinion. *Funü zazhi* (Ladies' Journal), *Dongfang zazhi* (Eastern Miscellaney), *Xin qingnian* (New Youth), and national newspapers like *Dagong bao* (The Observer) published capsule accounts of the thinking of diverse social theorists ranging from Comte, Spencer, Mill, Adam Smith, Montesquieu, Marx, Shimamura Tamizo, Kuriyakawa

Hakuson, and Lester Ward, to Havelock Ellis, Yosano Akiko, Robinson, Sanger, and Perkins-Gilman. Professionalized sociology shared with these vernacular predecessors the view that the historical catachresis of "society" is a real, tangible space that individuals occupy and where norms, conflicts, and relationships are mediated in family and other social collectivities. The point is that questions about how to live a good life are wedded to knowing about the new social scientific theories and to understanding personal experience through them. Social theory published in the mass media that presumes the existence of the social contract, introduces psychosocial dynamic theories of subjectivity, or invokes a "social question" is vernacular sociology. In my reasoning, the assumption that society is an epistemic given underpins middle-class, modernist thinking in Shanghai as elsewhere.

Two examples illustrate how these modernist vernacular sociological clichés were variously expressed. In 1921, Jun Zuo celebrated a sociological method he claimed was mushrooming among his classmates. Youth were thinking in new ways about social questions, he said, and they consequently required sociological theories to get a handle on the new realities of modern society. Jun's essay assigned a use value to theory itself, but more importantly it drew a clear link between the assumption that society is a thing and the belief that sociological theory explained the truths of society.[31] A mature example is Pan Guangdan, who shared with Carl Crow the assumption that society is a universal matrix composed of autonomous individuals, and that women should appear publicly in society as themselves. What that "self" was had yet to be established, of course, and particularly in regard to the question of women's future, modern personality captured the imagination of male and female theorists and social scientists in the interwar years.[32]

Later an illustrious eugenic social scientist, Pan first published vernacular style social theory in 1924, a twelve-page article in *Funü zazhi* titled "Research on Feng Xiaoqing" (Feng Xiaoqing kao), which he had drafted in 1922. Its first part, "Historical Xiaoqing" (Lishi de Xiaoqing), listed known facts about the girl poet: a fateful meeting with a nun who warned Xiaoqing's mother to keep the child illiterate, marriage as a child concubine into the Feng family, Feng's wife's vendetta against her, Xiaoqing's close relationship to her girlfriend Yang, Xiaoqing's death at age seventeen, the destruction of her poetic legacy by the jealous wife, the poet's eventual entombment, and the enshrining of her few remaining poems into a largely male literary cult. In part two, "Xiaoqing in Literature and Sexual Psychology" (Xing xinlixue de ji wenxue de Xiaoqing), Pan used Freudian psychoanalytic techniques to diagnose this sad history as a sociologically typical case of female narcissism.[33]

Part two began: "Sex is the origin of religion, literature and art, a point that modern, educated psychologists have said clearly and publicly." Indeed, psychoanalytic psychologists go so far as to say that "sexual desire explains everything about human behavior" (1710). Among the varieties of abnormal psychologies that Freudian analysis identified, Pan continued, is narcissism or *yinbian*, which in Xiaoqing's case meant that she had declined heterosexual and homosexual intimacy in favor of self-gazing activities, particularly writing, and had directed her libido into a pattern of subjective development typical of too many Chinese women. Given the paucity of evidence about her historical existence, Pan highlighted Xiaoqing's importance as a social signifier or icon of "Chinese society's attitude toward women" (1716). In expanded versions, the 1927 "An Analysis of Xiaoqing" (Xiaoqing zhi fenxi) and 1929 "Feng Xiaoqing: A Study in Narcissism" (Feng Xiaoqing: I jian yinbian zhi yanjiu), and smaller afterthoughts published over the 1930s, Pan expanded his theory.

Pan Guangdan's "historical research" into the female subject question using the poet Xiaoqing is consistent with vernacular sociological truism. It also usefully reflects a contemporary interlocked relation between the other scenes of use value in commercial advertising art and middlebrow social theory. Pan used the poet-painter Wen Yiduo's pretentiously highbrow rendition of the sexy Modern Girl icon to illustrate his book.[34] Wen's highbrow appropriation of commercial drawing reverses what I show in the next section as a common appropriation of highbrow theory into sexy Modern Girl iconography. Eugenics' association with the sexy Modern Girl worked downward into popular culture, too. A vulgarized version of the broad-spectrum eugenics theories that Pan used to ground sociology appear in a visually explicit Five Continents Pharmacy advertisement. Here the naked, sexy Modern Girl icon fan-dances with what appears to be a large sponge or placard extolling eugenics and female reproductive health (see figure 13.10). Less explicit, more European-style references to sexy Modern Girl icons and eugenics appear in the twenties and thirties in long-running, banalized ads for Tampax, Modess, Kotex, Comfort, Veramon, Santogen, Byla's Musculosine, Cryogenine-Lumiere, Hemegene Tailleur, and Agomensin-Sistomensin menstrual products.

In the explosion of theoretical writing that characterized the Chinese Enlightenment (1919–37), advertising itself became a topic of vernacular theory projects. In his lengthy introduction of contemporary theories of advertising social psychology, Shi Quan offered readers of *Eastern Miscellany* important new theoretical advances from the United States and Europe. Discussing at length the ideas of Hollingworth on advertising and selling, Scott on the psychology of advertising, and Starek on basic principles of advertising science, Shi concluded with a critique and an admonition. Shanghai stores should stop using crude ads and get more sophisticated while socially responsible Chinese

13.10 "Naked eugenics sexy girl dances with sponge board."
Funü yuebao, 10 October 1936.

people ought to learn more about the psychology and arts involved in advertising and catch up with the West. Shi Quan's awareness of the extra value that sophisticated advertising brought to commodities lends further credence to my point that while a commodity might sell in Shanghai because Flit really does kill bedbugs better than hot water, it might have appealed to enlightened consumers because buying soap stamped with the Colgate trademark or oat grain with the Quaker trademark reinforced attractive and increasingly widespread polemics on social evolution, progressive feminism, human sexuality, nuclear family formation, or contemporary motherhood.[35]

These examples suggest ways that making general arguments, which is to say *theorizing*, about the values of enlightened social thinking paralleled elements of the burgeoning advertising culture. But vernacular sociology and new commodity ads shared direct links, too. Crow (and probably other agencies) used product placement advertising to amplify the connection between commodities and the new social theory. His memoir references the chronic problem he had getting placements right, particularly in provincial media, where editors habitually clustered ads together by type of product.[36] But metropolitan advertisers and the major, monthly opinion journals seem to have been more responsive to this internationally developing advertising practice. Juxtaposed with the first page of a long, informative article by Liu Shuqin entitled "From Natural Sociology to Cultural Sociology," in an issue of *Eastern Miscellany* in November 1926, for instance, appears a striking advertisement for the Ford Motor Company.[37] In the familiar curlicue script of the Ford brand, the advertising copy lists the comfort and uses of the family auto and gives the price and address for a Ford car franchise in Shanghai. Just behind the engraved image, a modern Chinese couple is entering their apartment after a refreshing ride in their car. Liu's essay, meanwhile, asks what sociology is and how it can be defined and analyzes questions ranging from natural evolution to cultural social evolution.

Vernacular sociology and advertising copy instructions about how to use commodities (with libidinous illustrations) reinforced each other. After all, learning the various uses of such things as Brunner Mond chemical fertilizers or Sunmaid Raisins is not unlike learning the modernist values encoded in the powerful universalisms of the new vernacular social theory. These shared values included imported standards of cleanliness, personal and collective hygiene, evolutionary racial improvement, athleticism, modern sexual expression, aesthetic modernism, national sovereignty, and rapid modern economic development.[38] My underlying assertion here is that sociological theories and scientific advertising technologies shared the same assumptions and practical objectives. Each put a premium on gathering accurate information about an as yet undifferentiated mass, reflecting back information in a categorical framework of collective categories that resorted people into "classes," "sexes," and other social scientific categories.

Lurking behind Endo Ryukichi's abstractions about will and willed behavior, sexuality and sexual choices, race improvement and stories of degeneration, in other words, is the pressing matter of why individuals would buy Parker pens and Victrola brand record players, Two Gorgeous Girls toothpowder, Parisian hosiery, Viennese kerosene, Australian milk powder, American soap, and all the other trademarked commodities that elite consumers apparently regularly preferred to Chinese national products. Will, desire, emotion, and other new categories of vernacular sociology were theoretical ways to ask the question of what people want and how they get what they want. That certainly was also the central concern of advertising agents.

The Cutex Campaign

In the mid-1920s, an elaborate Cutex advertising campaign appeared in the major venue for vernacular sociology topics, the *Ladies' Journal* (see figure 13.11). Designed to establish its flashy trademark and brand name, each episodic drawing had a number in the lower right-hand corner, a Romanesque frame, a coupon etched with the number of the ad (allowing the agency to gather information about which scenes most captivated what kinds of readers), and three design elements. These consisted of a girl drawn into a social scene, a short text about the scene, and an unobtrusive drawing of the product with its logo clearly depicted. The Cutex campaign is a modification of that formula pervasive in interwar Shanghai advertising culture — the girl, mirror, and commodity ad. Although many advertising campaigns for transnational, branded commodities had a similar structure, the Cutex campaign is particularly compelling for three reasons. First, it explicitly placed the branded commodity into social evolutionary developmental time. Second, the written copy accompanying the series of images drew explicitly on vernacular sociological terms and neologisms (those newly created words that facilitated the translation of Japanese, European, and American social theory into modern Chinese). Third, more clearly than the many other national products and transnational commodity campaigns I have tracked, Cutex illustrates the powerful moment of the other scene of use value.

Keep in mind that in the mid-1920s when the Cutex fingernail and hand skin products campaign hit its stride, marketers were confronting the need to carve out a market in a cosmetic terrain where conventional beauty products already existed and, according to none other than Carl Crow, were widely used. Particularly imported luxury brands like Cutex confronted the need to invent a counterlogic that would justify buying something new and expensive. Social evolutionary dogma had become the prevailing elite truism in Chinese circles, as it had in educated communities in Europe, Latin America, the United States,

13.11 "School girl and school boy shake hands." *Funü zazhi* 11, no. 5 (May 1925).

and Japan. To create a campaign based on social evolution and on the role of commodity use in social progress exhibited a modernist sensitivity to the new theories of social life. Chinese social evolution itself forms the developmental logic linking the dozens of individual images together into a continuous story. The point to stress is that like so many other brand advertisers, the Cutex campaign made the sexy Modern Girl icon its dramatis persona in staging truisms current in vernacular sociological theories. The evolutionary story arc, which links each numbered cartoon cell to the campaign as a whole, narrates a tale about modernity growing organically out of a once graceful but ever more historically moribund Chinese beauty culture.

The campaign begins in the era of the mythic ruler Fu Xi (ca. 2850 BCE), and each successive cartoon cell documents the evolutionary development of nail enhancement. Ad cells 1–7 (I am referring to ads by the number assigned to them in the story arc) trace a trajectory from the archaic period through the Han dynasty (206 BCE to 220 CE), the Later Han dynasty (25–220 CE), and the Shu Han dynasty (221–263 CE), noting in each case that while tradition had its virtues, beauty culture way back when was not always perfectly safe and usually based on secret formulas the beauty took with her to the grave. To market a scientific commodity as both superseding old practices and as an evolutionary vehicle for social progress, the advertiser went after noncommodified or "traditional" nail care products for women. For instance, since time immemorial, according to ad cell 3, the use of balsa flower dyes for fingertips had been celebrated in poetry and practiced by all the great beauties.[39] But flower dyes are not real manicure items, nor is their use scientific, because in Fu Xi's time there was no science! Women today can get scientific Cutex manicure items in an adorable box that makes the Cutex manicure set your vanity table's best friend (many subsequent cells repeated this comparison and reiterated the stock phrase about Cutex being "the vanity table's best friend").

In ads set in times before modernity, artists often drew the traditional beauty or the Modern Girl inside each other's thought bubbles, placing the beauty in a scene and the sexy Modern Girl in the same episode. Ad cell 3, for instance, showed a Modern Girl at her vanity table in a bubble at the top of the screen. This sexy icon is gazing obliquely out of her bubble in a linear perspective beyond her vanity table mirror and thus directly into the cell's dominant scene, which shows a traditional fairy beauty in a garden, while the text draws a comparison between superseded practices and the happiness of the modern icon. The copy in cell 5, to give another example, castigates Li Zhuang, the Han Wudi emperor's (reigned 141–86 BCE) lady-in-waiting, whose failed treatment for maintaining her alabaster jade skin is compared unfavorably to today's products. There is no danger to the skin in the potion you can buy now, in either powdered or already mixed and bottled form, the legend reads. Ad cell 6 featured the fictive Wang Magu who took her beauty secrets with her when she became a celestial fairy. In this case, the copy says that, in comparison to Magu's exclusive or elitist beauty secrets, girls in modern society mingle democratically with boys and their beauty culture is open to the admiring eyes of all. When these ads illustrate the relationship between new consumer and outdated traditional beauty, they show how individual choices affect social development. They also specularize the immediate past, literally incorporating ghosts into a present where intelligent girls can prevail over the vestiges of a discredited history.

The point is established repeatedly that all societies evolve historically and they all begin with good traditional practices (made obsolete by science) but grow, as China is growing, into a market of universally available products that anyone can buy in a department store. Evolutionary developmental history overcomes the defunct (albeit, again, utterly praiseworthy) elite beauty practices of the past, and the Cutex timeline leads directly to the modern present. With time, the volume of contemporary vignettes and images increased and the archaic historical references declined. The campaign's story arc and objectives shifted to hammering home the difference between generic and branded modern manicure products. Social life and social evolution into the future come to rest on the application of science to everyday personal care.

The second point to be drawn from this long Cutex campaign is the tendency in interwar era advertising to draw on vernacular sociological theory and its modernist vocabulary. This style of campaign probably owes a debt to the popular illustrated fiction of the earlier part of the twentieth century. "Huabao"-style stories pictured curious girls in modernist social spaces for readers, a technique readily apparent in cell 10, which shows a girl and a boy shaking hands (see figure 13.11). She is wearing the fashion a la mode of chignon in the shape of a hair bob, earrings, and a two-piece proto-*qipao;* both figures are holding books. The text reads: "Coeducation of men and women and public intercourse involves shaking hands in greeting since this is now the fashion in society." The use of the neologism "society" here is significant, as is the association of "society" with the advanced space of the classroom. Of course, you will be utterly humiliated unless you are able to meet the gaze of other modern people, particularly because the school is one of those modern sectors of Chinese society where the comingling of women and men is moving progressively toward ending gender segregation.

In ad cell 11 we are in a colonial ballroom where heavily made-up girls dance with young men dressed in European suits, hair slicked back (no doubt with Staycomb) (see figure 13.12). Everyone is engaged in the mixed social inter-

13.12 "Sexy girl and sexy boy ballroom dancing." *Funü zazhi* 11, no. 7 (July 1925).

course of ballroom dancing. In this scene, the ad copy explains that while people in the olden days liked to keep their fingernails long, the new custom is to prefer them short. "In the field of social intercourse, no matter what sort of dress you have on your back you still want your makeup to look great. If your hands are coarse and your skin is flawed people will most surely laugh at you." The term to stress is "field of social intercourse" since it appears regularly in vernacular sociological writings. It is a place, like "society" where the progressive woman and man mingle in order to forward the aims of modern China and, not unimportantly, to select mates and form modern, procreative, eugenically sound families. To accomplish the evolutionary imperative, therefore, young people will need a good manicure.

One way the campaign asserted Cutex brand's ability to declare a modernist space to be modern comes in ad cells that show how commodity use transforms your social interactions. Ad cell 12 presents this vividly through Ms. Wang Balsa, whose name is a parodic wordplay on the use of balsa flowers by beauties in the past.[40] Wang Bal-sa's arrogance about her delicate, white hands has made her friend, Ms. Li Xiuying, weep with inferiority. One day while Ms. Li is reading the newspaper, she finds an ad in the paper for "such-and-such company," so she immediately sends off her postal coupon, and after waiting with great anticipation, she receives her goods. After that, Ms. Wang can no longer lord it over Ms. Li because the company in question is the oh-so-modern Cutex. Family hierarchy is yet another site for transformation in ad cell 9, "Private Chat in the Women's Quarters," in which a girl says, "Big Sis, look how ugly my nails are. How can I face people?" Big Sis replies that she has just gotten some "Really Cute Method of Manicure" product, which she has kept a secret. The pesky little sister replies that she will give anything to know about it. Big Sis laughs and says that if Lil' Sis tells her about her sweethearts and shares her love letters, she will disclose the secret of beautiful nails. In the end Lil' Sis learns that "really cute method of manicure" is just a descriptive term, and the trademark is, of course, "Cutex Manicure Products." Certainly, Big and Lil' Sis are sexy Modern Girls whose social relationships are being redefined through evolutionary commodity choices.

Third, the Cutex campaign helps expand a point raised earlier about the other scene of use value in commercial advertising culture. These drawings help to establish how the use of the commodity, Cutex, became fused to new forms of public erotic pleasure, which the sexy Modern Girl icon presents to readers as being indisputably modern and feminine. (A similar argument can be made for cars, cigarettes, chemicals, insecticides, medicines, kerosene, and the many cosmetics and hygienic products that flooded into advertising culture and China's contested commercial capitalism in these years.)[41] Of course, these advertisings involve mystification, since while the cartoon cell drawings depict stylized Modern Girl icons at play, the rationale given for using the product does not address the question of *whether* nail care makes the woman but *how* using Cutex products leads to an excellent progressive, modern femininity. As in the case of other girl practices or products — hair bobbing, toothpaste using, skin whitening, underarm deodorizing, and so on — Cutex ads inhabited contemporary consciousness of what it took to be modern and female. In that moment the ad becomes the sine qua non, the never fully articulated but always inhering basis, of everyday thinking about being a modern woman. Using the product realizes the promise. Using the product, even in fantasy, sutures the reader into a modern subject position.

Like all the other sexy advertising "girls," Cutex icons are desiring agents. They bring the fingernails and the skin of one's cosmetically altered hands to bear on what the advertising copy and vernacular theory both propose is social evolution. From the mid-twenties, Cutex's major selling points had to do with the application of modern science to the material body. The finger to which the polish would be applied was "miraculated" or made visible in a short, violent but legible vestment of tangibility into the modern or commodity body. The eroticized hand arises in some part as an effect of this product advertising campaign. But as the ad copy makes clear, Cutex is the scientific expression of a modern feminine aesthetic: this touch is antiseptic, desirous, self-willing, socially inventive, open to public scrutiny. Anyone with money and her wits about her can purchase it. On the other hand, anyone seeking to enter that sine qua non of modernity, the "society," will have to buy and apply the product. This association is not singular to Shanghai or even to China, of course. I fully agree with Agamben, who has noted that in Europe, in the 1920s "when the process of capitalist commodification began to invest the human body," even anticapitalist critics "could not help but notice a positive aspect to it, as if they were confronted with the corrupt text of a prophecy that went beyond the limits of the capitalist mode of production and were faced with the task of deciphering it."[42] These commodity adverts shifted the sources of bodily comfort and purchasable pleasures away from the ineffable body of traditional Chinese medical foods or general tonics and toward effable domestic commodities like bathtubs, kerosene-fueled heaters, hormonal birth control agents, antiseptic soaps, Cornflakes, all drawn as making the effable body feel good.

At the center of these Cutex stories is the mimetic sexy icon whose constant companions are the vanity table and cosmetics and whose arena is the metropolis of Shanghai. Her performance of the activity of self-improvement rests on the values of ease, comfort, safety, and evolutionary promise embedded in the industrial commodity. In every image, the user of the product is pleased. Her future looks good. Because she can handle the anxiety of scrutiny, the social life of modern times opens before her. The ads sketch out the pleasures of all girls in their self-directed yet educated use of the commodity. Hands are no longer the concern of emperors, husbands, or magical beings since they now belong to the modern woman herself. This illusory sense of self-ownership, personal pleasure, and the pleasure that others will take in her self-care, together with the sheer visibility of the bodily satisfaction she feels, justify commodity life as such. By the late 1930s, the photo image of the self-polishing woman's hands was as much a part of the scene in use value as other commodities that we associate with the Modern Girl icon.

The Iconic Self

In an advertisement appearing in the early twenties and endlessly thereafter, a woman who might be the Pond's girl sits facing the viewer, her gaze cast into a mirror mounted on a stand in front of her. She is gazing downward into her own reflection (see figure 13.13). In one hand she holds her artist's palette of European watercolors and in the other hand a brush. The ad catches her in the act of self-portraiture. The condensed classical language text explains that the delicate hand of the girl is tracing her own self-likeness. This is a remarkable advertising mise-en-scène for several reasons. Certainly no better illustration of mimesis is imaginable: girl, mirror, commodity, and self-representation, gazing at the self in the mirror while setting up the mise-en-abyme of the real and its representations. The self-desiring gaze of the painter reflects the same preoccupations as high-tide male-dominated vernacular sociological writing. The difference is how happy the sexy icon is. She is pleasurably and mimetically representing herself with the help of an industrially produced, scientifically crafted mirror, European paints, and Ribbon Dental Cream.[43]

In 1928, one year after the White Terror against the Chinese Communist Party, three years before the Japanese occupation of Northern China, and nine years before the Japanese Imperial Army occupied Shanghai and most of littoral China, Kotex joined other transnational corporations and began advertising in Chinese- and English-language venues. One of the most striking ads the

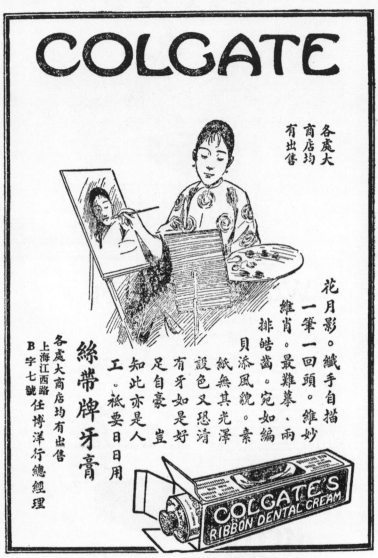

13.13 "Oil painting girl uses Colgate dental ribbon paste."
Funü zazhi 11, no. 2 (February 1925).

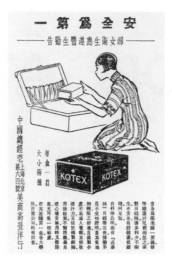

WOMEN! Safety First

Follow Doctor's Advice in Feminine Hygiene

TAKE no chances with your health when to be safe is so simple. No longer risk the dangers of *unsanitary* "sanitary pads" that may do more harm than good. They are not cheap at any price.

Science has perfected Kotex for you—a sanitary pad that the medical profession indorses. Kotex, made of softest materials, is utterly comfortable and scientifically designed to fit perfectly without revealing its presence.

It brings peace-of-mind because you know it is *5 times more absorbent than cotton*. And that means absolute protection. You dispose of it without bother—no laundry.

It deodorizes—and ends all fear of offense in that direction.

You owe it to yourself to try Kotex. Get a package today at any drug, dry goods or departmental store.

KOTEX
Sanitary Napkins

In 2 sizes: Kotex Regular and Kotex-Super; 12 to the package

Agents for China: Wm. Golding & Co., 64 Peking Road, Shanghai.

13.14 "Chinese modern girl finds Kotex in her suitcase."
Funü zazhi 14, no. 8 (August 1928).

13.15 "English modern girl finds Kotex in her suitcase."
North China Daily News, 6 December 1928.

campaign produced is the image of a Modern Girl stooped before a box of Kotex that she has lifted out of a suitcase (see figure 13.14). Consistent with the formula of the icon, the mirror, and the commodity, this girl (who looks like a curious girl, minus the braid) gazes right into the commodity with a literally speechless (since she has no mouth) intensity, as she seems to lift the package toward eye level. The image in the English-language version shows a similar girl icon (see figure 13.15). In both, the icon's gaze cannot be detached from the product. She looks into the box as if it is a mirror, fixed with longing for what it alleges to deliver. She is absorbed in the same mimetic self-cognition as the Ribbon dental paste painter, but she is making her body a publicly visible source of pleasure. In straightforward classical Chinese, the ad informs readers that in matters of hygiene, safety is the number one theme, so it is best to take health matters quite seriously. Homemade menstrual padding is more harmful than good, the copy says, because it is unhygienic, unsafe, and an obstacle to good health. This drawing is physically affecting because it literalizes the reproductive body. The object of the icon's gaze is not only unspeakably related to what makes her body singular, her menses; it also uses words that define and dissipate possible, delicate unease (about odor, blood, pain) while putting this unease irrevocably into public rhetoric. Focusing attention on the menstrual commodity, the ad seals the girl and the remedy to what becomes, through advertising culture, an openly, publicly secularized physical part of all women's everyday life. At least in theory: gazing at the menstrual pads hidden in the suitcase, the iconic sexed girl freezes in self-reflection, as if catching sight of her real self in a mirror. Perhaps she (and through her, the sutured viewer of the advertising image) is seeing in the transparent modern physiology of the menstrual cycle performed in a subtle other scene of use value.

It is not really surprising, then, that the pose of the Kotex girls is rather similar to a feminine performance of pleasure associated with movie actresses, or that gazing at commodities is a spectacle that advertising in these years repeated over and over. No image I have found better conveys this provocative cliché than the endlessly reiterated drama of the Sincere girl. Sincere Department Store, founded by an Australian Chinese overseas business family and one of the great wonders of Shanghai before Japanese bombing destroyed it, designed its own sexy Modern Girl icon in the company's heyday. "Material civilization discards the old and promotes the new," its banner reads (see figure 13.16). As the Sincere girl's efficiently drawn posture of delight captures visual attention, the text assures that the department store keeps you on an evolutionary track with all current commodities, which is why you should choose Sincere over the competition. While other iterations of this girl have her gazing in awe at a packaged ham, this one focuses on soaps and cosmetics. It is the

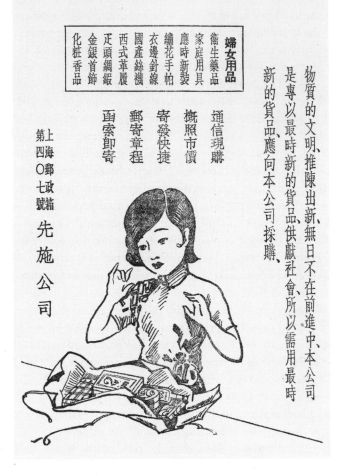

物質的文明、推陳出新、無日不在前進中、本公司是專以最時新的貨品供獻社會、所以需用最時新的貨品應向本公司採購、

婦女用品
僑生藥品
家庭用具
應時新裝
繡花手帕
衣邊針線
國產絲襪
西式革履
正頭綢緞
金銀首飾
化粧香品

通信現購
攝照市價
寄發快捷
郵寄章程
函索即寄

上海郵政
第四〇七號箱

先施公司

13.16 "Sincere Department Store girl icon gazes in awe."
Funü zazhi 17, no. 8 (August 1931).

relationship between the gaze of the ecstatic girl and the inert but intensely attractive commodity that charges the little drawing with emotion and thus draws us into the scene.[44]

Conclusion

Philosophy must be caught up in the "minutiae of everyday life," Lefebvre has argued, if it is to become more than ideology or class prejudice.[45] The relation of modernist vernacular sociology and the sexy Modern Girl icon — or, more broadly, philosophy and its visualization — is a mystery. Capitalist commodification of the human body brought with it the ambiguous redemption of women. That process has played out all over the world. But, as the evidence amassed here suggests, commodified eroticism came alive in the most banal fashion, in the pages of middle-class opinion journals and, in more bastardized form, at the physical margins of the leading daily newspapers. Littered inconspicuously in thumbnail images that framed the news columns of *Dagong bao* or *Shen bao*, tiny Cutex, Colgate, and Sincere Department Store ads combined fun with serious ideological work.

The sexy Modern Girl icon is in this sense a philosophical phenomenon. Consolidated in the tumultuous world of capitalist Shanghai, iconic commercial art naturalized the other scene or fantasy where the imagined use values of commercial commodities and modernist styles of eroticism fused. But the ideas, which I have called vernacular sociology here, are not so abstract as we might imagine, either. Like Balibar's other scene of politics, the other scene of use value was the moment when the passions shaping modern social behavior were given a visible form; where the commodity became the "modern" part of modernity. Vernacular sociology, sophisticated ideas about self and society, personhood, evolution, progress, and a future when China, as Japan already had, would belong to the family of advanced nations, shared the logic of the iconic sexy girl advertising scene.

This expression of philosophy through commercial minutiae means that lofty questions like "Who is a Modern Girl?" are better addressed historically within the ephemeral and tactile, outside the fake clarity of self-expression. Because, as Lefebvre put it, "philosophic categories" like "the subject," to raise a concern of this study, "can only be separated from social categories a posteriori." With attention to ephemera, "our consciousness of these things becomes transformed." Debris that has not been highly valued in its time, like these simple cartoon advertising images, loses its "triviality, its banality since in each thing we see more than itself — something else which is there in everyday objects, not an abstract lining but something enfolded within which hitherto we have been unable to see."[46] Here I have called this something the other scene of use value. It is the philosophic categories of Chinese colonial modernist sociology that saturate 1920s advertising culture. But it is in these sophisticated other scenes of use value starring Shanghai's sexy Modern Girl icon that this "something enfolded" in modernity was most powerfully expressed.

Notes

I gratefully acknowledge the intellectual generosity and careful reading of this chapter in draft form that Ruri Ito and Lynn Thomas provided. To Donald M. Lowe for his criticism of repeated drafts I am as always deeply grateful. Teresa Mares, Brandy Parris, Helen Schneider, Pamela Tang, and Mengliang Zhang have helped me a lot over the years in handling images and copy editing my prose.

1. "A use-value is a property that satisfies some human need, such that someone might want to purchase the commodity. An exchange-value is a quantitative measure of the value of a commodity in relation to other commodities. It is the possession of exchange-value that makes a product a commodity. To be produced as a commodity is to be produced *for exchange*. Commodity production is production for exchange." Osborne, *How to Read Marx,* 12–13.

2. Žižek, *The Sublime Object of Ideology,* 19. Žižek defines the "other scene" as a "form of thought whose ontological status is not that of thought" and thus is "external to the thought whereby the form of the thought is already articulated in advance." In Žižek's thinking, the other scene has a second element. That is an unconscious "theater," where modern personhood is staged psychically.

3. Balibar, *Politics and the Other Scene,* xiv. In this view such a locality is "not so much a concrete or theoretical place . . . as the moment where it becomes manifest that politics is not 'rational' (but is not simply 'irrational' either)." See also Lacan, "The Signification of the Phallus," 285.

4. Benton, Benton, and Woods, eds., *Art Deco 1910–1930,* 13.

5. Crow, *Four Hundred Million Customers,* 32.

6. Xu Junji, *History of Chinese Advertising,* 148–59. The longer version of this chapter (unpublished) lists an astounding number of ad agencies.

7. Laing, "The Fate of Shanghai Painting Style," 953–1003, 981. Her primary source is *Millard's Review,* 8 June 1919, 70.

8. Ibid., 983.

9. See Bacon, "Advertising in China," 745. Also consulted was the Chinareach Company profile, http://www.chinreach.com/profile.htm (visited 15 July 2002). Lin Zhenbin studied advertising and marketing at Rochester University and took his M.A. at Columbia. According to his son, Ling created his own campaigns.

10. Yi, Liu, and Gan, *Lao Shanghai Guangao,* 1–19; Cochran, *Big Business in China,* 1–9, 201–20; Cochran, "Marketing Medicine and Advertising Dreams," in Yeh, ed., *Becoming Chinese: Passages to Modernity and Beyond,* 62–97; and Cochran, "Transnational

314   TANI E. BARLOW

Origins of Advertising in Early Twentieth Century China," in Cochran, ed., *Inventing Nanjing Road*, 37–60.

11. See *Directory and Chronicle for China*, 193.

12. Laing, "The Fate of Shanghai Painting Style," 983, cites the *Weekly Review* (formerly *Millard's*), 30 December 1922.

13. Crow, *Four Hundred Million Customers*, 314. Crow established a coupon feedback system and ways of using newspaper distribution circuits to advantage clients. To compensate for illiteracy among clients (he cites a wealthy, illiterate carpenter who owned a private motor car), Crow hired high-priced artists to create drawings of beautiful women (175).

14. You Guoqing, *Byebye Old Style Advertising*, 23–108.

15. It reflected the international moment and development of the global advertising industry.

16. http://www.scvhistory.com/scvhistory/pioneer-asme-ii.htm (visited 29 June 2005).

17. Complex images like these appear in *Shenbao* (1872–1949), the foreign-owned, Chinese-language daily; *Liangyu huabao*, established in 1926 by overseas Chinese entrepreneurs; *Meishu shenghuo* (1934–37); as well as *North China News, South China Morning Post, Dongfang zazhi* (*Eastern Miscellany;* hereafter DFZZ), and *Funü zazhi* (*Ladies' Journal;* hereafter FNZZ), to list the venues that I or my assistants have examined. See Li Yensheng, *Zhongguo baokan tushi*, 1–64.

18. Bacon, "Advertising in China," 759.

19. Crow, *Four Hundred Million Customers*, 105 (my emphasis).

20. Ibid., 38.

21. Eclat girl advertisement, FNZZ 10, no. 6 (June 1924): n.p.

22. Colgate vanity, DFZZ 18, no. 10 (20 October 1921): n.p. Since the vanity table is an integral element of all contemporary Pond's ads, I am suggesting (1) that it is Crow's habit of recopying American corporate ads that "translated" the image into common commercial parlance in the banal line-drawing ad, and (2) that the process of imitation is the motile element in the creation of the sexy modern girl icon.

23. Laing, *Selling Happiness*, 144–45.

24. *Pepsodent ads:* FNZZ 10, no. 12 (December 1924); DFZZ 25, no. 7 (10 April 1928); FNZZ 11, no. 10 (November 1925). *Palmolive ads:* FNZZ 14, no. 7 (July 1928) and FNZZ 16, no. 7 (July 1930).

25. This section is indebted to Barlow, "Wanting Some," 312–50.

26. Marx, *Capital*, and Lowe, *The Body in Late Capitalist USA*.

27. Agamben, *The Coming Community*, 47–84. See also Zito and Barlow, eds., *Body, Subject and Power in China*, 1–102.

28. Lefebvre, *Critique of Everyday Life*, 159.

29. Yung-chen Chiang, *Social Engineering and the Social Sciences in China, 1919–1949*.

30. Endo, *Modern Sociology*.

31. Jun Zuo, "New Thought and New Art, Sociological Research Method" (Xin sixiang yu xin wenyi, shehuixue de janjiu fa), DFZZ 18, no. 21 (1922): 73–77.

32. Barlow, *The Question of Women in Chinese Feminism*, chap. 3.

33. Pan Guangdan, "Feng Xiaoqing kao," FNZZ 10, no. 11 (1924). See Ko, *Teachers of the*

Inner Chambers, 69, 91–112; Widmer, "Xiaoqing's Literary Legacy," 111–55; Jing Tsu, *Failure, Nationalism and Literature*, 149–53; and Zhang, "Literary Uses of Psychoanalytic Criticism by Chinese Psychologists," 132–39. I am particularly grateful to the latter.

34. See Barlow, "The Women in the Mirror," unpublished manuscript essay, "Family Values Workshop," Weissbourd Conference, Society of Fellows, University of Chicago, April 2005, on linking Pan Guangdan and the late imperial visual cliché of mirror gazing women. I gratefully acknowledge the help of Ellen Laing, Ann Waltner, and particularly Christine Tan.

35. Shi Quan, "Outline of Advertising Psychology" (Guanggao xinlixue gailun), DFZZ 21, no. 21 (1924).

36. Crow, *Four Hundred Million Customers*, 170–85.

37. Liu Shuqin, "From Natural Sociology to Cultural Sociology" (Cong ziran shehuixue xiang wenhua de shehuixue), DFZZ 23, no. 19 (1926): 57–70.

38. On hygiene and modernism, see Rogaski, *Hygienic Modernity*.

39. FNZZ 10, no. 6 (1924): n.p.

40. FNZZ 11, no. 8 (1925): n.p.

41. Barlow, "History and the Border," 8–32.

42. Agamben, *The Coming Community*, 46–47.

43. Elam, *Feminism and Deconstruction*, 27–66.

44. An advertisement for the Lihua department store visually conveys the commodity world's magic: a crowd sleepwalking toward the open door of the department store. With one exception, a man loaded with packages, the figures have their backs to the reader. While arresting, it does not have the force of the mise-en-scène of the icon and her gaze. DFZZ 23, no. 8 (1926): n.p.

45. Lefebvre, *Critique of Everyday Life*, 76, 74, 134.

46. Ibid., 159.

14

Fantasies of Universality?

Neue Frauen, Race, and Nation

in Weimar and Nazi Germany

UTA G. POIGER

In 1928, a U.S. advertising executive complained in the German professional design journal *Gebrauchsgraphik* that German graphic artists had developed a recognizable signature style. In particular he criticized Ludwig Hohlwein's ads for an American account: "The people in his posters were not American or cosmopolitan types, they were distinctly local types, peculiar to Germany, not idealized types."[1] Hohlwein was one of Germany's foremost graphic artists in the first few decades of the twentieth century, and in the 1920s he, like most of his colleagues, participated in the construction of images of Modern Girls, or *neue Frauen* and "girls," as German contemporaries frequently called them. In the early and mid-1920s, he was also successful in the United States.[2]

His ads did feature idealized types, but apparently not the "cosmopolitan" look that many U.S. advertisers, and some German ones as well, were striving for by the late 1920s. A cosmetics ad from 1924 signed by Hohlwein for the Kaloderma brand of powder, soap, and gel by the German cosmetics company F. Wolff and Sohn portrayed a young white woman with a wavy bob turning her dreamy gaze away from a vanity. The image of a recognizable

14.1 Not cosmopolitan? Ad for Kaloderma products of the
German F. Wolff and Sohn Company, designed by Ludwig
Hohlwein, from *Leipziger Illustrirte Zeitung*, 1924.

individual woman is drawn in what one can call a realist style (see figure 14.1).

Within the next couple of years, F. Wolff and Sohn replaced Hohlwein with
another artist, Jupp Wiertz, whose ads for the company one might indeed label
cosmopolitan. In one famous 1929 poster for Vogue, one of F. Wolff and Sohn's
perfumes, Wiertz too depicted a Modern Girl. In contrast to Hohlwein's Kaloderma ad, this woman was drawn in a more abstract and angular style. She had
an elongated body, stylized facial features, including almond-shaped eyes, and
a reddish brown bob.[3]

In 1935, two years after the Nazis had come to power, an ad for the same company featured yet a different format (see figure 14.3). In an ad for Kaloderma
soap, a photograph of a dark-haired white woman with painted lips, carefully
plucked eyebrows, and a gaze similar to Hohlwein's Kaloderma ad accompanied extensive copy that asked readers: "Why should you be less beautiful?"[4]

In this chapter, I ask what forces shaped such changing representations of
Modern Girls in Germany in the 1920s and 1930s. The three ads from F. Wolff
and Sohn span a period from the Weimar Republic to the first years of the Third

14.2 (top) Cosmopolitan aesthetic: 1929 poster for Vogue perfume by the F. Wolff
and Sohn Company, designed by Jupp Wiertz. Reprinted from Arnold Friedrich,
Anschläge: Deutsche Plakate als Dokumente der Zeit, 1900–1960 (Eberhausen:
Langewiesche-Brandt, 1963), 64. Courtesy of Langewiesche-Brandt.

14.3 (bottom) Vamp of the early Nazi era? Ad for Kaloderma Cream by F. Wolff and
Sohn Company, from *Leipziger Illustrirte Zeitung*, 1935.

Reich. Developing contextual layers for some of the German ads discussed in the collaborative chapter on global cosmetics advertising in this volume (chapter 2), I elaborate on the international frameworks, political stakes, and business logic that influenced changing representations of Modern Girls in Germany. I examine how Modern Girls were depicted in explicitly racialized, and often racist, advertising and cartoon imagery in Germany. More specifically, I trace the appearance and disappearance from the late 1920s to the early 1930s of what I call a cosmopolitan aesthetic, of which I see Wiertz's Vogue poster as one prime example.

The cosmopolitan aesthetic featured stylized and abstract images of women's bodies and faces. Frequently it depicted women who may be read as East Asian through the shape of their eyes and lips, or it combined a range of visual racial markers, such as almond-shaped eyes, brown or blond hair, and brown or white skin. These women were figured as modern through their fashions, hairstyles, and use of cosmetics. This cosmopolitan aesthetic was motivated, at least in part, I argue, by fantasies of universality. By fantasies of universality, I mean visions, textual or visual, that imagined different people in different parts of the globe reaching identical or nearly identical ways of living and looking. For corporations, including export-oriented German cosmetics companies, the cosmopolitan aesthetic could be part of efforts to express a business logic of universality in the short "golden twenties" before the onset of the Depression in 1929. I investigate how this cosmopolitan aesthetic and appeals to universality departed from some forms of racism in Germany, and I also examine the inherent limitations, exclusions, and contradictions of such appeals. Finally, I explore in what ways the rise of National Socialism impacted the preferred aesthetics of cosmetics advertisers in Germany. In short, I reflect on the visions of racial difference, as well as international connection, that Germans attached to changing representations of women.

So-called *neue Frauen* in Germany, like Modern Girls elsewhere, raised both hopes and fears about forces of modernity. Neue Frauen or "girls" in bobs, short, loose dresses, or sports outfits did indeed become a pervasive social presence across classes in 1920s Germany. To contemporaries, they could be indicators of increased leisure and wealth, of greater public roles for women, and of social health. Commentators also saw them as victims of commercial manipulation and "slaves of fashion," and as responsible for promiscuity, a low birthrate, and general decline. Often both positive and negative views were shaped by eugenic thought that interlinked the health of the individual and that of the nation. This range of opinions did not distribute neatly along political lines, but rather commentators across the political spectrum expressed some worries about the neue Frau. Such ambiguities meant that images of Modern Girls could be deployed for a range of ideological and commercial purposes.[5]

In exploring such deployments I read cosmetics ads in conjunction with reporting and visual images in the illustrated press and in professional graphic design journals. I also trace some of the material connections between Germany, the United States, and Japan that, I argue, generated specific representations of Modern Girls. These material connections ranged from the circulation of advertising images in design journals and books, to the international marketing strategies of U.S. and German cosmetics companies, to international advertising and press exhibits. Close attention to the imagery deployed in ads allows exploration of three issues often missing from the historiography of modern women in Germany and from the historiography of German consumer culture in the twentieth century more generally: changing visions of ethnic and national difference manifest in constructions of Modern Girls; depictions of interracial intimacy; and the international frameworks that contributed to the creation of such imagery.

As we have seen in chapters 1 and 2, one characteristic of cosmetics advertising was representations of various ethnic groups and adaptations of elements drawn from elsewhere. These developments were evident in 1920s Germany, as cosmetics advertisers made representations of Modern Girls central to much of their advertising — and to their efforts to create brand images, expand their markets, and make cosmetics a staple of everyday life and not just a luxury available to a wealthy few. In Germany, within a fairly short period of time, from the early 1920s to the 1930s, visual representations of Modern Girls changed in how they depicted both different racial groups and interracial intimacy. Representations associated with Modern Girls in German cosmetics ads included black and Chinese servants, harem women, and women with East Asian features. Changes in representations took place in conversation with changing ideas about colonial relations, race, and nationalism, as well as with changing business logics regarding consumption and access to domestic and foreign markets.

Colonialism and Racism after the Loss of Colonies

The advertisements that Hohlwein constructed for the brand Kaloderma by the F. Wolff and Sohn Company in the 1920s featured a distinct realist aesthetic style but had varying subjects and messages. The same year that the image of the modern woman in front of her vanity appeared, F. Wolff and Sohn ran another ad for Kaloderma shaving cream. A white man is shaving himself, looking into a mirror that is held by a smaller black adolescent. The ad depicts unequal power relations between blacks and whites in a situation of everyday life and relies on a racism based in colonial relations in advertising the product. At a time when Germany had lost formal control of its colonies with the Versailles Treaty of 1919, the image made reference to the history of German settler colonialism in Africa, where Germans employed black Africans in their households. However, such German colonial imagery did not necessarily relate specifically to German colonies but involved Germans in a discourse of European domination over non-Europeans. After World War I, Hohlwein had also drawn advertisements for other products, for example Riquet chocolates, that focused on diminutive figures, including Chinese, as servants, perhaps in reference to the former German colony in Tsingtao in China. As David M. Ciarlo has pointed out, racialized ad imagery coalesced into much repeated stereotypical representations in the years before World War I.[6] At the same time, such depictions were not the province of German advertising alone; racialized ad imagery with people of color serving whites also existed in other European countries, the United States, and Japan.[7] In his 1924 Kaloderma shaving cream ad, Hohlwein drew on a trope he himself had helped develop but also transformed it by depicting both the white man and the African servant in a realist fashion with fairly realistic proportions. The image thus both relied on and transformed racist conventions of German advertising.

Another advertisement from 1924 for a perfume and other toiletries named Tai Tai by the German Mouson Company likewise harked back to prewar advertising conventions: it figured a stereotypically portrayed diminutive, apparently Chinese servant (see figure 14.4). In contrast to Hohlwein's 1924 "realist" portrayal of the black servant, this depiction with its childlike proportions repeated the earlier Hohlwein image from 1920. In the 1924 rendition for Tai Tai, however, it was a modern woman, depicted with a bob, nude shoulders, and a long slim gown, who was served her perfume by the servant. Just as Germany had lost its formal overseas colonies and claimed to be humiliated by the presence of Senegalese French colonial troops in the Rhineland, advertisers appealed to racist longings for power over people of color. In the case of Tai Tai, they did so with a depiction of the Chinese servant whose kneeling posture was even more submissive than Hohlwein's 1920 image and figured the visibly Modern Girl as a central agent in such a colonial fantasy. Such a depiction of a Modern Girl likely had special resonance in early 1920s Germany, when the French occupation of the Rhineland, and the relations between German women and African men that resulted, had heightened anxieties about interracial sexual relations. The specific racism of the Tai Tai ad, especially the

14.4 Ad for Tai Tai toiletries by the German Mouson Company,
from *Leipziger Illustrirte Zeitung*, 1924.

control that the white Modern Girl exerted over the body of the servant, appeared to preclude the possibility of interracial sex.[8]

Other advertisements for Tai Tai from this period drew on a range of Orientalist images. Another newspaper ad from the same year figured a white
woman traveler with short hair and a cloche-like hat in a kimono-like gown
with her shoulder exposed in front of a Buddha and appealed to a longing for
access to the world outside of Europe (which had in fact become difficult even
for wealthy Germans in the war and postwar years). It also drew on long-
lasting stereotypes of the Orient as a place of sensuality, but in contrast to the
moralizing depictions of the Orient in mass circulation periodicals of the prewar period which had juxtaposed the restrained Western bourgeois housewife
with the lascivious female inhabitants of the harem, it figured the white woman's sensuality as opened up by travel to the Orient.[9]

A third German cosmetics company, Dr. M. Albersheim, likewise used the
image of the nonwhite diminutive servant in advertising for its Khasana per-

14.5 Ad for Khasana cosmetics by the German Dr. Albersheim Company, from *Berliner Illustrirte Zeitung*, 1925.

fume. In a cartoonlike ink drawing from 1924, a small servant with stereo-typical thick lips and turban served a much taller woman whose breasts were covered by a wreath of flowers and whose legs were showing through her "harem pants," a style made world-famous by the French designer Paul Poiret. Like other Western imagery, this depiction made the "inaccessible" woman of the harem visible and sexualized her. The accompanying brief copy described her not as a "slave of love" (a stereotypical Western label for women of the harem) but rather claimed that "even for those women who are the slaves of fashion, the eternal Khasana is and remains the most modern perfume." Apparently "modern" (implicitly Western) consumers were to be transported into a world of female sexual desire and mastery over people of color through Khasana.[10]

In another ad for Khasana from the following year, the Albersheim Company played openly with the conventions of the servant ads and the possibility of interracial sex: a muscular man with dark skin kneels in front of a white woman, averting his gaze and offering her a range of Khasana products (see figure 14.5). She is opening a large printed cloth to reveal her nude body, looking straight at the viewer. The combination of headdress, facial features, sandals, and jewelry on the upper arms locate her in antiquity, whereas her slim bodily proportions mark her as distinctly modern in the 1920s sense. While the black man's submissive posture cites other servant ads, the ad draws attention to his full-size nude body. The possibility that a white woman might desire sexual relations with a black man is not precluded here.[11]

The racist imagery of sexualized depictions of "the Orient" and of Chinese or black servants disappeared from German cosmetics ads over the following years. In the second half of the 1920s, one dominant theme used by Wolff und Sohn, Khasana/Dr. Albersheim, Mouson and most other German cosmetics companies was the white woman in a bob sitting by herself in a bath or in front of a vanity (see figure 14.1).[12] I can only speculate on the reasons behind this shift. In the 1920s, in the aftermath of World War I, discussions of good and bad colonialism were pronounced. In the treaty of Versailles, Germany had been explicitly labeled a particularly brutal colonial power and as a result had lost its colonies.[13] At the same time, multifaceted anti-imperialist movements made their voices heard. Moreover the German cosmetics industry was export oriented, and especially after 1924, it increased its involvement in foreign trade again.[14] Perhaps the servant images were not transferable to markets abroad, for example in China, India, or South Africa. While a possible renewal of German colonialism was explicitly discussed among liberals and the right wing in Germany, improved international communications may have made such racist depictions in ads a potential embarrassment for German companies abroad.

However, references to the Orient remained a feature of German cosmetics advertising and of portrayals of Modern Girls. A particularly interesting case is that of F. Wolff and Sohn, which by 1927 mostly used Jupp Wiertz as its signature artist. Wiertz drew a series of images for the company's hair tonic, Auxolin, which combined drawings of recognizable modern women in black bobs along with older motifs from East Asian art, such as a rising sun or stylized leaves.[15] Wiertz's style in the Auxolin and other ads was noticeably influenced by Aubrey Beardsley, whose art nouveau woodcuts had themselves been influenced by Japanese art. References to East Asia functioned here as ornamentation of the landscape. Like the majority of its German competitors F. Wolff and Sohn did not yet run ad campaigns with a unified message in visual imagery or copy, and Wiertz's style for Wolff was eclectic in the second half of the 1920s.

In 1929, Wiertz drew the poster for Vogue perfume by the Wolff company that featured a Modern Girl with heart-shaped mouth, elongated hands, and geometric earrings (see figure 14.2). A tight cap, reddish brown short hair, bathing-suit-like gown, and exposed arms adorned with jewelry all marked her as modern. Her hand position and the shape of her mouth may have been references to East Asian art. Perhaps her most outstanding features were her eyes. The combination of brown hair and stylized almond-shaped eyes marked the representation as a possible composite of white and East Asian features. (In chapter 1 we described this as one feature of "Asianization.") Such hybridity and the marking of different racial groups as unambiguously modern were two characteristics of the cosmopolitan aesthetic of the late 1920s and early 1930s.

It is impossible to know for certain whether the U.S. executive who called in *Gebrauchsgraphik* for "cosmopolitan types" would have approved of Wiertz's figures over Hohlwein's. (*Gebrauchsgraphik* had the subtitle *International Advertising Art* and published articles in both German and English, for audiences in Germany and abroad.) Wiertz published himself in the professional journal, was almost certainly a reader, and thus may have responded to the desires that some U.S. executives expressed.

The body shape of Wiertz's and other Modern Girls with broad shoulders and slim hips repeated images of women that circulated widely in Germany and other parts of the world. In the German context, such stylized, elongated body shapes of women could first be seen in prewar art nouveau and cigarette advertising. These representations of women also echoed the presentations of slim, dramatic womanhood that had made an actress like Sarah Bernhardt a controversial success in Europe and the United States. Such representations ran counter to notions of beauty and race promoted in some popular prewar hygiene manuals that claimed East Asian women had short limbs and African women broad shoulders compared to ideal "Middle European" beauties with longer limbs and wide hips. Such hygiene manuals labeled the female ideal as both beautiful and nonsensual.[16] Like some predecessors in art, advertising, and on the stage, cosmetics ads of the 1920s presented the allegedly undesirable slim body shape as sexual and attractive. Moreover, the context in which Wiertz depicted almond-shaped eyes, an ad for a perfume that urged viewers to emulate the figure represented also meant a departure from racist evaluations of East Asian eyes as sly.[17]

Wiertz's 1929 Vogue ad was in conversation with more abstract depictions of women that had become important in international art and advertising in the previous years. For example, in 1925 for the Paris exhibition that gave art deco its name, Siegel and Stockmann had designed mannequins, with brown golden "skin" and abstracted features, including eyes that could be read as East Asian, mannequins that were quite different from the previously used white wax figures.[18] Such abstractions of facial features had also become evident in much prewar art, for example in the works of Pablo Picasso (influenced by African sculpture) or in expressionist painting.[19] While Germans were not allowed to participate in the Paris exhibition, German artists participated in art deco styles and watched what artists elsewhere were doing. In 1927 *Gebrauchsgraphik* ran a special report on Japanese graphic art, and a year later Japanese advertisements were part of an international exhibit on the press in Cologne Germany, called Pressa.[20] One ad that may have circulated among graphic artists was from the Japanese cosmetics manufacturer Shiseido for a toothpowder from 1927 that featured a woman sitting on a divan (see figure 14.6). With blond hair and stylized eyes that may have been read as East Asian, this interpretation of an odalisque was clearly as ethnically ambiguous as Wiertz's creation for Vogue perfume.[21]

U.S.–produced ads were more pervasive than Japanese ones in Germany, and by 1927 they also featured ethnically ambiguous depictions of women. The *Annual of Advertising Art* that was compiled by U.S. advertising art directors from 1921 onward was distributed by *Gebrauchsgraphik* in Germany and thus was viewed by graphic designers such as Wiertz. The preface to the 1928 edition, for example, remarked that many ads were characterized by an "angularity, which is being discussed as modernism."[22] The 1927 volume and its successors featured a number of artists such as Helen Dryden, Edouard Benito, and Hans Schleger (Zero) who worked with angular lines, drew elongated bodies, and whose renditions of eyes could be read as East Asian. The work of some of these artists also appeared in ads for U.S. companies in Germany, for

14.6 Cosmopolitan aesthetic: 1927 poster for toothpowder by the Japanese Shiseido Company. Reprinted from Fraser, Heller, and Chwast, *Japanese Modern: Graphic Design between the Wars* (San Francisco: Chronicle Books, 1996), 82.

example in the work of Zero for the Richard Hudnut Company, and some of them were also featured in *Gebrauchsgraphik*.[23] "Modern" in late 1920s U.S. advertising meant women in bobs and with angular lines: in 1929, the U.S. professional journal *Printer's Ink Monthly* featured an ad for a lithography company that highlighted its use of "modernism" and the "modern motif." The ad was illustrated with multiple images of Modern Girls in bobs and stylized eyes.[24]

In Germany, Wiertz was not the only designer of the late 1920s to participate in the construction of a cosmopolitan aesthetic. The December 1929 issue ("The Newspaper") of *Die Reklame*, Germany's professional advertising journal, featured a woman drawn by Albert Rabenbauer with stylized features, whose eyes, lip shape, and black bob suggested that she might be East Asian (see figure 14.7). Her elongated hands held a selection of Western European and American newspapers.[25]

Was there a certain logic that made a cosmopolitan aesthetic with images of ethnically ambiguous and recognizably modern women attractive for advertisers of cosmetics and of the art of advertising itself? Perhaps this aesthetic and especially the depictions of eyes that can be read as East Asian were partially the result of a shift to angularity and abstraction among graphic

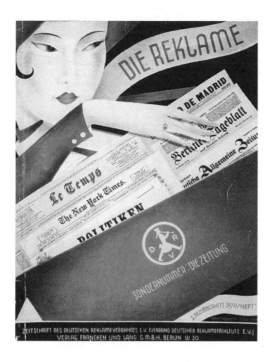

14.7 Cosmopolitan aesthetic: cover of the graphic design journal
Die Reklame, 1929, by Albert Rabenbauer.

artists. However, this aesthetic was also a part of international business and
power relations.

It is not by chance that Wiertz's work for Vogue perfume and Albert Rabenbauer's cover of *Die Reklame* appeared in the same period that an international
advertising congress convened in Berlin in the summer 1929 under the slogan
"Advertising—the key to the well-being of the world."[26] The slogan for the
meeting encapsulated a logic of universalism: advertising here was presented as
a tool of modernization that could help people around the world.

The way that Western Europeans and Americans portrayed Japan's position,
and the role of Japanese women, in the modern world was part of a vision of
modernization and perhaps one inspiration for Wiertz's Vogue and Rabenbauer's *Reklame* images. One major German illustrated weekly, for example,
ran an image in 1929 of "Miss Kahotura," Japan's "beauty queen" (see figure 14.8.). Kahotura was featured in swim gear and with a tight cap. The
existence of a beauty pageant and queen marked Japan as modern, and at the
same time the German press (like American commentators) planted the notion
that Japanese modernity was in some ways an imitation of the United States.

Auch Japan hat seine Schönheitskönigin.
Fräulein Kahotura, die preisgekrönte japanische Schönheit, die über Hunderte von
Mitbewerberinnen den Sieg davontrug.— Bemerkenswert erscheint es, daß die Wahl
offenbar unter dem Einfluß des amerikanischen Schönheitsideals getroffen wurde.

14.8 "Miss Kahotura," Japan's "beauty queen," from
Leipziger Illustrirte Zeitung, 1929.

The caption of the image noted, "It is remarkable that the selection happened apparently under the influence of the American beauty ideal."[27] Such reporting reflected a somewhat reluctant rearrangement of visions of civilization: by the late 1920s, Japan was the first nation outside of Europe or North America to be increasingly considered an industrialized, urbanized, civilized, and modern nation by the West. The suggestion that Japan imitated U.S. beauty ideals may also have been an expression of ambivalence about the perceived importance of the American "girl" for standards of beauty and behavior in Germany. At the same time, the international distribution of beauty standards through beauty contests and Hollywood films may have been another reason that the stylized almond-shaped eyes made sense as part of an effort to create a cosmopolitan aesthetic.

By the late 1920s, images of women who exposed their bodies in sports such as swimming and with short bobs became major signifiers of modern transformations in Germany and elsewhere in the German press. The tight dress of the Wiertz's Vogue woman may have been a reference to sports and specifically swimming. Her tight cap referred to a hat fashion similar to swim caps, like the one worn by Kahotura. In the late 1920s and early 1930s the

German illustrated press regularly featured depictions of women from Germany and abroad engaging in sports. Such images included, for example, a photograph in the *Leipziger Illustrirte* from 1929 of Turkish female students in bobs and short dresses doing gymnastics, or an image in *Die Dame* from 1930 of Japanese women in bathing suits and swim caps at a beach.[28] Such imagery was interlinked with contemporary concerns in eugenics. Images of women with exposed legs and arms and engaging in exercise served as indicators of the health of the population of a given locale and marked it as modern. Such imagery likely fed certain fantasies of universality. Some German commentators explicitly promoted such a vision. In 1930 a "taste columnist" in the German women's magazine *Die Dame* announced (not without some ambivalence) that "national characteristics were being abandoned in favor of international style."[29]

Related fantasies of universality were consciously fostered by advertisers and politicians in the United States and Germany in the second half of the 1920s. *Gebrauchsgraphik* commented in 1927 that "the size of today's commerce transcends all national boundaries and is assuming the character of world economics. This requires an international understanding of advertising, its most valuable expression." And future West German chancellor Konrad Adenauer called the 1928 Cologne Pressa exhibit that featured the international press and international advertising "an international pageant of civilization." In 1929 the former German chancellor Hans Luther used the occasion of the World Advertising Convention in Berlin to speak of advertising "as a language of the new world."[30] Advertising was clearly a major concern for Germans in this period. Not only did a former German chancellor speak to the convention but leaders of the liberal and conservative wings of the German women's movement, including Marie-Elisabeth Lüders and Gertrud Bäumer, served on the women's committee. Like all conceptions of universality, the one promoted by international advertising exhibits was implicitly or explicitly exclusionary: advertising and commentary on it continued to rely on distinctions between "primitive" and "civilized" people; the World Advertising Convention in Berlin included only Europeans and North Americans; and the December 1929 cover of *Die Reklame* revealed the same limits—the papers presented there were western and northern European as well as American (see figure 14.7).

Fantasies of universality did register ambivalence in Germany in the 1920s, even on the part of their supporters. Luther urged Germans to "learn from other countries who had more experience in this language" but also to "create a German dialect of this language in the German spirit and with German aesthetic feeling."[31] His words referred both to the model of U.S. and British advertising and to nervousness about losing German cultural distinctiveness,

COTY

DER SIEG DES GUTEN GESCHMACKES

14.9 "One human can be wrong, but not millions." Ad for face powder by the multinational Coty (with French roots) in *Die Dame*, 1930.

anxieties that the Nazis were to exploit over the following years. Luther's solution in the meantime was to plead for a special as yet undefined German role in this universal vision.

With their cosmopolitan aesthetic, Wiertz and the Wolff company and Rabenbauer for *Die Reklame* may also have been in conversation with a business logic of universality expressed in ads placed by some international companies in German illustrated magazines. U.S. companies regularly ran ads in Germany, claiming appeal for their products all over the world. The copy of a 1927 ad for Creme Elcaya, for example, told potential German consumers that the product was a creation of the New York–based Elcaya Company, "which is well known all over the world as one of the foremost beauty laboratories." This ad was accompanied by two images of women whose features were highly stylized.[32] A second U.S. company, Elizabeth Arden, stressed its reach by listing the international locales of its salons in its ads in the German illustrated press.[33] A cosmopolitan aesthetic fit well with a vision of international reach.

The tensions in this vision become particularly clear in another ad placed in 1930 in the German magazine *Die Dame*. The ad featured a black-and-white drawing of lips that made reference to East Asian art and stylized eyes (see figure 14.9). Coty, a company with French origins and world reach, advertised its face powder with the slogan "One human can be wrong, but not millions." The ad described Coty as a "top achievement of the cosmetic world industry, an indispensable beauty product of the well-groomed woman, her protection against smoke and weather." At the same time that the ad stressed that the cosmetics industry had global reach, it also appealed to the individuality of the consumer. The copywriters tried to strike a balance between mass appeal and individual expression. The "color and fragrance scale" of Coty Powder had the "finest nuances" and "offered a great variety of choices, the most perfect solution for your specific teint, for the essence of your personality." Coty represented "the victory of good taste."[34] The Coty ad made no reference to the French roots of the company, which some German women had apparently boycotted in previous years because of alleged anti-German statements by the former French owner of Coty, himself a member of the French right wing.[35]

Wiertz's ad for Vogue perfume and Rabenbauer's cover for *Die Reklame* may have been attempts to produce a cosmopolitan aesthetic for a marketing logic similar to that of Coty, Richard Hudnut, and other U.S. companies like Elizabeth Arden, all of which were export-oriented. What makes Wiertz's poster particularly hard to interpret is the lack of extensive copy. This lack of copy may have been part of an effort to create a universal language through advertising and graphic design. U.S. observers of German advertising complained repeatedly that German advertisers used little text but rather relied, as one executive from the U.S.–based J. Walter Thompson put it in 1928, on "art of the bold poster type of crashing display" and "bold lettering." The executive described the advertising style he saw in Germany as "extremely modern."[36] While I do not have direct knowledge of Wolff and Sohn's business strategies, there is some evidence that the combination of cosmopolitan aesthetics and international reach was used consciously also by German cosmetics companies, which had a history as strong exporters before 1914 and were increasing their exports again in the second half of the 1920s.

The Dr. Albersheim/Khasana company appears to have pursued this vision through a cosmopolitan aesthetic in 1929. An ad for its depilatory Dulmin featured a drawing of a stylized Modern Girl in an evening gown. Her large dark eyes and her dark hair referenced images of Middle Easterners, while her bob and nude shoulders marked her as modern. In contrast to earlier ads, the company now stressed its international reach: the ad gave its office locations as both Frankfurt/Main and London and described Dr. Albersheim as "the producer of the world-renowned 'Khasana products.'"[37] German companies, like U.S. and French companies, used a cosmopolitan aesthetic in the late 1920s to portray themselves as exporters to domestic and foreign audiences. For a brief period, they also put into the commercial mainstream aesthetic elements seen by some as an attack on bourgeois respectability or as a sign of racial decline.

A cosmopolitan aesthetic could also be found in images of Modern Girls on covers of the nationalist *Leipziger Illustrirte Zeitung* as late as 1933. Four days before Hitler's rise to power in January 1933, the magazine featured two modern women in ski pants and short hair tanning on the ski slopes. One is brunette with fairly dark skin, dark eyes, and a wide nose, with possible Middle Eastern or black features, the other one is white. Three weeks later, the magazine again featured two young women on the slopes, drawn by a different artist, R. Huèn (who was perhaps Chinese).[38] Both of them have what contemporaries may have read as East Asian eyes and one of them applies lipstick, glancing at a mirror while standing on her skis. The image focuses on bright red lipstick at a time when few cosmetics advertisers found it worth their while to advertise for lipstick, because lipstick had clear connotations of prostitution. Clearly this drawing represented modern East Asian girls. The fantasies of universality promoted in such visual representations countered notions of racial hierarchies in that they portrayed different ethnic groups as having legitimate access to modern luxuries such as cosmetics, tanning, and skiing, with proper equipment and stylish clothing. Such fantasies could generate nervousness on a number of counts. They depicted class privilege as the basis for cross-ethnic connection and elided the logic of hierarchies between "primitive" and "civilized," and the attending exclusion of that deemed "primitive" that universalism relies on. Likely, such images were designed to titillate German consumers by suggesting possibilities of identification with racialized others and the transgression of racialized and class-based conceptions of beauty. However, the creation of possibilities for identification and transgression in ads or other genres of visual representation did not mean recognition of others. Indeed, such representations made difference into a purely aesthetic issue that manifested itself simply in certain facial features. But such visual representations also have had great powers of attraction. In Germany, for example, Wiertz's Vogue image was revived in the 1970s in advertising, this time for gasoline.[39] In Nazi Germany, however, such cover art was to disappear as well.

Depression, National Socialism, and the End of the Cosmopolitan Aesthetic

Business strategies that lined up with a vision of universality receded in the aftermath of the stock market crash of 1929 and with the onset of the Great Depression, which was felt quickly in both the United States and Germany. With the withdrawal of many foreign loans, the German economy took a dramatic downturn, with production falling and unemployment rising dramatically. At the same time, efforts to insulate the German economy from world markets gained in strength.[40]

The change in business climate coincided with a dramatic shift in image strategy among many cosmetics companies, a shift to the use of photography in ads. Some ads attempted to transpose a cosmopolitan aesthetic to photographs. A 1930 Chlorodont ad featured a photo of a Filipino theater star, Juanita Fuentes, "known all over Europe for her embodiment of Madame Butterfly" — who was announcing that she used only Chlorodont toothpaste since her visit to Germany (see figure 14.10).[41] The photo of Fuentes combined the teeth-revealing smile of many Modern Girl representations with the Japanese kimono and hairstyle of her opera role but did not convey the glamour of stylized features and elongated bodies of so many drawings. Apparently the ad

Blendend weiße Zähne

Die berühmte orientalische Primadonna, Jovita Fuentes aus Manila, in ganz Europa durch ihre einzigartige Verkörperung der „Butterfly" bekannt, schreibt uns:

„Seit meinem Aufenthalt in Deutschland benutze ich zur Pflege meiner Zähne ausschließlich Ihr *Chlorodont* und bin mit dem Erfolg so zufrieden, daß ich keine andere Zahnpaste mehr gebrauchen werde." *Jovita Fuentes.*

Chlorodont-Zahnpaste   Chlorodont-Zahnbürsten   Chlorodont-Mundwasser

14.10 The Filipino theater star Juanita Fuentes in ad for German toothpaste Chlorodont, *Berliner Illustrirte Zeitung*, 1930.

was not judged to be successful, because it did not run for long nor did other companies try to emulate it.

German cosmetics companies that used photography already in the 1920s generally did not participate in constructing a cosmopolitan aesthetic or in eliciting exotic places or styles. Since the mid-1920s, Beiersdorf, the maker of Nivea products, had been among the first companies to build a fairly consistent campaign in the German illustrated press while using photography. In 1927, for example, the company advertised use of its cream for achieving "a bronze tone" in the summer with a photograph of a brunette at a lake. By the late 1920s, other German companies, in their ads for tanning products, likewise drew on photography to appeal to customers.

One such ad urged the identification of whites with blacks. In 1930, Creme Mouson published an ad for its sports cream that featured the photo of a man in a bathing suit who was applying cream to a Modern Girl's back. The slogan proclaimed "Braun wie ein Neger," "Brown like a Negro," and is the only ad I have found that makes a link between the tanning of a white European woman and "Negroes," a word that at the time referred to black Africans and black Americans.[42] The slogan gave a positive meaning to an expression that had negative racist connotations — where "brown" or "black" and "Negro" stood for dirty and primitive. Mouson's advertising strategy may have been an effort to draw on the great popularity of the African American dancer Josephine Baker and of jazz musicians in this period when some cultural critics saw blacks as the hope for Europe's renewal.[43] Such identifications were certainly a departure from the colonial racism expressed in Hohlwein's 1924 Kaloderma ad. But such identifications also involved some exoticization and frequently reinforced racist stereotypes. Apparently the vision of cosmopolitan identification on the part of Germans with blacks that the Creme Mouson ad suggested was judged not to be successful, for Creme Mouson did not continue the ad or make similar claims in ads that followed. As all cosmetics companies increased their ads for tanning products over the following years, they portrayed tanning as a prerogative for healthy, athletic, and sexy white women without any references to a logic of primitivism or blackness.

After 1930, references to ethnic ambiguity, to nonwhites, and to the international reach of German companies became rare in cosmetics ads. F. Wolff Sohn moved to the use of photography for its brands in 1931. That year its ads featured photographs of a young German film star labeled "internationally renowned" who endorsed Kaloderma soap in extensive copy.[44] Even such explicit references to the international reach of a German white star were soon to disappear from German cosmetics ads.

Soon after the Nazis came to power, one of Germany's journals for advertising professionals, *Die Reklame*, asked, "Are our women really the way they are represented in advertisements?" The author applauded the brand Nivea (which had German Jews among its founders, owners, and managers) for having used German motifs for a long time but was very critical of other advertisers who used only "film stars" and "dolls made up with shaved eyebrows and well-formed [*wohlgeschwungenen*] lips, often in coquettish positions." According to the author, "this type of woman has no trace of Germanness. The German woman is well-groomed, but she is not made up with shaving knife, lipstick, and powder." The author proclaimed it as the goal of advertising to "create the ideal image of the modern German woman and thus to influence the return to German ways and mores."[45]

As this quote shows, advertisers who were explicitly sympathizing with the Nazis saw the construction of a *modern* German woman as their goal. These constructions included many ambiguities. Evidence from the late 1920s suggests that the fashions of the neue Frau, including shorter skirts and the bob, had in fact become acceptable across political divides. A study of workers conducted by Erich Fromm in 1929 found that while Nazi workers were somewhat less likely than leftist workers to approve of the new fashions, two-thirds of them found them acceptable.[46] Further evidence that much of modern fashion was acceptable to most Nazis is the use of images of these fashions in anti-Semitic propaganda. A cartoon from a 1927 issue of the Nazi weekly *Der Stürmer* portrayed women in short slim clothes, bobs, and cloche hats as threatened by Jewish male seducers with stereotypical noses (see figure 14.11). The caption reads "It hurts my soul when I see you in this company." The cartoon accompanied an article against miscegenation that argued that Jews were an "alien race" who had mainly "Mongolian and Negro blood" in their veins. Sexual intercourse between Germans and Jews, figured here as interracial sex, would lead to a "degeneration" of the "German people's body." Such an article and image sent the message that Jews, Asians, and blacks could not be Germans and that German Modern Girls and the German nation were allegedly endangered by Jews, Asians, and blacks. This caricature was one among many in *Der Stürmer* over the following years that saw ethnic German "modern" women threatened by Jewish men.[47]

Whereas the fashions of the neue Frau proved largely acceptable (even as the Nazis promoted a constant search for modern "German" fashions), more hostility persisted toward women's use of certain cosmetics, especially lipstick. The 1929 study by Fromm reported that about 91 percent of men and 73 percent of women were, irrespective of political leanings, against the use of powder and lipstick. Creams were acceptable, color was not. At least one respondent in the Fromm study rejected the use of cosmetics as a "needless waste of our national wealth."[48] The 1933 statement about the transformation of women's images in advertising reiterated hostility toward such cosmetics use with its critique of lipstick and plucked eyebrows.

Cosmetics advertising continued under National Socialism and reveals some of the lines of continuity with the Weimar years as well as some ruptures. The makers of Nivea heavily advertised their cream with women in sporty outfits, before and after 1933. While one branch of the Nazi machinery held Nivea up as an example of proper representations of German women, others

14.11 Anti-Semitic cartoon from the Nazi *Der Stürmer* (1927), mobilizing
the image of a Modern Girl under attack by a Jewish man.

used anti-Semitism to attack the company. *Der Stürmer* ran a story about the
"Nivea-Creme-Jews," and a competitor tried to organize a boycott with the
slogan "Who buys Nivea, supports a Jewish company." Representatives of the
Mouson company, too, were involved in the distribution of anti-Semitic leaf-
lets against Nivea. Jewish members of the board of the Beiersdorf company
resigned or transferred out of Germany, while the firm continued to market
its Nivea products throughout the Nazi period, predominantly using blond
women to portray a message of health, modernity, and athleticism.[49]

Cosmetics ads of the Nazi era show a range of female types but within limits.
In this range they are similar to Nazi films. Ads for Kaloderma by F. Wolff and
Sohn featured the photograph of a dark-haired woman with plucked eyebrows
and painted lips in 1935 (see figure 14.3). Her looks resonated with images of

"vamps" whose sexuality had endangered men in dance and film since the beginning of the twentieth century. One of Wolff's directors, Walter Wolff, was in the meantime sitting on the Nazi-controlled supervisory council for advertising after 1933 that was to assure "cleanliness" in advertising and indeed helped to narrow options over the following years.[50] Also in 1935, Creme Mouson accompanied the slogan "Natural beauty is looking at you" with a frontal shot of a young woman who appeared to have her blond wavy hair pulled back in a bun. Both ads portrayed women as sensual.[51] Nivea, the brand repeatedly threatened by the anti-Semitic tactics of its competitors, perhaps came closest to "Aryan" or "Nordic" ideals in its ads that featured sporty, blond young women (see figure 2.21 in chapter 2). The Nivea campaign in the 1930s was designed by Elly Heuss-Knapp, who certainly did not consider herself a Nazi and who had entered advertising after her husband, the future West German president Theodor Heuss, had been dismissed from his professorship by the Nazis.[52]

Khasana/Dr. Albersheim, a company founded and owned by Jewish Germans, was one of few companies in the 1930s in Germany to advertise lipstick, a cosmetic product that Nazi leaders railed against repeatedly. Some of Khasana's ads appeared to be an effort to accommodate Nazi demands for a more restrained German woman. A 1935 ad, for example, showed a photo of a woman in front of a marble statue and advertised Khasana Superb Creme, which would add a "natural fresh look" to the cheeks. The ad also mentioned Khasana-Superb lipstick that "likewise beautifies the lips without attracting attention."[53] Other Khasana ads harked back more explicitly to the cosmopolitan drawings of the late 1920s, but without leaving any doubt that the depicted woman was white. In 1939, the company was "aryanized" and its name changed to Dr. Korthaus, while its Jewish owner emigrated to the United States.[54]

Cosmetics advertising under National Socialism showed less aesthetic variety than in the 1920s. In contrast to U.S. companies and in spite of continued ambitions for international expansion, German companies made no references to their international reach under National Socialism. While cartoons in Nazi publications regularly positioned Jews or blacks as inferior to ethnic Germans, major cosmetics companies in their ad campaigns in the illustrated press stayed away from making such visibly racist representations. Ads depicted a range of white types but did not cast doubt on the whiteness of their subjects. Wiertz's cosmopolitan aesthetic had already disappeared before 1933 from cosmetics ads, and he spent the years before his death in 1939 drawing highly regarded posters of landscapes and cities (which were often devoid of human faces) for transportation companies and the Nazi "Strength through Joy."[55]

The signature style of Ludwig Hohlwein, the creator of the realist ad for Kaloderma with which I began my discussion, proved compatible with Nazi messages, not least because of Hohlwein's political convictions. He had this to say in 1933: "Today, art as a cultural factor, is more than ever called upon to take a leading place in building up and conserving cultural values. It must take its place in the front rank of the legion which Europa has gathered to preserve her individuality against the onslaughts from the East."[56] Hohlwein's rhetoric was shared not just by Nazis but also by many conservatives, and one can only speculate whether the "onslaughts from the East" against which Hohlwein sought to defend "Europe" included Bolshevism, which was frequently labeled "Jewish" and "Mongol," as well as fears of the might of peoples of the East, Jews, Slavs, Mongols, and other members of the so-called yellow race. Perhaps they also included the Asian features that had been part of Wiertz's and others' cosmopolitan aesthetic around 1930. Hohlwein's Modern Girls in any case proved useful for portraying Nazi messages. Thus Hohlwein designed the poster for the 1934 National Sports Day of the Nazi girls' association (see figure 14.12): A muscular, tanned woman with a brown bob and shorts is running in front of a Nazi flag. As in much contemporary sports and dance imagery (but not advertisements), she is raising an arm and her head up to the sky.[57] The copy on the poster was in German script (Fraktur).

While such imagery has become important in illustrating the Nazi racial ideology, its frequent presence in today's textbooks should not lead one to conclude that the visual world of the Nazi period was dominated by such images. Representations of modern women in the press as well as in film under National Socialism did owe much to the imagery of the Weimar years, and to international images from the 1930s.[58] However, a cosmopolitan aesthetic and images that suggested explicit identification with ethnic "others" as part of an effort to portray modernity and international reach disappeared from German cosmetics ads with the onset of the Great Depression. While representations of women under National Socialism were multifaceted and the image of the Modern Girl in Germany proved highly malleable and usable for both commercial advertising and Nazi political propaganda, the range of what was aesthetically and ideologically acceptable narrowed considerably.

In this chapter, I have shown that German representations of modern women relied on changing references to people of color, an issue that has received scant attention in German historiography of modern women and of German consumer culture more generally. Representations of Modern Girls in cosmetics ads reveal how race and international relations manifested themselves in the everyday workings of capitalism. In the late 1920s at a time when modernization was not yet a widespread concept, universalistic fantasies and a business logic associated with a cosmopolitan aesthetic imagined growing numbers of people in increasing areas of the world in pursuit of the same commodities,

14.12 Poster for the 1934 National Sports Day of the Nazi Federation of German Girls by Ludwig Hohlwein. Reprinted from Aynsley, *Graphic Design in Germany, 1890–1945* (Berkeley: University of California Press, 2000), 186.

including modern fashions and cosmetics, striving toward a standardized way of living. The Modern Girl was perhaps the central icon of such fantasies. National Socialism was one of many possible reactions against such visions. However, in spite of repeated denunciations of "Girlkultur," the Third Reich did not simply leave the Modern Girl behind.

Notes

1. H. K. Frenzel in a conversation with Frederic Suhr, *Gebrauchsgraphik* 3, no. 10 (October 1928), quoted in Aynsley, *Graphic Design in Germany 1890–1945*, 134–35.

2. See Aynsley, *Graphic Design*, 84–85.

3. Vogue ad in Friedrich, *Anschläge*, 64, dated there 1929. On Wiertz, see *Die Femme Fatale im Tempo der Großstadt*.

4. Ad for Kaloderma soap, *Leipziger Illustrirte Zeitung* (hereafter LIZ), 1935.

5. On neue Frauen in the Weimar Republic, see especially von Ankum, ed., *Women in the Metropolis*; Grossmann, "Girlkultur, or Thoroughly Rationalized Female?"; Kessemeier, *Sportlich, sachlich, männlich*; Meskimmon and West, eds., *Visions of the "Neue Frau"*; Petro, *Joyless Streets*; von Soden and Schmidt, eds., *Neue Frauen*.

6. See Ciarlo, "Rasse konsumieren," esp. 147–48. For a reprint of the Riquet ad originally drawn in 1920, see LIZ, April 6, 1922, 319.

7. See, for example, McClintock, *Imperial Leather*; ad in permanent exhibit in Shiseido Company Museum, Japan, viewed September 2004.

8. On German debates about sexual relations between ethnic Germans and colonized people, see Wildenthal, *German Women for Empire, 1884–1945*; Campt, "Converging Spectres of An Other Within."

9. LIZ, 17 December 1925, 967.

10. LIZ, 9 April 1925, 553. On German depictions of the Orient, especially in the popular press of the nineteenth century, see Harnisch, "Der Harem in Familienblattern des 19. Jahrhunderts." For complex meanings of Orientalist dance and fashion and associated bodily images, see Studlar, "Out-Salomeing Salome," and Walkowitz, "The 'Vision of Salome.'"

11. Khasana ad, *Berliner Illustrirte Zeitung* (hereafter BIZ), 3 May, 1925.

12. See Khasana ad, BIZ, 3 July 1927; Creme Mouson ad, LIZ, 15 March 1928.

13. Compare Klotz, Introduction, and "Global Visions."

14. See Ausschuß zur Untersuchung der Erzeugungs- und Absatzbedingungen der deutschen Wirtschaft, *Die deutsche Seifen- und Parfümerienindustrie*.

15. See Auxolin ad in LIZ, 21 July 1927, 108.

16. On hygiene manuals, see Hau, *The Cult of Health and Beauty in Germany*, chap. 4.

17. On German visions of East Asians, see Goldfuß, "Die Gelben kommen."

18. See Finamore, "Fashioning the Colonial at the Paris Expositions, 1925 and 1931."

19. See, for example, Barkan and Bush, eds., *Prehistories of the Future*.

20. See Aynsley, *Graphic Design in Germany*, 141–43.

21. Figure 65 in Fraser, Heller, and Chwast, *Japanese Modern*, 82.

22. Roy S. Dursteine, "Foreword," *Seventh Annual of Advertising Art*, 1928; article on Benito in September 1929 issue of *Gebrauchsgraphik*.

23. Hudnut ad in *Die Dame*, no. 21 (1930): 43. Compare work by Zero in *Seventh Annual of Advertising Art*, 28.

24. Ad for Einson-Freeman Co., *Printer's Ink Monthly*, May 1929, 57. My thanks to Tani Barlow for alerting me to this ad.

25. Cover of *Die Reklame*, second December issue, 1929.

26. See Knapp, *Reklame, Propaganda, Werbung*.

27. *LIZ*, 11 July 1929, 64.

28. *LIZ*, 22 August 1929; *Die Dame*, no. 22 (1930): 5.

29. Anita, "Formlosigkeit als Gesellschaftsform," *Die Dame*, no. 26 (1930).

30. *Gebrauchsgraphik* 4, no. 1 (1927), quoted in Aynsley, *Graphic Design in Germany*, 129; Adenauer, quoted in ibid., 141; Hans Luther, "Geleitwort," in Knapp, *Reklame, Propaganda, Werbung*, 3–4. On the advertising convention, see also Westphal, *Werbung im Dritten Reich*, 1ff.

31. Luther, "Geleitwort."

32. Ad for Creme Elcaya, *BIZ*, 27 May 1927.

33. See, for example, *Die Dame*, no. 22 (1930): 41.

34. Coty ad, *Die Dame*, no. 10 (1930).

35. On hostility toward Coty, see "Parfümerie-Konkurrenz," *Deutsche Allgemeine Zeitung*, 4 October 1930, Hamburger Weltwirtschaftsarchiv (hereafter HWWA).

36. A. E. Hobbs, "Advertising in Germany," 10 January 1928, Marketing Report, Investigations, reel #232, J. W. Thompson Collection, Duke University. My thanks to Lynn Thomas for alerting me to this report.

37. Ad for Dulmin, *BIZ*, 13 January 1929, 68.

38. See covers of *LIZ*, 26 January and 16 February 1933.

39. See ad for Aral gasoline from 1975, reprinted in *Die Femme Fatale*, 24.

40. See James, *The End of Globalization*.

41. Ad for Chlorodont, *BIZ*, 12 October 1930.

42. Ad for Sportcreme Mouson, in *Die Dame*, no. 21 (1930).

43. See Ivan Goll, "The Negroes are Conquering Europe" (1926), in Kaes, Jay, and Dimendberg, eds., *The Weimar Republic Sourcebook*, 559–60.

44. Such ads followed JWT and Ponds who, in 1930, ran ads with German actresses, including Lil Dagover, endorsing Ponds creams. See *BIZ*, 13 July 1930, 1279.

45. *Die Reklame* 26 (1933): 392–93, quoted in Reinhardt, *Von der Reklame zum Marketing*, 408.

46. Fromm, *The Working Class in Weimar Germany*, 155.

47. Title page of *Der Stürmer*, no. 21 (May 1927).

48. Fromm, *The Working Class in Weimar Germany*, 161.

49. Gries, *Produkte als Medien*, 467–86; Bajohr, *Aryanisation in Hamburg*, 23–26; Claudia Hansen, *Nivea*.

50. On Wolff, see Westphal, *Werbung im Dritten Reich*, 165.

51. *LIZ*, 17 January 1935.

52. See Gries, *Produkte als Medien*.

53. Khasana ad, *LIZ*, 14 February 1935.

54. See http://www.aufbau-ffm.de/doku/Archiv/khasana.html (viewed 20 August 2004).

55. See *Die Femme Fatale*.

56. Ludwig Hohlwein, in *Gebrauchsgraphik* 10, no. 1 (January 1933), quoted in Aynsley, *Graphic Design in Germany*, 192.

57. Poster for Reichssporttag des BDM, 23 September 1934, designed by Ludwig Hohlwein, 1934, reprinted in Aynsley, *Graphic Design in Germany*, 186.
    Hohlwein apparently also provided some of the most notorious depictions of the healthy, Aryan German family. In 1938 he probably designed the cover of the calendar for the Reich's Racial Policy Office, featuring a blond, tanned German family, where a father protected a mother with long hair in a bun and a child: http://www.wolfsonian .fiu.edu/collections/(viewed 5 April 2005).

58. On the complexity of representations of women in the Third Reich, see Koepnick, *The Dark Mirror*; Ascheid, *Hitler's Heroines*; Dagmar Herzog, *Sex after Fascism*; Reese, *Growing up Female in Nazi Germany*; Guenther, *Nazi Chic*.

CONCLUDING COMMENTARIES

15

Girls Lean
Back Everywhere

⌒

KATHY PEISS

Girls lean back everywhere, showing lace and silk
stockings; wear low-cut sleeveless blouses, breathless
bathing suits; men think thoughts and have emotions
about these things everywhere . . . and no one is cor-
rupted. JANE HEAP, 1920

Over twenty-five years ago, when I began studying the history of
young working women in New York City, I never considered the
Modern Girl to be anything but an American phenomenon. British
New Women and French fashion may have influenced Americans,
I thought, but the breezy, flirtatious, made-up flapper could only
be home-grown. She was a creation of urban working-class women
in the years after 1910 who embraced fashion, found camaraderie
among their co-workers, and looked for romance and adventure in
dance halls and amusement parks. Her style became popularized
through magazines and movies, spreading across the United States in
the 1920s. My later research into the history of cosmetics seemed to
confirm this view: The takeoff of the American beauty industry was
inextricably tied to young women's experience of modernity, and the
ways that experience was interpreted and marketed in consumer culture. Then, in 1991, I happened to meet the historian Miriam Silver-

berg, who said she wanted to show me some remarkable images from Japanese magazines and advertisements of the interwar period. Looking at pages of drawings and photographs, I was stunned to see a familiar figure in a radically different context: the Modern Girl as *moga*.

I should not have been surprised. As this volume shows so well, the emergence of the Modern Girl in the 1920s and 1930s was a worldwide phenomenon. In France, Germany, South Africa, India, China, and Japan — countries with vastly different economies, political institutions, social relations, religions, and cultures — she was instantly recognizable. What made a slender, fashionable young woman, with bobbed hair, lipstick and rouge, a casual pose, broad smile, and come-hither gaze into a global image of modernity? On the surface, the Modern Girl might seem an unlikely figure for the study of world history, too frivolous, body-conscious, and self-absorbed. However, as these essays reveal, she turns out to be a fascinating tour guide, not only to the territory of gender and sexuality, as we might suppose, but also into unexpected places, into the history of nationalism, racial formations, global trade, and the transnational flow of people and ideas.

The essays in this volume belie the view that a simple or linear process of Americanization gave rise to the Modern Girl around the world. They point to the distinctive local situations, national debates, and transnational encounters that stimulated diverse forms of modern feminine identity. Still, questions remain: Why did flappers, moga, *neue Frauen*, *modeng xiaojie*, and other Modern Girls share a fascination with style, beautifying, and self-fashioning? Why did they make their appearance nearly simultaneously around the world? If Americanization is too simplistic an explanation, what then was the relationship of images and styles from the United States to the experience and perception of girls and young women elsewhere? And what was the impact of the Modern Girl in these and other countries, not only in the 1920s and 1930s, but in the long term?

The historians in this volume are careful to distinguish the interwar years, when the modern girl appeared, from the post–World War II era of American corporate dominance. Their comparative analysis of cosmetics advertising reveals the presence of American firms that had successfully cultivated a domestic U.S. market for beauty products, such as Ponds and Northam Warren, maker of Cutex nail-care products. The largest American advertising agency, J. Walter Thompson, which early saw itself as a player on the international scene, opened offices and hired personnel from London to New Delhi and Shanghai. They specialized in advertising that adopted a local idiom to sell hygienic and beauty products as a universal need. Nor were these efforts confined to large mass-market corporations. Such leading African American beauty businesses as the Madam C. J. Walker Company and Apex exported hair- and skin-care products to women of color in Latin America and Africa.

Still, American businesses were not the driving force behind the worldwide phenomenon of the Modern Girl. These firms gained a foothold in the early twentieth century but faced stiff competition from British and French corporations with an international reach, including Lever and Coty, as well as local entrepreneurs and regional businesses in India, China, and Japan. Moreover, it is hard to judge the extent and impact of these campaigns based solely on advertising in local newspapers and magazines. The advertising of Cutex in China seems to have been quite extensive, while Apex ads ran only fifteen months in South Africa's *Bantu World*. How successful were these and other products? To what extent did consumers buy into advertising images of youthful beauty?

The timing of the Modern Girl merits a closer look. Many of the marketing and advertising campaigns in India, China, Japan, and South Africa occurred in the late 1920s and the 1930s and might be understood as a *response* to the early presence of the Modern Girl. Advertisers' well-defined strategies aimed to promote and exploit a feminine style already appearing on the streets, in schools, and elsewhere. Fashioning the Modern Girl—and her distinct manifestations in diverse places—were unpredictable encounters and the rapid movement of images, people, and products across national lines.

Some of these encounters took place in the realm of commercialized leisure, where international travelers, musical and theatrical troupes, and motion pictures were particularly important. Hollywood obviously played an early and crucial role in circulating the image of vamps and flappers internationally. By the 1920s, such screen stars as Clara Bow and Joan Crawford epitomized the style of the Modern Girl, with her bobbed hair, frank gaze, and flirtatious manner. But even before the movies spread their flickering images around the world, the theater circulated such feminine "types" as the independent New Woman and the Modern Girl. The fashions and gestures of these types were readily copied by women in urban centers. French women took up the notion of the Anglo-American New Woman of the late nineteenth and early twentieth centuries but modified her "mannish" aspects into a vision of beauty and fashion; this emphasis on femininity carried over to the flapperish *garconne* after World War I, who shared with her older sister a devotion to aesthetics as an aspect of female modernity. In the 1920s, traveling bands and fox-trotting college students, working for the American Relief Administration, helped inaugurate the Jazz Age in Soviet Russia.

The transnational movement of individuals did not work in only one direction. Local entrepreneurs and cultural brokers traveled to the United States or

Western Europe and decided to import new fads, products, selling techniques, and images to their home countries. Arinobu Fukuhara, founder of the Japanese beauty company Shiseido, built an American-style pharmacy in Tokyo, complete with ice cream parlor; his son Shinzo studied at Columbia University, worked at a drugstore on Broadway, and delved into French modern design before he took the reins of the business in 1915. As Lynn Thomas shows, some South African women traveled to the United States and received training in African American beauty culture, then returned home to work as beauticians. In an ongoing newspaper debate, one of them defended the use of hair and skin products as a sign of black African modernity and respectability, arguing against those who saw the enhancement of appearance to be artificial and dangerous. By the 1930s, Max Factor was employing local women in the Philippines, the Middle East, Cuba, and elsewhere to demonstrate a line of makeup associated with Hollywood and at the same time serve as appropriate models of modern femininity and beauty specific to their milieu. Knowing more about these cultural brokers, who in various ways promoted the ideal and image of the Modern Girl in distinctive national, regional, and local circumstances, would be an important next step for research.

What did the Modern Girl mean in such vastly different local and national settings? This volume largely explores the question of meaning by focusing on representations, as they emerged and circulated in the domains of commerce, education, and politics. It seems that the sketchy image of the Modern Girl carried no fixed sense but rather offered a canvas for a multiplicity of ideologies as well as more fleeting thoughts and emotions.

The Modern Girl was variously a symbol of female social freedom, normative Western racial hierarchies, the universality of beauty, standards of hygiene and fashion, and a modernizing economy. Together these essays suggest that these were not always opposing or even separate elements but were closely related to each other. In the 1920s and 1930s, in such places as Germany, Australia, and the United States, the Modern Girl figured in struggles over racial and national identity. In the United States, the modern accoutrements of makeup and grooming products, diet, and hygiene reinvigorated the ideal of the white woman as a symbol of the supposedly "progressive" nature of racial nationalism and white supremacy. In contrast, German National Socialists scorned the sexualized, commodified flapper yet embraced another version of the Modern Girl—her healthy and athletic sister—as a symbol of a strong nation-state.

Yet this image could be read and used in many different ways, by modernizing nations, by anticolonial political movements, by racial minorities and, not least, by anxious men. For example, magazines and advertisements placed

Aboriginal women outside the boundaries of modern, civilized Australia by depicting them as primitive and unsightly, but other images undermined this racial divide by presenting well-groomed Aboriginal girls "placed" in white homes as wards and servants, wearing cast-off but modern clothing. Anti-colonial and independence movements often perceived the Modern Girl as a kind of Trojan horse, reinforcing a colonial psyche through the blandishments of consumption. Gandhi believed the Modern Girl was incompatible with India's *swadeshi* movement, with its emphasis on nonviolent struggle and employment of the poor through village manufactures. In China, the New Life Movement embraced a nationalist ideology that pushed the consumption of domestic goods; its "Brigades of Destroying the Modern" made the point by slashing Modern Girls' imported clothing.

One of the critical contributions of this volume, then, is that it places the Modern Girl in the world of political tensions, colonial struggle, racial conflict, and global capitalism. This departs from much of the literature on the Modern Girl in the United States, which tends to separate leisure, consumption, and marketing from the domain of formal politics. An exception is the new research on African American women, which reveals the close ties between the promotion of beauty and style as modern, on the one hand, and political and economic activity, on the other. For many black American women, beauty culture affirmed a sense of dignity and respectability in the face of demeaning racial and sexual stereotypes. It offered an entrée into a modern way of life, through employment opportunities and new leisure activities, especially in Northern cities. It also led women into political activism, with many beauticians and hairdressers taking part in campaigns for civil rights and economic justice in the twentieth century.

However, by presenting the Modern Girl as a figure who especially embodied "the complexity of global economic and cultural processes," we risk losing sight of her more quotidian character. The image of the Modern Girl would not have had such resonance politically and economically if she had not been, in the first place, a living presence, in the streets, in movie houses, in schools, and in homes. How did a fun-loving, smiling flapper with bobbed hair and red lips light the lives of young women in so many different countries? In the United States, this style seemed to spread inexorably — as the popular song went, "everybody's doing it." But being a Modern Girl really involved a choice — to refashion the body and embrace a new performance of self, sometimes in violation of community standards, church teachings, or parental commands. How did young women make this choice in Tokyo and Okinawa, in Shanghai and New Delhi, in Cape Town and Pretoria, in Berlin and Moscow? And what did it mean to them?

If these essays do not fully answer this question, they do provide some tantalizing hints. In the United States, it was young working-class women who pioneered many of the elements that constitute the Modern Girl; this seemed a style attuned to their entrance into wage work in factories, offices, and department stores, a way of declaring their autonomy and, for immigrant daughters, their American identity. Middle-class youth picked up the style in schools, movies, and magazines, and it quickly became normative. In contrast, in such places as South Africa, China, and India, the Modern Girl was identified in the first instance with the segment of women who were educated and members of the middle class or elite. The readers of *Bantu World* were educated in schools or Christian missions, and for them respectability was highlighted in the construction of the Modern Girl. For Okinawan women, travel to Tokyo for education and jobs exposed them to new ideas about womanhood which they brought back home. Schooling, even when directed to women's roles as wives and mothers, created possibilities for self-development and widening horizons. What difference did it make to the configuration of the Modern Girl that she emerged in the context of an expanding middle class and new emphasis on education for women? How were the investments in daughters and potential wives different for middle-class and poor families? How did these young women think about their present lives and possible futures?

Migration to urban centers, even for lower-class women, opened the prospect of a new sense of self, as women earned their own wages, navigated the city on their own, separated from families, and took pleasure in new places of leisure and entertainment. The Chinese ads for Cutex recognized these new conditions when they acknowledged the great tradition of Chinese beauty culture but insisted on the need for new hygienic practices as women enter into schools, ballrooms, and other spaces for social intercourse. A similar sensibility appears in beauty ads from the Weimar Republic and in the conduct of Soviet girls during the New Economic Policy. An air of cosmopolitanism blows across this terrain.

Indeed, the wish to claim a public space for herself especially marks the Modern Girl. The criticism of the Modern Girl as frivolous, shifting with the winds of fashion, is the other side of her own desire — to make her *self* visible and refashion how the world perceived her. Wherever she appeared, the Modern Girl professed herself an individual. This was not the individualism of liberal political theory, involving a claim to citizenship and political participation, but a more psychological notion of individuality, which was, in fact, more easily wedded to consumer culture and expressive sexuality. What did women risk when they made such a claim in countries with strong traditions of communalism or collectivism — whether rooted in older patterns of social organization or in the newer ideological formations of nationalism, communism, or fascism? In several cases, the Modern Girl was a hybrid, someone who fell in between existing categories of social status and identity. She was already, in a sense, a cultural problem. That at least some Modern Girls could turn a dilemma into fame suggests something of the dynamic possibilities of this time. The *sitara* film stars of India, themselves often of mixed parentage or Jewish background, offered a fluid and ambiguous racial and religious identity to Indian audiences; mediating perceptions of respectability and immorality, they found ways to signal simultaneously their adherence to tradition and embrace the modern, by the way they fixed their saris, or wore both makeup and the *bindi*.

What made the individualism of the Modern Girl so desirable and so troubling was its connection to the pleasures and unpredictability of the erotic — the narcissism of the mirror, the touch of a dance partner, the swoon of a saxophone, the glance of flirtation. Girls lean back everywhere: How they must have been a distraction to those building a collective society or engineering a eugenic population, how they must have enraged parents and confounded the expectations of suitors. The caricatures drawn by Chinese men of the Modern Girl as gold digger no doubt would have been understood by men around the world. For all that the Modern Girl was a marketing strategy of global capitalism, a lightning rod for nationalists, and the scourge of traditionalists, she was a figure taken up by real women and girls, however partially and briefly, who glimpsed in her something new, worldly, and accessible. Although the flapper with bee-stung lips and bobbed hair has long given way to other images, her leap into modernity, with its snares and possibilities, is one that women continue to make today.

Note

The title of this chapter quotes Jane Heap and pays homage to Edward de Grazia's book by the same name published in 1992.

16

After the Grand Tour

The Modern Girl, the New Woman,

and the Colonial Maiden

~

MIRIAM SILVERBERG

Memories of the Modern Girl:
From the Local to the Global and Back

Fifteen years have passed since I first documented the vibrant presence of the Modern Girl in Japan. "The modern girl," I wrote, makes only a brief appearance in our histories of prewar Japan. She is a glittering, decadent, middle-class consumer who, through her clothing, smoking and drinking, flaunts tradition in the urban playgrounds of the late 1920s. Arm in arm with her male equivalent, the *mobo* (Modern Boy) and fleshed out in the Western flapper's garb of the roaring twenties, she engages in *ginbura* (Ginza-cruising)."

How does one do justice when responding to this anthology? To do so one would have to elaborate the local specificity of each stop on what I am calling the Modern Girl's Grand Tour and then associate these distinctions with the global Modern Girl who ultimately is the heroine of this book. I have chosen instead to focus on aspects of the tour stops provided, for the most part, by the core members of the Modern Girl Working Group to illustrate how my earliest perspectives on the history of the Modern Girl can be rethought in light of their fresh insights.

The identity of the Modern Girl is based on her awareness that she may have always fashioned herself with a similar cosmopolitan "Modern Girl look" (Dong). As a marker of capitalist modernity, she was an advertising icon suffusing once banal objects with an intense aura and occupying new social thought through the positions she took in advertisements (Barlow). I would add to this that what the Japanese Modern Girl expressed in her own inimitable style was sometimes historically repressed or could be appropriated for differing ideological ends, just as her magic, sensual touch was used to animate all sorts of commodities. This seems common in many places where Modern Girls wrapped themselves in bright colors, painted their faces, as they discarded all semblance of propriety and fixed racial identity or hierarchy (Thomas), prowling not so much in search of boys but pleasure seeking in their masquerade, as Modern Girls (Weinbaum).

The masquerade is nimble, moving back and forth between the global and the local, acknowledging that one cannot have one without the other. Now fast forward, to the present — a time when images of a geisha with blue eyes are being projected in cities around the world at dizzying speed — a speed even faster than that of Japanese troops quickly conquering the cities of Southeast Asia during the Pacific War. And that old familiar syntax — with accompanying indeterminate Asian accent — "YOU WILL BECOME (PAUSE) GEISHA" is yet again there to haunt us (indeed, it never left). If there were a concordance to the Madam Butterfly canon, it would no doubt include the adverbs and adjectives to be found in a full-page ad for the film *Memoirs of a Geisha* in the 10 December 2005 copy of the *Los Angeles Times*; breathless, sumptuous, beguiling, ethereal, intoxicating, etc.

However, continuity in discourse notwithstanding, the "global" of then is not the current "global." Simultaneity, the Grand Tour tells us, works differently. If, as we have now learned, "East Asian eyes" in German advertising signified modern fantasies of universality (Poiger) during the earlier phase of globalization and, as I have found, Western-looking eyes in Japanese ads of the same years mirrored this sentiment, these blue eyes take on a different analytical significance. This anthology illustrates how ideologies of universalism could be quickly displaced by references to racial phantoms; one extreme could follow the other.

In both Germany and Japan, fantasies of universality were displaced by racializing of the other and of the self. One example is provided in a Japanese ad for a Modern Girl staple, face cream. The newfound racist sentiment expressed in an advertisement in November 1941 made clear that all fantasies blurring Japanese and Western identity, through identification with Hollywood, were no longer valid. In no uncertain terms it offered good cheer while putting race and time into a new order. The text read:

> If your country's different, your race is different
> If your race is different, your makeup is different
> As for long ago and now, the eras are different
> If the era is different, the make-up is different
> Throw different makeup clean away
> Be in good spirits.

Who were these Modern Girls? And to paraphrase the second question I raised fifteen years ago, why did they do what they did? The Modern Girl Research Group has convinced me that the commodity made them "do a lot of what they did." Moreover, the Grand Tour strategy the group has pioneered succeeds in the unlikely task of relaying the thrill of contact with new commodities without apologizing for capitalism. (How did they ever achieve this? Don't we usually spend our time apologizing for this too intimate relationship between commodities and modern young women?) But it has also encouraged me to change my mind about the Modern Girl in other ways, while helping me to resolve the problem that I had with her.

I must confess that while my early version of the Modern Girl was admirably free of any sentiment expressing even the slightest suggestion of race thinking, she has given me trouble over the years since I wrote the following: "The Modern Girl was a highly commodified cultural construct crafted by journalists who debated her identity during the tumultuous decade of cultural and social change following the great earthquake of 1923." I had meant that the "Modern Girl" was a phantasm projected onto the social landscape by male critics made increasingly anxious by the sociocultural change taking place all around them, change that included the politicization of women. But to deny live embodiment to the Modern Girl is to ignore the actual young women who were modern. And I will now concede that there are many ways to be modern. I would venture to presume that very few of the handful of young girls dressed in cosmopolitan Modern Girl uniform possessed any dedication to social change. But to say that there were no living, breathing Modern Girls in the sense that the media portrayed them is to deny a history to a second faction — the group of young women in bobbed hair who were aware of wanting to make cultural and social revolution. The third group of young women whom I hereby admit into my ranks is the women workers of the 1920s and 1930s, ranging from the professional journalist to the factory girl. I will concede that they can all be called Modern Girls, those whose commitment to change was limited to a change of clothing, those who were activists, and those whose everyday actions were a challenge to the order. These agents and the icon of the Modern Girl were all Modern Girls. These Japanese women adopted the global Modern Girl style documented so consistently in the Grand Tour.

This volume has convinced me that clothes could make the Modern Girl. To don modern clothing was to participate in the creation of radically new gestures and mores. It was one aspect of the radical break from traditions that marked gendered social relations that had been seen as a given before the Great Earthquake of 1923. At the same time we must bear in mind Barbara Sato's finely documented insight that class position dictated whether the women eagerly devoted to reading the mass magazines would have actual access to the consumer items pictured in the advertisements and featured articles of these magazines for women. Sato explains how those who could not afford to pay were still consumers—of visual culture and its associated fantasies. Kimura Ihee, the leading documentary photographer of the 1920s and 1930s, reported that in his business of photographing people, he constantly came across cases of young men whose style of clothing and hair came straight out of the movie magazines. Women also were appropriating fashions in clothing, hair, and cosmetics. Even more common was the direct adoption of fashion from the movies. Moreover, these young people did not merely mimic the styles of the stars as they had in earlier years. Instead, they matched the styles (Kimura used the word *kata*, a Kabuki term) of America, France, and Germany to their own individuality. And not only had young Japanese spectators begun to dress in movie style, according to Kimura. These moviegoers had also begun to speak in talkie conversational style, adopting—through a form of code switching—the pacing of speech and the spacing of laughter in the interstices between phrases found in the movies.

My conclusion about the Modern Girl remains the same as when I cited Natalie Davis in order to conclude that "the Modern Girl as multivalent symbol questioned relations of order and subordination and at the same time, through her cultural gender play and promiscuity, served 'to explore the character of sexuality' and of gender while also suggesting that order be preserved." What I did not make clear was that the Modern Girl I was referring to in my conclusion was the Modern Girl as icon. I would now elaborate on my category of Modern Girl to include icons and agents, and I have now agreed to place the Modern Girl squarely within consumer culture.

This is one very central reason why, contrary to others, I wish to hold on to the distinction between the New Woman and the Modern Girl; *pace* Ito, whose rich evocation of the colonial society of Okinawa terms the women intellectuals of that colony "Modern Girls." I do not see the two as interchangeable. While I agree with the Modern Girl group that the former cannot lay sole claim to political activism, and it is clear that Modern Girls were not the only consumers of free love and beauty for sale, there is a crucial question to be answered in the Japanese case, at least at that time. Why was there a need to have both New Women and Modern Girls and to keep the two categories so separate? My answer requires me to revise my original stance. My new position is that the agent who instigated "modern" changes, thereby threatening the order, was the New Woman even more so, possibly, than the Modern Girl.

The New Woman as Modern Girl

My apologies to the New Women of the pre-earthquake years. In my zeal to prove the Modern Girl militant, I rendered the New Woman immaterial. I blindly followed the lead of others who had not taken the New Woman seriously. The standard narrative has been that cerebral bourgeois women with literary pretensions were displaced by the lustful, threatening Modern Girl. If I (and others) had seriously bothered to look behind the Modern Girl, we would have encountered a formidable New Woman blocked from view by the Modern Girl's gyrations.

The scholars in this volume have tended to consider the New Woman as one manifestation of the Modern Girl. But I think that the coexistence of both terms, and both terms as clearly different in the case of Japan, should be taken seriously (Roberts). I am prompted to consider the New Woman as serious social threat, notwithstanding the existence of a small minority of women in Modern Girl style whose everyday life was defined by iconoclastic mores. In this formulation the Modern Girl icon was a rare means to take power away from the New Women who challenged political certainties and respectability (Thomas). (What better way was there to disempower woman than to call her "girl"?)

My premise is that the New Woman was an intellectual and a social theorist and was acknowledged as such. If the Modern Girl was to be seen, the New Woman was to be heard or at least read. Through their actions they illustrated Marx's discussion of the double-edged nature of the weight of the energy of the bourgeoisie. "New Women" were not sheltered. They were traveled and they were lovers, mothers, writers. (The most illustrious writers, Hiratsuka Raicho, Yosano Akiko, and Ito Noe, were all of the above.) Like the poet Yosano

Akiko, who expressed her desire "to make the mountains move" (in the first issue of *Seito*, the acknowledged journal by and for New Women), they took their opinions, and their passions, seriously. *Seitō* was a place for social commentary that aimed at the heart of the Japanese family system, a patriarchal order which through its civil code sustained the Japanese state and empire.

Recently, what I call the "new New Woman scholarship" demonstrates the political nature of the New Woman by encouraging us to place her in her time. For example, the verdict in the notorious trial of the anarchist Kotōtū Shūsui, Kanno Suga, and fellow enemies of the state, for a supposed attempt to assassinate the emperor, was handed down in January 1911, eight months before the inauguration of the Bluestocking (Seitō) organization of "New Women" and of its journal by the same name. These rich girls did not live in a vacuum or in a narcissistic fog leading them to theorize only about the "self" as has been emphasized. For example, are we to believe that they were deaf and blind to the fate of the anarchist woman Kanno Suga, one of the accused who was executed with Kotoku? Horiba Kiyoko talks about how stunned and moved she was when she realized that young women from the provinces throughout Japan had been Bluestocking members who sent letters and short stories into the *Seito* offices about their lives in the family system.

Ito Noe, interpreter of Emma Goldman's proclamations on traffic in women, and editor of *Seitō* following founder and leader Hiratsuka Raicho, was number seventy-eight on the list of members when she first made her pilgrimage to the offices as a young teenager, before she became the lover of the Dadaist Tsu Jun and then of the Anarchist theorist Osugi Sakae. And not only were the Bluestocking women intellectuals; they were also angry. The sarcasm and irony so central to the voice of the New Women is history forgotten (Ramamurthy), for it is clear from the media of the teens and early 1920s that women intellectuals were taken seriously both by those like the socialist Sakai Toshihiko, who praised the new woman workers, and by other established intellectuals. While the media took advantage of any gossip about the New Woman, the world of journalism was sufficiently perturbed by the "woman problem" to devote entire issues of magazines to analysis of the new phenomenon. I conclude that by turning this "New Woman" into a "girl" and by implying that she was not indigenous by using the lone word "modern," the establishment media could turn to the task of disempowering and displacing the New Woman.

We can only presume that when Ito Noe was murdered during the premeditated violence following the Great Earthquake of 1923, she was garbed in her usual bold fashion, in her usual cosmopolitan style topped by a cloche: an anarchist New Woman in Modern Girl style. The young Korean women who died during the state-sanctioned, grass-roots pogrom that saw the deaths of Ito,

Osugi, and six thousand colonial Koreans — who had been forced to seek a living in the metropole — remain anonymous. But through its discussion of racialization the Modern Girl Around the World Tour draws attention to another kind of "girl." I will call her the "Colonial Maiden."

The Colonial Maiden

The sophisticated theorization of race in this anthology has led me to my conception of the Japanese Colonial Maiden. At the time I was studying this volume I found her in the opening pages of Tanizaki Junichirō's book, which has been translated as *Naomi*. I recommend a close rereading of the work as a tale of racial masquerade that illustrates the racializing of women and men, the feminization of empire, and the eroticization of colonial power relations. The tawdriness of colonial eroticism is all too clear in the account of an obsession of a young white collar worker which gives us no access to the subjectivity of his girl turned woman. I am one who is guilty of equating Naomi (whose name, as the author tells us, could be Japanese, English, or Eurasian) with the attraction to the West during the modern years 1920s and 1930s. What demands attention as soon as we are made aware of the obvious is that, from beginning to end, this novel is about the racialized body of Naomi and the power relations projected onto it.

A meaningful study of the Colonial Maiden — around the world — would call for a discussion of girls of the "exterior" and the metropole. They would be the daughters of colonizers, the colonized (or one of each), collaborators, and adventurers. They would be fantasy or fictional figures and daughters of the rich and famous, as well as members of groupings of anonymous maidens. In the Japanese case, the most famous of the anonymous would be the comfort women. These were truly maidens — virgins — little girls.

But such a project belongs after the Grand Tour, the Modern Girl Around the World anthology, which I'm sure will inspire innumerable studies of considerable scope. The core authors of this project have kept their own stories in the background. And yet they have written a history of their mothers, mothers-in-law, and grandmothers (Ramamurthy). It seems to me that through their years of close collaboration, they may have created a new form of feminist scholarship.

I would like to come to an end here with a brief story, really a memory. Approximately fifteen years ago, I was privileged to attend a monthly meeting of a group of Japanese professional women in their thirties and forties — a designer, a travel agent, and so on. The group had dedicated itself to recording an oral history of a geisha and I believe that the geisha would have been a contemporary of Modern Girls around the world. (I remember that she recalled the pleasures of a Buster Keaton movie.) The session that I attended was nearing the end of her story, and the group members were excitedly planning a grand finale. They had tracked down the love of her life and, unbeknown to her, were orchestrating a reunion. The Modern Girl project of course differs from this group of professional women. In their dedication to recuperating a vision of the past, the contributors to this anthology are aware of method and the importance of weighing differences. They do not run away from the responsibility to explain more global findings or to talk about the place of fantasy in history. The volume speaks for itself and it is now time for the (Japanese) Modern Girl to return, from whence she came. For every Modern Girl must eventually withdraw from the fantasy of the universal, to go home. Let us leave with the battle cry of the New Woman in our archive. The words were voiced by Ito Noe: "Smash All Conventions!"

Thank you to each scholar in this book, for illuminating the multiplicity and the global nature of the Modern Girl around the world, through your shared histories. You have given us a new language and methodology, new theory, new imagery, new knowledge.

17

The Modern Girl
and Commodity Culture

TIMOTHY BURKE

In my book *Lifebuoy Men, Lux Women* (1996), I charted the history
of three strands of structure and practice that helped to weave commodity culture in modern southern Africa.[1] The first was the production of various forms of "common sense" within colonial society;
for the commodities I studied, the forms of common sense that addressed domesticity, hygiene, and physical appearance. The second
was an account of the growth of local manufacturing and retailing.
The third was an effort by advertisers and market researchers to describe and manipulate what they called the "African market." These
histories, I argued, were what gave structure to twentieth-century
assertions of needs and desires for different commodities, and which
changed the substantive content of material life in African communities. Tying these strands together was the answer to the question I posed at the outset: why and more importantly how did many
Africans in modern Zimbabwe come to experience deeply felt needs
and wants for commodities that they had neither previously needed
nor wanted?

I have slowly come to feel that some of the implications of my
answers to that question have even larger and more unsettling rever-
berations. In part, this sensation is a consequence of working on a new

project in which I have found myself at an increasing distance from some of the orthodoxies of Africanist historical writing and postcolonial theory.

"Modernity"—a word now used with near-meaningless abandon in scholarship—seems at the heart of my unease. Many words spread too broadly throughout scholarly writing but most are easily abandoned when they lose their specific meanings. Yet modernity cannot be left behind: much of what the term describes is indispensable. On one hand, the word references the history of particular political and economic institutions, social transformations, modes of personhood. Africanists and many other scholars are uneasy about this dimension of modernity because it seems to imply that there is but one road to the human present, that Western societies traveled there first, and that non-Western societies are at various points along the road to the same destination. Hence many scholars have turned to the idea of "multiple modernities," that every human society experienced some transition in the last two hundred years and that all contemporary societies are related in their current state. The problem with this usage is that modernity rapidly becomes little more than a synonym for "contemporaneity," a statement that all societies exist in an interrelated global present. This truism carries little analytic weight, because it says nothing constraining about the nature of that relationship. For modernity to mean anything, it has to reference particular social forms such as industrialization, nation-states, liberal individuality—and it needs to acknowledge when those forms have a history of dissemination from metropolis to periphery or of circulation back from periphery to metropolis.

One productive social form through which to consider modernity is the "Modern Girl." As this volume attests, her global distribution across the twentieth century is striking. The Modern Girl is a construct, a representation of personhood, identity, and practice. The difference between representations or social constructions and lived experience is real and meaningful, but representations form the raw material from which everyday life is shaped by human agents: representations in texts become repertoires of behavior and performance in everyday practice. There were Modern Girls in magazines and films, on stage and in the public arena of urban life, but there were also women who imagined themselves and their aspirations through and within such images.

Thinking about the Modern Girl and commodity culture, primarily but not exclusively in terms of southern Africa, suggests to me that the emancipatory value of both modernity and capitalism have been systematically underrated by a generation's worth of scholarship which dedicated itself, often appropriately, to correcting colonial ideology and capitalist mythmaking. The Modern Girl, both in life and in imagination, was defined as much by her clothing and her cosmetics, by the food she ate and the tobacco she smoked, and by the things she bought and did not buy. The Modern Girl is impossible to imagine without capitalist consumerism, and even if consumption did not describe more than a small part of her commitment to a lived identity, she could not have crafted that identity without it.

Broadly speaking, southern African urban communities had two different archetypical models for women seeking to self-identify as modern, each of which had a distinctive profile in commodified terms. The first were the "respectables," the second, to use the terminology offered by Dorothy Hodgson and Sheryl McCurdy, were the "wicked."[2] The respectable defined her commodified modernity through the idioms of colonial domesticity and in terms of material restraint. She had her origins in mission education from the 1920s to the 1960s, which offered an increasing focus over time on teaching domesticity and connected ideals of feminine behavior. Mission schools aimed to train a female elite charged with spreading their lessons to other women in rural and urban settings. The curricular content of mission schools was broadly replicated in propaganda and newspapers aimed by the colonial state at African audiences. The respectable was also envisioned as a woman outside the domain of the customary, though she might well be said to preserve the presumed virtues of the customary. The respectable's claims to modernity were, if not uncontested, grudgingly accepted in the same way that educated aspirant men compelled the colonial state to accept their existence if not respect their aspirations.

The vision put forth by respectable Modern Girls was often centrally defined by material practices. The ideology of mission domesticity simultaneously argued that women rather than men should have control over household finances and that the obligation of a modern woman was to demonstrate thrifty restraint in her consumption. A respectable should learn how to sew and mend her own clothing. She should never buy luxury items like gramophones and always cook simple, nutritional foods. She should avoid alcohol and try to prevent men from excess consumption of it. But at the same time, the respectable was also enjoined to be a consumer of manufactured goods, to buy soaps and detergents and deodorants, to have afternoon tea set at a proper table, to hang drapes on her windows, to have quintessentially modern furniture like beds and chairs, to live in a square rather than a round home.

For many self-identified respectables, particularly in urban townships, demonstrating one's commitment to modernity through consumption tended to stress the acquisition and display of proper commodities rather than habits of thrift. The value of thrift was more the emphasis preferred by white interlocutors who sought to discourage aspirant African women from competition with or close imitation of white material culture, thereby erasing important racial distinctions. However, commodified respectability, whether thrifty or not, was an important way for urban women to exercise control over their own identities. Precisely because it insisted that economic control over household finances was the business of the Modern Girl in her respectable incarnation, it made consumption central to her identity. This showed up not only in what she bought and displayed but also in how she commented on and disciplined the consumption of others.

The respectable's main rival, the other archetypical Modern Girl, was equally reliant on commodity culture to define and shape her public identity. The wicked Modern Girl embraced practices and signs that were characterized by the dominant order as transgressive, illicit, or immoral. The wicked girl might be little more than a momentary pose adopted for the thrill of it, or she might be someone whose entire social life and economic well-being centered on habits of consumption that ran intensely counter to dominant representations of propriety.

Historians obsessed with refuting colonial ideology have managed to overlook the degree to which some women adopted wickedness with considerable enthusiasm. For most scholars working on these subjects, this characterization was strictly a legal and moral construct used against women, to police their behavior or represent them as subjects legible to various juridical and moral sanctions. Diana Jeater, in her otherwise excellent history of the construction of colonial morality in Zimbabwe, argues that the construction of a moral domain within urban communities largely served to burden women with new forms of shame and restraint, while overlooking a significant constituency of women who exulted in acting outside of these constructs of shame.[3] In colonial townships, there were beer brewers, wealthy prostitutes, shady female entrepreneurs, famous dancers and singers, or, as David Coplan relates in a recent essay, women who associated with notorious urban gangsters to define a life of extended girlhood.[4]

Alongside these more stable examples of wicked Modern Girls, there were also women, many of them short-term migrants to the city, who adopted transgressive postures and attitudes while in the metropolis only to switch back to more sedately customary or respectable modalities when they returned to rural homesteads. Whether these were long-term identities or short-term performances, they were statements about autonomy, expressions of self-determination, even while they were also often demonstrably about constraints or desperation. And wickedness, whether reluctant or exultant, was defined through and by the use of particular commodities. This kind of Modern Girl, at least as she was often represented in the colonial public sphere, smoked cigarettes. She flaunted her expensive or unusual clothing and chased after the latest fashions. She wore cosmetics and used skin lighteners.

The respectable Modern Girl made colonial authorities nervous, because she—like her male counterparts—was exposing the tenuous fictions of the "civilizing mission" by enacting the part of civilized African with ease. The wicked Modern Girl drew explicit censure from not only white authorities but also (even more vehemently) black men. As an archetype, she appears again and again in literary and journalistic works by African men as seducer, betrayer, and complicit pawn of a corrupt social order. It is hard to pick through the ruins of representation to guess at how many urban women or migrants actually performed this role, with its repertoire of characteristic commodities, and how deep the performance ran into their experience of personhood. But, for example, I do know from materials produced by market research firms and manufacturers that cosmetics sold fairly well in urban African communities, despite the fact that their use was almost universally represented as salacious and immoral. Two young rural women I interviewed in 1990 told me something that I later heard from quite a few others, that they never wore cosmetics when they were at home, but that when they went to Harare to visit friends of their own age, they often carried an illicit stash to apply as soon as they arrived in town.[5]

The "turn to consumption" in historical scholarship has been criticized, sometimes justly, for its capacious ability to celebrate consumption as a free domain for social action, and for its representation of the world of goods as a set of free-floating, endlessly imaginative signifiers unattached to economic structures.[6] This concluding commentary may have some of that feel. For those who need to hear it, I offer the obligatory note of dour, pious warning about the very real material constraints and oppressions that African women under colonialism had to deal with. Whether individual young women lived everyday life largely within the stereotypical boundaries of respectability or transgression, or lived lives largely unencompassed by either trope, they all had to cope with a social world that was structurally hostile to their daily existence and a material world that was defined by scarcity and deprivation.

Yet the insistence that we recall the impoverishment of young African women (and men) under colonial and postcolonial rule often overlooks their informal strategies for generating income. Prostitution, beer brewing, and various forms of mutual aid associations are only the most obvious and well known of these. Theft from white employers or gifts from same were also important sources of symbolically potent luxury commodities. Nor does recalling the structural limitations on African consumption necessarily tell us much about the considerable symbolic authority of consumption in everyday life, the capacity of commodified practice and performance to create or embody social relations.

I honestly think that African women, whether respectable or wicked or indeterminately neither, often found through their identification with modernity new possibilities for social autonomy and freedom and expressed some of those possibilities through consumer choices. This, I would suggest, is a characterization whose validity carries well beyond the borders of southern Africa, and which carries with it another subversive implication. To argue that what young African women understood to be modern living was not merely another patriarchal trap is to defy the orthodox Africanist tendency toward nationalist mythography, in which modernity is always understood as a regrettable fall from indigenous grace, a thing imposed from outside. It is equally disturbing to certain paradigms to suggest that it is no coincidence that whatever degree of autonomy young African women found in modernity, they sometimes found it through capitalist commodity culture. In both conjectures it's important to remember that modernity *is* a thing whose historical genesis comes from outside African societies, just as capitalist commodity culture is. Both modernity and commodity culture have been localized and remade within particular African societies over time, but this does not elide the fact of their historical externality or their association with colonial conquest. The ultimately unsettling premise here is that the transformations of modernity mediated through colonialism were in a great many ways generative and even emancipatory for particular individuals, communities, and collectivities.

For those who understand "real" forms of freedom to be vested only within formal conceptions of politics or in terms of fundamental struggle over production, regarding choices over which products to buy and consume as important seems perverse. Clearly, I disagree with this characterization. What Modern Girls have done with consumption all over the globe is not inconsequential. Choices over what (and whether) to buy, what to do with what is bought, and how to connect the world of commodities with deeper expressions of personhood and desire are as meaningful as any choice we might care to identify. Meaningful in different ways than the actions we are more accustomed to seeing as expressions of individual and collective agency, to be sure. The pursuit of desire, the performance of aspiration, the work of self-fashioning are not the same kind of choices as strategic economic choices, choices about family life, or choices to flee repression or accept it. However, the fashioning of the Modern Girl in representation and practice through commodities, consumption, fashion, and performance is not by comparison trivial or subordinate to these "real" choices.

The subordination of one form of choice to the other, the assumption that consumerism and desire are more trivial expressions of liberty, ultimately goes back to Enlightenment moral philosophy and its deep ambivalence about the unleashing of material abundance in the human world, an ambivalence that led to an envisioned division between substantive individual liberties defined by the contractual and disciplinary framework of liberal society and trivial or superficial choices rooted in self-indulgence.[7] The difference between the kinds of modern identity and personhood that rights-bearing discourses invoke and the kinds that discourses of self-fashioning and self-indulgence point to are real and substantial. The commonsensical assumption that the former trumps the latter, on the other hand, is anything but commonsensical.

Southern African women who signified as Modern Girls also made other choices about their lives that were not unrelated to their self-fashioning. It is not an accident that what I regard as meaningful social and cultural choices for Modern Girls were vested (and remain vested) in capitalist commodity culture. In the end, the most provocative thought I can offer is that classical formulations of capitalist liberalism have, often unintentionally, defined even highly subjugated and marginalized subjects as *agents* precisely because they are forced to regard all known subjects as *consumers*, as people who make choices. Even when the choices of consumers are highly circumscribed and the local agents of capitalist enterprise are disinclined to see subject populations — including women — as capable of choice, the underlying liberal frame of post-Enlightenment commodity capitalism inevitably returns those agents to an unavoidable acceptance of those groups as acting.

If colonialism was marked by what David Scott has called a "flawed liberalism,"[8] it nevertheless introduced a liberal conception of individual subjects. At a time when antiglobalization activists speak in the name of local communities allegedly disenfranchised by the power of neoliberal economic policies, this complication may be worth recalling. We might (or might not) wish that Modern Girls all around the world had something more meaningful to express their identity through than consumer goods — but we should not let that wish blind us to the fact that access to the capitalist marketplace has been an important part of the Modern Girl's identity wherever she has appeared, and sometimes the only part of her self-definition over which she had some significant degree of meaningful agency.

Notes

1. Timothy Burke, *Lifebuoy Men, Lux Women: Commodification, Consumption, and Cleanliness in Modern Zimbabwe.*
2. Hodgson and McCurdy, eds., *"Wicked" Women and the Reconfiguration of Gender in Africa.*
3. Jeater, *Marriage, Perversion and Power.*

4. David Coplan, "You Have Left Me Wandering About."
5. Burke, *Lifebuoy Men*, chap. 6.
6. See Agnew, "Coming Up for Air."
7. See Appleby, "Consumption in Early Modern Social Thought," for a detailed intellectual history of early modern European thinking about consumption, abundance, and self-indulgence.
8. Scott, *Refashioning Futures*.

Bibliography

"Aboriginal Beauty." In *Modern Pictorial* Atlas. Melbourne: Sun News-Pictorial, ca. 1938.

Agamben, Giorgio. *The Coming Community*. Translated by Michael Hardt. Minneapolis: University of Minnesota Press, 2003.

Agnew, Jean-Christophe. "Coming Up for Air: Consumer Culture in Historical Perspective." In *Consumption and the World of Goods*, edited by John Brewer and Roy Porter, 19–39. New York: Routledge, 1993.

Akyeampong, Emmanuel. "'Wo pe tam won pe ba' ('You like cloth but you don't want children'): Urbanization, Individualism and Gender Relations in Colonial Ghana c. 1900–1939." In *Africa's Urban Past*, edited by David Anderson and Richard Rathbone, 222–34. Oxford: James Currey, 2000.

Alexander, Sally. "Becoming a Woman in London in the 1920's and 1930's." In *Metropolis: London Histories and Representations since 1800*, edited by David Feldman and Gareth Stedman Jones, 245–71. London: Routledge, 1989.

Allman, Norwood F. *Shanghai Lawyer*. New York: McGraw-Hill, 1934.

Anderson, Jervis. *A. Philip Randolph: A Biographical Portrait*. New York: Harcourt Brace, 1973

Anderson, Warwick, *The Cultivation of Whiteness: Science, Health and Racial Destiny in Australia*. Melbourne: Melbourne University Press, Carlton South, 2002.

Appleby, Joyce. "Consumption in Early Modern Social Thought." In *Consumption and the World of Goods*, edited by John Brewer and Roy Porter, 162–76. New York: Routledge, 1993.

Archer-Straw, Petrine. *Negrophilia: Avant-Garde Paris and Black Culture in the 1920s*. New York: Thames and Hudson, 2000.

Arnold, David. *The Problem of Nature: Environment, Culture and European Expansion.* Oxford: Blackwell, 1996.

Ascheid, Antje. *Hitler's Heroines: Stardom and Womanhood in Nazi Cinema.* Philadelphia: Temple University Press, 2003.

Auchmuty, J. J. "1810–1830." In *A New History of Australia*, edited by F. K. Crowley, 45–81. Melbourne: Heinemann, 1986.

Ausschuß zur Untersuchung der Erzeugungs- und Absatzbedingungen der deutschen Wirtschaft. *Die deutsche Seifen- und Parfümerienindustrie.* Berlin: Mittler & Sohn, 1931.

Aynsley, Jeremy. *Graphic Design in Germany, 1890–1945.* Berkeley: University of California Press, 2000.

Bacon, C. A. "Advertising in China." In *Chinese Economic Journal, Index.* Volume 5. Shanghai: Bureau of Industrial and Commercial Information, Ministry of Industry, Commerce, and Labor, National Government of the Republic of China, 1929, 754–66.

Bairoch, Paul. "Globalization Myths and Realities: One Century of External Trade and Foreign Investment." In *States against Market: The Limits of Globalization*, edited by Robert Boyer and Daniel Drache, 173–192. London: Routledge, 1996.

Bajohr, Frank. *Aryanisation in Hamburg: The Economic Exclusion of Jews and the Confiscation of Their Property in Nazi Germany.* New York: Berghahn Books, 2002.

Baldwin, Davarian. "Chicago's New Negroes: Race, Class, and Respectability in the Midwestern Black Metropolis, 1915–1935," Ph.D. diss., New York University, 2002.

Balibar, Etienne. *Politics and the Other Scene.* London: Verso Press, 2002.

Ball, Alan M. *Russia's Last Capitalists: The Nepmen, 1921–1929.* Berkeley: University of California Press, 1987.

Ballantine, Christopher. *Marabi Nights: Early South African Jazz and Vaudeville.* Johannesburg: Ravan Press, 1993.

Ballhatchet, Kenneth. *Race, Sex, and Class under the Raj: Imperial Attitudes and Policies and Their Critics, 1793–1905.* London: Weidenfeld and Nicolson, 1980.

Banks, Ingrid. *Hair Matters: Beauty, Power, and Black Women's Consciousness.* New York: New York University Press, 2000.

Barkan, Elazar, and Ronald Bush, eds. *Prehistories of the Future: The Primitivist Project and the Culture of Modernism.* Stanford, Calif.: Stanford University Press, 1995.

Barlow, Tani E. " 'What Is a Poem?': The Event of Women and the Modern

Girl as Problems in Global or World History." In *World-Scale Ambitions*, edited by David Palumbo-Liu and Nirvana Tanoukhi. Durham, N.C.: Duke University Press, forthcoming.

———. "History and the Border." *Journal of Women's History* 18 (2006): 8–32.

———. "Eugenic Woman, Semi-Colonialism, and Colonial Modernity as Problems for Postcolonial Theory." In *Postcolonial Studies and Beyond*, edited by Ania Loomba, Suvir Kaul, Matti Bunzl, Antoinette Burton, and Jed Esty, 359–84. Durham, N.C.: Duke University Press, 2005.

———. "Wanting Some." In *Women in China: The Republican Period in Historical Perspective*, edited by Mechthild Leutner and Nikola Spakowski, 247–83. Berlin: LIT Verlag, 2005.

———. *The Question of Women in Chinese Feminism*. Durham, N.C.: Duke University Press, 2004.

Barlow, Tani, ed. *Formations of Colonial Modernity in East Asia*. Durham, N.C.: Duke University Press, 1997.

Barrett, Charles. *Blackfellows of Australia*. Melbourne: Lawrence Kay for Pictorial Newpapers, 1936.

Barwick, Diane E. "And the Lubras Are Ladies Now." In *Woman's Role in Aboriginal Society*, edited by Fay Gale, 51–63. Canberra: Australian Institute of Aboriginal Studies, 1978.

Batty, Philip, ed. *Colliding Worlds: First Contact in the Western Desert, 1932–1984*. Melbourne: Museum of Victoria, 2006.

Bayly, Susan. *Caste, Society, and Politics in India from the Eighteenth Century to the Modern Age*. Cambridge: Cambridge University Press, 1999.

Bean, Jennifer, and Diane Negra. *A Feminist Reader in Early Cinema*. Durham, N.C.: Duke University Press, 2002.

Ben-Ghiat, Ruth. *Fascist Modernities: Italy, 1922–1945*. Berkeley: University of California Press, 2001.

Benton, Charlotte, Tim Benton, and Ghislaine Wood, eds. *Art Deco, 1910–1930*. London: Victoria and Albert Museum Publications, 2003.

Bergner, Gwen. "Who Is That Masked Woman? Or, the Role of Gender in Fanon's *Black Skin, White Masks*." *PMLA* 110, no. 1 (January 1995): 75–88.

Berry, Sarah. "Hollywood Exoticism: Cosmetics and Color in the 1930s." In *Hollywood Goes Shopping*, edited by David Dresser, 108–38. Minneapolis: University of Minnesota Press, 2000.

———. *Screen Style: Fashion and Femininity in 1930s Hollywood*. Minneapolis: University of Minnesota Press, 2000.

Bertrand, Ina. *Cinema in Australia: A Documentary History*. Kensington: New South Wales University Press, 1989.

Bezobrazow, Olga de. *La Femme nouvelle*. Paris: Société nouvelle d'éditions, 1896.

Bhaumik, Kaushik. "The Emergence of the Bombay Film Industry, 1913–36." Ph.D. diss., Oxford University, 2001.

Bi, Keguan, and Huang Yuanlin. *Zhongguo manhua shi*. Beijing: Wenhua yishu chuanshe, 1986.

Bickford-Smith, Vivian. *Ethnic Pride and Racial Prejudice in Victorian Cape Town*. Cambridge: Cambridge University Press, 1995.

Bisset, Andrew. *Black Roots and White Flowers: A History of Jazz in Australia*. Sydney: Golden Press, 1979.

Blackwelder, Julia Kirk. *Styling Jim Crow: African American Beauty Training during Segregation*. College Station: Texas A&M Press, 2003.

Blunt, Alison. *Domicile and Diaspora: Anglo-Indian Women and the Spatial Politics of Home*. Malden, Mass.: Blackwell Publishing, 2005.

Blyton, Enid. *The Three Golliwogs*. London: Dean and Son, 1969.

Bobryshev, Ivan T. *Melkoburzhuaznye vliianiia sredi molodezhi*. Moscow-Leningrad: Molodaia gvardiia, 1928.

Bois, Jules. *L'Eve nouvelle*. Paris: Chaillin, 1896.

Bonner, Philip. " 'Desirable or Undesirable Basotho Women?' Liquor, Prostitution and the Migration of Basotho Women to the Rand, 1920–1945." In *Women and Gender in Southern Africa to 1945*, edited by Cheryl Walker, 221–50. Cape Town: David Philip, 1990.

——. "The Transvaal Native Congress, 1917–1929: The Radicalisation of the Black Petty Bourgeoisie on the Rand." In *Industrialisation and Social Change in South Africa*, edited by Shula Marks and Richard Rathbone, 276–313. London: Longman, 1982.

The Book of Songs: The Ancient Chinese Classic of Poetry. Translated by Arthur Waley. New York: Grove Press, 1996.

Bordeaux, Henry. *La Vie au theater*. Vol. 3. Paris: Librairie Plon, 1913.

Bower, Daniel. " 'The City in Danger': The Civil War and the Russian Urban Population." In *Party, State, and Society in the Russian Civil War*, edited by Diane P. Koenker, William G. Rosenberg, and Ronald Grigor Suny, 58–80. Bloomington: Indiana University Press, 1989.

Bowlt, John E. "Constructivism and Early Soviet Fashion Design." In *Bolshevik Culture: Experiment and Order in the Russian Revolution*, edited by Abbot Gleason, Peter Genez, and Richard Stites, 203–19. Bloomington: Indiana University Press, 1985.

Bozzoli, Belinda. *Women of Phokeng: Consciousness, Life Strategy, and*

Migrancy in South Africa, 1900–1983. Portsmouth, N.H.: Heinemann, 1991.

Bradley, Carol. "A Change in Status for Aboriginal Women? Aboriginal Women in the Australian Workforce." *Aboriginal History*, 11, no. 2 (1987): 143–55.

Brandon, Ruth. *The New Women and the Old Men: Love, Sex and the Woman Question.* London: Secker and Warburg, 1990.

Brennan, Teresa, and Martin Jay, eds. *Vision in Context: Historical and Contemporary Perspectives on Sight.* New York: Routledge, 1996.

Brieux, Eugène. *La Femme seule: Comédie en trois actes.* Paris: P. V. Stock, 1913.

Broome, Richard. *Arriving (Series: The Victorians).* McMahon's Point, NSW: Fairfax, Syme and Weldon Associates, 1984.

Brumberg, Joan Jacobs. *The Body Project: An Intimate History of American Girls.* New York: Random House, 1997.

Bundles, A'lelia Perry. *On Her Own Ground: The Life and Times of Madam CJ Walker.* New York: Scribner, 2001.

——. *Madam C. J. Walker, Entrepreneur.* New York: Chelsea House, 1991.

Burke, Timothy. *Lifebuoy Men, Lux Women: Commodification, Consumption, and Cleanliness in Modern Zimbabwe.* Durham, N.C.: Duke University Press, 1996.

Burton, Antoinette. "Introduction: The Unfinished Business of Colonial Modernities." In *Gender, Sexuality and Colonial Modernities*, edited by Antoinette Burton, 1–16. New York: Routledge, 1999.

——. *Burdens of History: British Feminists, Indian Women, and Imperial Culture, 1865–1916.* Chapel Hill: University of North Carolina Press, 1994.

Campbell, Colin. *The Romantic Ethic and the Spirit of Modern Consumerism.* New York: Blackwell, 1987.

Campbell, James. *Songs of Zion: The African Methodist Episcopal Church in the United States and South Africa.* New York: Oxford University Press, 1995.

——. "T. D. Mweli Skota and the Making and Unmaking of a Black Elite." Unpublished paper presented to the University of the Witwatersrand History Workshop, 9–14 February 1987.

Campt, Tina. "Converging Spectres of an Other Within: Race and Gender in Prewar Afro-German History." *Callaloo* 26 (2003): 322–41.

Cao, Xuegin, and E. Gao. *Honglou meng* (Dream of the Red Chamber). Beijing: Renmin wenxue chubanshe, 1988.

Cappetti, Carla. *Writing Chicago: Modernism, Ethnography, and the Novel.* New York: Columbia University Press, 1993.

Carby, Hazel. *Reconstructing Womanhood: The Emergence of the Afro-American Woman Novelist*. New York: Oxford University Press, 1987.

———. "It Jus' Be's Dat Way Sometime: The Sexual Politics of Women's Blues." *Radical America* 20, no. 4 (June–July 1986): 9–24.

Chadwick, Whitney, and Tirza True Latimer, eds. *The Modern Woman Revisited: Paris between the Wars*. New Brunswick, N.J.: Rutgers University Press, 2003.

Chakrabarty, Dipesh. *Provincializing Europe: Postcolonial Thought and Historical Difference*. Princeton, N.J.: Princeton University Press, 2000.

Charlton, Susan. "In Living Memory." *Photofile: Contemporary Photomedia and Ideas* 78 (spring 2006): 34–37.

Chatterjee, Partha. *The Nation and Its Fragments*. Princeton, N.J.: Princeton University Press, 1993.

———. "The Nationalist Resolution of the Women's Question." In *Recasting Women: Essays in Colonial History*, edited by KumKum Sangari and Sudesh Vaid, 233–53. New Delhi: Kali for Women, 1989.

Chauvel, Charles, and Elsa Chauvel. *Walkabout*. London: W. H. Allen, 1959.

Chiang, Yung-chen. *Social Engineering and the Social Sciences in China, 1919–1949*. New York: Cambridge University Press, 2001.

Chicago Commission on Race Relations [Charles Johnson] (CCRR). *The Negro in Chicago: A Study of Race Relations and a Race Riot*. Chicago: University of Chicago Press, 1922.

Ciarlo, David M. "Rasse konsumieren: Von der exotischen zur kolonialen Imagination in der Bildreklame des Wilhelminischen Kaiserreichs." In *Phantasiereiche: Zur Kulturgeschichte des deutschen Kolonialismus*, edited by Birthe Kundrus, 135–79. Frankfurt am Main: Campus, 2003.

Cim, Albert. *Émancipées*. Paris: Flammarion, 1899.

Clark-Lewis, Elizabeth. " 'This Work Had a End': African-American Domestic Workers in Washington, DC, 1910–1940." In *"To Toil the Lifelong Day": America's Women at Work, 1780–1980*, edited by Carol Groneman and Mary Beth Norton, 196–213. Ithaca, N.Y.: Cornell University Press, 1987.

Cochran, Sherman. "Marketing Medicine and Advertising Dreams in China, 1900–1950." In *Becoming Chinese: Passages to Modernity and Beyond*, edited by Yeh Wen-hsin, 62–97. Berkeley: University of California Press, 2000.

———. "Transnational Origins of Advertising in Early Twentieth Century China." In S. Cochran, ed., *Inventing Nanjing Road*, 37–60.

———. *Big Business in China: Sino-Foreign Rivalry in the Cigarette Industry, 1890–1930*. Cambridge, Mass.: Harvard University Press, 1980.

Cochran, Sherman, ed. *Inventing Nanjing Road: Commercial Culture in Shanghai, 1900–1945*. Ithaca, N.Y.: Cornell University Press, 1999.

Cohen, Colleen, and Richard Wilk with Beverly Stoeltje. "Introduction: Beauty Queens on the Global Stage." In *Beauty Queens on the Global Stage: Gender, Contests, and Power*, edited by Colleen Cohen, Richard Wilk, and Beverly Stoeltje, 1–11. New York: Routledge, 1996.

Cole, Anna, "Unwitting Soldiers: The Working Life of Matron Hiscocks at the Cootamundra Girls Home." *Aboriginal History* 27 (2003): 146–61.

Collier-Thomas, Bettye. "Annie Turnbo Malone." In *Notable Black Women*, edited by Jessie Carney Smith, 724–27. Detroit: Gale Research, 1992.

Comaroff, Jean. "The Empire's Old Clothes: Fashioning the Colonial Subject." In *Cross-Cultural Consumption: Global Markets, Local Realities*, edited by David Howes, 19–38. New York: Routledge, 1996.

———. "Medicine, Colonialism, and the Black Body." In *Ethnography and the Historical Imagination*, edited by John L. Comaroff and Jean Comaroff, 215–33. Boulder, Colo.: Westview Press, 1992.

Comaroff, Jean, and John Comaroff. *Of Revelation and Revolution: The Dialectics of Modernity on a South African Frontier*. Vol. 2. Chicago: University of Chicago Press, 1996.

Comaroff, Jean, and John Comaroff, eds. *Modernity and Its Malcontents: Ritual and Power in Postcolonial Africa*. Chicago: University of Chicago Press, 1993.

Conor, Liz. *The Spectacular Modern Woman: Feminine Visibility in the 1920s*. Bloomington: Indiana University Press, 2004.

———. "The Beauty Contestant in the Photographic Scene." *Journal of Australian Studies* 71 (2001): 33–44.

Cooper, Carol. "The Aboriginal Welfare Board Photographs: Fact and Fiction." *Australian Aboriginal Studies* 1 (1985): 65–69.

Cooper, Frederick. "What Is the Concept of Globalization Good For? An African Historian's Perspective." *African Affairs* 100 (2001): 189–213.

Coplan, David. "You Have Left Me Wandering About: Basotho Women and the Culture of Mobility." In *"Wicked" Women and the Reconfiguration of Gender in Africa*, edited by Dorothy Hodgson and Sheryl McCurdy, 188–211. Portsmouth, N.H.: Heinemann, 2001.

Couzens, Timothy. *The New African: A Study of the Life and Work of H. I. E. Dhlomo*. Johannesburg: Ravan Press, 1985.

———. "'Moralizing Leisure Time': The Transatlantic Connection and Black Johannesburg (1918–1936)." In *Industrialisation and Social Change in South Africa: African Class Formation, Culture, and Consciousness, 1870–1930*, edited by Shula Marks and Richard Rathbone, 314–37. New York: Longman, 1982.

———. "A Short History of 'World' (and other Black SA Newspapers)." *Insipan Journal* 1, no. 1 (1978): 69–92.

Cowling, Donald S. "Will the Vogue for Tan Last?" *Printers' Ink Monthly*, August 1929.

Cox, Randi. "All This Can Be Yours! Soviet Commercial Advertising and the Social Construction of Space, 1928–1956." In *The Landscape of Stalinism: The Art and Ideology of Soviet Space*, edited by Evgeny Dobrenko and Eric Naiman, 125–62. Seattle: University of Washington Press, 2003.

Craig, Maxine. *Ain't I a Beauty Queen? Black Women, Beauty, and the Politics of Race*. Oxford: Oxford University Press, 2002.

Crow, Carl. *Four Hundred Million Customers: The Experiences — Some Happy, Some Sad of an American in China, and What They Taught Him*. New York: Harper and Brothers, 1937.

Damon-Moore, Helen. *Magazines for Millions: Gender and Commerce in the Ladies' Home Journal and the Saturday Evening Post, 1880–1910*. Albany: State University of New York, 1994.

Dangarembga, Tsitsi. *Nervous Conditions: A Novel*. Seattle: Seal Press, 1989.

David-Fox, Michael. "The Fellow Travelers Revisited: The 'Cultured West' through Soviet Eyes." *Journal of Modern History* 75 (June 2003): 300–335.

Davis, Angela. *Blues Legacies and Black Feminism: Gertrude "Ma" Rainey, Bessie Smith, and Billie Holiday*. New York: Pantheon Books, 1998.

Davis, Simone Weil. *Living Up to the Ads: Gender Fictions of the 1920s*. Durham, N.C.: Duke University Press, 2000.

Dean, Carolyn J. *The Frail Social Body: Pornography, Homosexuality, and Other Fantasies in Interwar France*. Berkeley: University of California Press, 2000.

Dhlomo, Rolfes Robert Reginald. *An African Tragedy*. Alice: Lovedale Institution Press, 1920.

Die Femme Fatale im Tempo der Großstadt: Der Meister-Designer Jupp Wiertz, 1888–1939. Aachen: Suermundt-Ludwig-Museum, 2003.

Dikobe, Modikwe. *The Marabi Dance*. London: Heinemann, 1973.

Directory and Chronicle for China, Japan, Corea, Indo-China, Straits Settlements, Malay States, Siam, Netherlands India, Borneo, the Philippines, &c. Hong Kong: Hong Kong Daily Press Office, 1930.

Doan, Laura. *Fashioning Sapphism: The Origins of a Modern English Lesbian Culture*. New York: Columbia University Press, 2001.

Donham, Donald. *Marxist Modern: An Ethnographic History of the Ethiopian Revolution*. Berkeley: University of California Press, 1999.

Dovesti do kontsa bor'bu s nepmanskoi muzykoi. Moscow-Leningrad: Gos. Muzykal'noi izdatel'stvo, 1931.

Drake, St. Clair, and Horace Cayton. *Black Metropolis: A Study of Negro Life in a Northern City.* 2 vols. New York: Harper and Row, 1945.

Driscoll, Catherine. *Girls: Feminine Adolescence in Popular Culture and Cultural Theory.* New York: Columbia University Press, 2002.

Du Bois, Marie. "The Sun-Tan Mode Arrives: What It Is Doing to a Score of Industries." *Advertising and Selling,* 1 May 1929.

——. "What Is Sun-Tan Doing to Cosmetics?" *Advertising and Selling,* 12 January 1929.

Duncan-Kemp, A. M. *Where Strange Paths Go Down.* Brisbane: W. R. Smith and Patterson, 1964.

Duranty, Walter. *Duranty Reports Russia.* New York: Viking Press, 1934.

Eales, Kathy. "Patriarchs, Passes, and Privilege: Johannesburg's African Middle Classes and the Question of Night Passes for African Women, 1920–1932." In *Holding Their Ground: Class, Locality, and Culture in Nineteenth- and Twentieth-Century South Africa,* edited by Philip Bonner, Isabel Hofmeyr, Deborah James, and Tom Lodge, 105–39. Johannesburg: Witwatersrand University Press, 1989.

Edgar, Robert. *An African-American in South Africa: The Travel Notes of Ralph J. Bunche, 28 September 1937–1 January 1938.* Athens: Ohio University Press, 1992.

Edwards, Brent. *The Practice of Diaspora: Literature, Translation, and the Rise of Black Internationalism.* Cambridge, Mass.: Harvard University Press, 2003.

Edwards, Louise. "Policing the Modern Woman in Republican China." *Modern China* 26, no. 2 (April 2000): 115–47.

Edwards, Paul. *The Southern Urban Negro as Consumer.* 1932. New York: Negro Universities Press, 1969.

Ehrenburg, Ilya. *Memoirs: 1921–1941.* Translated by Tatania Shebunia. New York: Grosset and Dunlap, 1966.

Elam, Diane. *Feminism and Deconstruction.* New York: Routledge, 1994.

Ellinghaus, Katherine. "Absorbing the 'Aboriginal Problem': Controlling Interracial Marriage in Australia in the Late Nineteenth and Early Twentieth Centuries." *Aboriginal History* 27 (2003): 183–207.

Endo, Ryukichi. *Modern Sociology* (Jindai shehuixue). Translated by Tan Shougong. Shanghai: Taidong tushu yinshuguan, 1920.

Enstad, Nan. *Ladies of Labor, Girls of Adventure: Working Women, Popular Culture, and Labor Politics at the Turn of the Twentieth Century.* New York: Columbia University Press, 1999.

Erenberg, Lewis A. *Steppin' Out: New York Nightlife and the Transformation of American Culture, 1890–1930*. Westport, Conn.: Greenwood Press, 1981.

Erlank, Natasha. "Gender and Masculinity in South African Nationalist Discourse, 1912–1950." *Feminist Studies* 29, no. 3 (2003): 653–71.

Erlmann, Veit. " 'A Feeling of Prejudice': Orpheus M. McAdoo and the Virginia Jubilee Singers in South Africa, 1890–1898." In *African Stars: Studies in Black South African Performance*, 21–53. Chicago: University of Chicago Press, 1991.

Evans, Linda. "Claude Barnett and the Associated Negro Press." *Chicago History: The Magazine of the Chicago Historical Society* 12, no. 1 (spring 1983): 44–56.

Ewing, Elizabeth. *History of Twentieth Century Fashion*. London: B.T. Batsford, 1974.

Fabian, Johannes. *Time and the Other: How Anthropology Makes Its Object*. New York: Columbia University Press, 1983.

Fehrenbach, Heide, and Uta G. Poiger, eds. *Transactions, Transgressions, Transformations: American Culture in Western Europe and Japan*. New York: Berghahn Books, 2000.

Felski, Rita. *The Gender of Modernity*. Cambridge, Mass.: Harvard University Press, 1995.

Ferguson, James. *Expectations of Modernity: Myths and Meaning of Urban Life on the Zambian Copperbelt*. Berkeley: University of California Press, 1999.

Fields, Mamie Garvin. *Lemon Swamp and Other Places: A Carolina Memoir*. New York: Free Press, 1983.

Finamore, Michelle Tolini. "Fashioning the Colonial at the Paris Expositions, 1925 and 1931." *Fashion Theory* 7 (2003): 345–360.

Finnegan, Margaret. *Selling Suffrage: Consumer Culture and Votes for Women*. New York: Columbia University Press, 1999.

Fischer, Lucy. *Designing Women: Cinema, Art Deco, and the Female Form*. New York: Columbia University Press, 2003.

Flashback: Cinema in the Times of India. Bombay: Times of India, 1990.

Foley, Barbara. *Spectres of 1919: Class and Nation in the Making of the New Negro*. Urbana: University of Illinois Press, 2003.

Forbes, Geraldine. *Women in Modern India*, Cambridge: Cambridge University Press, 1996.

Foucault, Michel. "Technologies of the Self." In *Technologies of the Self: A Seminar with Michel Foucault*, edited by Luther H. Martin, Huck Gutman, and Patrick Hutton, 16–49. Amherst: University of Massachusetts Press, 1988.

Frank, Stephen P. "Simple Folk, Savage Customs? Youth, Sociability, and the Dynamics of Culture in Rural Russia, 1856–1914." *Journal of Social History* 25, no. 4 (1992): 711–36.

Fraser, James, Steven Heller, and Seymour Chwast. *Japanese Modern: Graphic Design between the Wars*. San Francisco: Chronicle Books, 1996.

Friedrich, Arnold. *Anschläge: Deutsche Plakate als Dokumente der Zeit, 1900–1960*. Eberhausen: Langewiesche-Brandt, 1963.

Fromm, Erich. *The Working Class in Weimar Germany: A Psychological and Sociological Study*. Lemington Spa: Berg, 1984. Originally published in German in 1929.

Fujinkai, ed. *Yūgaku Annai: Tokyo no Jogakkō* (Guide for Studying in Girls' Schools in Tokyo). Fujinkai Rinji Zokan vol. 2, no. 5. Tokyo: Fujinkai, 1903.

Fynn, H. F. *The Diary of Henry Francis Fynn*. Edited by James Stuart and D. McK. Malcolm. Pietermaritzburg: Shuter and Shooter, 1950.

Gallichio, Marc. *The African American Encounter with Japan and China: Black Internationalism in Asia, 1895–1945*. Chapel Hill: University of North Carolina Press, 2000.

Gandhi, M. K. *Women and Social Injustice*. Ahmedabad: Navjivan Publishing House, 1947.

Gaonkar, Dilip. "On Alternative Modernities." *Public Culture* 11 (1999): 1–18.

Gardner, Viv, and Susan Rutherford, eds. *The New Woman and Her Sisters: Feminism and Theatre, 1850–1914*. New York: Harvester Wheatsheaf, 1992.

Garga, B. D. *So Many Cinemas: The Motion Picture in India*. Mumbai: Eminence Designs, 1996.

Gates, Henry Louis Jr., and Gene Andrew Jarrett, eds. *The New Negro: Readings on Race, Representation, and African American Culture, 1892–1938*. Princeton: Princeton University Press, 2007.

Gems, Gerald. "Blocked Shot: The Development of Basketball in the African American Community of Chicago." *Journal of Sports History* (Summer 1995): 135–48.

Giles, Judith, and Tim Middleton. *Studying Culture*. Oxford: Blackwell, 1999.

Gill, Tiffany. "Civic Beauty: Beauty Culturists and the Politics of Female African American Entrepreneurship." Ph.D. diss. Rutgers University, 2003.

Glazier Schuster, Ilsa M. *New Women of Lusaka*. Palo Alto: Mayfield Publishing Company, 1979.

Glenn, Susan. *Female Spectacle: The Theatrical Roots of Modern Feminism*. Cambridge, Mass.: Harvard University Press, 2000.

Glennie, Paul. "Consumption within Historical Studies." In *Acknowledging Consumption,* edited by Daniel Miller, 164–203. London: Routledge, 1995.

Glosser, Susan L. " 'The Truth I Have Learned': Nationalism, Family Reform, and Male Identity in China's New Cultural Movement, 1915–1923." In *Chinese Femininities, Chinese Masculinities: A Reader,* edited by Susan Brownell and Jeffrey N. Wasserstrom, 120–48. Berkeley: University of California Press, 2002.

Goldfuß, Gabriele. "Die Gelben kommen: Große Massen, kleine Füße — Körperbilder des Asiaten." In *Fremdkörper — Fremde Körper: Von unvermeidlichen Kontakten und widerstreitenden Gefühlen,* 210–17. Ostfildern-Ruit: Haatje Cantz, 1999.

Goldsmith, Meredith. "Shopping to Pass, Passing to Shop: Bodily Self-Fashioning in the Fiction of Nella Larsen." In *Recovering the Black Female Body: Self-Representations by African American Women,* edited by Michael Bennett and Vanessa D. Dickerson, 97–120. New Brunswick, N.J.: Rutgers University Press, 2001.

Goodhew, David. *Respectability and Resistance: A History of Sophiatown.* Westport, Conn.: Praeger, 2004.

——. "Working-Class Respectability: The Example of the Western Areas of Johannesburg, 1930–55." *Journal of African History* 41, no. 2 (2000): 241–66.

Goodman, Bryna. "The Vocational Woman and the Elusiveness of 'Personhood' in Early Republican China." In *Gender in Motion: Divisions of Labor and Cultural Change in Late Imperial and Modern China,* edited by Bryna Goodman and Wendy Larson, 265–86. New York: Rowman and Littlefield, 2005.

——. "Semi-Colonialism, Transnational Networks and News Flows in Early Republican Shanghai." *China Review* 4 (2004): 55–88.

Goomilevsky, Lev. *Dog Lane.* London: 1927.

Gorsuch, Anne E. *Youth in Revolutionary Russia: Enthusiasts, Bohemians, Delinquents.* Bloomington: Indiana University Press, 2000.

——. " 'A Woman Is Not a Man': The Culture of Gender and Generation in Soviet Russia." *Slavic Review* 55, no.3 (fall 1996): 636–60.

Goscilo, Helena. "Keeping A-Breast of the Waist-Land: Women's Fashion in Early Nineteenth-Century Russia." In *Russia. Women. Culture*, edited by Helena Goscilo and Beth Holmgren, 31–63. Bloomington: Indiana University Press, 1996.

Grewal, Inderpal. *Home and Harem: Nation, Gender, Empire, and the Cultures of Travel.* Durham, N.C.: Duke University Press, 1996.

Gries, Rainer. *Produkte als Medien: Kulturgeschichte der Produktkommunikation in der Bundesrepublik und der DDR.* Leipzig: Leipziger Universitaetsverlag, 2003.

Grigorov, G., and S. Shkotov. *Staryi i novyi byt.* Moscow: Molodaia gvardiia, 1927.

Gronow, Jukka. *Caviar with Champagne: Common Luxury and the Ideals of the Good Life in Stalin's Russia.* Oxford: Berg, 2003.

Grossmann, Atina. "Girlkultur, or Thoroughly Rationalized Female?" In *Women in Culture and Politics: A Century of Change,* edited by Judith Friedlander, 62–80. Bloomington: Indiana University Press, 1986.

Guenther, Irene. *Nazi Chic? Fashioning Women in the Third Reich.* Oxford: Berg, 2003.

Guo, Jianying. *Modeng Shanghai: 30 niandai de yangchang baijing.* Edited by Chen Zishan. Guilin: Guangxi shifan daxue chubanshe, 2001.

Gyp. *Autour de mariage.* Paris: Calmann-Levy, 1883.

Halberstam, Judith. *Female Masculinity.* Durham, N.C.: Duke University Press, 1998.

Hall, Stuart. "Race, Articulation and Societies Structured in Dominance." In *Black British Cultural Studies: A Reader,* edited by Houston A. Baker, Manthia Diawara, and Ruth H. Lindborg, 16–60. Chicago: University of Chicago Press, 1996.

———. "Encoding and Decoding." In *Culture, Media, Language,* edited by Stuart Hall, Dorothy Hobson, Andrew Lowe, and Paul Willis, 128–38. London: Unwin Hyman, 1980.

Handbook on the Protection of Trade-Marks, Patents, Copyrights and Trade-Names in China. Shanghai: Kelly and Walsh, 1924.

Hansen, Claudia. *Nivea: Evolution of a World-Famous Brand.* Hamburg: Beiersdorf, 2001.

Hansen, Karen Tranberg, ed. *African Encounters with Domesticity.* New Brunswick, N.J.: Rutgers University Press, 1992.

Harlan, Louis, and Raymond Smock. *The Booker T. Washington Papers.* Vol. 2, *1911–1912.* Urbana: University of Illinois Press, 1981.

Harnisch, Antje, "Der Harem in Familienblättern des 19. Jahrhunderts: Koloniale Phantasien und Nationale Identität." *German Life and Letters* 51 (July 1998): 325–41.

Harootunian, Harry. *History's Disquiet: Modernity, Cultural Practice, and the Question of Everyday Life.* New York: Columbia University Press, 2000.

———. *Overcome by Modernity: History, Culture, and Community in Interwar Japan.* Princeton, N.J.: Princeton University Press, 2000.

Harrison, Mark. *Climates and Constitutions: Health, Race, Environment and British Imperialism in India, 1600–1850.* New York: Oxford University Press, 1999.

Hart, Gillian. "Denaturalizing Dispossession: Critical Ethnography in the Age of Resurgent Imperialism." Paper presented at Center for Place, Culture and Politics, CUNY Graduate Center, New York, 15–17 April 2004.

Harvey, David. *The Condition of Postmodernity: An Enquiry into the Origins of Cultural Change.* Oxford: Blackwell, 1989.

Haskins, Victoria, " 'A Better Chance?' — Sexual Abuse and the Apprenticeship of Aboriginal Girls under the NSW Aborigines Protection Board." *Aboriginal History* 28 (2004): 33–58.

Hau, Michael. *The Cult of Health and Beauty in Germany: A Social History, 1890–1930.* Chicago: University of Chicago Press, 2003.

Hause, Stephen. *Women's Suffrage and Social Politics in the French Third Republic.* Princeton, N.J.: Princeton University Press, 1984.

Hawes, C. J. *Poor Relations: The Making of a Eurasian Community in British India, 1773–1833.* London: Curzon, 1996.

Hayase, Toshiyuki. *Marie Louise: Kyūtei Fukusō Komon* (Marie Louise: Dress Advisor to the Court). Tokyo: Kōdansha Shuppan Service, 2003.

Healy, Dan. *Homosexual Desire in Revolutionary Russia: The Regulation of Sexual and Gender Dissent.* Chicago: University of Chicago Press, 2001.

Heath, Stephen. "Joan Riviere and the Masquerade." In *Formations of Fantasy*, edited by Victor Burgin et al., 45–61. London: Methuen, 1986.

Held, David, Anthony McGrew, David Goldblatt, and Jonathan Perraton. *Global Transformations: Politics, Economics, Culture.* Stanford, Calif.: Stanford University Press, 1999.

Heller, Steven, and Louise Fili. *German Modern: Graphic Design from Wilhelm to Weimar.* San Francisco: Chronicle Books, 1998.

Hellmann, Ellen. *Rooiyard: A Sociological Survey of an Urban Native Slum Yard.* Cape Town: Oxford University Press, 1948.

———. "Native Life in a Johannesburg Slum Yard." *Africa* 8, no. 1 (1935): 34–62.

Herzog, Dagmar. *Sex after Fascism: Memory and Morality in Twentieth-Century Germany.* Princeton, N.J.: Princeton University Press, 2005.

Hewitt, Kathleen Douglas, ed. *Us Women: Extracts from the Writings of Marjorie Mensah.* London: Elkin Mathews and Marrot, 1933.

Higa, Mitsuko. *Sugao no Iha Fuyū* (An Unretouched Portrait of Iha Fuyū). Naha: Niraisha, 1997.

Higginbotham, Evelyn Brooks. *Righteous Discontent: The Women's Move-*

ment in the Black Baptist Church, 1880–1920. Cambridge, Mass.: Harvard University Press, 1993.

Hinz, Manfred O., Helgard Patemann, and Arnim Meier, eds. *Weiss auf Schwarz: 100 Jahre Einmischung in Afrika: Deutscher Kolonialismus und afrikanischer Widerstand.* Berlin: Elefanten Press, 1984.

Hodgson, Dorothy, and Sheryl McCurdy, eds., *"Wicked" Women and the Reconfiguration of Gender in Africa.* Portsmouth, N.H.: Heinemann Books, 2001.

Hoffmann, David L. *Stalinist Values: The Cultural Norms of Soviet Modernity.* Ithaca, N.Y.: Cornell University Press, 2003.

Hoffmann, David L., and Yanni Kotsonis, eds. *Russian Modernity: Politics, Knowledge, Practices.* New York: St. Martin's Press, 2000.

Hofmeyr, Isabel. *The Portable Bunyan: A Transnational History of "The Pilgrim's Progress."* Princeton, N.J.: Princeton University Press, 2004.

Hoggart, Richard. *The Uses of Literacy.* London: Chatto and Windus, 1957.

Hokama, Shuzen. *Okinawa no Gengoshi* (The History of Okinawan Language). Tokyo: Hōsei Daigaku Shuppankyoku, 1971.

Hokama, Yoneko, and Ryūkyū Shimpōsha, eds. *Jidai wo Irodotta Onnatachi: Kindai Okinawa Joseishi* (Notable Women of an Era: Modern Okinawan Women's History). Naha: Niraisha, 1996.

Hollinsworth, David, *Race and Racism in Australia,* Katoomba, NSW: Social Science Press, 1998.

Horiba, Kiyoko. *"Inaguya Nanabachi": Okinawa Joseishi wo Saguru.* "Inaguya Nanabachi" (Women are born with seven penances): Exploring Okinawan Women's History. Tokyo: Domesu Shuppan, 1990.

Hosoi, Wakizō, and Toshio Takai. *Watashi no jokō aishi.* Tokyo: Horupu Shuppan, 1983.

Hostetler, Ann E. "The Aesthetics of Race and Gender in Nella Larsen's *Quicksand.*" *PMLA* 105 (1990): 35–46.

Huggins, Jackie, " 'Firing on in the Mind.' " *Hecate* 13, no. 2 (1987–88): 5–23.

Hughes, Athol, ed. *The Inner World and Joan Riviere: Collected Papers, 1920–1958.* London: Karnac Books, 1991.

Hullinger, Edwin Ware. *The Reforging of Russia.* New York: E. P. Dutton, 1925.

Hunt, Lynn. *Politics, Culture, and Class in the French Revolution.* Berkeley: University of California Press, 1989.

Hunter, Monica. *Reaction to Conquest: Effects of Contact with Europeans on the Pondo of South Africa.* London: Oxford University Press, 1936.

Hutchinson, George. "Subject to Disappearance: Interracial Identity in Nella Larsen's *Quicksand.*" In *Temples for Tomorrow*, edited by Genevieve Fabre and Michel Keith, 177–90. Bloomington: Indiana University Press, 2001.

——. "Nella Larsen and the Veil of Race." *American Literary History* 9, no. 2 (Summer 1997): 329–49.

Hutt, Jonathan. "La Maison D'or—The Sumptuous World of Shao Xunmen." *East Asian History* 21 (June 2001): 111–42.

Iha, Fuyū, with Majikina Ankō. *Okinawa Joseishi* (History of Okinawan Women). Tokyo: Heibonsha, 2000.

Iha Fuyū Seitan Hyakunen Kinenkai, ed. *Seitan Hyakunen Kinen Arubamu Iha Fuyū* (Album of Iha Fuyū, Commemorating His 100th anniversary). Naha, 1976.

Iliffe, John. *Honour in African History.* Cambridge: Cambridge University Press, 2005.

Indian Cinema: Contemporary Perceptions from the Thirties. Jamshedpur: Celluloid Chapter, 1993.

Indian Cinematographic Committee Report, 1927–28, Madras: Government of India, 1928

Isaacs, Nathaniel. *Travels and Adventures in Eastern Africa.* 1836. Edited by Louis Herrmann and Percival Kirby. Cape Town: C. Struik, 1970.

Jackson, Jerma. "Testifying at the Cross: Thomas Dorsey, Sister Rosetta Tharpe and the Politics of African-American Sacred and Secular Music." Ph.D. diss., Rutgers University, 1995.

Jacobsen, Matthew Frye. *Whiteness of a Different Color: European Immigrants and the Alchemy of Race.* Cambridge, Mass.: Harvard University Press, 1998.

James, Harold. *The End of Globalization: Lessons from the Great Depression.* Cambridge. Mass.: Harvard University Press, 2001.

Jami, Irène. "*La Fronde* (1897–1903) et son rôle dans la défense des femmes salariées." Mémoire de Maîtrise, Université de Paris I, 1981.

Jeater, Diana. *Marriage, Perversion and Power: The Construction of Moral Discourse in Southern Rhodesia, 1894–1930.* New York: Oxford University Press, 1993.

John, Mary, and Janaki Nair. Introduction to *A Question of Silence: The Sexual Economies of Modern India,* edited by Mary John and Janaki Nair, 1–51. New Delhi: Kali for Women, 1998.

Johnson, James Weldon. *Along This Way: The Autobiography of James Weldon Johnson.* New York: Viking Press, 1933.

Jones, Andrew. *Yellow Music: Media Culture and Colonial Modernity in the Chinese Jazz Age.* Durham, N.C.: Duke University Press, 2001.

Joshi, Sanjay. *Fractured Modernity: Making of a Middle Class in Colonial North India*. New Delhi: Oxford University Press, 2001.

Jun Zuo. "New Thought and New Art, Sociological Research Method" (Xin sixiang yu xin wenyi, shehuixue de janjiu fa). *DFZZ* 18, no. 21 (1922): 73–77.

Kaes, Anton, Martin Jay, and Edward Dimendberg, eds. *The Weimar Republic Sourcebook*. Berkeley: University of California Press, 1994.

Kaestle, Carl K. "The History of Readers." In *Literacy in the United States: Readers and Reading since 1880*, edited by Carl F. Kaestle, Helen Damon-Moore, Lawrence C. Stedman, Katherine Tinsley and William Vance Trollinger Jr., 33–74. New Haven, Conn.: Yale University Press, 1991.

Kagan, A. G. *Molodezh' posle gudka*. Moscow-Leningrad: Molodaia gvardiia, 1930.

Kataoka, Teppei. *Modan Gāru no Kenkyu* (A Study of Modern Girl). Tokyo: Kinseidō, 1927.

Katayama, Seiichi. *Kindai Nihon no joshi kyōiku*. Tokyo: Kenpakusha, 1984.

Kawabata, Tokurō, et al., eds. *Himeyuri no Kaori* (The Scent of Star Lily). Naha: Himeyurikai, 1937.

Kelly, Catriona, and Vadim Volkov. "Directed Desires: *Kul'turnost'* and Consumption." In *Constructing Russian Culture in the Age of Revolution, 1881–1940*, edited by Catriona Kelly and David Shepard, 241–313. Oxford: Oxford University Press, 1998.

Kemp, Amanda. " 'Up from Slavery' and Other Narratives: Black South African Performances of the American Negro (1920–1943)." Ph.D. diss., Northwestern University, 1997.

Kenez, Peter. *Cinema and Soviet Society, 1917–1953*. Cambridge: Cambridge University Press, 1992.

Kerr, Joan, ed. "Vic Cowdroy." In *Heritage: The National Women's Art Book*. Sydney: Craftsman House, 1995.

Kessemeier, Gesa. *Sportlich, sachlich, männlich: Das Bild der "Neuen Frau" in den Zwanziger Jahren: Zur Konstruktion geschlechtsspezifischer Körperbilder in der Mode der Jahre 1920 bis 1929*. Dortmund: Edition Ebersbach, 2000.

Kiaer, Christina, and Eric Naiman. *Everyday Life in Early Soviet Russia: Taking the Revolution Inside*. Bloomington: Indiana University Press, 2005.

Kinjō, Seitoku, and Takara Kurayoshi. *Iha Fuyū: Okinawashizō to sono Shisō* (Iha Fuyū: His Image of Okinawan History and Thoughts). Tokyo: Shimizu Shoin, 1972.

Kinjō, Yoshiko. *Okinawa wo Kataru* (On Okinawa). Naha: Niraisha, 1988.

———. *Naha Onna Ichidaiki* (Life Story of a Naha Woman). Tokyo: Horupu, 1980.

Klejman, Laurence, and Florence Rochefort. *L'Egalité en marche: Le Féminisme sous la Troisième République*. Paris: des femmes, 1989.

Klotz, Marcia. Introduction and "Global Visions: From the Colonial to the National Socialist World." Special issue on German colonialism, *European Studies Journal* 16 (fall 1999): 1–8, 37–68.

Knapp, Alfred. *Reklame, Propaganda, Werbung: Ihre Weltorganisation*. Berlin: Verlag fuer Presse, Wirtschaft und Politik, 1929.

Knauft, Bruce M., ed. *Critically Modern: Alternatives, Alterities, Anthropologies*. Bloomington: Indiana University Press, 2002.

Ko, Dorothy. *Teachers of the Inner Chambers: Women and Culture in Seventeenth-Century China*. Stanford, Calif.: Stanford University Press, 1994.

Ko, Ikujo (Hung, Yuru). "Shokuminchi Taiwan ni okeru Fashion to Kenryoku (Fashion and Colonial Power in Taiwan)." *Setsuzoku* 4 (2004): 2–20.

Koenker, Diane P. "Men against Women on the Shop Floor in Early Soviet Russia: Gender and Class in the Socialist Workplace." *American Historical Review* 160, no. 5 (December 1995): 1438–64.

Koepnick, Lutz. *The Dark Mirror: German Cinema between Hitler and Hollywood*. Berkeley: University of California Press, 2002.

Kohiyama, Rui. "Not Imitation but Practicality: Missionary Higher Education for Women and the Modern Girl." In *Interim Report on the Research Project "Modern Girl and Colonial Modernity in East Asia (2003–2006),"* 7–24. Tokyo: Ochanomizu University, 2005.

Kolesnikov, L. *Litso klassovogo vraga*. Moscow: Molodaia gvardia, 1928.

Komagome, Takeshi. *Shokuminchi Teikoku Nihon no Bunka Tōgo* (Cultural Integration in the Japanese Colonial Empire). Tokyo: Iwanami Shoten, 1996.

Kostrov, T. "Kul'tura i meshchantsvo." *Revoliutsiia i kul'tura*, 3–4 (1927): 110.

Kracauer, Siegfried. "Photography." In *The Mass Ornament: Weimar Essays*, translated, edited, and with an introduction by Thomas Levin. Cambridge, Mass.: Harvard University Press, 1995.

Kumar, Radha. *The History of Doing*. New Delhi: Zubaan, 2003.

Lacan, Jacques. "The Signification of the Phallus." *Ecrits*. Translated by Alan Sheridan. New York: W. W. Norton, 1977.

Laing, Ellen Johnston. *Selling Happiness: Calendar Posters and Visual Culture in Early Twentieth-Century Shanghai*. Honolulu: University of Hawaii Press, 2004.

———. "The Fate of Shanghai Painting Style in Early Twentieth-Century Printed Advertising." In *Hai pai hui hua yan jiu wen ji* (Studies on Shanghai School Painting). Shanghai: Shanghai shuhua chubanshe, 2001.

Lake, Marilyn. *Getting Equal: The History of Australian Feminism.* St. Leonards, NSW: Allen and Unwin, 1999.

La Nauze, J. A. *Alfred Deakin.* Vol. 1. Melbourne: Oxford University Press, 1962.

Landau, Paul S., and Deborah D. Kaspin. *Images and Empires: Visuality in Colonial and Postcolonial Africa.* Berkeley: University of California Press, 2002.

Langford, Ruby, and Susan Hampton. *Don't Take Your Love to Town.* Ringwood, Victoria: Penguin, 1988.

Larkin, Brian. "Indian Films and Nigerian Lovers: Media and the Creation of Parallel Modernities." *Africa* 67 (1997): 406–40.

Larsen, Nella. *"Quicksand" and "Passing."* Edited by Deborah E. McDowell. New Brunswick, N.J.: Rutgers University Press, 1986.

Latham, Angela J. *Posing a Threat: Flappers, Chorus Girls, and Other Brazen Performers of the American 1920s.* Hanover, N.H.: University Press of New England for Wesleyan University Press, 2000.

Latsis, A. E., and L. Kellina. *Deti i kino.* Moscow: Tea-kino-pechat,' 1928.

Laurence, Patricia. *Lily Briscoe's Chinese Eyes: Bloomsbury, Modernism, and China.* Columbia: University of South Carolina Press, 2003.

Lebina, N. B. "Molodezh i NEP: Ot konflikta k edinstvu subkul'tur." Paper presented at the conference "Youth in Soviet Russia, 1917–1941," Marburg, Germany, May 1999.

Ledger, Sally, and Scott McCracken, eds. *Cultural Politics at the Fin de Siècle.* Cambridge: Cambridge University Press, 1995.

Lee, Robert. *Orientals: Asian Americans in Popular Culture.* Philadelphia: Temple University Press, 1999.

Lefebvre, Henri. *Critique of Everyday Life.* Translated by John Moore. Vol. 1. New York: Verso Press, 1991.

Leyda, Jay. *Kino: A History of the Russian and Soviet Film.* 3rd ed. Princeton, N.J.: Princeton University Press, 1983.

Li Yensheng. *A Bibliographic History of Chinese Newspapers and Periodicals* (Zhongguo baokan tushi). Hankou: Hubei renmin chubanshe, 2005.

Lidin, Vladimir. *The Price of Life.* Translated by Helen Chrouschoff Matheson. Westport, Conn: Hyperion Press, 1973.

Liechty, Mark. *Suitably Modern: Making Middle-Class Culture in a New Consumer Society.* Princeton, N.J.: Princeton University Press, 2003.

Lindesay, Vane. *Drawing from Life: A History of the Australian Black and White Artist's Club.* Sydney: State Library of New South Wales Press, 1994.

Liu Shuqin. "From Natural Sociology to Cultural Sociology" (Cong ziran shehuixue xiang wenhua de shehuixue). *DFZZ* 23, no.19 (1926): 57–70.

Lo, Jiu-jung, "Historical Narrative and Literary Representation: The Death of a Woman Spy in the Discourse of Modern Chinese Nationalism and Gender Relations." *Jindai Zhongguo funu shi yanjiu* 11 (December 2003): 47–98.

Locke, Alain. *Voices of the Harlem Renaissance.* New York: Albert and Charles Boni, 1925.

Looking Back, 1896–1960. New Delhi: Directorate of Film Festivals, 1981.

Lott, Tommy I. *The Invention of Race: Black Culture and the Politics of Representation.* Oxford: Blackwell, 1991.

Lowe, Donald M. *The Body in Late Capitalist USA.* Durham, N.C.: Duke University Press, 1995.

Ludden, David. *India and South Asia: A Short History.* Oxford: Oneworld Publications, 2002.

Lutes, Jean Marie. "Making Up Race: Jessie Fauset, Nella Larsen, and the African American Cosmetics Industry." *Arizona Quarterly* 28, no.1 (spring 2002): 77–108.

Lydon, Jane. *Eye Contact: Photographing Indigenous Australians.* Durham, N.C.: Duke University Press, 2005.

Ma, Guoliang. *Liangyou yi jiu: Yijia huabao yu yige shidai.* Beijing: Sanlian shudian, 2002.

Maezato, Taizan. "Yabu no naka no Kanaria" (A Canary in the Bush). *Aoi Umi* 12, no.1 (1981): 32–37.

Majumdar, Neepa. "Female Stardom and Cinema in India, 1930s to 1950s." Ph.D. diss., Indiana University, 2001.

Makiminato, Tokuzō. *Gensō no Machi, Naha* (Naha, the City of Fantasy). Tokyo: Shinjuku Shobō, 1986.

Maltby, Richard, ed. *Dreams for Sale: Popular Culture in the Twentieth Century.* London: Harrap, 1989.

Mann, Susan. "Grooming a Daughter for Marriage: Brides and Wives in the Mid-Qing Period." In *Chinese Femininities, Chinese Masculinity: A Reader*, edited by Susan Brownell and Jeffrey N. Wasserstrom, 93–109. Berkeley: University of California Press, 2002.

Marchand, Roland. *Advertising the American Dream: Making Way for Modernity, 1920–1940.* Berkeley: University of California Press, 1985.

Marcus, Julie. *A Dark Smudge upon the Sand: Essays on Race, Guilt and National Consciousness.* New South Wales: Lhr Press, 1999.

Margueritte, Paul, and Victor Margueritte. *Les Femmes nouvelles.* Paris: E. Plon, Nourrit et Cie, 1899.

Margueritte, Victor. *La Garçonne.* Paris: Flammarion, 1922.

Marks, Patricia. *Bicycles, Bangs and Bloomers: The New Woman in the Popular Press.* Lexington: University of Kentucky Press, 1990.

Marks, Shula. "Patriotism, Patriarchy and Purity: Natal and the Politics of Zulu Ethnic Consciousness." In *The Creation of Tribalism in Southern Africa*, edited by Leroy Vail, 215–40. Berkeley: University of California Press, 1991.

Martin, Wendy. "Remembering the Jungle: Josephine Baker and Modernist Parody," 310–325. In *Prehistories of the Future: The Primitivist Project and the Culture of Modernism*, edited by Elazar Barkan and Ronald Bush, 310–25. Stanford, Calif.: Stanford University Press, 1995.

Matthews, Jill Jilius. "Building the Body Beautiful." *Australian Feminist Studies* 5 (summer 1987): 17–34.

Maxwell, Anne. *Colonial Photography and Exhibitions: Representations of the "Native" and the Making of European Identities*. London: Leicester University Press, 1999.

Mayakovsky, Vladimir. *The Bedbug and Selected Poetry*. Edited by Patricia Blake. New York: Meridian Books, 1960.

Maynes, Mary Jo, Brigitte Søland, and Christina Benninghaus. *Secret Gardens, Satanic Mills: Placing Girls in European History, 1750–1960*. Bloomington: Indiana University Press, 2005.

McCabe, Tracy. "The Multifaceted Politics of Primitivism in Harlem Renaissance Writing." *Soundings* 80, no. 4 (winter 1997): 475–97.

McClintock, Anne. *Imperial Leather: Race, Gender, and Sexuality in the Colonial Conquest*. New York: Routledge, 1995.

McLees, Ainslie Armstrong. *Baudelaire's "Argot Plastique": Poetic Caricature and Modernism*. Athens: University of Georgia Press, 1989.

Meech, Julie, and Gariel Weisberg, eds. *Japonisme Comes to America: The Japanese Impact on the Graphic Arts, 1876–1925*. New York: Abrams, 1990.

Meskimmon, Marsha, and Shearer West, eds. *Visions of the "Neue Frau": Women and the Visual Arts in Weimar Germany*. Brookfield, Vt.: Ashgate, 1995.

Miki, Takeshi, ed. *Naha Onna no Kiseki: Arakaki Mitoko 85 sai Kinen Shuppan* (The Itinerary of a Naha Woman: For the Commemoration of the 85th Anniversary of Arakaki Mitoko). Naha: Ushio no Kai, 1985.

Mil'chkov, Al. *Pervoe desiatiletie. Zapiski veterana komsomola*. Moscow: Molodaia gvardiia, 1965.

Mitchell, Sally. *The New Girl: Girls' Culture in England, 1880–1915*. New York: Columbia University Press, 1995.

Mitchell, W. J. T. *Picture Theory: Essays on Verbal and Visual Communication*. Chicago: University of Chicago Press, 1994.

Mizejewski, Linda. *Ziegfeld Girl: Image and Icon in Culture and Cinema*. Durham, N.C.: Duke University Press, 1999.

Modern Girl Around the World Research Group (Tani E. Barlow, Madeleine Y. Dong, Uta G. Poiger, Priti Ramamurthy, Lynn M. Thomas, and Alys Eve Weinbaum). "The Modern Girl around the World." *Gender and History* 17, no. 2 (2005): 245–94.

Mofokeng, Santu. "The Black Photo Album." In *Anthology of African and Indian Ocean Photography*, 68–75. Paris: Revue Noire, 1998.

———. "Trajectory of a Street-Photographer: South Africa 1973–1998." In *Democracy's Images: Photography and Visual Art after Apartheid*, edited by Jan-Erik Lundström and Katarina Pierre, 42–45. Umeå, Sweden: BildMuseet, 1998.

Mohan, Reena. *Of Wayward Girls and Wicked Women: Women in Indian Silent Feature Films.* Mumbai: Majlis, 1996.

Mongold, Jeanne Conway. "Annie Minerva Turnbo Malone." In *Notable American Women: The Modern Period*, edited by Barbara Sicherman and Carol Hurd Green, 700–702. Cambridge, Mass: Harvard University Press, 1980.

Moreton-Robinson, Aileen. *Talkin' Up to the White Woman: Aboriginal Women and Feminism.* St. Lucia: University of Queensland Press, 2000.

Morrow, Willie. *400 Years without a Comb.* San Diego, Calif.: Black Publishers, 1973

Moses, Claire. *French Feminism in the Nineteenth Century.* Albany: State University of New York Press, 1984.

Moses, Wilson. *The Golden Age of Black Nationalism, 1850–1925.* Hamden, Conn.: Archon Books, 1978.

Mphahlele, Ezekiel. *Down Second Avenue.* Garden City, N.Y.: Anchor Books, 1971 [1959].

Museum of Victoria. *Daughters of the Dreaming: A Photographic Exhibition of Koori Women of Southeast Australia.* 2nd ed. Melbourne: Museum of Victoria, 1994.

Muta, Kazue. " 'Ryosai Kenbo' Shiso no Hyori: Kindai Nihon no Katei Bunka to Feminizumu" (The Two Sides of 'Good Wife, Wise Mother': Modern Japanese Home Culture and Feminism). In *Onna no Bunka* (Women's Culture), Kindai Nihon Bunkaron Vol. 8, edited by T. Aoki et al., 23–46. Tokyo: Iwanami Shoten, 2000.

Muzak, Joanne. " 'The Things Which Money Could Give': The Politics of Consumption in Nella Larsen's *Quicksand.*" *Agora: An Online Graduate Journal* 2.1 (winter 2003): 1–18.

Nagamine, Shigetoshi. *Zasshi to dokusha no kindai.* Tokyo: Nihon Editor's School, 1997.

Nagoran Dōsōkai, ed. *Nagoran, Gojunen Kinenshi* (Nagoran, Fiftieth Anniversary of Alumni Association, Former Prefectural Girls' Higher School No. 3). Naha: Nagoran Dōsōkai, 1971.

Nahashi Joseishi, Henshu Iinkai, Nahashi Sōmubu Joseishitsu, eds. *Naha, Onna no Ashiato, Naha Joseishi (Kindai hen)* (Naha, Footsteps of Women. Naha Women's History [Modern Period]). Tokyo: Domesu Shuppan, 1998.

———. *Naha Joseishi Shōgenshu: Nuchinu Akashi* (Testimonies on Naha Women's History: Vindications of Life). Naha: Naha shi, 1994.

Nahashi Kikakubu Shishi Henshūshitsu, ed. *Naha Shishi Shiryōhen vol. 2, no. 7, Naha no Minzoku* (The History of Naha City, vol. 2, no. 7, Folklore of Naha). Naha: Nahashi Kikakubu Shishi Henshsūhitsu, 1979.

Naha Shuppansha, ed. *Shashinshū Mukashi Okinawa* (Album of Okinawa in the Old Days). Naha: Naha Shuppansha, 1978.

Naiman, Eric. "Revolutionary Anorexia (NEP as Female Complaint)." *Slavic and East European Journal* 37, no. 3 (1993): 542–44.

Newell, Stephanie. "White Cargoes/Black Cargoes on the West Coast of Africa: Mabel Dove's *A Woman in Jade*." In S. Newell, *Literary Culture in Colonial Ghana: "How to Play the Game of Life,"* 119–34. Bloomington: Indiana University Press, 2002.

———. *Ghanaian Popular Fiction: "Thrilling Discoveries in Conjugal Life" and Other Tales.* Athens: Ohio University Press, 2000.

———. "An Incident of Colonial Intertextuality: The Adventures of the Black Girl in her Search for Mr. Shaw." In Newell, *Ghanaian Popular Fiction*, 70–87. Athens: Ohio University Press, 2000.

Noma, Seiji. *Watashi no hansei.* Tokyo: Chikura shōbo, 1936.

Ntantala, Phyllis. *A Life's Mosaic.* Berkeley: University of California Press, 1993.

Ognyov, N. (Mihail Grigorevich Rozanov). *The Diary of a Communist Undergraduate.* Translated by Alexander Werth. New York: Payson and Clarke, 1929.

———. *Diary of a Communist Schoolboy.* Translated by Alexander Werth. New York: Payson and Clarke, 1928.

Oguma, Eiji. *Nihonjin no Kyōkai: Okinawa, Ainu, Taiwan, Chōsen, Shokuminchi Shihai kara Fukki Undō made* (The Boundary of Japanese: Okinawa, Ainu, Taiwan, Korea. From Colonial Rule to Reversion Movement). Tokyo: Shinyōsha, 1998.

Ohmann, Richard. *Selling Culture: Magazines, Markets, and Class at the Turn of the Century.* London: Verso, 1996.

Okinawaken Joshi Ichikōjo Dosokai. *Himeyuri: Joshi-Ichikōjo Enkakushi* (Himeyuri: The History of Okinawa Prefectural Women's Normal School and Girls' Higher School No.1). Naha: Okinawaken Joshi Ichikōjo Doso-kai, 1987.

Ōkōchi, Kazuo. *Nihonteki chūsan kaikyū*. Tokyo: Bungei shunjū shinsha, 1960.

Okuda, Akiko. "Shokugyō fujin no tanjō." In *Mainoritii toshite no joseishi*, edited by Akiko Okuda. Tokyo: Keisō shobō, 1997.

Oliver, Paul. *Songsters and Saints: Vocal Traditions on Race Records*. New York: Cambridge University Press, 1984.

———. "Research on Feng Xiaoqing" (Feng Xiaoqing kao). *FNZZ* 10, no. 11, November 1924.

Osborne, Peter. *How to Read Marx*. New York: W. W. Norton, 2005.

Pan Guangdan. *Feng Xiaoqing: A Study in Narcissism* (Feng Xiaoqing: Yibian yinjian de yanjiu). Shanghai: Xinyue shudian, 1929.

———. *An Analysis of Feng Xiaoqing* (Xiaoqing zhi fenxi). Shanghai: Xinyue shudian, 1927.

———. "Research on Feng Xiaoqing" (Feng Xiaoqing kao). *FNZZ* 10, no. 11, November 1924.

Park, Robert Ezra. "Mentality of Racial Hybrids." *American Journal of Sociology* 36, no. 4 (January 1931): 534–51.

———. "Human Migration and the Marginal Man." *American Journal of Sociology* 33, no. 6 (May 1928): 881–93.

———. "Behind Our Masks." *Survey Graphic* 56 (May 1926): 135–39.

———. "The Negro Race Consciousness as Reflected in Race Literature." 1923. In *Race and Culture*, edited by Robert Ezra Park, 284–300. Glencoe Ill: Free Press, 1950.

———. "Race Prejudice and Japanese-American Relations." 1917. In *Race and Culture*, 223–29. Glencoe, Ill: Free Press, 1950.

———. "Racial Assimilation in Secondary Groups with Particular Reference to the Negro." *Publications of the American Sociological Society* 9 (July 1914): 66–83.

Patterson, Tiffany Ruby, and Robin D. G. Kelley. "Unfinished Migrations: Reflections on the African Diaspora and the Making of the Modern World." Special Issue on the Diaspora, *African Studies Review* 43 (April 2000): 11–45.

Peiss, Kathy. "Educating the Eye of the Beholder — American Cosmetics Abroad." *Daedalus* 131 (fall 2002): 101–10.

———. "On Beauty . . . and the History of Business." In *Beauty and Business: Commerce, Gender and Culture in Modern America*, edited by Philip Scranton, 7–23, New York: Routledge, 2001.

——. *Hope in a Jar: The Making of America's Beauty Culture*. New York: Metropolitan Books, 1998.

——. *Cheap Amusements: Working Women and Leisure in Turn-of-the-Century New York*. Philadelphia: Temple University Press, 1986.

Pellegrini, Anne. *Performance Anxieties: Staging Psychoanalysis, Staging Race*. New York: Routledge, 1997.

Petro, Patrice. *Joyless Streets: Women and Melodramatic Representation in Weimar Germany*. Princeton, N.J.: Princeton University Press, 1989.

Peukert, Detlev J. K. *The Weimar Republic: The Crisis of Classical Modernity*. Translated by Richard Deveson. New York: Hill and Wang, 1992.

Phillips, Ray. *The Bantu in the City: A Study of Cultural Adjustment on the Witwatersrand*. Lovedale, South Africa: Lovedale Press, 1938.

Poole, Deborah. *Vision, Race, and Modernity: A Visual Economy of the Andean Image World*. Princeton, N.J.: Princeton University Press, 1997.

Pratt, Mary Louise. *Imperial Eyes: Travel Writing and Transculturation*. New York: Routledge, 1992.

Prévost, Marcel. *Les Demi-Vierges*. Vol. 2, *Léa*. Paris: Alphonse Lemerre, 1900.

——. *Les Demi-Vierges*. Vol. 1, *Frédérique*. Paris: Alphonse Lemerre, 1894.

Radway, Janice. *Reading the Romance*. Chapel Hill: University of North Carolina Press, 1991.

Rafail, M. *Za novogo cheloveka*. Leningrad: Priboi, 1928.

Raheja, Dinesh, and Jitendra Kothari. *Indian Cinema: The Bollywood Saga*. Bombay: Roli Books, 2003.

Rajadhyaksha, Ashish, and Paul Willemen, eds. *Encyclopaedia of Indian Cinema*. London: British Film Institute; New Delhi: Oxford University Press, 1994

Reekie, Gail. *Tempations: Sex, Selling and the Department Store*. St. Leonards, NSW: Allen and Unwin, 1993.

Reese, Dagmar. *Growing Up Female in Nazi Germany: Social History, Popular Culture and Politics in Germany*. Ann Arbor: University of Michigan Press, 2006.

Reinhardt, Dirk. *Von der Reklame zum Marketing: Geschichte der Wirtschaftswerbung in Deutschland*. Berlin: Akademie-Verlag, 1993.

Renan, Ernest. "What Is a Nation?" In *Nation and Narration*, edited by Homi Bhabha, 8–22. New York: Routledge, 1990.

Reswick, William. *I Dreamt Revolution*. Chicago: H. Regnery, 1952.

Reynolds, Henry. *Frontier: Aborigines, Settlers and Land*. Sydney: Allen and Unwin, 1987.

Rice, Shelley, ed. *Inverted Odysseys: Claude Cahun, Maya Deren, Cindy Sherman*. Cambridge, Mass.: MIT Press, 1999.

Rich, Doris L. *Queen Bess: Daredevil Aviator*. Washington: Smithsonian Institution Press, 1993.

Richards, Thomas. *The Commodity Culture of Victorian England: Advertising and Spectacle, 1851–1914*. Stanford, Calif.: Stanford University Press, 1990.

Riviere, Joan. "Womanliness as Masquerade." In *Formations of Fantasy*, edited by Victor Burgin et al., 35–44. London: Methuen, 1986.

Robb, Peter, ed. *The Concept of Race in South Asia*. Delhi: Oxford University Press, 1995.

Roberts, Kimberly. "The Clothes Make the Woman: The Symbolics of Prostitution in Nella Larsen's *Quicksand* and Claude McKay's *Home to Harlem*." *Tulsa Studies in Women's Literature* 16, no.1 (spring 1997): 107–30.

Roberts, Mary Louise. *Disruptive Acts: The New Woman in Fin-de-Siècle France*. Chicago: University of Chicago Press, 2002.

———. *Civilization without Sexes: Reconstructing Gender in Post-War France, 1917–1927*. Chicago: University of Chicago Press, 1994.

———. "Samson and Delilah Revisited: The Politics of Women's Fashion in 1920's France." *American Historical Review* 98, no. 3 (June 1993): 657–83.

———. " 'This Civilization No Longer Has Sexes': *La Garçonne* and Gender Ambiguity in Postwar France." *Gender and History*, 4, no. 1 (spring 1992): 49–69.

Robinson, Gwendolyn. "Race, Class and Gender: A Transcultural, Theoretical, and Sociohistorical Analysis of Cosmetic Institutions and Practice to 1920." Ph.D. diss., University of Illinois, Chicago, 1984.

Robinson, Shirleene. " 'We do not want one who is too old': Aboriginal Child Domestic Servants in Late Nineteenth and Early Twentieth Century Queensland." *Aboriginal History*, 27 (2003): 162–82.

Rofel, Lisa. *Other Modernities: Gendered Yearnings in China after Socialism*. Berkeley: University of California Press, 1999.

Rogaski, Ruth. *Hygienic Modernity*. Berkeley: University of California Press, 2005.

Rogin, Michael. *Blackface, White Noise: Jewish Immigrants in the Hollywood Melting Pot*. Berkeley: University of California Press, 1996.

Rooks, Noliwe. *Hair Raising: Beauty, Culture, and African American Women*. New Brunswick, N.J.: Rutgers University Press, 1996.

Rose, Phyllis. *Jazz Cleopatra: Josephine Baker in Her Times*. New York: Doubleday, 1989.

Rothstein, Robert A. "Popular Song in the NEP Era." In *Russia in the Era of*

NEP: Explorations in Soviet Society and Culture, edited by Sheila Fitz-patrick, Alexander Rabinowitch, and Richard Stites, 268–94. Bloomington: Indiana University Press, 1991.

———. "The Quiet Rehabilitation of the Brick Factory: Early Soviet Popular Music and Its Critics." *Slavic Review* (September 1980): 373–88.

Ruane, Christine. "Clothes Shopping in Imperial Russia: The Development of a Consumer Culture." *Journal of Social History* 28 (summer 1995): 765–82.

Rubenshtein, M. M. *Iunost.' Podnevnikam i avtobiograficheskim zapisiam.* Moscow: Izd. Vysshikh pedagogicheskikh kursov pri Moskovskom vysshem tecknich. uchilishche, 1928.

Russkaia sovetskaia estrada, 1917–1929. Moscow: Iskusstvo, 1976.

Sachs, Wolf. *Black Hamlet.* Baltimore: Johns Hopkins University Press, 1996 (1937).

Sandler, Stephanie. "Pleasure, Danger and the Dance: Nineteenth-Century Russian Variations." In *Russia. Women. Culture*, edited by Helena Goscilo and Beth Holmgren, 247–72. Bloomington: Indiana University Press, 1996.

Sarcey, Francisque. *Quarante Ans de théâtre.* Paris: Bibliothèque des Annales Politiques et Littéraires, 1902.

Sato, Barbara. *The New Japanese Woman: Modernity, Media, and Women in Interwar Japan.* Durham, N.C.: Duke University Press, 2003.

Scales, Rebecca. "Frivolous Objectives: Manipulating Gender and Genre in Marguerite Durand's *La Fronde*." M.A. thesis, University of Georgia, Athens, 2000.

Schapera, Isaac. *Married Life in an African Tribe.* New York: Sheridan House, 1941.

Schoeman, Karel. *The Face of the Country: A South African Family Album, 1860–1910.* Cape Town: Human and Rousseau, 1996.

Schuster, Ilsa M. Glazer. *New Women of Lusaka.* Palo Alto, Calif.: Mayfield Publishing, 1979.

Scott, David. *Refashioning Futures: Criticism after Postcoloniality.* Princeton, N.J.: Princeton University Press, 1999.

Semashko, N. *Iskusstvo odevat'sia.* Moscow-Leningrad: Gosudarstvennyi izdatelsvo, 1927.

———. "Nuzhna li shenstvennost.' " *Molodaia gvardiia* 6 (1924): 206.

Serov, S., and L. Lebedev. *Molodezh' nu sude.* Moscow-Leningrad: Molodaia gvardiia, 1927.

Shahani, Roshan G., ed. *Pramila: Esther Victoria Abraham.* Mumbai: Sound and Picture Archives for Research on Women, 1998.

Sheperd-Barr, Kirsten. *Ibsen and Early Modernist Theatre, 1890–1900.* Westport, Conn.: Greenwood Press, 1997.

Shih, Shu-Mei. *The Lure of the Modern: Writing Modernism in Semicolonial China, 1917–1937*. Berkeley: University of California Press, 2001.

——. "Gender, Race and Semicolonialism: Liu Na'Ou's Urban Shanghai Landscape." *Journal of Asian Studies* 55 (1996): 934–56.

Showalter, Elaine. *Sexual Anarchy: Gender and Culture at the Fin de Siècle.* New York: Penguin Books, 1990.

Shūkan, Asahi. *Zoku-nedan no Meiji, Taisho, Showa fūzoku shi.* Tokyo: Asahi Shinbunsha, 1981.

Silverberg, Miriam. "The Cafe Waitress Serving Modern Japan." In *Mirror of Modernity: Invented Traditions of Modern Japan*, edited by Stephen Vlastos, 208–25. Berkeley: University of California Press, 1998.

——. "The Modern Girl as Militant." In *Recreating Japanese Women, 1600–1945*, edited by Gail Bernstein, 239–66. Berkeley: University of California Press, 1991.

Silverman, Debora. *Art Nouveau in Fin-de-Siècle France: Politics, Psychology and Style.* Berkeley: University of California Press, 1989.

Simmel, Georg. "The Metropolis and Mental Life." In *Cities and Society*, edited by Paul K. Hatt and Albert J. Reiss, 635–46. Glencoe, Ill.: Free Press, 1957.

Singh, Nikhil Pal. "Culture/Wars: Recoding Empire in an Age of Democracy." *American Quarterly* 50 (September 1998): 471–522.

Sinha, Mrinalini. *Gender and Nation*. Washington: American Historical Association, 2006.

——. "Refashioning Mother India: Feminism and Nationalism in Late-Colonial India." *Feminist Studies* 26, no. 3 (2000): 623–44.

——. *Colonial Masculinity : The "Manly Englishman" and the "Effeminate Bengali" in the Late Nineteenth Century.* Manchester: Manchester University Press, 1995.

Sivaramakrishnan, K., and Arun Agrawal. "Regional Modernities in Stories and Practices of Development." In *Regional Modernities: The Cultural Politics of Development in India*, 1–62. Stanford, Calif.: Stanford University Press, 2003.

Skinner, Elliot. *African Americans and the U.S. Policy toward Africa, 1850–1924*. Washington, D.C.: Howard University Press, 1992.

Skota, Mweli. *The African Yearly Register: Being an Illustrated National Biographical Dictionary (Who's Who) of Black Folks in Africa (Contributions by the Leading Native Ministers, Professors, Teachers, and Doctors).* Johannesburg: R. L. Esson, 1930.

Slater, Don. *Consumer Culture and Modernity.* Cambridge: Polity Press and Blackwell, 1997.

Slepkov, Vl. "Rytsari skorbi i pechali." In *Obyvatel'shchinu na pritsel! Sbornik statei i fel'etonov.* Leningrad: Krasnaia gazeta, 1928.

Smart, Judith. "Feminists, Flappers and Miss Australia: Contesting the Meanings of Citizenship, Femininity and Nation in the 1920s." *Journal of Australian Studies* 71 (2001): 1–16.

Smith-Rosenberg, Carroll. *Disorderly Conduct: Visions of Gender in Victorian America.* New York: Alfred A. Knopf, 1985.

Smith-Rosenberg, Carroll, and Charles Rosenberg. "The Female Animal: Medical and Biological Views of Women and Their Role in Nineteenth Century America." In *From Fair Sex to Feminism: Sport and Socialization of Women in Post-Industrial Eras,* edited by J. A. Mangan and Robert J. Park, 13–37. London: Frank Cass, 1987.

Søland, Birgitte. *Becoming Modern: Young Women and the Reconstruction of Womanhood in the 1920s.* Princeton, N.J.: Princeton University Press, 2000.

Stamp, Shelley. *Movie-Struck Girls: Women and Motion Picture Culture after the Nickelodeon.* Princeton, N.J.: Princeton University Press, 2000.

Stanichinskaia-Rozenberg, E. "Vliianie kino na shknol'nika." *Vestnik prosveshcheniia* 2 (1927).

Stansell, Christine. *American Moderns: Bohemian New York and the Creation of a New Century.* New York: Henry Holt, 2000.

Starr, Frederick. *Red and Hot: The Fate of Jazz in the Soviet Union, 1917–1980.* New York: Oxford University Press, 1983.

Steele, Valerie, and John S. Major. *China Chic: East Meets West.* New Haven, Conn.: Yale University Press, 1999.

Stevens, Jacqueline. *Reproducing the State.* Princeton, N.J.: Princeton University Press, 1999.

Stevens, Sarah E. "Figuring Modernity: The New Woman and the Modern Girl in Republican China." *NWSA Journal* 15, no. 3 (fall 2003): 82–103.

Stevenson, Michael, and Michael Graham-Stewart. *Surviving the Lens: Photographic Studies of South and East African People, 1870–1920.* Vlaeberg: Fernwood Press, 2001.

Stites, Richard. *Russian Popular Culture, Entertainment and Society since 1900.* Cambridge: Cambridge University Press, 1992.

———. *The Women's Liberation Movement in Russia: Feminism, Nihilism, and Bolshevism, 1860–1930.* Princeton, N.J.: Princeton University Press, 1990.

Strikhenova, T. *Iz istorii sovetskogo kostiuma.* Moscow, 1972.

Strogovoa, Ekaterina. "Womenfolk: Factory Sketches." In *An Anthology of Russian Women's Writing, 1977–1992,* edited by Catriona Kelly, 282. Oxford: Oxford University Press, 1994.

Studlar, Gaylyn. " 'Out-Salomeing Salome': Dance, the New Woman, and Fan Magazine Orientalism." In *Visions of the East: Orientalism in Film*, edited by Matthew Berrnstein and Gaylyn Studlar, 99–129. New Brunswick, N.J.: Rutgers University Press, 1997.

Switzer, Les. "*Bantu World* and the Origins of a Captive African Commercial Press." In *South Africa's Alternative Press: Voices of Protest and Resistance, 1880s-1960s*, edited by Les Switzer, 189–212. Cambridge: Cambridge University Press, 1997.

Takaki, Ronald. *Strangers from a Different Shore: A History of Asian Americans*. Boston: Little, Brown, 1989.

Tamrakar, Shriram. "Film Tarikaon ki Aakaashganga." In *Parade ki Pariya, 1913–1990*. Bombay: Naiiduniya Visheshank, 1990

Taylor, Ula. "From White Kitchens to White Factories: The Impact of World War I on African-American Working Women in Chicago." *Ufahamu: Journal of the African Activist Association* 14, no. 3 (1985): 5–50.

Thomas, Lynn M. *Politics of the Womb: Women, Reproduction, and the State in Kenya*. Berkeley: University of California Press, 2003.

Thompson, Dorothy. *The New Russia*. New York: Holt, 1928.

Tinayre. *La Rebelle*. Paris: Calmann-Levy, 1905.

Tonkinson, Myrna. "Sisterhood or Aboriginal Servitude? Black Women and White Women on the Australian Frontier." *Aboriginal History* 12, no. 1 (1988): 27–40.

Torgovnick, Marianna. *Gone Primitive: Savage Intellects, Modern Lives*. Chicago: University of Chicago Press, 1990.

Tramp, M. "Pod fonarem El'dorado." In *Obyvatel'shchinu no pritsel! Sbornik statei i fel'etonov*. Leningrad: Krasnaia gazeta, 1928.

Trimborn, Jüergen. *Leni Riefenstahl: A Life*. New York: Faber and Faber, 2007.

Tsing, Anna Lowenhaupt. *Friction: An Ethnography of Global Connection*. Princeton, N.J.: Princeton University Press, 2005.

Tsu, Jing. *Failure, Nationalism and Literature: The Making of Modern Chinese Identity, 1895–1937*. Stanford, Calif.: Stanford University Press, 2005.

Upton, Florence Kate. *The Adventure of Two Dutch Dolls and a Golliwogg*. London: Bodley Head, 1895.

Vainstein, Ol'ga. "Female Fashion, Soviet Style: Bodies of Ideology." In *Russia, Women, Culture*, edited by Helena Goscilo and Beth Holmgren, 64–93. Bloomington: Indiana University Press, 1996.

von Ankum, Katharina, ed. *Women in the Metropolis: Gender and Modernity in Weimar Culture*. Berkeley: University of California Press, 1997.

von Hagen, Mark. *Soldiers in the Proletarian Dictatorship: The Red Army and the Socialist State, 1917–1930.* Ithaca, N.Y.: Cornell University Press, 1990.

von Soden, Kristine, and Maruta Schmidt, eds. *Neue Frauen: Die zwanziger Jahre.* Berlin: Elefanten, 1988.

Walkowitz, Judith. "The 'Vision of Salome': Cosmopolitanism and Erotic Dancing in Central London, 1908–1918." *American Historical Review* 108 (April 2003): 336–76.

———. *City of Dreadful Delight: Narratives of Sexual Danger in Late-Victorian London.* Chicago: University of Chicago Press, 1992.

Wall, Cheryl A. *Women of the Harlem Renaissance.* Bloomington: Indiana University Press, 1995.

Walton, Jean. *Fair Sex, Savage Dreams: Race, Psychoanalysis, Sexual Difference.* Durham, N.C: Duke University Press, 2001.

Ward, Janet. *Weimar Surfaces: Urban Visual Culture in 1920s Germany.* Berkeley: University of California Press, 2001.

Wardlow, Holly. " 'Hands-Up'-ing Buses and Harvesting Cheese-Pops: Gendered Mediation of Modern Disjuncture in Melanesia." In *Critically Modern: Alternatives, Alterities, Anthropologies,* edited by Bruce Knauft, 144–72. Bloomington: Indiana University Press, 2002.

Webb, Colin de B., and John B. Wright, eds. and trans. *The James Stuart Archive of Recorded Oral Evidence Relating to the History of the Zulu and Neighbouring Peoples.* Vols. 1–5. Pietermaritzburg: University of Natal Press, 1976, 1979, 1982, 1986, and 2001.

Weinbaum, Alys Eve. *Wayward Reproductions: Genealogies of Race and Nation in Transatlantic Modern Thought.* Durham, N.C.: Duke University Press, 2004.

Weinbaum, Alys Eve, and Brent Hayes Edwards. "On Critical Globality." *Ariel: Review of International English Literature* 31, no. 1 (2000): 255–74.

Welfelé, Odile. "*La Fronde:* Histoire d'une entreprise de presse." Thèse du doctorat, Ecole de Chartres, 1982.

Westphal, Uwe. *Werbung im Dritten Reich.* Berlin: Transit, 1989.

Wexler, Laura. *Tender Violence: Domestic Visions in an Age of U.S. Imperialism.* Chapel Hill: University of North Carolina Press, 2000.

White, Luise. *The Comforts of Home: Prostitution in Colonial Nairobi.* Chicago: University of Chicago Press, 1990.

White, Shane, and Graham White. *Stylin': African American Expressive Culture from Its Beginnings to the Zoot Suit.* Ithaca, N.Y.: Cornell University Press, 1998.

Wickham, James. "Working-Class Movement and Working-Class Life: Frankfurt-am-Main during the Weimar Republic." *Social History* 8, no. 3 (October 1983): 315–43.

Wicksteed, Alexander. *Life under the Soviets.* London: John Lane, 1928.

Widmer, Ellen. "Xiaoqing's Literary Legacy and the Place of the Woman Writer in Late Imperial China." *Late Imperial China* 13 (1992): 111–55.

Wildenthal, Lora. *German Women for Empire, 1884–1945.* Durham, N.C.: Duke University Press, 2001.

Wilk, Richard. "The Local and the Global in the Political Economy of Beauty: From Miss Belize to Miss World." *Review of International Political Economy* 2 (1995): 117–34.

———. "Consumer Goods as Dialogue about Development." *Culture and History* 7 (1990): 79–100.

Willan, Brian. *Sol Plaatje: South African Nationalist, 1876–1932.* Berkeley: University of California Press, 1984.

Willett, Julia. *Permanent Waves: The Making of the American Beauty Shop.* New York: New York University Press, 2000.

Williams, Raymond. *Marxism and Literature.* Oxford: Oxford University Press, 1977.

Williams, Rosalind. "The Dream World of Mass Consumption." In *Rethinking Popular Culture: Contemporary Perspectives in Cultural Studies*, edited by Chandra Mukerji and Michael Schudson, 198–235. Berkeley: University of California Press, 1991.

Winter, Ella. *Red Virtue.* London: Victor Gollancz, 1933.

Wipper, Audrey. "African Women, Fashion, and Scapegoating." *Canadian Journal of African Studies* 6, no. 2 (1972): 329–49.

Wolcott, Victoria. *Remaking Respectability: African American Women in Interwar Detroit.* Chapel Hill: University of North Carolina Press, 2001.

Woodward, James P. "Marketing Modernity: The J. Walter Thompson Company and North American Advertising in Brazil, 1919–1939." *Hispanic American Historical Review* 82, no. 2 (2002): 257–90.

Woollacott, Angela. "White Colonialism and Sexual Modernity: Australian Women in the Early Twentieth Century Metropolis." In *Gender, Sexuality and Colonial Modernities*, edited by Antoinette Burton, 49–63. New York: Routledge, 1999.

Xu Junji. *History of Chinese Advertising* (Zhongguo guanggao shi). Beijing: Zhongguo quanmei daxue chubanshe, 2006.

Xu, Xinqin. "Shidai xiaojie de jianglai." *Shidai manhua* 1 (1934). Reprinted in *Shidai manhua: Lao Shanghai qikan jingdian*, edited by Cheng Depei, 6. Shanghai: Shehui kexue yuan chubanshe, 2000.

Xueqin, Cao. *Dream of the Red Chamber*. Beijing: Renmin wenxue chubanshe, 1998.

Yakabi, Osamu. "Kindai Okinawa ni okeru Mainoritî Ishiki no Hensen" (The Metamorphosis of Minority Consciousness in Modern Okinawa). In *Bessatsu Kan*, vol. 6, Ryūkyūken to wa Nanika (What Is Ryūkyūken?). Tokyo: Fujiwara Shoten, 2003.

Yamakawa, Kikue. "Gendai shokugyō fujin ron." In *Nihon fujin mondai shiryō shūsei- shisō*, vol. 8, edited by Hideko Maruoka, 334–44. Tokyo: Domesu Shuppan, 1976.

Ye, Qianyu. *Manhua daguan*. Shanghai: Zhongguo meishu, 1931.

Yeh Wen-hsin, ed., *Becoming Chinese: Passages to Modernity and Beyond*. Berkeley: University of California Press, 2000.

Yi Bin, Liu Wenming, and Gan Zhenhu. *Old Shanghai Advertising* (Lao Shanghai guangao). Shanghai: Shanghai huabao chubanshe, 1995 and 2000.

Yoshida, Aya. "Kōto Jogakkō to Joshi Gakusei: Seiō Modan to Kindai Nihon" (Girls' Higher Schools and School Girls: Western Modern and Modern Japan). In *Onna no Bunka* (Women's Culture), Kindai Nihon Bunkaron, vol. 8, edited by T. Aoki et al., 123–40. Tokyo: Iwanami Shoten, 2000.

Yoshihara, Mari. *Embracing the East: White Women and American Orientalism*. New York: Oxford University Press, 2003.

You Guoqing. *Byebye Old Style Advertising* (Zaijian lao guangao). Tianjin: Baihua wenyi chubanshe, 2004.

Youngblood, Denise J. *Movies for the Masses: Popular Cinema and Soviet Society in the 1920s*. Cambridge: Cambridge University Press, 1992.

———. "The Fate of Soviet Popular Cinema during the Stalin Revolution." *Russian Review* 50 (April 1991): 148–62.

Yu, Henry. *Thinking Orientals: Migration, Contact, and Exoticism in Modern America*. New York: Oxford University Press, 2001.

Yuval-Davis, Nira, and Floya Anthias. Introduction. *Women-Nation-State*, 3–10. London: Macmillan, 1989.

Zelenko, Anna. *Massovye narodnye tantsy*. Moscow: Rabotnik prosveshcheniia, 1927.

Zhang Henshui. *Shanghai Express*. Translated by William A. Lyell. Honolulu: University of Hawaii Press, 1997.

Zhang, Jingyuan. *Psychoanalysis in China: Literary Transformations, 1919–1949*. Ithaca, N.Y.: Cornell University East Asia Program, 1992.

Zhang, Zhen. *An Amorous History of the Silver Screen: Shanghai Cinema, 1896–1937*. Chicago: University of Chicago Press, 2005.

Zito, Angela, and Tani E. Barlow, eds. *Body, Subject and Power in China*. Chicago: University of Chicago Press, 1994.

Žižek, Slavoj. *The Sublime Object of Ideology*. New York: Verso Books, 1989.

Contributors

MODERN GIRL AROUND THE WORLD RESEARCH GROUP is a collective based at the University of Washington, Seattle. Its members are Alys Eve Weinbaum, Lynn M. Thomas, Priti Ramamurthy, Uta G. Poiger, Madeleine Yue Dong, and Tani E. Barlow.

DAVARIAN L. BALDWIN is an associate professor of history and African and African Diaspora Studies at Boston College. The chapter in this volume comes from his larger project *Chicago's New Negroes: Modernity, the Great Migration, and Black Urban Life* (2007).

TANI E. BARLOW is a professor of history and women's studies at the University of Washington, Seattle. She is the author of *The Question of Women in Chinese Feminism* (Duke, 2004) and "Wanting Some" in Mechthild Leutner and Nikola Spakowski, eds., *Women in China: The Republican Period in Historical Perspective* (2005).

TIMOTHY BURKE is a professor of history at Swarthmore College. He is the author of *Lifebuoy Men, Lux Women: Commodification, Cleanliness and Consumption in Modern Zimbabwe* (Duke, 1996) and co-author of *Saturday Morning Fever: Growing Up with Cartoon Culture* (1999). He also maintains a blog, Easily Distracted, at http://weblogs.swarthmore.edu/ burke.

LIZ CONOR is the author of *The Spectacular Modern Woman: Feminine Visibility in the 1920s* (2004), and has recently completed a postdoctoral fellowship in the Department of Culture and Communications at the University of Melbourne. She is the former editor of *Metro Magazine* and *Australian Screen Education,* and her present research is concerned with racialized childhood.

MADELEINE YUE DONG is an associate professor of history and international studies at the University of Washington. Her most recent publications include *Republican Beijing: The City and Its Histories* (2003), and she is co-editor (with Joshua Goldstein) of *Everyday Modernity in China* (2006).

ANNE E. GORSUCH is an associate professor of history at the University of British Columbia. She is the author of *Youth in Revolutionary Russia: Enthusiasts, Bohemians, and Delinquents* (2000) and co-editor (with Diane P. Koenker) of *Turizm: The Russian and East European Tourist under Capitalism and Socialism* (2006).

RURI ITO is a professor of migration and gender studies at the Graduate School of Social Sciences, Hitotsubashi University, Tokyo. She has published extensively on minority movements in the interstate system, including Britanny, France, and Okinawa. Her most recent work is on gender and inter-Asian migration.

KATHY PEISS is the Roy F. and Jeannette P. Nichols Professor of American History at the University of Pennsylvania. Her books include *Cheap Amusements: Working Women and Leisure in Turn-of-the-Century New York* (1986) and *Hope in a Jar: The Making of America's Beauty Culture* (1998).

UTA G. POIGER is an associate professor of history and adjunct associate professor of women's studies at the University of Washington, Seattle. She is the author of *Jazz, Rock, and Rebels: Cold War Politics and American Culture in a Divided Germany* (2000), co-editor (with Heide Fehrenbach) of *Transactions, Transgressions, Transformations: American Culture in Western Europe and Japan* (2000), and co-editor (with Volker Berghahn) of *Documents in German History,* volume 8, *1945–1961,* an online collection for the German Historical Institute, Washington. Currently she is working on a book titled *Beauty and Business in Germany: An International History*.

PRITI RAMAMURTHY is an associate professor of women's studies at the University of Washington, Seattle. Her essays on feminist critiques of international development, agrarian transitions, consumption and commodity cultures, and transnational feminism have been published in *Cultural Anthropology, Feminist Studies, Feminist Theory, Society and Natural Resources, Women's Studies Quarterly,* and *World Development*. She is working on a book entitled *100% Cotton: Gender, Globalization and Agrarian Change in South India*.

MARY LOUISE ROBERTS is a professor of history at the University of Wisconsin, Madison. She is the author of *Civilization without Sexes: Reconstructing Gender in Post-War France, 1918–1928* (1994) and *Disruptive Acts: The New Woman in Fin de Siècle France* (2002). She is currently at work on a book concerning relations between the American GIs and French civilians during the Second World War.

BARBARA SATO is a professor of history at Seikei University in Tokyo, Japan. She is the author of *The New Japanese Woman: Modernity, Media, and Women in Interwar Japan* (Duke, 2003), "Commodifying and Engendering Morality: Self-Cultivation and the Construction of the Ideal Woman in 1920s Mass Women's Magazines," in *Gendering Modern Japanese History* (2005), and numerous articles on the Modern Girl in Japanese and English.

MIRIAM SILVERBERG was a professor of history at the University of California, Los Angeles. She wrote many books, most recently *Erotic Grotesque Nonsense: The Mass Culture of Japanese Modern Times* (2007). Her prescient 1991 essay "The Modern Girl as Militant" opened discussion of the Modern Girl phenomenon and influenced a generation of research.

LYNN M. THOMAS is an associate professor of history and adjunct associate professor of women's studies at the University of Washington, Seattle. She is the author of *Politics of the Womb: Women, Reproduction, and the State in Kenya* (2003) and co-editor (with Jennifer Cole) of *Love in Africa* (forthcoming). Her current research focuses on the transnational history of skin lighteners.

ALYS EVE WEINBAUM is an associate professor of English at the University of Washington, Seattle. She is author of *Wayward Reproductions: Genealogies of Race and Nation in Transatlantic Modern Thought* (Duke, 2004) and co-editor with Susan Gillman of *Next to the Color Line: Gender, Sexuality, and W. E. B. Du Bois* (2006).

Index

5.5); Dhlomo's role at, 99, 106–9, 112, 115–16; elongated Modern Girl body depicted in ads, 3 (figure 1.1); founding of, 97; influence of, 97; languages used in, 97–99, 111, 111 (figure 5.4); progressive/moderate agenda of, 97, 108; on racial uplift or shame, 96, 112, 116; Valmor Products ads in, 112–13; women's pages of, 97–99

Bardot (clothing chain), 237n.30

Barlow, Tani, 6–7, 12, 355

Barnett, Claude, 72

Barnum, P. T., 100–101

Barrès, Maurice, 80

Barrett, Charles, 227

Barwick, Diane E., 233

Bäumer, Gertrud, 331

Beardsley, Aubrey, 208, 326

beauty contests, 100–101, 227, 330. *See also under* racial respectability in South Africa

beauty culture. *See* black beauty culture; C. J. Walker Company

beauty and seduction as power, 81–84, 83 (figure 4.2), 85

Bedbug, The (Mayakovsky), 192–93n.57

beggar's balls, 126, 127–28 (figures 6.5–6.7)

"Behind Our Masks" (Park), 134–38, 145n.16

Beiersdorf, 47–48, 49 (figure 2.21), 336, 338

Benito, Edouard, 327

Bennett, Joan, 48

Bennett, Tony, 283–84

Berlin, consumerism in, 264

Berliner Illustrirte Zeitung, 27

Bernard, Jack ("Jolly"), 110–11

Bernhardt, Sarah, 326

Betty Boop, 288

bhadramahilas, 158

Bharat naris (respectable Indian women), 163, 171

Bich (Rowdy; USSR), 174, 176 (figure 8.1)

Bickford-Smith, Vivian, 97–98

Bilimoria, Dinshaw, 147, 156 (figure 7.6)

bindis, 149 (figure 7.2), 157, 158 (figure 7.7), 162

Birbal, 160

Birell, Tala, 48

black beauty culture, 55–76; American, generally, 18, 21; as desire for whiteness, 60–61; emergence of, 56–57, 74; employment opportunities via, 351; hair straightening, 63, 108, 140; influence in South Africa, 110–15, 350; naturalness vs. excessive adornment/artifice, 57–58, 60, 68–69, 108; and New Negro movement, 58 (figure 3.1), 66–71, 74; political activism within, 351; and professionalization, 71–72, 74; and racialization of "girl," 11; re-creation of black women, and class, 56–60, 58 (figure 3.1); and selling blackness, 56, 61–66, 65 (figure 3.3); slaves' hair styles and treatments, 59–60; vs. white aesthetic, 18. *See also* C. J. Walker Company

Black Consciousness, 52n.4

Black Egypt as archetype of civilization, 44

blackface, 124, 236n.3

blackness, 44, 56, 61–66, 65 (figure 3.3), 330

blacks: assimilation in United States, 137–38; Great Migration by, 60, 66–67; re-creation of, and gender/class, 57–60, 58 (figure 3.1); use of term, 116n.1

Chinese Commercial Press (Shanghai), 291

Chinese Enlightenment, 300

Chinese Modern Girls, 352; in cartoons, 13, 17, 20, 199–201, 199 (figure 9.2), 201 (figure 9.3), 206–14, 209–13 (figures 9.5–9.12), 353; class boundaries disrupted by, 12; consumer agency of, 21 (figure 1.8); criticism of, 204, 214–17, 351; feminist critique of, 214, 216; free love by, 206; gender relations challenged by, 12; as ideal modern woman, 202–6, 203 (figure 9.4); look of, and class boundaries, 196–202, 198–99 (figures 9.1–9.2), 201 (figure 9.3); and male perspective, 195; marriage goals of, 204–6, 216; and modern urban men, 205–14, 209–13 (figures 9.5–9.12), 217; vs. New Women, 215; overview of, 194–95; superficiality of, 195, 214–17; Westernized, 203–4, 215; and women's liberation, 197, 199, 216. *See also* Shanghai advertising, sexy Modern Girl icon in

Chlorodont ad, 334, 335 (figure 14.10), 336

Chocolate Kiddies, The, 178

Chopin, Kate, 78

Ciarlo, David M., 322

cigarette ads, 34, 326

Cim, Albert, 80

Cinema Girl, 153

Cinema ki Rani, 153

C. J. Walker Company, 119n.80, 348–49; ads for, 37 (figure 2.13), 43–44, 48, 70 (figure 3.4); black womanhood's makeover by, 11, 57, 59–65, 68–69; Walker Hair

Culturists' Union, 57, 61–62, 64, 69, 71, 110

class, 286n.44; and Chinese Modern Girl look, 196–202, 198–99 (figures 9.1–9.2), 201 (figure 9.3); cultural variations within classes, 284; and natural vs. artificial beauty, 106; and re-creation of race womanhood, 57–60, 58 (figure 3.1). *See also under* consumerism in mass women's magazines

Clausen, Beryl (*pseud.* Madhuri), 162, 167

Clemenceau, Georges, 81

cloche hats, 13, 18, 131, 132 (figure 6.12), 179–80, 323, 337, 359

Club cosmetics, 279, 280 (figure 12.8)

clubwomen, 57, 62

Coleman, Bessie, 67–68

Colgate, 295, 296 (figure 13.9)

College Humor, 203

colonial racism, 320–25, 323–24 (figures 14.4–14.5), 336

"coloured," use of, 27, 52n.4

Comfort, 300

commodification, attacks on, 264

commodities: commodity capitalism, 9–10, 12, 19–20, 307, 356, 368; erotic, 1; Modern Girls and commodity culture, 362–69; overview of, 1, 18–20, 21 (figure 1.8)

common sense, 362

communists vs. Modern Girls, 14, 17, 175–77, 185–89

connective comparison, 4–7, 6 (figures 1.3–1.4), 14, 20, 26, 50

Conor, Liz, 11, 19–20

consumerism in mass women's magazines, 263–88; advertisements, 278–79, 280–81 (figures 12.7–

torian/conventional, 57, 83, 90.
    See also masculinity
feminists: activism of, 78–79, 81;
    British imperial, 170; Chinese
    Modern Girls critiqued by, 214,
    216; Hollywood films critiqued
    by, 165; internationalism of, 221
Femme seule, La (Brieux), 89
Femmes nouvelles, Les (Paul and
    Victor Margueritte), 80, 89
Femmes savantes, Les (Molière), 80
Feng Xiaoqing, 299–300
Fields, Mamie Garvin, 61
Figaro, Le, 81
film stars: athleticism of, 68; beauty
    contests as means of discovering,
    101; in cosmetics ads, 34, 34 (fig-
    ure 2.9), 43, 343n.44; exotic skin
    tones of, 48; Indian Modern Girls
    as, 152–60, 155–56 (figures 7.3–
    7.6), 158 (figures 7.7–7.8); Mod-
    ern Girl style of, 349; product
    endorsements by, 336, 343n.44
fin de siècle, 86, 90
Five Continents Pharmacy ad, 300,
    301 (figure 13.10)
flappers, 9. *See also* Soviet Modern
    Girls
Ford Motor Company, 302
Fort Hare College (Eastern Cape,
    South Africa), 107
fox trot, 178, 182–84, 188
Frank, Stephen, 192n.45
Freckle Wax, 41–42, 43 (figure 2.18)
free love, 10, 79, 81, 206, 216, 249,
    257, 358
French Modern Girls, 77–95; and
    all-women's community, 89; and
    beauty/seduction as power, 81–
    84, 83 (figure 4.2), 85; and Don-
    nay's *Les Éclaireuses*, 78, 85–91;
    and Durand's aesthetic politics,

81–85, 82–83 (figures 4.1–4.2),
    90; and feminist activism, 78–79,
    81; vs. garçonnes, 10, 90–92, 349;
    New Woman's emergence and
    reception in France, 78–82,
    93n.10; overview of, 77–78
Fromm, Erich, 337–38
"From Natural Sociology to Cultural
    Sociology" (Liu), 302
Fronde, La, 84–85, 89–92
Fuentes, Juanita, 334, 335 (figure
    14.10)
Fu'ermosi (Sherlock Holmes; China),
    27, 197
Fujin geijutsu (Women and Art;
    Japan), 286n.38
Fujin kaizō (Women's Reform;
    Japan), 286n.38
Fujin kōron (Women's Review;
    Japan), 277, 286n.38
Fujin kurabu (Woman's Club;
    Japan), 276
Fujin no Tomo (Japan), 246
Fujin sekai (Women's World; Japan),
    265, 276
Fujokai (Woman's Sphere; Japan),
    265, 267, 269, 276, 280 (figures
    12.7–12.8), 283, 287n.49
Funü shibao (China), 291
Funü zazhi. See *Ladies' Journal*
Furen huabao (Women's Pictorial;
    China), 202–5, 203 (figure 9.4),
    206–7
futsūgo (standard Japanese lan-
    guage), 244, 259n.12
F. Wolff and Sohn, 32, 325; artists
    used by (*see* Hohlwein, Ludwig;
    Wiertz, Jupp); cosmopolitan aes-
    thetic of, 332–33; under National
    Socialism, 338–39; photography
    used by, 336. *See also* Kaloderma
    ads; Vogue perfume

Galien, Blanche, 84

Gandhi, Mohandas Karamchand, 159–60, 351

Garçonne, La (Margueritte), 92n.1

garçonnes, 10, 77, 92n.1, 349. *See also* Modern Girls

Garga, B. D., 157, 169

Garson, E., 111

Garvey, Marcus, 71, 101–2. See also *Negro World*

Gasper, Iris (*pseud.* Sabita Devi), 162, 167

Gebrauchsgraphik, 317, 326–28, 331

gender: and Indian nationalism (*see under* Indian Modern Girls); and re-creation of race womanhood, 57–60, 58 (figure 3.1); relations reconfigured in families of Okinawa New Women, 254, 257; Victorian norms explored in theater, 79, 90

George, Louis, 59

German Modern Girls, 317–44; and American beauty ideals, 329–30; and colonial racism, 320–25, 323–24 (figures 14.4–14.5), 336; cosmopolitan aesthetic's appearance, 319 (figure 14.2), 320, 326–34, 328–29 (figures 14.6–14.7), 332 (figure 14.9); cosmopolitan aesthetic's disappearance, 320, 334–42, 341 (figure 14.12); elongated, stylized bodies in representations of, 326–27; and eugenics, 320, 331; fashions of, 337; vs. ideal German women, 336–37; and interracial sex, 323, 325; and Japanese references, 328–30; and modernity/modernism, 320, 327–28; and National Socialism's effects on cosmetics ads' aesthetics, 320; and Oriental refer-

ences, 323, 325–26, 333–34; overview of, 317–21; racial groups depicted in ads associated with, 321; sports images of, 330–31; and universalistic fantasies, 320, 331–32, 334, 340, 342, 355

Germany: colonies lost by, 322, 325; cosmetics industry in, 325 (*see also specific companies*); cosmopolitan aesthetic in, 15; cultural distinctiveness of, fear of losing, 331–32; Depression's effects on, 334; Fascism in, 8; Japanese-produced ads in, 327; modernity in, 264 (*see also under* German Modern Girls); tariffs by, 8; territorial expansion by, 8; U.S.-produced ads in, 327–28, 332; women's movement in, 331. *See also* National Socialism

Giles, Judith, 272

Ginza (Tokyo), 272, 273 (figure 12.3), 274

"girl," use of, 8–12

Glennie, Paul, 279, 282

globalization, 5. *See also* connective comparison; multidirectional citation

Glosser, Susan, 205

Gohar, "Glorious" (*aka* Goharbai Mamajiwala), 154, 157, 158 (figure 7.7), 162, 167–68

Goldman, Emma, 359

golliwog figures, 221, 236n.3

Goodhew, David, 98

Goomilevsky, Lev, 188

Gorsuch, Anne E., 14, 17, 19, 21–22

Gramsci, Antonio, 284

Grand, Sarah, 78, 81

Great Depression, 8, 15, 18–19, 320, 334, 340

Hunt, Lynn, 174–75
Hunter, Monica, 100
hygiene, scientific, 31–32
hygiene manuals, 326–27

Iaroslavskii, Emel'ian, 188
Ibsen, Henrik, 81; *A Doll's House*, 79, 86, 208
ICC Report (Indian Cinemato-graphic Committee report), 152–54, 161–62, 164–65
Ichikōjo (Prefectural Girls' Higher School; Okinawa), 244–45, 247, 258, 260n.24, 261–62n.46. *See also* Joshi-shihan
icons. *See* Shanghai advertising, sexy Modern Girl icon in
Iha Fuyū, 260n.26, 261n.29, 261n.32, 261n.38; *Koryūkyū*, 248; *Okinawa Joseishi*, 248
ILDP (International League of Darker Peoples), 71
Iliffe, John, 98
Illiustrirovannaia Rossiia (Illustrated Russia), 179–80
Illustrated Weekly of India (Bom-bay): cosmetics ads in, 28, 30, 30 (figure 2.5), 33 (figure 2.7), 42 (fig-ure 2.17), 49; film/commodity ads in, 152; film industry coverage by, 152, 154–55, 155 (figure 7.3), 162–63, 167–68
Immigration Act (U.S., 1924), 44–45, 126
Immigration Restriction Act (Aus-tralia, 1901), 222
Imperial (India), 151
"in-betweens" (ethnicity), 44–45, 45 (figure 2.19), 46
India: Anglo-Indian difference in, 160–62, 166–67, 169–70; Brit-ish colonialism/interests in, 150,

159, 159 (figure 7.9), 161, 164–66, 169–70; cinema in, 151–53, 164–67, 169 (*see also* Indian Modern Girls); domestic-market growth in, 8; Hindu middle class in, 162; interracial unions in, 161; languages of, 151; skin color hierarchies in, 40–41, 169
Indian Cinematographic Committee report. See *ICC Report*
Indian Federation of University Women, 165
Indian Modern Girls, 147–73, 352–53; attire of, 149 (figure 7.2), 155–56 (figures 7.4–7.5), 157–58, 158 (figure 7.7), 159 (figure 7.9), 162; vs. bhadramahilas, 158; and Bharat naris, 163, 171; con-sumer agency of, 21 (figure 1.7); and courtesans, 162; ethnicity of, 160–61; and feminist critique of Hollywood films, 165; Gandhi on, 159–60, 351; and Indian national-ist modernity, 150, 160, 164–66, 170–71; and Indianness, 150, 160, 163–64, 166, 170–71; kiss-ing in cinema, 154; vs. New Women, 159–60, 159 (figure 7.9); overview of, 147–51; racially ambiguous and erotic images of, 14; as sitaras (starlets), home-grown, 160–64; sitaras as nationalist symbols, 166–71; sit-aras' eclipsing, 14, 17, 148, 150, 166, 170; source material on, 151–52; worldly and wicked film stars, 152–60, 155–56 (figures 7.3–7.6), 158 (figures 7.7–7.8)
Indira B.A., 153–54
Indira M.A., 153–55, 157
"In Living Memory: Surviving Pho-tographs from the Records of the

MODERN GIRL AROUND THE WORLD RESEARCH GROUP
is a collective based at the University of Washington, Seattle. Its members are
Alys Eve Weinbaum, Lynn M. Thomas, Priti Ramamurthy,
Uta G. Poiger, Madeleine Yue Dong, and Tani E. Barlow.

LIBRARY OF CONGRESS CATALOGING-IN-PUBLICATION DATA

The modern girl around the world : consumption, modernity,
and globalization / the Modern Girl Around the World Research Group.
p. cm. — (Next wave : new directions in women's studies)
Includes bibliographical references and index.
ISBN 978-0-8223-4299-1 (cloth : alk. paper)
ISBN 978-0-8223-4305-9 (pbk. : alk. paper)
1. Young women. 2. Girls. 3. Girls in popular culture. 4. Consumption
(Economics) — Social aspects. 5. Women consumers.
HQ1229.M694 2008   305.242'20904 — dc22
2008028481

An earlier version of chapter 2 and sections of chapter 1 appeared as Modern Girl Around the World Research Group, "The Modern Girl Around the World: A Research Agenda and Preliminary Findings," *Gender and History* 17, no. 2 (2005): 245–94.

Chapter 3, Davarian Baldwin's essay, was previously published in his book *Chicago's New Negroes* (2007). It is printed here in revised form with permission from the University of North Carolina Press.

A longer version of chapter 5 appeared as Lynn M. Thomas, "The Modern Girl and Racial Respectability in 1930s South Africa," *The Journal of African History* 47, no. 3 (2006): 1–30. It is reprinted here with permission from Cambridge University Press.

Parts of chapter 7 were originally published in "The Modern Girl in India in the Inter–War Years: Inter–Racial Intimacies, International Competition, and Historical Eclipsing," *WSQ* 34, no. 1/2 (spring 2006): 197–226. It is reprinted here by permission of the author and the Feminist Press at CUNY.

Chapter 8 originally appeared as "Flappers and Foxtrotters" in Anne Gorsuch, *Youth in Revolutionary Russia: Enthusiasts, Bohemians, Delinquents* (2000), 116–38. It is printed here in revised form with permission from the University of Indiana Press and the author.

Chapter 10 originally appeared as "The 'Primitive' Woman in the Late Colonial Scene" in Liz Conor, *The Spectacular Modern Woman: Feminine Visibility in the 1920s* (2004), 175–208. It is printed here in revised form with permission from the University of Indiana Press and the author.